THE POWER OF PLACE, THE PROBLEM OF TIME

Aboriginal Identity and Historical Consciousness in the Cauldron of Colonialism

The Indigenous communities of the Lower Fraser River, British Columbia (a group commonly called the Stó:lō), have historical memories and senses of identity deriving from events, cultural practices, and kinship bonds that had been continuously adapting long before a non-Native visited the area directly. In *The Power of Place, the Problem of Time*, Keith Thor Carlson re-thinks the history of Native-newcomer relations from the unique perspective of a classically trained historian who has spent nearly two decades living, working, and talking with the Stó:lō peoples.

Stó:lō actions and reactions under colonialism were rooted in their pre-colonial experiences and customs, which coloured their responses to events such as smallpox outbreaks or the gold rush. Profiling tensions of gender and class within the community, Carlson emphasizes the elasticity of collective identity. A rich and complex history, *The Power of Place, the Problem of Time* looks to both the internal and external factors that shaped a society during a time of great change, and its implications extend far beyond the study region.

KEITH THOR CARLSON is an associate professor in the Department of History at the University of Saskatchewan.

The Power of Place, the Problem of Time

Aboriginal Identity and Historical Consciousness in the Cauldron of Colonialism

KEITH THOR CARLSON

UNIVERSITY OF TORONTO PRESS

Toronto Buffalo London

© University of Toronto Press Incorporated 2010
Toronto Buffalo London
www.utppublishing.com
Printed in Canada

ISBN 978-0-8020-9839-9 (cloth)
ISBN 978-0-8020-9564-0 (paper)

Printed on acid-free, 100% post-consumer recycled paper with
vegetable-based inks

Library and Archives Canada Cataloguing in Publication

Carlson, Keith Thor
The power of place, the problem of time : aboriginal identity and historical
consciousness in the cauldron of colonialism / Keith Thor Carlson.

Includes bibliographical references and index.
ISBN 978-0-8020-9839-9 (bound)   ISBN 978-0-8020-9564-0 (pbk.)

1. Indians of North America – British Columbia – Fraser River Valley –
Historiography.   2. Indians of North America – British Columbia –
Fraser River Valley – Social conditions.   3. Indians of North America –
British Columbia – Fraser River Valley – Government relations.   4. Indians of
North America – First contact with Europeans – British Columbia –
Fraser River Valley. I. Title.

E78.B9C364 2010   305.897′071137   C2010-903159-8

University of Toronto Press acknowledges the financial assistance to its
publishing program of the Canada Council for the Arts and the
Ontario Arts Council.

 Canada Council   Conseil des Arts   ONTARIO ARTS COUNCIL
for the Arts   du Canada   CONSEIL DES ARTS DE L'ONTARIO

University of Toronto Press acknowledges the financial support for its
publishing activities of the Government of Canada through the Book
Publishing Industry Development Program (BPIDP).

This book has been published with the help of a grant from the
Canadian Federation for the Humanities, through the Aid to Scholarly
Publications Program, using funds provided by the Social Sciences and
Humanities Research Council of Canada.

To Albert Jules McHalsie,
(also known as Sonny and as Ná:xáxalhts'i)
I couldn't ask for a more thoughtful companion with whom to
travel down the path of cross-cultural understanding.

And to the memory of Ernest Wilfrid Carlson
For inspiring me to choose Clio as my muse.

Contents

Foreword

It's pretty awesome to see so many of the things Keith Carlson and I have discussed so often over the years appear in this book. Keith's long and close relationship with us, the Stó:lõ of the lower Fraser River watershed, has given him insights and sensitivities to our culture that other scholars have lacked. As an outsider who came in and applied his academic training and analysis to our history and culture, Keith places us in Canadian history, but he also places Canada in our history. Through the things he's published he's started conversations that add to the bigger picture and the larger project of cross-cultural understanding and reconciliation. He brings academic training and expectations but does so in a way that is respectful to the Stó:lõ, and respectful to the people who lived in the past. He's done this in a way that contributes to broader understandings of Aboriginal identity that should appeal to people interested in the human experience as lived in the cauldron of colonial encounters. He shows us that colonialism unfolded in Aboriginal society in ways that were often unanticipated or even contrary to colonial officials' expectations. This is ethnohistory at its best and its relevance goes well beyond the specific Stó:lõ examples examined.

Over the past two centuries, since Simon Fraser first arrived in our territory in 1808, we've had a lot of different people come and try to understand us – fur traders, missionaries, government agents, surveyors, educators, social workers, anthropologists, and historians. Usually, they were trying to understand us so that they could change us. Fur traders thought we would be like Aboriginal people on the other side of the Rocky Mountains and decided we should trap and trade beaver instead of catch and trade salmon; missionaries decided we were heathens and that our spirituality wasn't the right spirituality and they tried to make us

Christians; government agents recognized that we were fishermen and
so decided we didn't need large land reserves – and then later they took
away our right to trade our salmon; educators thought that our education system wasn't adequate and that our children needed to be taken
away from their parents and sent to residential schools; anthropologists
decided that we were a dying race and that we couldn't fit within Western society, and so they tried to preserve a snap-shot image of our culture by collecting our masks and carvings from our living communities
and conserving them in museums; historians relegated us to the first
chapters of their books on the development of the Canadian state; social
workers argued that we were people with a problem, and so they put our
children in non-Native families where they could be raised without our
important cultural influences.

Ironically, sometimes scholars' descriptions of our culture were really
efforts to critique their own Western culture. The result, too often, was
a portrayal that was static, romantic, a description of a world where everything was wonderful. And even if this was better than earlier portrayals
where we were shown as savages they were still wrong – and wrong depic-
tions are in nobody's interest. This book is different.

Keith isn't just another academic who comes to visit our communities.
He's lived with us in our territory, and for nearly a decade, from 1992 to
2001, he worked with us and for us in our offices. During that time, he,
his wife Teresa, and their sons Liam and Ben became 'siyá:ye' – a word
that my Elder Rosaleen George translated as meaning friends who are so
close they are considered family. Keith went to winter dance and sxwóyxwey ceremonies, played cards, went to birthday celebrations, visited fish
camps, came to funerals, participated in wedding ceremonies, dropped
by for coffee, and then invited our families back to his house for meals
and visits. In return, he shared parts of his own culture and beliefs with
us. I learned from him the importance that faith plays in any culture.
He and his family became a part of our community. This book is part of
his way of giving back to us, and even now that he's moved away to the
University of Saskatchewan, he still comes to visit us and work with us.

The Power of Place, the Problem of Time is scholarship that is open to different ways of seeing the past. It shows that Keith respects our beliefs and
traditions, and does this without trying to become Stó:lō himself. This
openness has allowed him to work with us in a respectful way. Here's an
example that I think shows Keith's character properly. We have a belief
that ancestor spirits become active in the evenings when the sun goes
down. And the ancestor spirits are hungry and a little lonely. The spirits

are attracted when food is shared when families gather for a meal, and if
you are not careful, the spirits might see someone they were really close
to when they were alive, and the spirits might want to take that living
person's spirit back with them to the spirit world. To help protect people, we have a custom of closing our blinds at night when we're eating.
That way the spirits outside won't see what's going on inside the house
and people will be safe. Years ago Keith saw my family doing this, and
he asked about it and we discussed it in great detail. I was happy when
we came to his house for dinner one night and I saw him going around
closing all his curtains and blinds before we sat down to eat. I don't know
if he believed that the spirits were there, but he knew that we did and
he was being respectful – to both us and to the spirits. I know that now
he closes his blinds during meals at night even if a Stó:lō person isn't
present, because he knows that we believe the spirits are there and even
if that isn't part of his own family's teachings he honours it in case our
Stó:lō ancestral spirits are there outside his house.

When Keith first came to work with us at the Tribal Council office
back in 1992, I quickly discovered that he was a person I could get along
with. We'd had some other non-Native people working with us who did
things or said things that I thought were disrespectful and problem-
atic. They didn't necessarily know they were doing that. They probably
thought they were being helpful. When Keith came to work at the Tribal
Council we had a conversation where we agreed that communication was
going to be important. We decided that we would let one another know
if one of us said or did something inappropriate. That's really worked
out. There were a few times early on where I let Keith know that I didn't
think what he said or did was proper. And I could see that he respected
me for pointing those things out – even if it made him feel bad or un-
comfortable. But that showed that he really cared. And he's done the
same for me.

We have conversations that go on for months and even years. Keith
calls these 'sustained conversations,' I call them 'deep talks' – they're different from shallow discussions where people just skim over the surface.
We'll pick up a conversation and we'll go deeper and deeper into a subject each time we meet. Sometimes we'll start with something an Elder
has shared with us, with something we've found in the archives, or with
something that comes from an ethnographer's fieldnotes, and we'll have
deep conversations about that. This book in large part has come from
those sessions of deep thinking and 'sustained conversations.'

Keith has thanked me for helping him work through certain ques-

tions, and Keith's deep thinking has encouraged me as well. He's helped
me refine the way I think. There have been many times when he's asked
me questions about Stó:lō history and society and it has been really clear
that he's spent a lot of time thinking about the subject, and I have to
say, 'OK Keith, let me think about this and get back to you tomorrow,'
because oftentimes it was about something I'd never thought about, or
at least never thought about in that way. Spending so much time living
and working with our people, Keith has taken in so much of our culture
and traditions that he is able to ask these really interesting and deep
questions. Comparing past and present, Keith has seen the way traditions change in his own culture, and this has given him insights that help
him understand changes to our traditions and belief systems. I can see
that understanding in the way Keith handles the topics in each of these
chapters. I don't think many people will have thought so deeply about
the history of our common Stó:lō collective identity.

When Keith started working with us, he brought a whole new way of
looking at research. Our experience with some other academics was not
as honest, and sometimes they would just tell us what they thought we
wanted to hear. They showed our present and our past as romantic, and
showed us as simple victims in history. Early on, Chief Ned of Sumas told
Keith: 'Tell us what we need to hear, not what we want to hear.' Keith
took that seriously. And he did this in a way that let us know that he respected us, because he knew that we respected him.

Keith also went a lot deeper in his research than I was used to seeing, for instance, when he was asked in 1993 to research the lynching of
Louie Sam in 1884. We had a few documents and a little oral history, but
we didn't have the full story. He took the initiative to go to the archives
in Victoria and Bellingham and then he carried out new research in
our own communities. From that moment on I saw the value of Keith's
research and the way he used creative and original ways to look at these
things. How he does research is different because he sees new ways of
taking sources and getting more information from them. He looks for
and asks different questions than other historians have. And I've learned
many of my own research methods from Keith not only because he
shared the results of his research with us, but also because he shared
the process he went through to get those results. It was from Keith that I
learned to appreciate context, to read between the lines, and to appreciate the little things that are buried in books and documents. Now I have
a huge library in my own house and Keith and I have also spent many
hours together visiting archives and used book stores.

Keith has also shared with me the importance of trying to believe and appreciate things you can't always see – an important theme in this book. To be honest, I didn't understand the importance of faith or what Elders meant when they talked about it. Then one year Keith explained that he had been fasting for Lent and invited me to attend the Easter Mass. He said I had shared so much with him, such as *sxwōyxwey*, winterdance, and burnings, that he wanted to share some of his faith with me. He said he wasn't trying to convert me, he just wanted me to know him better. So I went and I watched. After that we had deep conversations and he talked about his struggles to believe that during the mass the wine and bread change into the body and blood of Christ. And we talked about a similar transformation in my Stó:lō culture. We believe that the food burned at burning ceremonies changes into food for our ancestor spirits. I saw faith in a new way. I had a better understanding of the importance of faith in my culture and how cultures could share different ways of having faith without forcing it on somebody.

Before this, I used to set myself aside from the old stories, sort of the way the old anthropologists had done. I'd say, 'Our elders say this ...' But I didn't connect myself to it. I had heard my Elders Rosaleen George and Peter Dennis Peters say they were real stories, but it wasn't until after my conversation with Keith that I understood the importance of my faith and belief in the stories. So it's funny that in a way he was actually teaching me about how to understand what the Elders were telling me. He's told me that our conversations have helped him better understand his own Catholic faith and those conversations have been really useful and enriching.

It's not just that Keith Carlson has been working with and within Stó:lō communities for a long time that makes this book special. Others before him have spent long periods of time trying to know and understand our society and our history. Sometimes these relationships have worked out, but the results haven't always been rewarding. What sets Keith and this book apart is the way he mixes respect for our culture, curiosity in his research, and his interpretions of the way things are seen. He shows our more complex history where we're more than romantic victims or people whose main story is the struggle against colonialism. The history he shares includes anthropology and the voices of our Elders so that he creates a story of Stó:lō collective identity and relationships that are vibrant and changing. In this book my ancestors are not portrayed as a people frozen in the past and unable to adapt to what academics call modernity. In this book my ancestors are depicted as living a rich and changing history that is full of meaning. Keith is not shy about looking at the importance of the internal pressures that existed within Stó:lō society and between people of different status and different genders. He shows how we reacted to colonialism differently depending on perspectives that changed over time. He shows how ancient patterns guided our ancestors as we encountered European diseases and colonial policies. In doing this he also shows that colonialism wasn't just one thing. It took many forms, some of which my ancestors resisted, some of which my ancestors turned to their advantage. The tensions that our communities face today are mostly products of both these earlier internal divisions in our communities and the later colonial forces. For these reasons, this book has valuable lessons that contemporary chiefs and family leaders should be reminded of, and that government officials should be introduced to.

Some people, for example, won't like hearing that the band, or tribe, or First Nation has not always been (and should not always be) the most important collective unit or political entity in Stó:lō culture and history. This book will rattle what some people have come to think is right and proper. Keith has made the idea of Stó:lō identity more complicated, and shows that there have always been forces pulling communities apart and forces pushing things together. Each chapter of Keith's book shows real unity among Stó:lō people even though there are forces working to pull or push us in other directions. What the most important collective unit was, was not always the same for everyone. Sometimes those forces pulling our communities apart were not colonial, but actually ancient Stó:lō divisions. Today there are tensions and divisions between the Stó:lō Tribal Council and Stó:lō Nation, between the central and upper Fraser Valley Stó:lō First Nations and the Yale First Nation in the Fraser Canyon, and so on. This book shows that conflicts have histories and that by looking at the tensions within our societies we can learn things about ourselves and about our relations with others.

We shouldn't be afraid of the power of bands, or First Nations, or the broader Stó:lō Nation in how they relate to one another. They don't have to be a threat to each other. The most interesting thing Keith argues in this book is the elasticity of identity. Identity is ancient and the history of identity helps us to understand not only who we are, but how we got here. We have a long history of nested political and social authority, and of how we form and reform our identity. All through this book Keith shows that we remain the Aboriginal people of the lower Fraser River watershed. People have to understand how important each of our identities is, and that means recognizing that over time the differ-

ent ways we express ourselves has shifted and changed. It's our strength
that we can adapt that way. And although the government would love to
divide and conquer us, some of the changes have been our choices and
haven't always been forced on us by outsiders.

This book is a story warning people about going too far down the road
to band or family identity, on the one hand, or tribal or national identity, on the other. We have to recognize the forces that pull and push
against each other and the importance of changing voices. It's important
to see how government, economics, and religion have been used to divide Stó:lō identity and to make certain ideas and beliefs more important
that others – those that were the most agreeable to colonizers. But Keith
shows how we've found new and innovative ways to be different and distinct. The history presented in *The Power of Place, the Problem of Time* shows
how we have reacted and responded to these internal and external pressures. And that is an important thing for our leaders and community
members to read and know.

Albert 'Sonny' McHalsie
Co-director and Cultural Adviser, Stó:lō Research and Resource
Management Centre

Acknowledgments

What lies ahead on these pages started as a question, turned into an idea, developed into a series of conversations, took the form of a dissertation, and then was transformed into this book. There are many who contributed at points along the way and who deserve credit for whatever strengths and merits this volume might have:

First and foremost, my patient and supportive wife, Teresa, and sons, Liam and Benjamin. Also my parents, John and Elizabeth, and my sister, Stormy.

My Coast Salish colleagues, friends, and *siyá:ye*, especially Albert J. 'Sonny' McHalsie, Grand Chief Clarence Pennier, Gwendolyn Point, Grand Chief (and Lieutenant Governor of British Columbia) Steven Point, Patricia Charlie, Michelle Julian, William 'Tunny' Charlie, Grand Chief Doug Kelly, Fern Gabriel, Tim Peters, Dalton Silver, Chief Maureen Chapman, Joe Hall, Kelsie Charlie, Grand Chief Sam Douglas, Denise Douglas, Sid Douglas, Corky Douglas, Marcie Peters, Anette Peters, Herb Joe, Hellen Joe, Tracey Joe, Larry Commodore, Darwin Douglas, Winona Victor, Willy Hall, Tim Peters, Carol Peters, Marlyn Gabriel, Darren Charlie, Chief Willy Charlie, Maggie Pettis, Earl Commodore, Evelyn McHalsie, Bill McHalsie, Danny Charlie, Ernie Crey, Ken Malloway, Bruce Sam, Stan Greene, Patricia John.

My Xwelítem friends and colleagues, especially David Schaepe, John Lutz, David Smith, Ron Denman, Wendy Wickwire, Dana Lapofsky, Tia Halstadt, Jody Woods, Sarah Eustace.

My Coast Salish mentors and *siyá:m*, especially Grand Chief Wesley Sam, Andy Commodore, Grand Chief Archie Charles, Frank Malloway, Myra Sam, Ralph George, Robert Thomas, Grand Chief Joe Gabriel, Rina Point-Bolten, Matilda Guiterrez, Alan Guiterrez, Jimmie Charlie, Rosaleen George, Harol Wells, Lena Johnny, Minnie Peters, Maureen

Gabriel, Hugh Kelly, Ray Silver, Nancy Phillips, Edna Douglas, Bertha Peters, Henry Pettis, Tiny Pettis, Shirley Julian, Jeff Point, Minnie Silver, Bill Pat-Charlie, Sophie Pat-Charlie, Aggie Victor, James Fraser, Moody Michelle, Buster Joe, Patricia Campo, Vincent Stogan, Anna McGuire, Vi Hilbert.

My academic mentors and guides, especially Arthur Ray, Bruce Miller, Diane Newell, Kerry Abel, Brian Dippie, Ted Wooley, J.R. Miller, Kenneth Coates, Dave Debrou, Jay Miller, Dan Boxberger, Cole Harris, Mike Kew, Hamar Foster, Julie Cruikshank.

Those Coast Salish people from an earlier era who saw fit to share their knowledge with ethnographers and others who would preserve their voices for others of subsequent generations to access, especially, George Chehalis, Robert Joe, Albert Louie, Joe Capilano, Peter Pierre, Simon Pierre, William Sepass, Patrick Charlie, Dan Milo, Hank Pennier, Jason Alard, Amy Cooper, John Wallace.

Those early observers, recorders, and ethnographers who made the effort to record, and then make available, their observations and recordings of Coast Salish history and culture, especially, George Vancouver and his officers, Simon Fraser, James Douglas, John Work, James McMillian, Gilbert M. Sproat, Franz Boas, Charles Hill-Tout, James Teit, Homer Barnett, Dianmond Jenness, Wilson Duff, Norman Lerman, Marian Smith, Elanor Leacock, Oliver Wells, Sally Snyder.

Jan Perrier for her artful design and cartography.

Those archivists and librarians who take care of, and facilitated my access to, manuscript collections in the BC Archives, UBC Special Collections, Stó:lō Nation Archives, Stó:lō Research and Resource Management Centre, Libraries and Archives Canada, Hudson Bay Company Archives, Chilliwack City Archives, American National Archives – Regional Branch, Bellingham, Washington, Center for Pacific Northwest Studies at the University of Western Washington, Oblates of Mary Immaculate Archives in Rome, Oblate of Mary Immaculate Archives Dechatles in Ottawa, Oregon Historical Society, Bancroft Library University of California Berkley, British National Archives (formerly Public Record Office), British Newspaper Library, Provincial Crown lands Vault Victoria BC, Royal Anthropological Institute in London, Vancouver Museum.

The anonymous reviewers with the University of Toronto Press who provided thoughtful comments and suggestions for revisions.

The people at University of Toronto Press who worked so hard to make this book look and read as well as it does, especially Len Husband, Frances Mundy, and Kate Baltais.

People who read earlier drafts, assisted with citations, engaged in conversations, or in other ways assisted in the thinking and writing that went into this monograph, especially John Porter, Amanda Fehr, Omeasoo Butt, Rob Algrove, Andrée Boiselle, Ana Novacovic, Stephanie Dalyluk, Mark Ebert, Julie DaSilva, Gordon Mohs, Brian Thom.

Katya MacDonald for creating the index to this volume.

SSHRC for a doctoral fellowship.

The University of Saskatchewan for a grant to cover the costs of producing maps and securing images.

SECTION ONE

Introduction

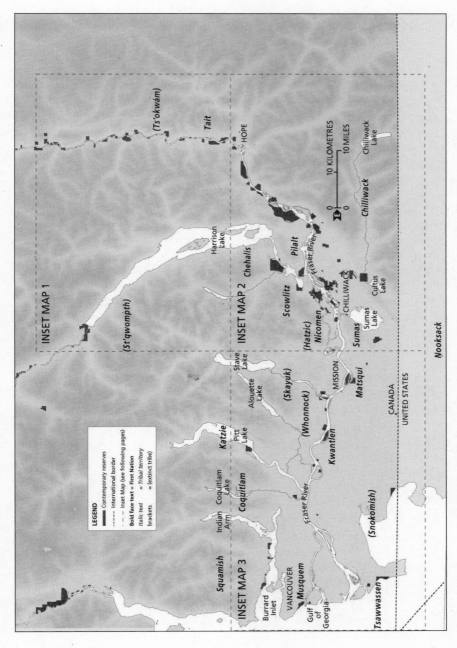

Map 1. First Nation Indian Reserves of the Lower Fraser River Watershed Region.

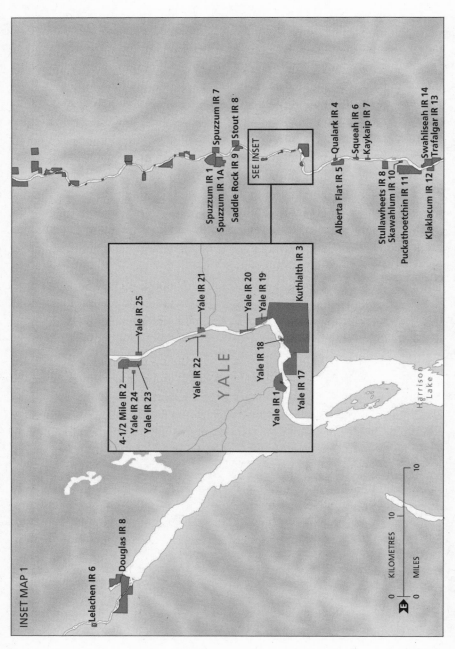

INSET MAP 1

SEE INSET

Spuzzum IR 7
Spuzzum IR 1
Spuzzum IR 1A
Saddle Rock IR 9
Stout IR 8

Alberta Flat IR 5
Qualark IR 4
Squeah IR 6
Kaykaip IR 7

Stullawheets IR 8
Skawahlum IR 10
Puckathoetchin IR 11
Klaklacum IR 12
Swahliseah IR 14
Trafalgar IR 13

Yale IR 21
Yale IR 25
Yale IR 20
Yale IR 19
4-1/2 Mile IR 2
Yale IR 24
Yale IR 23
Yale IR 22
YALE
Yale IR 18
Kuthlalth IR 3
Yale IR 1
Yale IR 17

Lelachen IR 6
Douglas IR 8

Harrison Lake

E

0   KILOMETRES   10
0   MILES   10

Map 2. Inset map 1 (see Map 1).

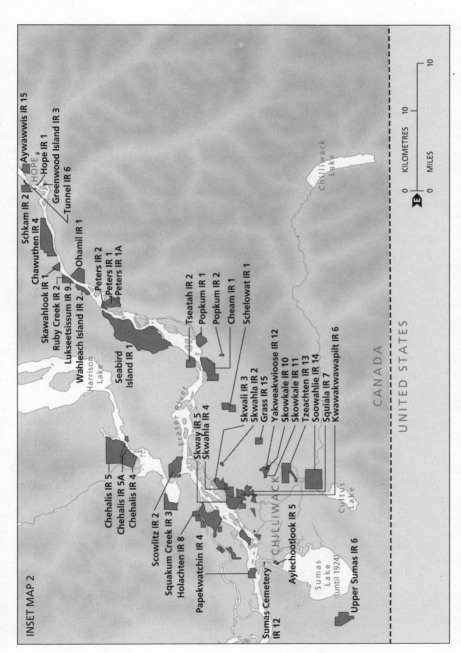

INSET MAP 2

Aywawwis IR 15
Schkam IR 2
HOPE
Hope IR 1
Chawuthen IR 4
Greenwood Island IR 3
Skawahlook IR 1
Tunnel IR 6
Ruby Creek IR 2
Lukseetsissum IR 9
Ohamil IR 1
Wahleach Island IR 2
Peters IR 2
Peters IR 1
Peters IR 1A
Seabird Island IR 1
Harrison Lake
Tseatah IR 2
Popkum IR 1
Popkum IR 2
Cheam IR 1
Schelowat IR 1
Chehalis IR 5
Chehalis IR 5A
Chehalis IR 4
Skwali IR 3
Skwahla IR 2
Grass IR 15
Yakweakwioose IR 12
Skowkale IR 10
Skowkale IR 11
Tzeachten IR 13
Soowahlie IR 14
Squiala IR 7
Kwawkwawapilt IR 6
Scowlitz IR 2
Squakum Creek IR 3
Holachten IR 8
Skway IR 5
Skwahla IR 4
Fraser River
CHILLIWACK
Aylechootlook IR 5
Papekwatchin IR 4
Cultus Lake
Sumas Cemetery
IR 12
Sumas Lake (until 1924)
Upper Sumas IR 6
Chilliwack Lake

CANADA
UNITED STATES

0   10   KILOMETRES   10
0   MILES   10

Map 3. Inset map 2 (see Map 1).

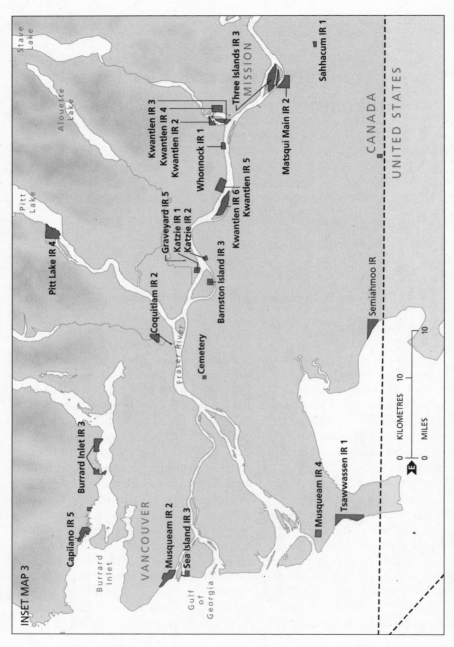

INSET MAP 3

Stave Lake

Alouette Lake

Pitt Lake

Kwantlen IR 3
Kwantlen IR 4
Kwantlen IR 2
Three Islands IR 3
MISSION
Whonnock IR 1

Pitt Lake IR 4

Graveyard IR 5
Katzie IR 1
Katzie IR 2
Kwantlen IR 5
Kwantlen IR 6
Kwantlen IR 2
Sahhacum IR 1

Coquitlam IR 2

Matsqui Main IR 2

Cemetery

Barnston Island IR 3

Fraser River

Burrard Inlet IR 3

Capilano IR 5

VANCOUVER

Musqueam IR 2

Sea Island IR 3

Burrard Inlet

Gulf of Georgia

Musqueam IR 4

Tsawwassen IR 1

Semiahmoo IR

CANADA
UNITED STATES

KILOMETRES
0   10   10

MILES
0   10

Map 4. Inset map 3 (see Map 1).

Chapter One

Encountering Lower Fraser River Indigenous Identity and Historical Consciousness

White men go about with a veil over their eyes and do not think as we
think.

– Chief Joe Capilano, Squamish, 1910[1]

Tunnels, Reserves, and Other Identity Shapers

Special tunnels link various sites on the Indigenous landscape of southwestern British Columbia's lower Fraser River watershed. Although they
cannot be found on government-produced maps, and are not readily visible to casual travellers, for those who know the history and know where
to look, the tunnels are real. Local Native Elders explain that you do not
need to be Aboriginal to find them, nor do you even need to believe in
their reality to be affected by them. People occasionally travel through
these mystical portals, but the journey is inevitably dangerous. Stories tell
of corpses being found near the exits of tunnels many kilometres from
the sites where the living persons were last known to be, proof that the sojourners died before reaching a tunnel's end. Others are more fortunate.
Those who survive the journey inevitably receive enhanced powers and
ultimately prestige. Travel through these tunnels is almost instantane-
ous, and as such their existence shapes Indigenous views of the physical
landscape by bending time. This transforms places that might otherwise
appear geographically distant into locations that are adjacent. The tunnels shape and inform Aboriginal views of collective identity and affiliation – the subjects of this book. Through the tunnels, settlements that
might otherwise seem far apart are brought together; much closer than
they appear on Western maps. The social affiliations of the people living

at either end of such tunnels are, thus, much closer than might be otherwise assumed.

While these tunnels connect Indigenous places and Indigenous people, they do not appear to link Indian reserves and Indian bands with one another. Indian reserves are creations of the British colonial and Canadian federal governments. They constitute property held in trust for Aboriginal people by the Crown. Reserves are associated with Indian bands, which are local Indigenous governing bodies with restricted powers and registered membership lists, are also creations of non-Native authorities. While Indian bands and Indian reserves are associated with particular Aboriginal communities, most of which are products of ancient social and geographical affiliations, they privilege a decidedly European notion of what constitutes a legitimate collective social and political unit: bands and reserves reflect an assumption that the most meaningful collective identity and affiliation is the one derived from proximity of residence, which in turn can be equated with local and exclusionary propriety rights over nearby natural resources.

Just as the tunnels are not readily visible to those untrained in the ancient ways, so too Indian reserves are invisible to those who are unfamiliar with government surveys and maps. As with the tunnels, you do not need to believe in the reality and legitimacy of Indian reserves to be affected by them. Reserve boundaries demarcate Native space from newcomer space, and Indian bands from one another like islands within a sea. Reserves transform places, which through mystical tunnels might otherwise appear adjacent, into locations that are distant from one another. Thus, reserves and bands shape and inform Indigenous views of collective identity and affiliation, and as such, these views are often hotly contested.

The tunnels and reserves are particularly illustrative because each represents identity-shaping forces that certain people on opposite sides of a cultural divide either refuse to accept or are incapable of appreciating. For Salish people, the proximity that tunnels create between otherwise distant bands shapes not only time and space, but social affiliations. Tunnels make neighbours of people who to non-believers are apparently distant; they keep relatives close. Indeed, people need not make regular use of the tunnels – tunnels are far too dangerous for most people to even consider using. It is enough that believers know they are there, just as their ancestors did; it is enough to realize that the tunnels can still be made operational by suitable people at suitable times.

Some who believe in the power of tunnels are frustrated and even angry at other people's certainty concerning the power of Indian reserves.

They see the reserve boundaries as arbitrary and oppressive and consider the band membership lists restrictive and insensitive to the ways of Salish families and society. They simply do not believe in reserves and reject the thinking behind them.

Thus, the tunnels and reserves give meaning to two distinct and competing imagined communities, but unlike the imagined communities studied by Benedict Anderson, these do not share an epistemological basis for their existence.[2] Rather, they represent cosmologies thrown together in the cauldron of colonialism – with all the power imbalance inevitably found in such contexts. Metaphysics and modernity compete with one another, and with other imagined communities, for legitimacy in the eyes and historical consciousness of Coast Salish people. Therefore, the British and Canadian governments are not the only external forces that contributed to the creation and reification of particular expressions of Aboriginal collective identity that are out of step with Indigenous historical understandings. Just as powerful as the invisible lines demarcating Indian reserves, and seemingly just as intractable as Ottawa's imposed system of band membership and governance, are the intellectual legacies of earlier generations of ethnographers, anthropologists, and historians. Salvage ethnographers, for instance, considered Indigenous people a disappearing race whose frozen-in-time culture needed to be documented; historians generally regarded Aboriginals as interesting only to the extent that they either contributed to, or served as foils for, the story of Western settlement and nation building; and anthropologists for decades were wed to the interpretive paradigm of structural functionalism and therefore interested principally in discerning forces within Salish society that served to maintain social order and equilibrium.

To these academics, and the voices of popular culture who occasionally turned to them for inspiration, mystical tunnels and affiliations forged through ancient stories were of no particular interest. Their role in shaping Aboriginal responses to colonial overtures thus has gone unappreciated. Scholarly literature on Coast Salish collective identity tended to emphasize either the importance of autonomous family households and corporate kin groups (in the case of anthropologists) or the significance of settlement and 'tribal' collectives (in the case of historians) to the near exclusion of those other competing identities and affiliations to which Salish people themselves often refer. Indeed, one of the most striking features of Coast Salish society is the effort the people put into maintaining a host of identity options; options that can be deployed or operationalized at a moment's notice to serve a range of personal or collective objectives. Sometimes, as during fishing season, what is most important is being able to show that one is a member of a particular extended family with ownership rights to a productive salmon fishing site. At other times, as when contemplating revenues from forestry resources, it is more important to emphasize one's affiliation with a particular tribal cluster. On still other occasions, as when requesting funding from the Canadian Mortgage and Housing Corporation, what really matters is being able to show that one is on a particular First Nation's band membership list. If one is seeking special spiritual helpers and powers an identity one might need to be able to demonstrate is genealogical connection to a legendary ancestor and/or membership in a particular spirit dance 'longhouse.' For *Sxwó:xwey* mask dancers, what matters is not only one's position as a dancer (inherited principally by men and primarily through their mother's line), but which division of the society one is associated with by virtue of affiliation with one of nine possible spirit helpers. Regardless of the situation, what matters most is that one has the training and knowledge to be able to shift and apply the relevant identity when the circumstances warrant and demand. (See Map 5.)

Composing scholarship that Aboriginal readers will find meaningful and through which they can see themselves, while retaining a critical analytical gaze, is a daunting task for an outsider. Fortunately, several sensitive and thoughtful researchers in both the social sciences and humanities have crafted works that serve as inspiration and upon which this study aspires to build. A growing body of ethnohistorical literature identified perhaps most closely with the work of Keith Basso among the Apache has begun, for example, to examine the intimate relationships Native people forge with the natural environment as a foundation for shared identity. Along similar lines the anthropological works of Julie Cruikshank in the Yukon and Jay Miller, Brian Thom, and Crisca Bierwert in Washington State and British Columbia illustrate the extent to which scholars are increasingly interested in studying the metaphysical underpinnings of culture to better appreciate the flavours that give identity local meaningfulness. Meanwhile, historians as diverse as Alexandra Harmon and Aletta Biersack are alerting us to the subtle ways Indigenous identity shifts in the face of colonial overtures – often along lines that are not always what those at the core of the imperial–periphery relationship anticipate or desire. Likewise, cultural studies scholars like Paige Raibmon and Philip Deloria remind us of the power that popular perceptions have to shape both non-Native and Native people's conceptions of what

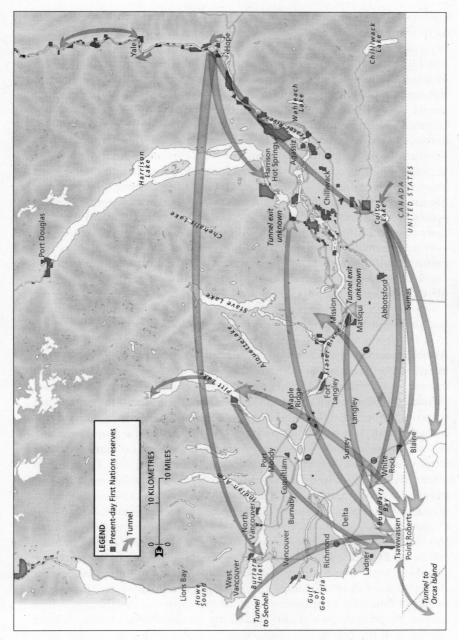

Map 5. Mystical tunnels transform spatial distance and inform social distance.

constitutes authentic or real indigeneity, while recent innovative works
as diverse as John Lutz's study of Aboriginal labour in British Columbia, Gary Zellar's analysis of racial identities among the African Creeks,
Jeff Oliver's recent examination of Stó:lō historical geography, which
bears directly on this study but which appeared in print too recently to
influence the writing and content of this book, and Sarah Carter's examination of the manipulation of Native gender on the northern plains,
remind us of the mutable nature of Aboriginal collective affiliations
across time and geography. In a more violent context, Diane Nelson's
provocative study of identity formation in Guatemala drives home the
importance of examining indegeneity in the context of colonial power
structures. Even more significantly, Marshall Sahlins has breathed new
life into ethnohistorical studies by alerting us to the interdisciplinary elephant in the room that no one seemed to want to talk about, namely,
the complex and poorly understood relationship between structure and
event. With such scholarship to build from, this study aspires to a more
complex and holistic engagement with Aboriginal history and historical
consciousness, one that, to borrow from Clifford Geertz's cited works,
offers a thicker description than has been the case so far.[3]

Encountering the Stó:lō[4]

Although inevitably influenced by powerful colonial forces, Coast Salish
people have been remarkably resilient in asserting their own identities
on their own terms, while rejecting the neat cultural and political boxes
others have attempted to put them in. When I first began my association
with the Stó:lō Coast Salish of the lower Fraser River watershed, in 1992,
I was immediately struck by, and indeed puzzled by, the diversity of collective identities and affiliations. Fresh out of a Master of Arts program,
where I had examined the history of decolonization in the Philippines,
while also participating in the university's Graduate Co-op Work Pro-
gramme where I spent two terms conducting archival research for the
Department of Indian Affairs (DIA), I was contracted by the Stó:lō Tribal
Council (STC) for six months to research the question of 'traditional
Stó:lō leadership.' Representing nine Stó:lō First Nations (or bands),
STC's goal was to provide the member communities then operating un-.
der the DIA system of 'municipal-style' elections with information that
could be used to reintroduce (through the 'customary code' provisions
of the Indian Act) a form of self-governance more in keeping with their
ancestral traditions. It was anticipated that the results of the study would
also inform the future development of broader supratribal self-govern-

ance.[5] In the course of my research I was provided with the names and contact information for over two dozen Elders. On recommendations from those Elders I subsequently contacted and consulted six additional cultural experts.

Stó:lō is the Halq'eméylem word for river, and I was told by Stó:lō Tribal Council staff and Elders alike that all the Indigenous people living along the lower 190 kilometres of western Canada's greatest river were 'Stó:lō,' or 'River People.' For a variety of reasons, however, less than a third of the region's twenty-nine Indian bands were members of the STC; twelve other bands belonged to a competing tribal organization called Stó:lō Nation Canada (SNC), while the remainder identified as 'independent' or unaffiliated. To my eyes there was no obvious geographical or cultural pattern informing the two tribal councils' memberships, though those First Nations on the eastern and western edges of the territory showed the least inclination to affiliate with other Stó:lō communities. None of the bands in the Greater Vancouver district, for example, were members of either organization, although at least one prominent Elder from Musqueam (near the University of British Columbia campus in Vancouver) assured upriver people that his community 'was Stó:lō.'[6] On the far eastern side of what was identified as Stó:lō territory, at the entrance to the Fraser Canyon, the Yale First Nation was also independent. In fact, Yale's relations with other lower Fraser bands were particularly strained. They were then currently involved in litigation against the Lower Fraser Fishing Authority[7] (an amalgam of the Stó:lō Tribal Council, Stó:lō Nation Canada, and several independent bands) which had been formed under the auspices of the federal Department of Fisheries and Oceans' controversial 'Aboriginal Fisheries Strategy.' Yale did not want to be part of a Stó:lō fisheries regime. A few years later the Yale First Nation again went to court over similar issues, this time declaring in their affidavits that not only were they not part of the cultural group anthropologists had identified as 'Stó:lō,' they were also not even Coast Salish. Rather, they asserted that the Yale people were an intermediate transition group between the Coast and Interior Salish. The terse rejoinder from Stó:lō chiefs' and fishermen was that the Yale were indeed Stó:lō, and that the canyon fishery in the region immediately upriver of Yale was central to Stó:lō identity and society.

If simple geographical propinquity failed to fully account for Stó:lō affiliations, I soon learned that what were popularly referred to as 'tribal' groupings – clusters of affiliated settlements – proved equally puzzling. An earlier generation of non-Native explorers, government agents, and social scientists had grouped (or divided, depending upon one's perspective) the Stó:lō into a number of tribal assemblages. There has never been a definitive agreed-upon listing of lower Fraser tribal communities, and indeed current scholarly orthodoxy tends to minimize both the historicity and cultural meaningfulness of Coast Salish 'tribes' as political units. Many Aboriginal people maintain that there were some two dozen Stó:lō tribes prior to European contact, and that these clusters of affiliated villages were politically significant expressions of shared identity. Generally speaking, the earliest European explorers and settlers, the salvage ethnographers, and contemporary Native oral traditions have all identified the tribe as having constituted an important Coast Salish affiliation. The bond linking members of a particular tribe together was the sense of common descent from one or more 'original people' – heroic ancestors or genealogical founders – shared among residents of associated settlements. Members of the Chilliwack Tribe in the central Fraser Valley, for example, trace their collective history back to four bear brothers named Wileliq, Thelachiyatel, Yexweylem, and Siyamches. These brothers are regarded as binding the Chilliwack people's collective past and future together through powerful metaphysical forces. Nevertheless, as I discovered upon starting my research, four of the bands making up the Chilliwack Tribe belonged to the Stó:lō Tribal Council, three to Stó:lō Nation Canada, and two were independent. More perplexing still was the fact that the bands in the vicinity of the non-Native city of Chilliwack had recently come together and registered themselves as a non-profit organization called 'The Chilliwack Tribe' whose mandate initially included submitting a 'statement of intent' to the B.C. Treaty Commission.[8] Among the member groups of the Chilliwack Tribe were two bands that historically and ethnographically have been identified as members of the neighbouring Pilalt Tribe; moreover, the chief of one of the Pilalt communities was elected chairman of the Chilliwack Tribe.

Similar instances of creative affiliating were to be found up and down the lower Fraser. While the Kwantlen Tribe had a reserve in New Westminster, its Band Office was on McMillan Island near Fort Langley, and (with government sanction) in the first decade of the twentieth century it annexed the reserves of the Whonnock Tribe near Maple Ridge. The Seabird Island Band near Agassiz, to take another still different example, wass a member of the Stó:lō Tribal Council and claimed to be part of the Tait ('upriver') Tribe. Yet within that community circulated stories of how their ancestors had relocated downriver to their present location from settlements beyond Stó:lō territorial limits in the Fraser Canyon in search of modern agricultural and wage labour opportunities. Similarly, Popkum, another registered Indian Act band near Agassiz and a member of the Stó:lõ Tribal Council, was considered by some to be an independent tribe and by others to be a member of the Tait Tribe, but was generally referred to simply as the Popkum First Nation. In 1993 Popkum had a population of nine people, more than half of whom, including the chief, lived off the reserve.

Clearly, the relationships between contemporary Indigenous place, space, and identity were complex – and history made them the more so. The passing of time and the occurrence of historical events inevitably called for innovative responses from Aboriginal people that challenged particular expressions of geographically nested identity. Even the historical and ethnographic legitimacy of a shared 'Stó:lõ' collective identity was a matter of heated Indigenous debate. Some Elders asserted that the lower Fraser people had always thought of themselves as an affiliated Stó:lõ community. According to this line of historical discourse, families within a village or cluster of villages had formerly gathered to select one man to be their tribal spokesman (*Siyá:m*). Every summer, during the salmon fishing season, while people gathered in the Fraser Canyon, the various Siyá:m met to discuss important issues of mutual concern. Paramount to these discussions was the selection of, or recommitment to, an overall supratribal Stó:lõ leader.[9] To exercise their power (either collectively or individually) the Siyá:m typically urged, occasionally cajoled, and in similar ways persuaded others to follow their leadership by demonstrating the wisdom of their ideas. Unlike a chief elected under the Indian Act, the Siyá:m, I was told, had no institutionally backed political authority.

In these regards, I was hearing essentially the same messages the anthropologists Wilson Duff and Wayne Suttles had recorded half a century earlier: that 'the concept of tribal unit was neither clearly defined, nor important in the native mind' and that 'neither village nor tribe had any formally separated machinery of government.'[10] But, whereas this earlier scholarship had emphasized the periods of stability where leadership functioned without the trappings of formal political authority, the Indigenous people I was speaking with appeared interested in discussing the disruptive events and powerful leaders who had periodically shaken this system.

Contemporary tensions were causing people to look back into the past for precedents – lessons that could inform contemporary decisions. Traditional hereditary control over prominent fishing and gathering sites meant that social influence had been backed by economic power, and at

times such economic power manifested itself as formal political authority. Also, I was told, at times tribal and supratribal identity had been of
vital importance, and leadership had been centralized and potent. If this
were the case, then it would seem that reconstructing a history of the
shifts and tensions within the various collective identities would prove
an important academic exercise – and one that might be meaningful
particularly to Aboriginal people.

The degree to which an historical examination of collective identity
would resonate within the Aboriginal community became increasingly
apparent as I learned how passionately certain people felt about the very
idea of a shared Stó:lō identity. While Elders had convinced both Suttles
and Duff that 'Stó:lō' identity was 'ancient' and that Stó:lō was the 'name
... which the natives prefer and use themselves,' certain contemporary
lower Fraser Aboriginal people openly rejected the historicity of Stó:lō
collective identity, arguing that it was an anthropological fiction – the
product of creative or nefarious academic theorizing and projection.
These detractors have suggested that the existence of competing oral
traditions supporting the idea of an ancient meaningful regional Stó:lō
affiliation said more about the ability of modern politics and academics to influence Indigenous historical consciousness than they did about
past historical realities. For people of this opinion, it was tribes and villages that were most commonly referred to as the genuine, and ancient,
meaningful collectives.

To help me make sense of these tensions I supplemented my oral history research with archival enquiry. Over the coming years I came to
appreciate the extent of primary documents generated prior to the proclamation, in 1858, of the Crown Colony of British Columbia. Within that
massive body of evidence I could find not a single reference to a group
of Aboriginal people referred to as Stó:lō. As far as I could determine,
the first written references to a Stó:lō identity appeared in the late nineteenth-century writing of ethnographer James Teit and in the French-
language publications of the Catholic Oblate Missionaries (see Chapter
7 in this volume). Yet within the archival documents left by even earlier
non-Native observers there were hints corroborating Elders' oral history
of a prominent and ancient Stó:lō collective mindset that preceded the
influence of missionaries.

My report on traditional leadership was submitted to the Stó:lō Tribal
Council in the fall of 1992, and although I felt it served the purposes of
providing culturally anchored alternatives to the divisive Indian Act election system, I remained personally frustrated by my inability to reconcile

the disparate voices concerning local and regional Aboriginal collective identities. Meanwhile, now hired as a salaried employee, I embarked on various new research initiatives for the STC, as around me the politics of identity continued to unfold. In 1994 the leadership of the STC and the SNC put aside their differences and with their supporters united to become the Stó:lō Nation. Although the motivations behind the merger were many, principally it was done to facilitate the assertion, within the recently established framework of the British Columbia treaty process, of a single collective Aboriginal title to the entire lower Fraser River watershed.

The newly merged body represented twenty-four of the twenty-nine bands/First Nations of the lower Fraser watershed. One of the Stó:lō leadership's first priorities was the drafting of a Stó:lō Nation constitution. This was accomplished and implemented incrementally, and eventually resulted in the establishment of a new legislative body called the Lalem ye Stó:lō Siyá:m ('House of Respected Stó:lō Leaders'), which was made up of the chiefs and councillors of the various member bands/First Nations. This body, in turn, chose from among itself an executive called the Council ye Siyá:m ('Council of Respected Leaders'). The executive was led by the Yewal Siyá:m (Most Respected Leader), and included a vice president-like figure known as the Stó:lō Siyám ('Respected Stó:lō Leader') and various 'portfolio chiefs' who were responsible for overseeing the Stó:lō Nation's programs and initiatives (e.g., community development, child welfare, fisheries, Aboriginal rights and title, finance and administration). Both the legislature and the executive were relatively non-cohesive groups, and the authority of the Yewal Siya:m in relation to either body was limited principally to his or her ability to persuade. Moreover, to the puzzlement of many non-Native observers among the general public and local media, certain members of the executive council often appeared to interact with the Stó:lō Yewal Siyá:m more like members of a parliamentary opposition party than as members of a prime ministerial cabinet.

Some of the unaffiliated lower Fraser River First Nations interpreted the Stó:lō Nation's treaty claim to the entire region as a provocative action – a challenge to their own sovereign tribal or band authority. To reduce apprehension, we as the staff of the Stó:lō Nation's leadership argued that the Stó:lō Nation's collective assertion of title to lands claimed by non-affiliated First Nations was not meant to be a usurping of tribally based title, but rather as an invitation to revive a broader system of governance based on supratribally shared interests. Contemporary

expressions of local First Nation/band and tribal boundaries were insuf-
ficiently nuanced, the Stó:lō Chiefs asserted, to account for the various
interests of people residing within one tribe's or band's territory in the
resources within another tribe's or band's core territory. Too many social, economic, genealogical, metaphysical, and historical links bound
communities together to allow any divisions between them to become
exclusionary. Canadian government policy, argued the Stó:lō Nation's
leadership, had solidified boundaries and memberships that had previously been more fluid, and as a result, future Indigenous governance
and management would require cross-tribal cooperation and planning.
In an attempt to indicate their sincerity, the Stó:lō leadership explained
that within their newly constructed government buildings they had in-
stalled sufficient chairs for representatives of all Stó:lō communities, and
not only those who had already formally declared themselves members
of the Stó:lō Nation.

The 1994 Stó:lō statement of intent submitted to the British Columbia Treaty Commission (BCTC), as with the architectural design and
layout of the new government buildings, expressed a resolve not to be
confined by preconceived ideas concerning the supposed relationship
between Indigenous identity, proximity to land and resources, and political authority. These were explicit efforts to decolonize the processes
of securing the recognition of Aboriginal title and self-determination.
Moreover, although they were bold and somewhat controversial moves,
Stó:lō leaders were quick to point out that they were not without precedent. In fact, their statement was substantively very similar to the expression of shared identity and Aboriginal title that their ancestors had
made to Joint Indian Reserve Commissioner Gilbert Malcolm Sproat in
1878 (see Chapter 9).

In 1878 Commissioner Sproat was visiting Aboriginal communities
throughout Canada's Pacific province, assessing and determining Aboriginal people's perceived territorial needs, and assigning reserve lands.
The effects of his activities, of course, had more far-reaching implications.
In creating Indian reserves, Sproat was effectively binding Indigenous
people to decidedly European notions of residence and governance.
Once a reserve land base was established it was possible for the Canadian
government to apply the assimilationist Indian Act. Prior to the creation
of reserves the government had no effective means of monitoring the
day-to-day lives of Indian people. Reserves, in other words, facilitated
systems of colonial surveillance, and through surveillance, manipulation
and control. Without fixed reserve boundaries it was difficult for authorities to regulate Aboriginal movements and activities. More importantly

for the purpose of understanding Aboriginal collective identity, until reserve boundaries were set, it was impossible for the government to create band membership lists, and without lists of names to associate people with particular land bases the Dominion had no recognized chief and council through which an appointed Indian agent could administer his authority or make policy with regard to local land use and resource development, or even service delivery.

Perceived through this lens, the process of creating Indian reserves facilitated and necessitated the creation of Indian bands, Indian chiefs, and Indian band membership lists. This process was simultaneously empowering for, and compromising of, Indigenous identity and governance. The Canadian federal government regarded an Indian reserve not merely as a portion of an Aboriginal community's traditional land, but also as Crown land. An Indian band was not merely a Dominion government-recognized expression of pre-existing Indigenous collective identity, it was also an administrative unit within the Canadian federal bureaucracy as defined in the Indian Act. An Indian chief, be he or she elected, appointed, or a recognized hereditary or 'customary' leader, was nonetheless by definition an agent of the minister of Indian Affairs, and as such his or her power and authority were in large part defined in, and subject to, the assimilationist Indian Act.[11] Regardless of how earnestly and sincerely Indian chiefs may have tried to use their positions to advance and protect their constituents' rights and interests, and no matter how closely Indian Act band governance might have reflected and paralleled certain older traditional expressions of collective identity and governance, the system was inherently contradictory. The inescapable irony of history is that although chiefs and councillors ostensibly represented their communities' voice against the Canadian government and its citizenry, it was through those same chiefs and councillors that the Department of Indian Affairs attempted to impose its will on band members and reserve lands. The chiefs of contemporary First Nations operating under the Indian Act continue to wrestle with, and continue to be compromised by, these contradictions.

Today, for example, just as in the late nineteenth century, the omnipresent and oppressive Indian Act provides no mechanism for someone who is not a registered member of an Indian band to formally influence band decisions – and it is only the band that the federal and provincial governments recognize as the legitimate (and hence funded) Aboriginal collective and government. Indeed, until the 1999 Supreme Court decision in *Corbiere* v. *Canada* even those registered members of an Indian band who happened to reside off reserve were not guaranteed the right to participate in elections for their own chief.[12] Moreover when people transfer their registration from one band list to another they are effectively denied any government-recognized means of influencing events or participating in decision-making processes in their original band. As far as the Canadian government is concerned, it does not matter if one's mother resides on another reserve, or if one has been initiated into a winterdance longhouse community on another reserve, or if one's hereditary rights to a fishing site are located on another reserve and had been affirmed through a potlatch. It does not even matter if a mystical tunnel connects a person's place of residence directly to a site on another reserve. Unless you are registered on the Canadian government's band membership list for a particular reserve, you have no legally recognized interests in the affairs of that land.

If Commissioner Sproat had previously been unaware of how certain Indigenous interests in lands reached well beyond the confines of local reserves, he certainly was made aware of this when he met with the chiefs of the lower Fraser River in the autumn of 1878. In a letter composed in a rain-soaked canvas tent, Sproat wrote to Prime Minister John A. Macdonald explaining: 'as the Indians on this Lower portion of the river are one people, and though claim to belong to particular villages, move about constantly from one place to another ... I propose before assigning land to any of the tribes to ascertain who *are* Lower Fraser Indians, and to take a view as to the people as a whole.'[13]

Given the historical and racial context in which Sproat was operating, his observation that the people of the lower Fraser were one people was as insightful as his desire to ascertain the nature of their collective identity and shared interests before assigning reserve land was refreshingly respectful. His sudden retirement the following year, however, prevented him from ever coming to a full appreciation of the relationship between identity, geographically dispersed land resources, and historical migrations among the lower Fraser people; and his successor, A.W. Vowell, as has been well documented by historical geographer Cole Harris and others, shared neither Commissioner Sproat's intellectual curiosity nor his concern for crafting Indian policy that was meaningful and intelligible to Aboriginal people.[14] Consequently, a system of reserve allocation and governance that was in sync with Aboriginal collective identity and that reflected broader regional affiliations never took hold. Instead, subsequent government agents and visiting scholars alike would concentrate their policy and enquiry respectively on the winter village community at the expense of the broader affiliations – this despite the fact that regardless of the imposition of band membership lists, most of the region's Aboriginal population continued to spend much time each year residing and living outside of their winter settlement in differently constituted social amalgams.

Certainty and Identity

The 1994 unification of the Stó:lō Tribal Council and the Stó:lō Nation Canada into the Stó:lō Nation did not signal the eclipse of more localized tribal or settlement-based affiliations and identities. A mere ten years later, in the summer of 2004, the organization was to again split along fault lines essentially the same as those that had prevailed before the amalgamation. Indeed, both tension and flexibility were hallmarks of the Stó:lō Nation organization from the beginning, but even this flexibility was strained by competing ethnographic and legalistic definitions of community that equated every band a First Nation, but only certain First Nations a tribe.

In addition to those lower Fraser River First Nations who remained unaffiliated, certain founding members of the Stó:lō Nation disassociated themselves soon after 1994. Some, like the Union Bar Band located near Hope, simply never showed up at any of the Stó:lō Nation's meetings. Others, like the Cheam near Chilliwack, participated fully for a time before expressing dissatisfaction with some of the strategies the Stó:lō chiefs were adopting towards securing and defending collective rights and title, and so they decided to pursue a more independent course. Others still, like the Popkum or Kwantlen, tended not to be particularly active in day-to-day aspects of Stó:lō Nation governance, but remained firmly committed to 'the Nation' as a concept and agent for advancing a shared political vision. Nonetheless, the Kwantlen, like the Scowlitz, Sumas, and Lakahaman, among others, also never allowed their support and commitment to the Stó:lō Nation to distract them from pursuing more localized initiatives, or from strongly asserting a claim to specific tribally based rights to lands and resources within the broader Stó:lō-claimed territory. The Kwantlen and Lahahaman bands, in their capacity as First Nations and tribes, also earnestly defended their particular title claims to provincial Crown lands that fell somewhat beyond what appeared to have been their immediate pre-contact tribal territories – lands that previously were associated primarily with neighbouring tribes such as the Skayuks and Xatsuk, who were rendered 'extinct' following the devastating smallpox epidemic of the late eighteenth century – but,

of course, survivors of this epidemic did relocate to be with their relatives in the Kwantlen and Lakahaman tribes. Finally, some Stó:lō Nation
member communities, such as the Seabird Island and Soowahlie First
Nations, remained very politically active at the 'national' level while they
simultaneously assumed local band-level responsibility for the delivery of
most social, economic, and education services – services that the Stó:lō
Nation provided to many of its other members.

To many outside observers, and indeed some Aboriginal people, regional Coast Salish politics and identity in the 1990s was confusing and
only getting more mysterious. In the pages of the prestigious *Journal of
Ethnohistory* a debate raged between defenders of the non-centralized
interpretation of Coast Salish political authority and those who argued
that the classic interpretation overemphasized social networks at the expense of political bonds, and still others who posited that both of these
positions were inadequate inasmuch as they were 'unsituated, overly
democratic, and woefully irreligious.'[15] Local newspapers reported on
the growing, and seemingly irreconcilable gulf between the Yale First
Nation and the Stó:lō Nation over who had the more 'traditional' right
to exercise jurisdiction over the lucrative canyon salmon fishery.[16] More
recently archaeological evidence has been brought to bear on this increasingly interdisciplinary discussion.[17] All the while, well-meaning el-
ementary school teachers regularly contacted the Stó:lō Nation office
asking whether there were resources they could use in class to help pu-
pils understand the distinctions between Salish households, bands, First
Nations, tribes, and nations. They asked whether metaphors that equate
the Stó:lō Nation with the Canadian federal government and the various constituent First Nations/bands and tribes with Canadian provinces
were more appropriate than ones that associated the powers of the Stó:lō
Nation with a provincial-style entity and its constituent members with
municipalities. In such cases, as staff, we generally thanked the teachers
for their interest and efforts, but advised that both metaphors were ultimately inadequate, before providing them with contact information for
Aboriginal spokespersons who were willing to go to the schools to talk
with students directly about these issues.

Government and industry too, were puzzled. By the late 1990s non-
Natives, such as those sitting on the provincial government's Regional
Treaty Advisory Council, and in particular representatives of various
resource extraction industries, repeatedly expressed frustration at the
apparent ongoing ebbing and flowing of Stó:lō political authority. With
whom, they asked, were they supposed to consult: the Stó:lō Nation or

the local band/First Nation who was located nearest their operations and therefore apparently more likely to be most affected by their actions?

The B.C. treaty process was meant to bring 'certainty' to the province by clarifying the nature and extent of Aboriginal rights and title, including the right to self-government. 'Certainty' however, was, and remains, for many non-Natives, a euphemism for the extinguishment of Aboriginal title, and self-government a synonym for Aboriginal municipality. Even for non-Natives familiar with the academic writings of Paul Tennant, Hamar Foster, and Cole Harris, or the savvy journalism of the *Vancouver Sun*'s Steven Hume (and who therefore could foresee alternative and less assimilative visions of 'certainty'), the fluid nature of Stó:lō Nation membership and political authority were genuinely disconcerting. Front page stories in local Fraser Valley newspapers implicating some Stó:lō leaders in fiscal mismanagement or political interference in service delivery programs did not help matters.

As staff historian I was regularly asked by the Stó:lō leadership to make public presentations to non-Native groups about the nature of Stó:lō rights, title, and identity. As such, I made it a point to keep informed about the attitudes and assumptions many non-Natives held towards the Stó:lō. Cross-cultural education and dialogue were identified as major components of my job description, and towards that end I was intimately involved in the editing and authoring of several publications through the Stó:lō Heritage Trust. Each of these was informed by provincial curriculum guidelines as well as community objectives. These projects involved community intellectuals, a broad spectrum of professional staff in the Stó:lō Nation office, and academic colleagues at various universities. The first, titled *You Are Asked to Witness: The Stó:lō in Canada's Pacific Coast History* (1997), is a collection of essays discussing Stó:lō cultural traditions and significant events and issues in the history of Stó:lō–newcomer relations. The second, *I Am Stó:lō: Katherine Explores Her Heritage* (1999), is a children's textbook written in collaboration with Sonny McHalsie and his family; it examines racial stereotypes and Stó:lō traditions through a fictionalized story centring on young Katherine McHalsie and thus is a contribution advancing an important subtheme of this volume, the definition of community identity. Finally, in 2001 we produced *A Stó:lō-Coast Salish Historical Atlas*, where, through a series of map-based plates, we attempted to convey a sense of the temporal dimensions of lower Fraser River Aboriginal collective identity and 'nation building,' as well as the relationship between identity and resources.

Despite these and parallel efforts by some of my Aboriginal colleagues, who specialized in more dynamic communicative realms such as public speaking and artistic initiatives, I commonly encountered from non-Aboriginal residents of the Fraser Valley statements such as: '*They* [the Natives] are going to have to get their act together if they want to have real self-government,' 'There has to be accountability with *my* tax dollars,' and 'If *they* want to have self-government or special rights they should go back to living in the forest and catching fish with spears,' but perhaps most troubling of all, '*We* won the war didn't we?' or 'Why should we have to pay for the sins/crimes of our grandparents?'

Of course, there never was a war where the Stó:lō or any other B.C. Aboriginal group lost their title to their lands. Moreover, the financial and political shenanigans of the then (1990s) governing provincial New Democratic Party (NDP) and federal Liberals rendered, in my mind at least, Western politics more suspect and more corrupt than anything I'd witnessed among the Stó:lō. Thus, moved in part to further address the lack of awareness among the public, and by a growing personal desire to develop a richer temporal understanding of Aboriginal collective identity, I cut back my hours at the Stó:lō Nation office and embarked on doctoral studies at the University of British Columbia. There I was provided the opportunity to conduct deeper research than I hitherto had undertaken into the question of the history of Coast Salish collective identity.

The Problem of Time

Not all Aboriginal people of the lower Fraser River watershed will agree with the conclusions I arrive at in this book, a revised version of my 2003 dissertation. The power of place – expressed through variously constituted geographical signifiers of shared identity – is profound. Some expressions of identity inevitably become privileged over others. Furthermore, as people invest themselves into a particular collective identity, they develop vested interests in preserving that collective identity. Hence tensions inevitably exist between advocates of various overlapping, and sometimes competing, identities. I do not deny the validity or meaningfulness of any such affiliations. What I challenge is the notion that certain collective affiliations are necessarily more traditional or legitimate than others because they have always been so. I argue that the passage of time presents problems for collective affiliations, and these problems cause shared identities to be periodically reconstituted upon new lines.

Historical philosopher R.G. Collingwood discussed a good half-century ago how change can be interpreted in at least two, opposite, ways: as negative by those who oppose it and as positive by those who promote or embrace it.[18] Aletta Biersack, historical anthropologist of Oceania, more recently argued that to the degree that Indigenous societies are not static, analysis of tensions and conflicts within and between Native groups (and between these same communities and European colonizers) provides forums for determining which aspects of society promoted identity stasis and which were open to innovation.[19] The complexity and lack of consensus among the lower Fraser River Salish as to how to best define their own shared identity makes fascinating a historical examination of the methods and mechanisms by which the proponents of various expressions of Coast Salish collective identity advanced their sometimes competing objectives throughout the first century of contact and colonial disruption.

Regarding history as the arbitrator of identity and authority is, of course, neither an exclusively Stó:lō, nor even Aboriginal, phenomenon. As Patrick Geary demonstrates in *The Myth of Nations: The Medieval Origins of Europe* (2002), competing assertions over the historical legitimacy of ethnic communities to land and resources lie at the heart of many of the contemporary world's more violent and contentious conflicts.[20] Closer to home, Wayne Suttles has identified conflict and authority as understudied features of Coast Salish cultural expressions.[21] As such, determining how and why certain expressions of collective identity took situational precedence over others among the lower Fraser River Indigenous population engages and builds upon a large and diverse body of scholarly literature in both the social sciences and the humanities. Indeed, the implications of local ethnohistorical study may well generate insights that prove useful for understanding the context of various global phenomena, for if one thing is clear, it is that despite the power of global colonialism Indigenous people have been remarkably creative in finding new ways to be different, all the while remaining decidedly the same.

Clearly, then, no single collective identity is ever the only one that people associate themselves with. It is now a commonplace to state that identities are forged in relationships, and that to endure the boundaries between different identities require constant maintenance.[22] We could not be Canadians if there were not citizens of other nation states against whom we could compare and define ourselves. We could not be parents if there were not children, and we could not be non-Native newcomers if there were not Native Indigenous people. Without someone to 'other' there would be no 'us.' Furthermore, we are never simply Canadians, parents, or others. We are simultaneously many things even when we are temporarily primarily one thing. Importantly, as we other others, others other us.[23] Push-pull factors, which sociologists refer to as identity boundary maintenance, are at work. No matter how hard we might try to insist that particular others are, in fact, us or that we are, in fact, not certain others, there will be those who disagree: think, for example, of Quebecois separatists in Canada, members of the resistance in occupied France, a frustrated father who disowns a son.

Different situations require us to activate, or deploy, or operationalize certain relational identities. This book presents a history of the variously operationalized collective identities of the Indigenous people of the lower Fraser River beginning in the late eighteenth century (just prior to the first smallpox epidemic) and running through to 1906 (the beginning of the age of contemporary west coast Aboriginal politics), when political identities had been reified at the band level, service delivery and community governance likewise consolidated within the band, and where supratribal affiliations and actions were likewise regularized along particular lines that recognized the auonmy of constitutent bands. It documents the tensions that existed between various contemporaneous expressions of collective identity, but principally this book is interested in the processes of identity formation associated with conflict resolution that emerged as changing circumstances caused certain forms of collective affiliation to be challenged by certain others.

Identity, in the context of this study, should not necessarily be associated with formal political authority. I am not seeking to overturn the classic model of Coast Salish culture first and most clearly articulated in the academic literature by Wayne Suttles. Indeed, I consider myself largely to be working within the Suttlean tradition. But I also believe the historical evidence suggests that ethnographic descriptions sometimes tell us more about the structures and rules of Aboriginal society than about the society's actual workings and practices. In this regard I am reminded of the apparent contradictions I perceived many years ago between two undergraduate European history courses. In one, taught by a political historian, I was told that late nineteenth-century Germany was best understood within the context of increasingly centralized power and the rise of powerful individuals such as Otto Von Bismarck. In contrast, in the social history course it was explained that the fragmented nature of the various German principalities necessitated characterizing the region and times as a classically decentralized political order.

Such differing views are not only the product of different interpretive paradigms; they can also result from focusing one's analytical gaze on particular features of a topic. Imagine, for example, the different pictures of Christianity that would emerge depending upon whether one's focus was on the rules of the faith as revealed in the Gospels, and in particular the Sermon on the Mount, or on the actions of Christian Crusaders and Inquisitionists. Such an example is not so absurd. In the history of relations between Australian Aboriginals and newcomers a prominent scholar recently posited that the pioneers of Tasmania could not have been as cruel towards the local Indigenous population as some historians have suggested simply because they were Christians.[24]

Event and Structure

When it comes to writing ethnohistory, there is a disciplinary elephant in the room that few people are talking about: the exaggerated opposition between structure and event, and the way each influences the other. Marshall Sahlins rightly contends that for too many anthropologists and historians 'it seemed that "event" and "structure" could not occupy the same epistemological space. The event was conceived as antistructural, the structure as nullifying the event.'[25] Too often, Sahlins observes, structure is situated as being to event 'as the social is to the individual, the essential to the accidental, the recurrent to the idiosyncratic, the invisible to the visible, the lawful to the aleatory, the quotidian to the extraordinary, the silent to the audible, the comparable to the unique and so on.'[26] Sahlins challenges us to invert our theoretical praxis and recognize that historical events can become ethnographically intelligible through the study of change rather than stasis. Instead of looking for continuity in change he challenges us to seek change in continuity.[27] This is a principal objective of this work.

If historical events can be made ethnographicaly intelligible, the question, for some still remains: can they be made important to our interpretation of societies? The Annales school of historical enquiry, most popularly associated with Fernand Braudel's magisterial *The Mediterranean and the Mediterranean World* (1949) wherein the ocean replaces human actors as the main character with historical agency, has now for more than half a century argued that individuals and events are of secondary importance to the social structures and economic forces that shape and constrain human actions.[28] For Braudel, as with most twentieth-century anthropologists, the important thing was *la longue durée* – structural time, continuity. But as Raymond Fogelson points out, the peculiar historical circumstances surrounding Native–newcomer contact in North America and the rapid changes wrought Aboriginal society render scholastic enquiry into the Native past somewhat special. A structural approach alone cannot fully account for human experiences and understandings when introduced change was so sudden and profound. But likewise, a study of the event itself neglects the structural integrity that we know existed.[29] As such, the potential benefits of reconciling event-centred analysis and biography with processual examinations of social structures are significant. Indeed, there is a growing awareness of the value of contrasting and combining analysis of the 'rules of society' with examinations of certain important 'happenings' and personalities. This is serendipitous for, as will be shown, historical events and individuals also figure prominently in Stó:lō people's understanding and recounting of their own history.

Thus, Stó:lō identity needs to be conceived not only as situationally created through relationships, but also as emerging from unexpected historical events that alter or affect social structures. More importantly still, existing structures shape the way events are understood, while events cause changes to structures. The two inform one another profoundly. Certainly, this is an important aspect of the way Stó:lō people themselves describe and define their identity. This study builds from Sahlins' approach to event-centred analysis and accepts his definition of a genuine 'historical' event as a complex happening with specific significance in terms of both meaning and importance. Interpreted this way, 'not every action is an historical event ... [only] those which change the order of things.'[30] An historical event is not a common activity acted out within a culture, but an unanticipated action or happening that stands out against a backdrop of known predictability: 'It is a difference and it makes a difference.'[31] Put another way, 'It [an historical event] is a relation between a happening and a structure.'[32] It is important, therefore, to document carefully the earliest structures of lower Fraser River Aboriginal culture as they relate to identity, and to then identify stress points within those structures to better perceive the connection between historical event and subsequently altered expressions of identity. Of particular interest here are the ways structures shape the manner in which events are understood and reacted to, and how events likewise alter the structures within which they are interpreted. Particular individuals, classes, and genders inevitably regarded certain events as opening doors of opportunities even as they challenged the way things were. Their agency is central to this study, for as Sahlins points out, while 'structures and events cannot be reduced to the other ... yet each is somehow determining the other.'[33]

Resituating Aboriginal History

It will no doubt surprise some people to learn that non-Natives are not necessarily always the most important thing in Indigenous historical consciousness, let alone Indigenous history. Ethnohistory requires historians to explore not only the story of Natives in newcomer history, but also the saga of newcomers in multiple Aboriginal histories. It requires the construction of new chronologies and interpretive frameworks that go beyond the story of Aboriginal people in Canadian history; stories that are sensitive to, but not necessarily centred upon, the role and place of colonialism within Aboriginal history.

Once history is resituated so that Aboriginal people can be appreciated not only as minor players on the stage of Indian–white relations but as leading characters in plays that they increasingly co-author if not compose outright themselves, interesting images of the dynamics within Indigenous society emerge. Too often the racial and/or ethnic issues of Native–newcomer history work to obscure important class and/or status and gender issues within Indigenous society. Sensitivity to the historical injustices done to Indigenous people at the hands of non-Natives has understandably resulted in reluctance on the part of scholars to turn too critical an eye to the tensions within Indigenous society for fear of doubly victimizing a people already grievously wronged. Nevertheless, in generally overlooking the significance of gendered and class-based differences and tensions, historians and social scientists alike have inadvertently muted the voices of the most marginal of the marginal. Examination need not imply criticism, and as one of my Aboriginal mentors regularly reminds me, all people have things in their history that are not regarded as positive by contemporary measures; the point is not to deny their existence or explain them away, but rather to engage them respectfully and learn from them.[34] This study is interested in the critical points of tension within Aboriginal history.

Thus, while it is impossible to provide the equivalent of a literature review of Indigenous Coast Salish historical consciousness, the local Aboriginal discourse makes clear that divisions in Coast Salish identity revolve around fundamental tensions, certain dimensions of which Western scholars have largely overlooked. For example, it is generally accepted that tension remains between geographically nested identities and more regionally dispersed affiliations – the latter being for the most part products of human movements over the geography. What has not been adequately highlighted, however, is the degree to which the tension between geographical stasis and movement and migration has gender and class dimensions. In the period during and preceding this study, for example, the upper class of one village community had much more in common with the nobles of neighbouring tribes than they did with the propertyless commoners and slaves within their own settlement and tribe. Moreover, while elite women inevitably felt greater affiliation with the men of their own station than with the female slaves who relieved them of having to perform manual labour, nonetheless, the effects of elite polygamy and patrilocal residence patterns resulted in both high-class women and lower-class free men often being more interested in the affairs of people outside of their winter village than would have been the case for either elite males or slave women.

The historical reasons for these cross-gender/cross-class alliances, while generally overlooked, are relatively straightforward. To this day, high-status men typically derive much of their authority and status by publicizing genealogical ties to heroic ancestors who, near the beginning of time, were transformed into large stones or other objects located near their ancestral settlement. These stones serve as identity anchors around which prominent men build settlement- and tribally based affiliations among their followers. High-status women, on the other hand, typically relocated to live in their husbands' settlements after entering an arranged marriage. Important signifiers of a woman's status and identity therefore remain located in the immediate vicinity of her parents' homes or, as inevitably occurred, travelled with her sisters to their husbands' locales. My research reveals that throughout the contact and colonial periods, new opportunities emerged for people to take advantage of older gender- and status-based divisions to promote change that was set in stark opposition to particular expressions of identity and authority. Thus, within lower Fraser River Salish history and society, identities – like population movements – flow from fluid, predictable processes (which are linked to social structures) , and they also emerge from unexpected, punctuating historical events and personalities.

What Follows

Ultimately, collective identity is like a mask; a person puts it on or takes it off depending upon changing circumstances. For members of the sacred

Stó:lõ sx̱wó:ox̱wey fraternity, for example, it is literally a mask that signifies the spiritual brotherhood connecting each person privileged to wear it. The place of Coast Salish individuals and collectives in the human universe was decidedly different in 1906 from what it had been in 1780 (the temporal book ends of this study), but past precedent and understandings of how the world functioned informed all changes. Certain older social networks that had previously been relatively inactive rose to the fore of Indigenous political life, while other formerly more political expressions of identity either subtly shifted to accommodate changed colonial circumstances or, conversely, slipped into the background of Aboriginal political consciousness. This volume explores the process through which Indigenous people negotiated these changes, and it does this by taking Indigenous epistemology seriously.

The following is as much a journey through Indigenous historical consciousness as it is history. I am interested not only in what happened, but how people understood what happened, and how, over time, they came to reinterpret what happened in light of new experiences and understandings. To this end, the next two chapters examine some of the key forces that shaped local, and competing regional, expressions of collective Aboriginal identity immediately prior to the disruption caused by contact and colonialism. They situates the Stó:lõ within a broader ethnographic and ethnohistorical context by elucidating the geographical, technological, spiritual, and economic underpinnings of Stó:lõ collective identity as they existed immediately prior to contact. It is posited that these factors worked to emphasize the linkages between settlement and tribally based communities. Also introduced in these chapters are the gendered and class-based roots of differences in perspective over the expression and importance of collective identity.

Collectively chapters 2 and 3 establish the geographical, economic, environmental, and spiritual context for the various expressions of late eighteenth-century Stó:lõ collective identity. Individually, these topics have captured the interest of several earlier generations of anthropologists and historians working in the Coast Salish region. But here these matters are studied within the context of their relationship to one another. They are approached as components of an integrated whole whose modules cannot be fully understood in isolation from each other. As such, these chapters represent less a summary introduction to past scholarship than a fresh look at the way various factors influencing identity relate to one another. They also include fresh primary research and new conclusions. Chapter 2 invites readers to reconceptualize

rivers and watersheds so as to accommodate Coast Salish cosmology and,
in particular, to see the ecological and economic position of the lower
Fraser Canyon in broader regional Coast Salish epistemology. Chapter
3 examines the spiritual and cultural protocols surrounding not only
the transmission of historical narratives but their composition for what
they reveal about the role of past happenings in present understandings.
The various spiritual entities residing within each Coast Salish individual
are highlighted as semi-independent actors in the theatre of collective
identity building, just as the various 'myth-age' actors of the ancient narratives worked in tandem to 'make right' a world that was chaotic and
unaffiliated.

Chapters 4 and 5 together examine the previously overlooked role
of movement and migration in the formation of Coast Salish collective
identities in the early European-contact era through to the late nineteenth century. This is done by exploring the way historical events and
social structures inform one another and transform one another – all
the while working to constrain one another. Chapter 4 resituates the
Coast Salish response to the smallpox epidemic of 1782 within the context of earlier legendary stories of similar eventful disasters to illuminate
its place as a precipitator of mass migrations and community amalgamations (such as occurred among the upper and lower Chehalis). Chapter 5 investigates a subsequent category of migrations that resulted in a
range of community fractures and amalgamations. Some, like the Chilliwack Tribe's migration from the mountains to the valley floor, involved
complex negotiations with neighbouring groups. Others were more explicitly expressions of class conflict, as when the slaves from a village near
Hope left their masters and established their own 'tribal' identity farther
downriver in a region recently depopulated by smallpox. This chapter
also examines the significance and consequences of population migrations that resulted in entire communities relocating to be nearer opportunities for economic advancements, as in the movement of residents
of both downriver and upriver Kwantlen settlements to Fort Langley.
Finally, also explored are the mid-to-late nineteenth-century migrations
that resulted in the dissolving of certain upriver tribal identities and the
amalgamation of others. Towards a reflection of Indigenous historical
consciousness, the analysis reveals that the very fact that movement occurred is often more important than the expression it took, for within
Stó:lō society movement from one location to another is fundamentally
both an act and a process charged with power.

The process of identity fracture and contraction (i.e., the emphasis of localized or segmented expressions of gendered collective identity by specific colonial encounters) is the subject of chapters 6 and 7. Commencing with the international 1858 gold rush to the Fraser Canyon, relations with representatives of Western society and, increasingly, official representatives of state and ecclesiastic authorities, resulted in renewed tensions between village (primarily elite male) and pan-tribal (predominantly elite female and lower-status males and females) expressions of collective identity. Occurring initially within Stó:lō territory and then spreading rapidly up the Fraser River and into the B.C. interior, the gold rush also tipped the scales of military and political power between Aboriginal and non-Native populations.

Together, chapters 6 and 7 investigate the effect of reserve creation and the imposition of municipal-style elected band offices that acted to reinforce settlement and tribally based identities at the expense of more regional expressions. The role of the Roman Catholic Church in creating a regionally centralized residential school for all Stó:lō tribes, and in sponsoring petitions and other collective actions is also studied. The Church's interaction with the Stó:lō illuminates the role of syncretism (the blending of previously separate ideologies and beliefs) as a counterpoint to the forces of boundary maintenance as reflected in such acts as the banning of the potlatch and the prohibition put on sales of non-tidal (riverine) caught salmon. Both the ban of the potlatch and salmon fishing regulations led directly to escalations in the tensions over conflicting historical interpretations of identity while eliminating one of the key regulatory mechanisms for conflict resolution.

Much has been made of the value of bringing Native history 'out of the background,' and of emphasizing the Indigenous significance of events that to contemporary Western observers have often appeared small or insignificant.[35] However, we need not look in the historical shadows to catch glimpses of the rise of supratribal Stó:lō identity in the late nineteenth century. The Stó:lō and their Salish neighbours orchestrated and conducted some of the largest and best-documented political rallies in western Canada, not because they had necessarily always acted in a politically coordinated fashion, but because circumstances required it, and because the underlying social mechanism existed to facilitate it. Stó:lō people sought a collective response to the systematic alienation of their land and resources. This experience set a precedent for the quasi-military response to the lynching of a young Stó:lō boy by American vigilantes in 1884, as described in Chapter 8. The fact that these events and their Indigenous political significance have not become part of the non-

Native historical consciousness says more about the way history has been written than about Aboriginal participation in the making of history.

Colonial efforts to craft constricted Aboriginal identities were simultaneously countered by a subversive rise in supratribal political identification, and this process is examined in chapters 8 and 9. The Aboriginal response to colonial injustice and haphazard Indian administration was to make efforts to become genuinely self-governing and to have their relations with provincial and federal authorities governed by predictable rules of law.

The concluding chapter begins with a brief account of the 1906 Coast Salish delegation to London. This epic political journey to the most important non-Native urban centre in the world is placed within the context of the previous 130 years of identity formation. The sojourn's implications for the emergence of the more formal supratribal affiliations and political authority, so much a focus of Indigenous politics later in the twentieth century, are thereby made explicit.

Popular perceptions to the contrary, the history of Aboriginal collective identity is the story of a complicated process of change. To the extent that Aboriginal people have not only survived the homogenizing forces of corporate globalization and the assimilative policies of Canadian Indian policy, but have actually found new ways to be different, reveals the significance of local studies to our understanding of national and international issues. By adapting their expressions of collective identity, Aboriginal people along the coveted lands of the lower Fraser River watershed have successfully ensured their role as major players in a drama of cross-cultural relations whereby they continue to make decisions that shape the way distant manifestations of political and corporate power operate. To be meaningful to Indigenous people, and intelligible to non-Native newcomers, the recounting of Aboriginal history needs to reflect these realities. Ultimately, this book is an effort to construct a dialogue across cultures and with the past that will enable mystical tunnels and other uniquely Aboriginal features of contemporary Coast Salish epistemology to be placed alongside such matters as colonial land policy to reveal their individual and combined roles in identity-shaping events and processes in Aboriginal society, and thereby Aboriginal historical consciousness.

SECTION TWO

The Underpinnings of Stó:lõ Collective Identities

Chapter Two

Economics, Geography, Environment, and Historical Identity

As Geography without History seemeth a carkasse without motion; so History without Geography wandreth as a Vagrant without a certaine habitation.
                                                            – John Smith, 1624[1]

The Continuum

The Stó:lō of the lower Fraser River are part of a broader cultural and linguistic group known as the Coast Salish who historically have occupied the lands draining into the Strait of Georgia, Puget Sound, and the Strait of Juan de Fuca.[2] Coast Salish territory is remarkable for its physical and environmental diversity. Vertically, it ranges from tidal salt waters to glacial capped mountains. A healthy adult can hike from sea level to the subalpine in less than a day from almost any point in Coast Salish territory.[3] The region's vegetation was dense, however, and prior to non-Native urban and industrial development, travel by foot was largely restricted to a system of well-worn trails.[4] As a result, the canoe was the predominant means of transportation.

In addition to the unparalleled opportunities for wind-drying salmon that the Fraser River's lower canyon provided, Coast Salish territory was set apart from that of their more northerly neighbours by an abundance of lowland meadows on the rich alluvial soils of the Fraser Valley and the eastern coast of Puget Sound and southwestern Vancouver Island. Thus, while salmon was the principal food source, and wind-dried salmon the most reliable of winter stores, large and small game were also abundantly available, as were a host of vegetables and fruits, in particular wild potatoes and blueberries which, like salmon, could be preserved when harvested in the summer and stored for winter consumption.

Wayne Suttles, the leading figure in Coast Salish anthropology, pointed out that at the 'time of white settlement' the various marital, economic, and ceremonial ties linking the villages of central Coast Salish territory 'made the whole region a social and biological continuum.'[5] Contemporary Halkomelem language speakers living on the mainland of southwestern British Columbia and southeastern Vancouver Island refer to the people of this continuum as *Xwélmexw* (human beings, or literally 'People of Life'[6]). To be Xwélmexw it was not necessary to live in a settlement on the banks of the Fraser River and its tributaries, or even to speak Halkomelem. Rather, it was necessary to be part of either an extended family, a corporate kin group, a tribe, or some other social and/or economic affiliation that regarded it to be important to maintain associations with others who were likewise oriented to the lower Fraser River and in particular the lower canyon salmon fishery. As such, Squamish-, Nooksack-, and Saanich-speaking people were just as Xwélmexw as the Halkomelem-speaking Cowichan on Vancouver Island and the Chilliwack in the centre of the Fraser Valley – so long as they could demonstrate meaningful social, ceremonial, or economic connections to other Fraser River families and resources.

Farther away from the Fraser, people were increasingly 'different' (*lats'umexw*) in terms of culture, language, and economic orientation – a characterization that has grown less meaningful as the greater strangeness of European newcomers has eclipsed what once seemed to be such pronounced and important differences between Indigenous communities. It is clear that local and regional Salish people had ways of identifying 'others' long before Europeans arrived.

The earliest professional ethnographic observers failed to appreciate the extent of the region's social interconnectedness and instead regarded the autonomous Coast Salish winter villages as the most meaningful collective affiliation. Frans Boas, the father of modern North American anthropology, noted, in contrasting the Coast Salish (whom he theorized were relative newcomers to the salt water) with the more northern coastal people : 'While the [northern tribes] were divided into clans, the idea that was present to the minds of the Salish people was that of village community; and it is clear, therefore, that the traditions which developed would be of such character that each village would have one mythical ancestor.'[7]

Reflective of the settlement-based focus then current in anthropology, and undoubtedly influenced by the writings of prominent American ethnographer Lewis Henry Morgan (who in 1877 insisted that all North

American Aboriginal people were essentially 'barbarian' at the time of contact, that is, disorganized or in a state somewhere between 'savagery' and 'civilization'), anthropologists such as Thomas T. Waterman and Harlan Smith subsequently reinforced Boas' view of the Coast Salish.[8] Although at least one early ethnographer, Charles Hill-Tout, was sensitive to the significance of multivillage tribal clusters, and even claimed to have sources demonstrating the existence of pre-contact 'tribal confederacies' in the central Fraser Valley, his work was largely ignored and eclipsed by Boas' monumental university- and museum-based studies.[9] Hill-Tout's highly speculative theories about tribal origins and evolutionary development, moreover, kept his keen ethnographic observations on the periphery of North America's rapidly developing field of professional anthropology.[10]

Watershed Affiliations

The first academic to appreciate the significance of the connections linking certain Coast Salish settlements was Columbia University anthropologist Marian Smith. In 1940 Smith devised a spatial model to assess concepts of social unity among the Coast Salish of southern Puget Sound. Her statistical analysis illustrated the significance of river-based tribal associations. Smith's work in some ways represented coming full circle in the writings on the Coast Salish, for in emphasizing the role of landscape and ecology in fashioning human relationships she was corroborating the hitherto overlooked observations of the earliest European chroniclers such as Hudson's Bay Company (HBC) Chief Factor James Douglas.[11] Smith concluded that it was from the 'geographical concept of the drainage system that the Coast Salish derived their major concept of social unity. Thus, peoples living near a single drainage system were considered to be knit together by that fact if by no other.'[12] Based on quantified interviews with 178 informants, Smith determined that 'lacking the formal paraphernalia of political organization, the tie which ... [Puget Sound Salish] recognized as most binding, as most closely paralleling with what we know as political allegiance, was based upon this geography of the drainage system.'[13]

Smith's research demonstrates that each of the major rivers or inlets within the Coast Salish region was the domain of at least one tribe (a cluster of associated settlements). Moreover, some of the larger river systems, like the Puyallup in present-day Washington State, had significant tributaries of their own and were, therefore, home to more than one tribal group.[14] She learned that the Puget Sound Salish considered the Puyallup River from its mouth to the point where it divides into roughly two equal parts at Carbon, Washington, as distinct rivers from each of its forks above that point.[15] More importantly, broader groups of people (essentially clustered associations along drainage systems such as those groups based along the many rivers flowing into Puget Sound), although not formally organized, were, in her informants' words – as in those of James Douglas a century earlier – 'held to be one people.'[16] Smith recognized that 'the Indians of ... [the Puget Sound] region were supremely conscious of the nature of the country in which they lived. They were completely aware of its character as a great watershed.'[17] As such, Smith's research hinted at the existence of supratribal networks of collective identity, but she did not conduct the research necessary to verify their existence or to describe their expressions.

The implications of Smith's watershed-based identity thesis have not been adequately explored within the more northern Canadian Fraser River context.[18] This book examines the implications of the fact that within Coast Salish territory the massive lower Fraser River drainage system stands apart, acting as connector to no less than twenty-four sub-watersheds. Most of these smaller tributary rivers individually rival in scale and significance those around which are anchored other Coast Salish tribal communities in the Puget Sound and Strait of Georgia regions (recently renamed the Salish Sea). Indeed, each of the rivers running into the lower Fraser was home to a separate and distinct tribal community. Thus, *Stó:lō* (literally 'river') is the umbrella term that most of the many interconnected lower Fraser River tribal groups use to collectively distinguish themselves as what an Elder in the early years of the twentieth century termed the 'river of rivers.'[19]

Extended Family, Corporate Kin Groups, and Economic Niches

If Stó:lō was understood to mean the 'river of rivers' it is only a small step to appreciate that when conceived within a social rather than geographical context, Stó:lō can also be regarded as meaning 'tribe of tribes.' The idea of Stó:lō affiliation assumes special meaning when read in light of Wayne Suttles' insight that the people whose lives oriented around the Fraser River constituted a social continuum. Whereas Smith had studied settlements and tribes and inferred broader regional connections, twenty years later Suttles made the focus of his research the regional networks linking settlement- and/or tribally based communities. His analysis revealed a series of overlapping collective identities based on kinship and marriage that were at their heart economic relationships.[20] According to Suttles, neither the village nor the tribe have ever necessarily been the most important collective units. Indeed, Suttles went so far as to argue that villages were not 'communities' in any meaningful sense of the word.[21]

Approaching collective identity from the perspective of family rather than winter residence, Suttles identified the non-discrete, non-localized kin group as the most important collective affiliation. 'It was this group, or its head, rather than any of the residential groups,' Suttles maintains, 'that owned the most important ceremonial rights and the most productive natural resources.'[22] Cast in this light, the potlatch and other well-documented Coast Salish regional ceremonial activities were really responses to temporal and geographical fluctuations in food supplies. Put another way, what collective identity existed beyond the local house group and village settlement was inherently informal and based upon strategies designed to secure access to relatively scarce resources while building stores of what today would be referred to as social capital that could be cashed in during times of need. Thus, it was the extended family, and in particular in-laws (affines) through which such resources were accessed and shared, that constituted in Suttles' eyes the most meaningful network of intergroup affiliation within Coast Salish society.

To explain this thesis, Suttles drew attention to the fact that the environment of the people whose lives revolved around the lower Fraser River in the generation before contact 'was characterized by a variety of types of natural resources, local diversity and seasonal variations in their occurrence, and year-to-year fluctuation in their abundance.'[23] Significantly, as Suttles notes, a wide range of vegetables, shellfish, fish, birds, and land and sea mammals were available throughout the region, but the occurrence and abundance of these resources varied within ecological locales, and even within the localized areas there were seasonal variations as well as larger year-to-year fluctuations: 'All things were not available everywhere at all times so that they could simply be had for the taking. On the contrary, everything useful was available more at one place than another, and more in one season than another, and often more in one year than another.' Coast Salish social structures and ceremonialism, Suttles posited, were only 'intelligible in light of these variations.' He regarded this as the basis of an economy 'coping with abundance' with the alternating gluts and scarcities of individual resources in various seasons and specific locales.[24]

Suttles' model is remarkable for the way it helped to reorientate Coast Salish anthropology, but its full social implications only become apparent when resource availability is considered within the context of food procurement and processing technologies. Map 6 is a chart and schematic that illustrates comprehensively the relationship between resource availability and collective identity, taking into account the regional variations in the technology for salmon processing. Within this framework, resource procurement and processing are explored in terms of four distinct geographical/biological and 'food processing' niches. The first niche includes all tributary river systems flowing directly into salt water, and the second, those sub-watershed river systems entering directly into the Fraser River within the Fraser Valley. The third niche encompasses the lower Fraser Canyon where the main river narrows sufficiently to become, symbolically, a tributary watershed itself, not unlike those in niches 1 and 2. The fourth incorporates all subalpine parkland mountainous regions. Each of the four niches contains special resources that would appeal to people living outside its boundaries. Thus, to ensure access to a diversity of resources, people living in the lowland niches were motivated to forge various cross-niche alliances with those residing in niche 3 – which the residents of niche 3 were pleased to accommodate, securing as they did their access to valley and tidal food resources.

Pre-contact technologies allowed the Stó:lō to catch and process migrating salmon (in particular sockeye) in all but niche 4, but nowhere as easily and in such abundance as in the lower Fraser Canyon (niche 3). Likewise, prior to the adoption in the nineteenth and twentieth centuries of first salting, then glass-jar canning, and eventually artificial refrigeration and freezer technology, only in the canyon did climatic conditions make wind drying consistently possible. Wind drying was also dependent upon biological changes within the bodies of migrating salmon. As salmon ascend the river towards their spawning grounds they burn fat. Wind drying is simply impossible when salmon retain too high a fat content. Only when sockeye salmon – the fattest species – reach the canyon do they have the appropriate reduced, or diminished, fat content for effective wind drying. In the other lowland niche, salmon processing in pre-contact times depended upon smoking or sun drying – neither of which was as rapid, efficient, or reliable as wind drying. (See Figures 1, 2, and 3.)

Niches 1 and 2 also have distinctive biological characteristics. Unique to niche 1 are ocean resources such as marine mammals, shellfish, and

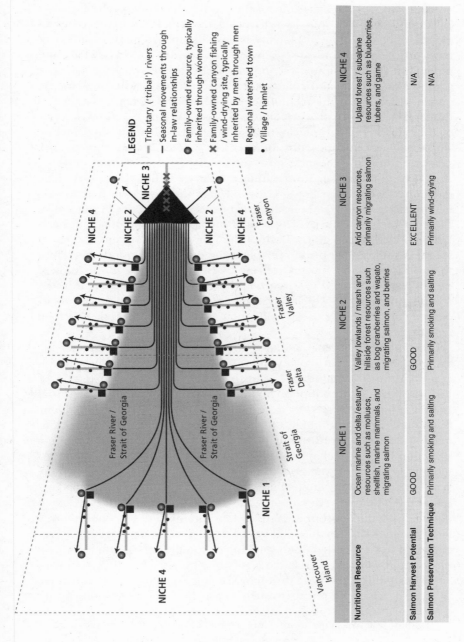

LEGEND

- Tributary ('tribal') rivers
- Seasonal movements through in-law relationships
- Family-owned resource, typically inherited through women
- X Family-owned canyon fishing / wind-drying site, typically inherited by men through men
- ■ Regional watershed town
- • Village / hamlet

	NICHE 1	NICHE 2	NICHE 3	NICHE 4
Nutritional Resource	Ocean marine and delta/estuary resources such as molluscs, shellfish, marine mammals, and migrating salmon	Valley lowlands / marsh and hillside forest resources such as bog cranberries and wapato, migrating salmon, and berries	Arid canyon resources, primarily migrating salmon	Upland forest / subalpine resources such as blueberries, tubers, and game
Salmon Harvest Potential	GOOD	GOOD	EXCELLENT	N/A
Salmon Preservation Technique	Primarily smoking and salting	Primarily smoking and salting	Primarily wind-drying	N/A

Map 6. Ecological niches.

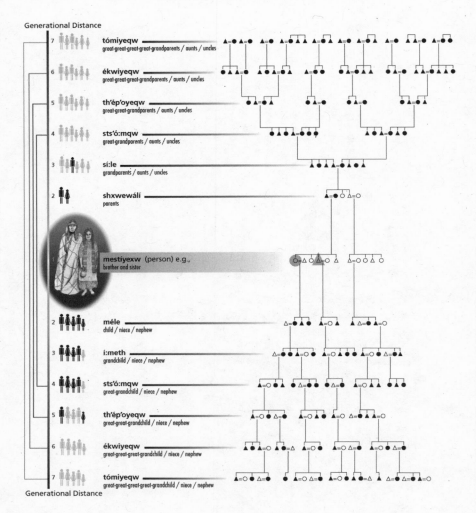

1. Identity across generations. Note parallel of kinship terms in past and present generations.

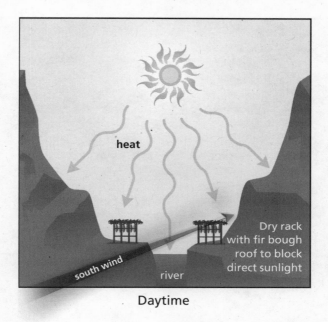

Daytime

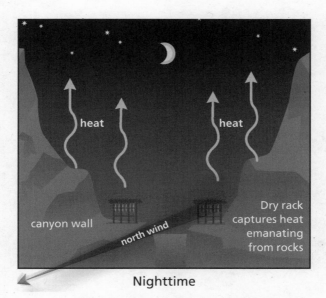

Nighttime

2. Unique climatic, biological, and geological circumstances make the lower Fraser Canyon ideally suited to processing salmon.

3. Stó:lō woman at fish camp near Yale, c. 1938. Note butchered salmon hanging to dry on racks beneath bark and boughs used to shade meat from direct sun. Photo by David Martin, Courtesy of Donna Dippie.

molluscs. Likewise (prior to widespread habitat destruction during the colonial era) cranberries and wild potatoes were plentiful and easily accessible only in the ponds and sloughs of niche 2. Cross-niche relationships, and especially those linking niches 1 and 2 with niche 3 were essential to prosperity.

Ethnographic evidence indicates that most of the resource sites that were subject to geographical, seasonal, or yearly variations and fluctuations were owned or controlled. Not all sites, but certainly the best, were the collective property of families, settlements, or tribes, their access and regulation controlled by specific individuals recognized as having a degree of authority over the collective unit. Resources that were readily available without regard to fluctuations over time or regional diversity were generally held to be open to all, or as George Gibbs characterized it more than a century ago, 'Land and Sea appear to be open to all with whom they are not at war.'[25] These were sometimes exploited by clusters of people associated by neither kith nor kin ties – communities referred to in the social science literature as corporate kin groups and households.

As Stó:lō Elders explained to the anthropologist Wilson Duff in 1950, 'Exclusive tribal or village ownership of resource areas was practically unknown among the Upper Stalo ... Such patterns of apparent ownership as did develop grew out of customary use rather than claims of exclusive right.'[26] Thus, people preferred to access and acquire plentiful resources from sites near their home settlements.

Extended families owned the best and most productive berry patches, camas beds, fern beds, wapato ponds, clam beds, duck net sites, and salmon fishing sites (individual dip net sites in the canyon, and entire streams or sloughs in the lower valley). Within the families, certain individuals exercised regulatory controls.[27] Fixed fish weirs or fences, such as the sturgeon weir at Musqueam, and reef nets found along the shores of the Gulf Islands were also regulated in this fashion. Typically, the individual who exercised control over the site (i.e., regulated access) lived in a nearby or adjacent settlement. The smokehouses used to preserve the salmon, which were located near the weirs and traps, were the property of the families who built them, as were the wind-drying racks used for similar purposes in the lower Fraser Canyon.[28] In the early to mid-nineteenth century, the Chilliwack Tribe similarly asserted the exclusive right to hunt in the forests within their claimed territory.

Certain types of resources belonged not to specific families, but to entire settlements or tribal communities.[29] For example, the cranberry bog immediately south of Allouette Lake belonged to the entire Katzie Tribe, while the bogs north of Sturgeon Slough and on Widgeon Creek belonged only to the people of the single Katzie settlement on Pitt Lake.[30] Similarly, people recognized that the giant sturgeon weir across the Sumas River was the collective property of all members of the tribe, in this case the Sumas Tribe,[31] as were most salmon weirs if they were large enough to traverse an entire river as opposed to simply smaller family-owned streams.

Resource ownership and access were directly linked to collective leadership, and by extension, collective identities. Jay Miller reminds us that Coast Salish society operated along lines of 'special interest groups,' who joined together to perform certain tasks under the leadership of situational and vocational specialists. Formerly referred to in the academic literature as task masters (*siateluq* in the Halq'eméylem dialect[32]) these interest group leaders were coordinated in their activities by village or tribal chiefs – men who carried prominent hereditary names derived from ancient community founders and who, as Marian Smith learned, were experts in human affairs.[33] As Miller explains, the 'intermesh of [special interest group leaders] with a chief had far-reaching consequences, since it provided a plan for larger, inter-tribal undertakings when called for.'[34] Along the lower Fraser River, for example, prominent family leaders who owned and controlled valuable resource sites (such as salmon streams, cranberry bogs, and camas patches) were generally referred to as *sxwsiyá:m* ('wealthy men with property'). The action of sxwsiyá:m were coordinated by men who carried hereditary tribal leaders' names (men whose positions were variously recorded as *hi'weqw siyá:m* (head chief) or 'master of the whole country'[35] or *yewal siyá:m* (first chief).[36]

Notably, the leaders of the variously constituted families, settlements, and tribes did not necessarily acquire their rights through direct inheritance. Suttles recorded that men from other tribes who had married Katzie women headed (i.e., controlled access to) two of the eighteen family-owned food sites in Katzie territory.[37] Hill-Tout reported that 'as a rule [a bride] confers her father's status and privileges upon her husband ... The chieftaincy of the tribe may be acquired by marriage of a chief's daughter ... as are the rights and privileges of the sxwõyxwey [mask].'[38] Likewise, while Duff speculated that prior to contact most of the owners of canyon fishing sites probably lived in the adjacent settlements, at the time of his investigations (1950) at least one owner lived as far away as Musqueam at the Fraser's mouth.[39]

Unless a state of war existed, families were obliged to allow visitors access to their property, but preferential access was the privilege of those with either blood or in-law connections to the site's owners. In a world where food resources were so unevenly distributed on the landscape and so subject to periods of seasonal abundance and absence, and where processing and storing foods demanded short intense bursts of labour activity, being able to demonstrate meaningful connections to a variety of property owners was of vital importance. Family ties, therefore, formed the economic base of people's most important collective identities. As a result, families with valuable canyon fishing and/or processing sites (niche 3) sought marriage alliances with families who owned complementary valley or ocean resources (niches 1 and 2), and so on. To emphasize closeness within the current generation, relatives as distant as fourth cousins were referred to as siblings. To make similar connections explicit across multiple generations, identical terms were used to describe the relationships between the living and people who were between four and seven generations removed in either temporal direction. For example, the word for great-grandchild/niece/nephew is the same as the term for great-grandparent/aunt/uncle and so on to the point of great-great-great-great grandchild/niece/nephew being the same as that for great-great-great-great grandparent/aunt/uncle (as in Figure 1). Likewise, the distinct terms used to describe relations with in-laws with whom the connecting individual had died illustrate the cultural imperative of keeping affinal groups together even after a death had ruptured the connecting link between families. Once newly forged ties of marriage reconnected in-laws the special descendant terms were replaced with the original terms for affines.[40]

High-status families, referred to as *smelá:lh* ('worthy people'), were those who knew their genealogical history and, therefore, knew who were their relatives and ancestors and could demonstrate their right to access important resource sites. The low-status *s'téxem* (literally 'worthless people') were considered to have 'lost or forgotten their history' and with it their rights to important resources. Polygamy functioned to make residence patterns among high-status families patrilocal. This situation worked to prevent insults from being perceived as would happen if a husband appeared to value one wife's family's resources over another's by choosing to reside with a particular wife's parents. However, a man (especially a man with only one spouse, it would seem) who chose to live in his wife's home community suffered no loss of status, and indeed, men often assumed ownership of property within their wives' families' home territories as part of their dowry. As Suttles explains:

In bilateral societies like the Coast Salish ... affinal ties in one generation lead to consanguineal [blood] ties in the next ... Marriage between two families in one generation reduces the number of potential mates in the next. To maintain affinal bonds between two communities for several generations requires that each [settlement or tribal] community be composed of several family lines alternating with each other in their marriages ... Since each community contained several 'owners' of productive resources, there was no special advantage in marrying one rather than another among the good families of a neighbouring community.[41]

From a functional perspective, therefore, collective identity and regional political authority could be regarded as being principally outgrowths of the need to secure access to regionally dispersed food resources and food-processing technology opportunities.

Thus, within the realm of economics, a system of constant movement existed between tribal communities in the three ecological niches where winter settlements were located. Elite women, through marriage, typically moved to live permanently with their husbands, but elite women's parents' families moved seasonally to visit their daughters and to access the resources that the marriage secured. Likewise, the elite woman's parents' families acted as hosts to visits from their son-in-law's family and provided its members with access to their resources. Occasionally these visits among affines lengthened into permanent reallocations of entire families.[42]

Although different families moved to visit and access their in-laws' resources, they also generally participated in at least two other seasonal visits to important resource sites regardless of whether they had family connections. These journeys were to the tuber patches near the mouth of the Pitt River, and to an even greater extent to the dry-rack fishing sites in the lower Fraser Canyon within the territory of the now-dispersed Ts'okwám Tribe. As a result, the lower Fraser Canyon represented a special place in Stó:lō society and geography. Each year, as the early Hudson's Bay Company records demonstrate, literally thousands of people from as far afield as Vancouver Island travelled to the canyon to procure wind-dried salmon.[43] If they had in-law connections they arrived to take their turns at the fishing stations and to exchange gifts; without such connections they still came, only their goal was to barter for what their lack of marriage alliances prevented them from acquiring more cheaply. Due to the size and scope of this migration, the lower canyon assumed the role of a regional trade centre where a plethora of other resources collected from other regions were also traded. For example, people arrived at the canyon with canoe-loads of dried and smoked molluscs and other such regionally specific resources with the intention of trading them to people who may not have been permanent winter residents of the canyon district, but rather visitors from other far-off places. The canyon provided an opportunity for the exchange of a diverse collection of goods that would have been impossible to procure had people been forced to travel widely to a host of different sites to exchange and acquire the variety of goods needed for winter sustenance and subsequent potlatch exchange. The lower canyon was a trade and social network hub.

Profit, River Currents, and Social Cohesion

While Marian Smith's drainage system analysis hinted at the existence of sophisticated cross-tribal networks, and Wayne Suttles' economic and ecological studies outlined the structural basis upon which they functioned, it was not until 1989 when Bruce Miller applied communication theory to his analysis of Coast Salish social networks that the significance of intercommunity networks was statistically demonstrated.[44] Miller examined five modes of social exchange and determined that the Puget Sound Salish region was indeed far more heavily integrated than the earliest anthropological literature implied. As such, Miller's work serves as a mathematical confirmation of Suttles' metaphorical analysis, and shows conclusively that meaningful collective identities and expressions of authority exist in forms other than the heretofore notably absent formal expressions of supratribal chiefly political power. Moreover, Miller's' findings helped resolve the problem of determining if a particular social institution existed in response to a particular problem or issue. In this case, Miller was able to demonstrate that intercommunity networks, as Suttles had hypothesized, did indeed serve to alleviate the geographical problem associated with periodic shortages of food supplies.

In addition to corroborating earlier theories, however, Miller's mathematical study also provided new insights into the way collective affiliations were constituted within Coast Salish society, which have important implications for this study. Miller showed that beyond the extended family there existed a broader 'corporate family group' which brought the labour and skills of certain unrelated people into any particular family's socioeconomic network. It was the corporate family that served as the real fabric linking various clusters of Coast Salish people together. It was from this body that various expressions of political authority and collective identity emerged. For example, Miller's work revealed a heretofore overlooked correlation between certain expressions of exchange and social relationships. Trade, ritual, and coalition ties were not dependent upon close kinship, as had been supposed. Rather, they served to strengthen network affiliation between people who were *not* related.[45]

My own subsequent research into the dynamics of Stó:lō exchange systems confirmed Miller's findings, but also revealed that close kinship ties with distant people could likewise work to a family's disadvantage, especially if a kin group held ownership rights over a particularly valuable resource with a unique geographical expression, such as Fraser Canyon fishing sites.[46] Coast Salish exchange with close kith and kin was reciprocal, but trade with strangers was designed to turn a profit.[47] Both Miller and I have demonstrated that, if a family possessed resources that could not be had anywhere else, they could expect to derive greater benefits by exchanging their wealth with strangers than in sharing it through reciprocal exchange with visiting family. The previously unknown (to outsiders) massive network of rock walls linking immediate pre-contact era settlements in the Fraser Canyon, which Grand Chief Archie Charles pointed out to David Schaepe and I in 1998, reveal, as Schaepe's subsequent study of these features has demonstrated, a profound degree of social and political cooperation most likely derived from the foundations of the corporate family group structure.[48] Schaepe's analysis astutely posits that construction of the walls and their coordinated use during attacks suggests that strongly centralized political leadership characterized the region. But the degree to which the walls were designed not only to protect the region's population from regular late summer and autumn attacks by aggressive coastal raiders but also to visually communicate power and inspire awe in order to help facilitate orderly summer visits with non-related coastal customers looking to exchange ocean and estuary goods for dried salmon remains to be explored.

Thus, regarded from a perspective that better takes into account both Indigenous rules of behaviour as well as practice, the geography of the lower Fraser River assumes new significance. For eighteenth- and nineteenth-century Coast Salish people who measured distance in terms of 'a day's canoe ride,' the Fraser provided unparalleled opportunities for those living along its tributaries to visit in-laws and attend potlatch ceremonies – activities that inevitably reinforced and supported the non-political affine networks as well as corporate kin group associations – well beyond those available to other Coast Salish groups in settlements located in tribal watersheds that drained directly into salt water. The opportunities for supratribal identification, such as might derive from opportunities for intertribal visits, were consequently also without parallel vis-à-vis the rest of Coast Salish territory. Whereas a Coast Salish canoe traveller on Puget Sound or the Strait of Georgia might realistically hope to pass the mouths of two to five watersheds (and therefore two to five tribes) in a single day, a person travelling down the Fraser could easily visit the entrances to well over a dozen tribal watersheds in the same time span. In travelling upriver, giant swirling oval-shaped back eddies, some more than half a kilometre in circumference, were used to rocket a canoe upstream by taking advantage of centrifugal force. Together with side channels, these eddies enabled a skilfully manoeuvred canoe to traverse the mouths of roughly ten tribal drainage systems in a day.[49]

Coast Salish people generally regard ocean waters as free, and open passageways for transportation and communication (although families own specific fishing sites[50]). In contrast, rivers are considered to be more restricted avenues controlled by the local watershed's occupants. In this capacity, rivers represent the core of potentially larger tribally claimed watershed-based territories. One of the earliest ethnographic observers of Coast Salish life was the Pacific Railroad surveyor-turned-settler, George Gibbs. He arrived among the Coast Salish of Puget Sound in 1854 and then served in a variety of official government capacities that involved trying to understand Coast Salish thought and society. In 1877, after working as secretary for the Washington Territory Treaty Commission, Indian agent, and published ethnographer, Gibbs reported: 'Tribes are ... somewhat tenacious of territorial right, and well understand their respective limits; but this seems to be merely as regards their title, and they never, it is believed, exclude from them other friendly tribes. It would appear also that these lands are considered to survive to the last remnant of a tribe, after its existence as such has in fact ceased ... Land and sea appear to be open to all with whom they are not at war.'[51]

The lower Fraser River (below the seven-kilometre length of the lower Fraser Canyon) is distinct from all other Coast Salish river systems in that, symbolically, it represents for Aboriginal people an extension of the ocean – or perhaps it is more accurate to say that the ocean represents an extension of the lower Fraser River. This fact, unappreciated in the earlier literature, is of vital importance because, when accounted for, it forces us to reassess the social geography of the entire region. For example, discussions that categorize the lower Fraser simply as a single Coast Salish river system have failed to recognize it as a parallel social geography to the open salt waters of Puget Sound to the south, Strait of Georgia to the north, and the Strait of Juan de Fuca to the west. As Smith explained, for the Puget Sound Salish as a whole the concept of broad pan-tribal identity, that is, of being 'one people,' stemmed from the fact that 'their country [the Sound drainage] all flowed in the same direction.'[52] Similarly, Wayne Suttles learned that among the Coast Salish of the Strait of Georgia 'the cardinal directions are not named.' Such directional indicators were important to Europeans interested in travelling across ocean systems, or to plains Indigenous people moving over vast tracts of prairie land, but they were clearly less significant to the coastal people of the protected waterways of Puget Sound and the Strait of Georgia. Thus, as Suttles records, Coast Salish direction is determined in relation to the axis of water travel routes: 'The northwestern end of Georgia Strait seems to be equated with "upstream" and the southeastern end with "downstream."'[53]

If, as Smith demonstrated, the people living along the shores of Puget Sound and the Strait of Georgia consider these ocean channels as cohesive riverlike waterways around which a loose collective supratribal identity is based, it is easy to imagine how much more this feeling informs the thinking of the lower Fraser Stó:lō communities whose country all literally flows together through their common river from mountains to ocean. While various Stó:lō tribal communities claim tributary side channels and even certain stretches of the shoreline of the mighty lower Fraser as their exclusive tribal territories, the ever-flowing central body of water is generally conceived of as belonging to all, or perhaps more accurately, to no single tribe. This collective riverine transportation route serves as the geographical nexus for collective Stó:lō identity.

The hegemony of Western concepts of geography has prevented scholars from appreciating that, for the Stó:lō, the banks of the Fraser River below the canyon are more properly regarded as continuations of the ocean shores – or, once again, given the linquistic evidence already discussed above, perhaps a more apt metaphor is to say that the north-running expanse of the Strait of Georgia, the easterly channel of the Strait of Juan de Fuca, and southern waters of Puget Sound are extensions of the lower Fraser River. Members of the various regional tribes travelled from the Fraser estuary upriver without feeling that they were trespassing. Indeed, this occurred on a large scale every summer during the salmon fishing season, when literally thousands of people headed upriver and then back down from the canyon drying racks. Even non-local communities with hostile intentions, often referred to by twentieth-century Elders as 'Coastal Raiders,' frequently passed up the Fraser en route to attack or exact revenge on particular Stó:lō tribal or village or family communities without being challenged or stopped by those farther downstream. Occasionally, collective efforts were made to repel intruders, but more frequently, as is reported in contemporary oral histories as well as ones collected at the beginning of the twentieth century, members of lower Stó:lō tribes sometimes simply watched the raiders as they made their way upriver to their chosen destination.[54] Often, Elders explain, the raiders' beautiful and powerful hypnotic war songs rendered the bystanders powerless to act in any case.[55]

Thus, from an Aboriginal perspective, Coast Salish territory is best conceived of as a four-pointed star with each of the four major open water systems – the Strait of Georgia, Puget Sound, the Strait of Juan de Fuca, and the Fraser River – constituting one of its points. (See Map 7.) Within the boundaries created by the star's coastlines relatively fluid movements of people, and therefore ideas and goods, occurred. Individual tribal communities naturally felt greater affinity and identified more closely with those with whom they interacted most frequently. Distance, as Suttles recorded, consequently played a key role in shaping a sense of shared identity. As it was often easier to travel across the star's points than through the star's centre and into another point, each of the clustered set of tribal communities in the points felt to varying degrees a sense of being 'one people' – a conception made stronger by the kin and other non-residence ties fostered across and between the various tribes. In terms of the opportunities they offered for developing common identities, however, the star's points were not equal. For the reasons outlined above, on the eve of European contact the social and political cohesion of the Fraser tribes exceeded that of the star's other points.

Geography, environment, and economics commingled in the minds and history of lower Fraser River Salish people in a manner that is not necessarily obvious to twenty-first century observers whose views of the river and ocean are primarily restricted to glimpses out of the windows of passing cars, and whose understanding of the relationships between a husband's and wife's two sets of parents is shaped primarily by the annual negotiations surrounding Christmas visits.

Individual tribes held within their local watershed-based territories a number of special resources that were obtainable only at specific times and found only in specific locations. Certain resources were available in greater quantities and for longer periods in different tribal homelands. These economic realities motivated people to forge complex webs of as-

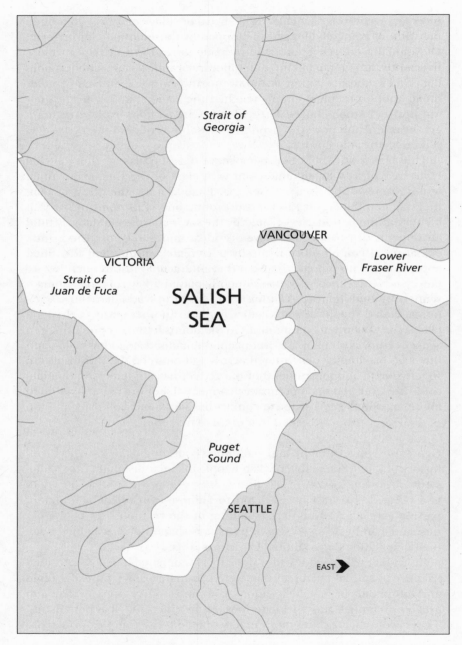

Map 7. Fraser River as an extension of the Salish Sea, or the Salish Sea as an extension of the Fraser River?

sociation across large and diverse geographies that went beyond related members of extended families. This pattern was common throughout all Coast Salish territory, but the special geography of the lower Fraser River with its numerous tribal sub-watersheds and unique salmon-catching and -preserving opportunities in the canyon, along with the upriver transportation facilitated by giant swirling eddies, created unrivalled opportunities for communication and the solidifying of various human relations and affiliations.

The physical geography of the region and the biological realities of the lower Fraser River's flora and fauna did not operate in a cultural vacuum. But, it was the belief systems of people who sought community and affiliation that gave meaning to the physical world. For the Coast Salish inhabitants living along the lower Fraser River in the later eighteenth century, geography and biology were but the outward manifestations of an active and dynamic metaphysical world in which humans were but one active partner. Indeed the Coast Salish living at the time of contact appear not to have held a notion of the individual in the sense that it has come to be understood in the post-Enlightenment Western world. Rather, dynamic spirit forces animated not only the landscape and waterscapes, but the social-scape associated with human activity. The objective of humans was to create situations where the various potential free agents of the Salish universe could be harmonized so as to minimize conflict and maximize collective strength. Accomplishing this, as we shall see, required that a great deal of energy be devoted to fostering social cohesion, and that meant people and spirits alike needed to be able to move frequently and freely across a storied landscape.

Chapter Three

Spiritual Forces of Historical Affiliation

The river is holy; it journeys day and night, coming no man knows whence, and travelling no man knows whither. Pray to it. Tell it that you are striving to be a medicine man, that for a long time you are going to fast, and ask it to help you. Then come back into the house.

        – Old Pierre's mother to her young son, c. 1860[1]

'Keeping the Stories Straight':
Spirituality and Indigenous Historiography

A fundamental tension in the writings about Coast Salish people re-volves around the utility of either a material and/or ecological basis for social and political affiliation or a spiritual basis. When contemporary lower Fraser River Indigenous people speak among themselves there is a pressure to foreground spiritual approaches to defining community. Perhaps this is in part a response to the contemporary economic mar-ginalization of Indigenous people, and the pervasiveness of popular Western discourse that has consistently portrayed Aboriginal people as essentially spiritual, non-economic beings.[2] Consequently, while fore-grounding spirituality risks reinforcing the image of Indigenous people as exclusively 'otherworldly,' allowing metaphysics to lie as an icing upon a cake of geography, biology, and economics risks creating scholarship that is not only disconnected from Aboriginal realities but within which Aboriginal people cannot recognize themselves. This book refuses to fall on one or the other side of this debate.

  Many of the most important indicators of Stó:lõ collective identity tran-scend time and place. One of the most central is a concept of connection through the unifying power of a supreme spiritual force responsible for creating the universe and providing it with life and sustaining that life through the distribution of power. Typically, Stó:lō people today refer to this creative energy as either *Chíchelh Siyá:m* (Chief Above) or 'Creator.' In 1936 Old Pierre of Katzie, one of the last of the formally trained Stó:lō shamans and a key informant for the anthropologist Diamond Jenness, explained that in English he preferred the names 'Most High Respected Leader' or 'Lord Above,' whereas one of Charles Hill-Tout's late nineteenth-century informants from near Fort Langley elaborated that while the Supreme Being was indeed Chíchelh Siyá:m, He was addressed in prayer as *Cwaietsen,* meaning 'parent, Father or Creator.' Such diversity in address continues today.

Academics have long struggled to determine whether the name Chíchelh Siyá:m, and much of the idea and ceremonial worship associated with it, show evidence of having been introduced or at least heavily influenced by early missionaries. Most have concluded that the idea and name are foreign and their adoption by the Coast Salish relatively recent.[3] Stó:lō people, however, do not necessarily share this opinion. They generally explain that the belief in, and worship of, a Supreme Being predated European contact. As such, many regard the academics' efforts to separate Christian beliefs from Indigenous ones as efforts to undermine Aboriginal belief in the one true God.[4]

Historicizing the belief in a Supreme Being is difficult. Thomas Crosby, a Methodist missionary who began his proselytization work in 1862 and quickly became fluent in the Halq'eméylem language, learned that the Stó:lō he spoke with 'believed in a Great Spirit, who created all things and was all-wise, but who was not actively concerned for them, and whom they never called upon except in cases of great difficulty or distress.'[5] Royal Navy officer R.C. Mayne shared this opinion. In his 1862 publication *Four Years in British Columbia and Vancouver Island,* Mayne argues that 'it is certain that the Indians here [Coast Salish] have some idea of a Supreme Being; and that this idea, no doubt, dates before the appearance of any priest among them.'[6] Likewise, the Anglican Bishop of British Columbia, in travelling through Salish territory en route to the Cariboo gold rush in 1860 notes in his diary: 'Most of the Indians profess to know of the Sackally Tyhee Papa, Great Chief Father. They point upwards; they say He sees all, is all-wise, and strong and good, and never dies. I found out to-day, from two Indians of this place, that Skatyatkeitlah is the same as Squaquash Suokum, or the sun. The sun is the Sackally Tyhee Papa. Klanampton, the moon, is his wife, and the stars their children.'[7]

In 1881 retired Hudson's Bay Company officer, Joseph William McKay, provided even greater insight into the nineteenth-century Coast Salish belief system. McKay lived much of his life in HBC posts along the lower Fraser River and on the adjacent shores of Vancouver Island, interacting both professionally and socially with Stó:lō and other Coast Salish people. When asked by a now long-forgotten aspiring academic about Coast Salish religious beliefs and observances McKay explained:

> [The Coast Salish] believed in Scha-us the Creator and ruler of the universe. The Missionaries have clumsily translated the name of our Diety into 'Chief Above' [Chíchelh Siyá:m]. This they readily identify with Scha-us. Their original idea of the Creator who pervades ~~through all space and~~ who rules the universe and is everywhere is better than the idea of the ~~local~~ Missionary's Deity who is localized to a certain extent by being styled the Chief Above. Scha-us ~~con~~ is a word which in this idiom conveys an idea which may be ~~represented expressed~~ translated by the English word First [or] primary. X-us means new in their Vernacular and the prefix S would [be] the Superlative of new i.e. newest or first ... Scha-us, the great first cause of the Cowichans [Halkomelem speakers] is omnipresent and Omnipotent and [in] his control over demons and all other powers he ~~was~~ is the great Creator. His name implies Newest and may be translated The first as Ha-us is equivalent to the English word new. (The Cowichan language has no equivalent for our word first. It has the words l.kha-la before and Ha-us New. Ha-us is nearest in significance to our word ~~new~~ first.) His existence at present is more a passive than an active one, the demons and other subordinate forces are ~~not~~ only occasionally interfered with in the exercise of their functions ... [Other spiritual forces] remain under the power and check of the Great First.[8]

Collectively, these historical voices do not discredit the anthropological interpretation. They do, however, suggest that the belief in a Supreme Being held by more contemporary Coast Salish people was shared by their nineteenth-century ancestors. Furthermore, they suggest that if the idea of a supreme creative power was adopted from newcomers it likely was a modification of older Indigenous understandings and that Native ideas, like Native history, could change to account for new information and new historical experiences without ceasing to be Aboriginal in nature.

Continuity in oral traditions relating to creative and transformative spiritual events is something Coast Salish people take seriously: not only is it regarded as improper to change or modify sacred stories such as those pertaining to ancient transformations and collective tribal origins, it is dangerous. Protocols pertaining to the integrity of historical narratives suggest that the concept of the Great First is unlikely to have been borrowed or introduced without provoking a major debate within the Indigenous community – and such a debate would likely have been remembered by future generations. This is not to say that the concept of a Supreme Being did not undergo a certain degree of modification (as McKay suggested when describing how missionaries were encouraging the idea of God as residing in the sky). Rather, the cultural imperative typically expressed as an obligation to 'keep the [sacred] stories right' in unaltered form, is sufficiently powerful within Stó:lō and all Coast Salish society, especially among the social and spiritual elite, to render it unlikely that such a prominent idea could have been borrowed so recently without there remaining an account of the borrowing.

Indicative of the obligation on Coast Salish historians to maintain the integrity of sacred historical narratives are the protocols and sanctions Sally Snyder observed and recorded in 1963 among even her 'acculturated' Skagit informants: people she described as being 'compulsive about telling stories "right."' As Snyder discovered, 'If a story was imperfectly recalled it was wrong for ... [people] to "guess," meaning to pad, improvise, paraphrase or omit. It was better not to tell it at all for it was dangerous to omit scenes and to shorten myths. Nubile women in the audience might then give birth to deformed children, incomplete or malformed like the abbreviated or truncated story. And shortening of myths would shorten the lives of all listeners.'[9]

On numerous occasions, both informal and ceremonial, contemporary Stó:lō people have clearly and forcefully articulated the conviction that it is wrong to modify or alter even slightly stories about the Creator or the actions of the transformers and the origins of the Stó:lō people. Good Stó:lō historians, they explain, use oral footnotes to legitimize their knowledge in the eyes of their audience; they explain to their audience from whom they acquired their information and how. And while people seldom chastise a person to his or her face for telling a story 'wrong,' they do speak within their circles of family and friends about offending individuals as people who come from a 'low class' family (that is 'worthless' because they have 'lost' or 'forgotten their history') and in so doing undermine the legitimacy of both the teller and the tale. The Stó:lō typically regard those who tell stories incorrectly as 'people who don't know right from wrong' or, and perhaps more tellingly, as people who have been too influenced by white society. One respected authority on cultural protocols explained: 'Some of our own people have the idea that our transformer and origin stories are like fairy tales; things you can make up or change. They aren't. This seems to be especially the case with those of our people who have gone off to university and gotten degrees.'[10]

Old Pierre of Katzie explained that prior to non-Native hegemony, whenever a dispute arose as to the proper form and content of an historical narrative, it became necessary to 'summon two old men who belonged to different villages but were both well versed in local histories' to discuss and reconcile the different historical interpretations.[11] Severe differences in historical interpretation, Old Pierre maintained, such as arose in the case of a dispute over the hereditary right to use a name, required the defender of a particular version of history to enlist two additional 'lawyers' to plead his case, after which, as anthropologist Diamond Jenness recorded, the adjudicating 'old men retired to consult in private. Whatever decision they reached was final.'[12] Recently, in discussing the matter of the integrity of historical narratives, two elderly, fluent Halq'eméylem-speaking women explained to me that in the past there were people who were recognized as the keepers and communicators of sacred histories. Such a person, typically a man, was referred to as *sxá:sls*, meaning 'One who keeps track of everything.'[13]

Protocols discouraging people from altering stories by guessing at content or omitting key components should not, however, be equated with a prohibition on acquiring new or forgotten information to supplement existing sacred historical narratives or from acquiring entirely new stories for the Indigenous literary canon or historiography. Change, refinement, and supplementation do occur within Stó:lō Coast Salish Indigenous historiography. Properly trained people can acquire new sacred historical information through special means. Transformation narratives, though largely about the distant past, are not exclusively about ancient occurrences. Rather, they are a distinct set of historical discourses, and some of the information they convey pertains to the very recent past, potentially as recent as a few moments ago. Properly trained or particularly gifted individuals can acquire certain types of sacred historical knowledge, not by referring to documents, but by travelling to particular sites on the landscape where they access metaphysical tunnels that lead to special locations in the spirit world where knowledge and information can be 'remembered': the land itself was, and is, the Stó:lō archive.

Put another way, accepting that the concept of a Supreme Being, or Great First, pre-dates contact is not to say that the Indigenous under-

standing of who or what the Great First is or was did not undergo alterations or refinements over the past two centuries. Indeed, the relationship
between Stó:lō people and the Great First likely was modified over time,
especially inasmuch as the Stó:lō likely came to regard the Great First in
more Christian-like terms (i.e., as a fatherly entity residing in the more
localized spiritual geography of Heaven above). Historian John Milloy's
account of the Plains Cree's shift towards greater monotheism following
their migration from the forest lands of the northern Canadian Shied to
the open bison-dominated prairies may provide a model for conceiving
of subtle but important changes in Stó:lō theology among those living
in the generations after the great smallpox epidemic of the late eighteenth century. Perhaps the survivors who migrated found it important to
place greater emphasis on their relationship with the Great First vis-à-vis
those with other lesser spiritual forces and entities.[14] Hence, although
the Great First was presumably understood to be a more 'passive' force
prior to contact, nonetheless, He (She, They, It?) could, and presumably did, occasionally exercise a prerogative to 'interfere' in the lives of
humans and 'other subordinate forces,' especially during those times,
as the Methodist Reverend Crosby pointed out, 'when people were confronted with great difficulty or distress.'[15]

Precedent and Sacred History:
Affiliation through Narratives of Movement

Ultimately, as the shared belief in the Great First indicates, cohesion
within and among tribal groups was not exclusively a factor of watershed-
based geography, residence proximity, or economic strategies to cope
with periodic shortages of food. Indeed, for the Stó:lō, geography appears to have been more commonly thought of as the product of tribal
cohesion rather than its source. It is genuine past precedence as reflected
in sacred narratives describing the formation of the contemporary world
that bring meaning to the pragmatic and practical materialist and ecological networks described above. The origins of tribal identities are found
in ancient stories of transformations accounting for how the world came
to be in the form and state it is today. Identities, therefore, are in at least
one important way primordially based in Aboriginal cosmology, making
discussion of their historical expressions a sensitive issue.

Stó:lō people classify their historical narratives into two categories:
sqwélqwel, often translated as 'true stories' or 'real news' which seem to
tell of recent happenings; and *sxwōxwiyám*, which often appear to de-

scribe the distant past when X̱exá:ls (the transformers) and the *tel swayel* (sky-people) transformed the chaotic world of creation into the stable and permanent form it takes today.[16] This classification of two types of history, both considered true accounts of past happenings, corresponds with what Jan Vansina has documented as a relatively common expression of Native cosmologies elsewhere.[17] However, while this classification accounts for aspects of the way people shared historical narratives, the dichotomy Vansina describes between a distant past that was mythical and a recent past that was real inadequately reflects Coast Salish ways of knowing.

To better bridge the gulf between Stó:lō and Western epistemology I previously assisted in the construction of metaphor-defining Stó:lō history as a series of sometimes unrelated happenings occurring simultaneously within the different rooms of a house. Hallways were grey areas where human and supernatural beings from the various rooms met and experienced things that would not have occurred had they remained in their separate rooms.[18] In deference to Clifford Geertz's notion that bridging the gulf of understanding between cultures requires continually re-evaluating and refining metaphors of understanding, I offer here a revised interpretation of Coast Salish history inspired by a rereading of Sally Snyder's unpublished analysis of Coast Salish oral traditions, and subsequent ruminations over information shared by Stó:lō friends and consultants.

Imagine Stó:lō historical understanding as a single play unfolding simultaneously on two separate stages separated by a passageway. On the first stage occurs the drama of the familiar physical world. On the second are depicted the actions of the x̱á:x̱a (sacred or taboo) realm of the spirit world. The spiritual actors on the second stage are able to observe the actions on the first, but the physical actors on the first cannot see the characters and happenings of the second. Actors from one stage can, and occasionally do, pass behind the curtain and enter the action on the other stage. Access points for beginning the journey are found at various x̱á:x̱a places located throughout the physical landscape, but only specially trained people can successfully negotiate the arduous and danger-fraught journey into the spirit world. Spirit actors, meanwhile, can and still do enter the drama of humans, often emerging into the physical world through these same x̱á:x̱a portals. Sometimes their visits are short; other times their stays are lengthy. The play's author and director is Scha-us (Chíchelh Siyá:m / the Great First / the Creator / the Lord Above). However, Scha-us has only revealed the drama's full script to the spirit beings on the second stage, and so only the shamans who have made the journey behind the curtain to the spirit world understand His directions. These shamans may occasionally hear the director's instructions, but more often they learn of the intentions of Scha-us second-hand from their associates in the spirit world. Thus, Stó:lō history is filled with significant points of interpenetration between the two dimensions. In the ancient past the penetrations were so frequent as to make the two dramas essentially indistinguishable – the division between the stages was eliminated, so to speak. This is the era anthropologists have typically described as the 'myth-age,' what fluent Halq'eméylem speakers refer to as *sxwōxwiyám*. More recently the drama occurring in the spirit realm has played a slightly less prominent role in the ongoing drama of Stó:lō human history or *sqwélqwel* in a world already 'made right' by the earlier work of the transformers.

From the late nineteenth through the early twentieth century ethnographers such as Franz Boas, Charles Hill-Tout, and Diamond Jenness collected stories from Stó:lō Elders such as Chief George and Mary Anne of the Chehalis Tribe on Harrison River, Pat Joe of the Scowlitz Tribe at the junction of the Harrison and Fraser rivers, and Old Pierre of the Katzie Tribe on Pitt Lake, describing how the world was once in a chaotic state where trees could talk to animals and where dangerous men and women (evil Indian doctors) with incredible powers caused harm and despair. Into this world the Great First sent the *tel swayel* people who fell from the sky at particular places to become the original leaders of either individual settlements or entire tribal communities. Swaniset 'The Great Benefactor' was one such person, who 'was planted on Sheridan Hill' adjacent to Pitt Lake. Another was Sumqeameltq, who parachuted from the sky at Scowlitz near the junction of the Harrison and Fraser rivers. According to the Indigenous histories, these and other sky-people possessed special powers, which they used to fix the world, set it straight, and make things predictable. Their modern-era descendants, such as the Elders who spoke with the ethnographers, inherited special rights of leadership and prestige. In this way, as Old Pierre explained, 'each village community had its own set of ancestral names (some for males only, others only for females) …a man's lineage connected him with several communities, he often received one name in his father's village and another in his mother's.'[19]

The Elders described how in addition to the sky-people, the early sxwōxwiyám age also witnessed the slightly later arrival of Xexá:ls (three bear brothers and their sister). Xexá:ls were the orphans of Red-Headed

Woodpecker and Black Bear (who had been killed by Red-Headed Woodpecker's jealous second wife, Grizzly Bear). Tellingly, the name Xexá:ls is derived from the same proto-Salish root as the verb 'to write'or 'to enscribe.' Together, they travelled throughout the world performing miraculous events of transformation that permanently inscribed stories into the landscape and skyscape – rewarding certain good people by transforming them into the 'First People' of additional tribes, or into a valuable component of the regional ecosystem or prominent celestial features in the night sky. They punished some evil people by turning them into giant stones or other features of the landscape. Some of the transformations they performed were not linked to moral causes but were motivated simply by Xexá:ls' desire to demonstrate their power. Together Xexá:ls traversed the world 'making things right.'[20]

The stories describing the ancient past, as recorded by earlier anthropologists, make apparent that not everyone knew all the details or full narratives describing the beginning of time or the travels and works of Xexá:ls and the sky-people. Chief George and Mary Anne of the Chehalis Tribe independently explained to both Boas and Hill-Tout that Xexá:ls, the transformers, started their journey in the mountains at the northern end of Harrison Lake.[21] From there they travelled downriver to the point where the Harrison River joins the Fraser River. Turning eastward, they travelled up the Fraser into the canyon, making transformations as they sojourned. Chief George did not know the details of Xexá:ls' journey after their departure from the Stó:lō region of the lower Fraser Canyon, but he knew that they eventually reached the sunrise where they began a journey through the sky with the sun until they reached the sunset. Once at the western horizon they began travelling eastward again until they eventually arrived at the mouth of the Fraser River. From the moment the transformers reached this point Chief George again knew many of the details of their actions. He explained that, from the Fraser estuary, the transformers travelled upriver again, passing through the Fraser Valley and tributary watersheds all the while continuing the process of fixing the world and putting all the individual tribal components in order until eventually they journeyed back up through the Fraser Canyon and disappeared once again into the sunrise, this time never to be seen again.[22] (See Map 8.)

Like Chief George and Mary Ann, Old Pierre of Katzie had also been taught that Xexá:ls' and the sky-people's' actions occurred as part of a coherent narrative in which the actions central to one tribal community were necessary to inform the historical development of another. His

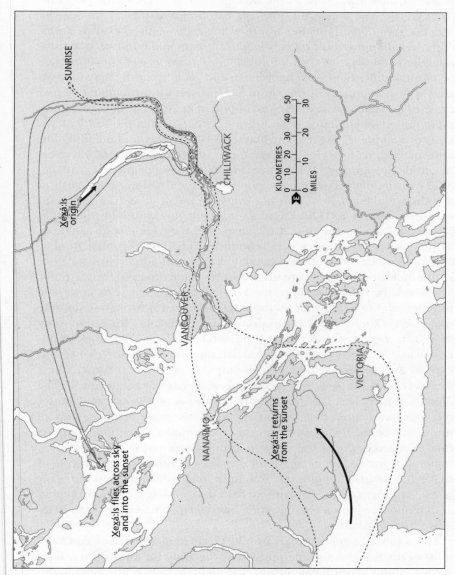

Map 8. The journeys of X̱exá:ls, the Transformers – a lower Fraser River watershed perspective.

knowledge base, however, was much deeper than either Chief George's or Marry Anne's in terms of the metaphysical world of spirit power associated with the life-giving power of the Great First, or 'Lord Above,' and the sky-people. This was not so much a difference between Katzie and Chehalis epistemology, as Charles Hill-Tout and other early anthropologists sometimes assumed,[23] but rather a reflection of the difference between vocationally based knowledge and geographically based knowledge within a single cultural group. As Hill-Tout's informants explained in the 1890s, and as Old Pierre corroborated in 1936, for example, while everybody learned the general stories, only specially trained healers, known as *shxwlá:m*, received the hereditary knowledge and full initiation into the body of esoteric experience and knowledge that enabled them to travel through the mystical spiritual dimension of the xá:xa realm. That journey enabled them to receive the true and full stories of creation and the spirit world.[24]

Chief George's and Old Pierre's stories encompass broad geographical regions, but both men's narratives are more detailed for the territory closest to their respective winter residences. Hill-Tout's Scowlits' informant, Pat Joe, by way of contrast, related a Xexá:ls story that had nothing to do with the immediate vicinity of his home. Instead, his narrative described the transformers' actions at Point Roberts on the coast just south of the Fraser River's mouth. Elders living today explain that in the past intercommunity gatherings provided opportunities for stories to be shared in a context that emphasized the need for connections to distant places. The stories themselves are about travels and movements, and they are fully appreciated in the context of the travels of the story-tellers themselves who moved and spoke with audiences from geographically diverse homes, and who apparently also possessed vocationally and/or status-based differences in knowledge. Thus, while learning the full meaning behind the stories was often restricted to vocational experts such as shxwlá:m, and the detailed connections and overlaps between regional stories retained by historians know as sxá:sls, the process of sharing the stories among the general populace emphasized the unity of the broader region, for without knowledge of sxwōxwiyám relating to neighbouring tribal communities, one's own tribal stories were themselves incomplete.

The Swaniset stories related by Old Pierre exemplify the role of the unity of the broader region in providing meaning for local stories. They are not simply about Katzie history and identity; indeed, Swaniset is also claimed by the people of the Kwantlen Tribe near Fort Langley as one of their original people.[25] Swaniset's travels and important actions and experiences in Puget Sound mean that places and resources far from Pitt Lake are of vital importance to Katzie concepts of self. It was in the interest of Katzie people to develop and maintain relations with people living abroad to ensure the Katzie's continued relationship with places and people far from their tribal homeland – places of vital importance to their understanding of how the world was put into its contemporary form and of the sacredness of certain human and social relations between geographically distant settlements. Once relationships were formed, the process of repeated intercommunity story-sharing formed a bridge that then reinforced the need to maintain those same relations. Thus, while sxwōxwiyám transformation narratives are ostensibly about tribal origins and identity, they also serve as the basis of many Salish people's sense of supratribal identity.

In addition to creating distinct First People for the various tribes and settlements, Old Pierre explained that the Lord Above also gave to the leaders of families around whom tribes coalesced a 'special rite or ceremony (cexwte'n) to increase... [its] joy or comfort in grief.'[26] These ceremonial rites, sometimes referred to as 'entertainments' or 'magic playthings,' were central aspects of tribal identities. Prohibitions barred people who were not members of the community who had received them from performing them.[27] In this way each tribe, and even villages within tribal clusters, claimed a distinct and special power and attribute derived from the spirit world at the beginning of time. Significantly, however, the privilege and authority to perform the rite spread to many different tribes through intercommunity marriages. Jenness recounts that, according to Old Pierre, for the Musqueam people at the mouth of the Fraser River and a community farther upriver, the tribal ritual was the masked sxwō:yxwey dance.[28] For a neighbouring group that had subsequently merged with the Musqueam, the tribal ritual involved 'an entertainment with two dolls that are called xa'malca and xa'pxep.'[29] For the Chilliwack Tribe, it was a rite involving the skins of fishers that were referred to as sxwamecen,[30] and tlukel.[31] Hill-Tout learned from people at Scowlitz that their special tribal rite was a feathered ring called *celmoqtcis*.

Contemporary Stó:lō corroborate the continuing importance of these special tribally specific 'gifts,' although with the exception of the masked dance ceremony, people generally explain that the associated characteristic of the gift – the gift's legacy, if you will – is of greater importance than the physical manifestation of the gift itself. Indeed, as Old Pierre observed more than half a century ago, most of the special rites have 'dropped out of memory' and are no longer practised. My own fieldwork corroborates this. For example, the unique ritual of the Shxw'ōwhámél community just downriver from Hope is the sturgeon dance. In the 1990s at least two Elders had a vague knowledge of this rite (one of whom explained that he has acquired as much of his information about the sturgeon dance through conversations with deceased ancestors during dreams as from his own childhood memories).[32] The sturgeon rite, although not performed for nearly a century, continues to inform a sense of distinctiveness among members of the Shxw'ōwhámél community.

In a similar fashion, certain members of particular tribal communities claim tribally based rights of supratribal political authority, arguing that leadership ability is innately theirs as a legacy of the events and bestowed gifts from the transformers as revealed through the sxwōxwiyám narratives. More than a hundred years ago this claim was expressed to Hill-Tout by members of both the 'Royal' Kwantlen Tribe near Fort Langley and the Chehalis Tribe near Harrison Hot Springs. More recently, members of a central Fraser Valley band have made the same claim with respect to themselves.[33]

Significantly, for the purpose of tracking change over time, the one remaining actively practised tribally based rite, the masked sxwó:yxwey dance, has come to foster and represent a collective identity that transcends its original tribal specificity. Within Coast Salish society, hereditary rights are traced bilaterally, that is, through both mothers and fathers. This system sets Coast Salish culture apart from the more northern, and often better known, matrilineal Northwest Coast cultural groups that trace hereditary rights through mothers. As such, although residence patterns for elite Coast Salish families were generally patrilocal, with the wife coming to live with her husband, children inherited rights from both their father's and their mother's family. As Old Pierre explained to Jenness, the right to perform certain tribally anchored rights therefore 'spread through intermarriage until nearly every community had within it someone who claimed legitimate right to the ritual.'[34] The spiritual link that exists among all members of the sacred sxwó:yxwey ritual fraternally binds male dancers of different communities together through shared ancestral connections.[35] While all dancers are members of their fraternity, each of the different spiritual expressions the individual dancers assume forms a distinct subcommunity within the spirit world. Wayne Suttles identifies the following as various sources of sxwó:yxwey spirit helper power: Thunder, Raven, Sawbill, Snake, Two-Headed Snake, Beaver, Spring Salmon, Owl, Ghost, Buzzard, Eagle, Bear, and Clown.[36]

As the example of the sxwó:yxwey illustrates, understanding Coast Salish definitions of 'community' is an extraordinarily complicated proposition. Beyond associations of families who trace their rights to ancient tribal rituals or gifts, or even the connections people form with guardian spirit helper communities, Coast Salish collective identity emerges at its most basic level from the belief that each individual has within him or her a community of up to seven distinct types of spirit entities, each of which has radiating relationships outside of its anchored physical human host. There is no tight consensus among all Stó:lō or Xwélmexw people as to the nature, expression, form, and function of each spirit expression, but there is a generally shared understanding in the basic matters.[37] Once again, differences in interpretation appear to be less reflections of regional or tribal distinctiveness than distinctions between various individuals' depth of knowledge. Put another way, certain knowledge is vocational in nature; acquired through specific training related to the pursuit of a particular career. For comparative purposes, we might think of the distinction between how a contemporary lay Catholic might explain the distinction between the human soul, mind, and intellect, or the distinction between angels and spirits or saints, and how a priest or theologian might define the same concepts.

According to Old Pierre, seven spirit entities reside within each Stó:lō person. One is a 'soul' (shxwelí), which at death returns to the Great First, who may reassign it to be reincarnated in one of the deceased's descendants. Another is the 'vitality' (smestíyexw), which is responsible for a person's conscious thought. A third is a 'talent or power' (swia'm), which is closely associated with the vitality/thought and is sometimes difficult to distinguish from it, and which perishes with the physical body at death. A 'shadow' or 'reflection' (qey'xene'?ten) is literally the spirit associated with one's shadow cast by the sun or moon. Then there is a 'shade' or 'ghost' (spoleqwíth'a), which is the merging of the vitality and shadow after death, and which roams invisible in the neighbourhood of its old home, being a source of great concern among surviving relatives who fear it may entice away a living person's vitality. The sixth are the 'guardian spirits' (syúwél or ó:lkwlh), which are generally acquired from birds, animals, or natural elements and which manifest themselves during the winterdance, and which were associated with professional or vocational skills and abilities. Finally, there are the spirits, which impregnate one's breath with power (sle'qwem).

Old Pierre not only listed the seven classes of spirit entities residing within each Coast Salish person, he also described in detail how they functioned, sometimes autonomously, and other times in unison and harmony with one another. While descriptions and explanations similar to Old Pierre's continue to be shared among Coast Salish people and in particular Coast Salish shxwlá:m, the one that Jenness recorded from Old Pierre in 1936 remains the most comprehensive and well-integrated extant account. As such, it forms the core of this discussion.

Old Pierre explained that, according to traditions he learned during his training, all plants and animals possess shadows, vitality (or thought), and special powers or talent. They had souls during the age of transformations, but when Xexá:ls transformed them into their permanent form their souls were sent back to the Great First. As a result, of all living things, only human beings and sockeye salmon, which are really regarded as humans whose home is far out to sea, retained their souls.[38] Humans and sockeye are together distinct from all the rest of creation. Each year it is imperative that the bones, skin, and intestines of the first-caught sockeye salmon be cast back into the water; by this means all sockeye souls accompany the bones back to their home where they take on a new body so they can return the following year. In like fashion, many people's souls are reincarnated, but only if a deceased person is mourned unceasingly. In such cases the Great First sends the soul back to be born in a new baby, who then possesses all the same features as its predecessor. A person's shadow or reflection might also end up being reincarnated, but unless the soul accompanies it, the infant will bear only a general resemblance to its predecessor. In this manner, powerful, shared identities are forged across temporal gulfs and between generations.

In the generation before contact it appears that it was universally believed that the sun provided people with vitality (or thought). In the winter, vitality left the limbs and trunks of trees and retired into the roots. That is why, Old Pierre explained, leaves fade and drop. Evergreens, made directly by the Great First, retain their vitality better than the deciduous trees Xexá:ls made. Evergreen trees continue to be used in rituals to transfer vitality to people and increase their strength. Cut trees, dead animals, and harvested plants have no vitality, as with dead humans. Unlike the soul or shadow, whose departure brings instant death, vitality can leave the body for short periods. Vitality is also responsible for memory. Vitality can travel through the spirit world to a xá:xa (sacred or taboo) place and there acquire knowledge, or reacquire lost knowledge (forgotten memories). A person's vitality could also acquire power or talent during its travels. However, if not returned within a reasonable period, a person without vitality goes crazy and dies.

When vitality leaves a person's body it takes the person's power and talent with it.

Old Pierre had been taught that people's vitality and power weaken with age. He explained that these forces also weaken during the winters when the sun is distant. Winterdances (*smílha*, also commonly referred to as 'spirit dances') serve the purpose of enabling people to rejuvenate themselves. Dancing itself, however, was not sufficient. Dancers depend upon the power or talent they receive from special animal or bird spirit 'partners,' or helpers, who come from the mountains to assist them. The power received from these sources wells up inside people causing them to sing and dance and thereby regain health and vigour. In earlier times, these helpers provided people with vocational direction and professional expertise. [39] Healers, warriors, clairvoyants, and others all acquired special vocational skills and powers from their guardian spirits. Mosquitoes and wind, therefore, were common spirit associations for *shxwlá:m* ('Indian doctors' or shamans) who were required to 'blow' their medicinal power into people to effect a cure, or likewise to 'suck' or 'pull' malevolent spirits from their patients. Interestingly, *stó:méx* (warriors) also sought the spirit power of mosquitoes and other tenacious creatures such as wasps to provide them with ferocity in combat. [40] Warriors and healers, therefore, were often joined through their identical mosquito spirit helpers as part of a spirit-based single community. In this way, individual Coast Salish spirit winterdancers, like the separate sxwó:yxwey dancers, formed collective identities with members of the animal world, and also with other unrelated humans who shared their animal partners. In the early 1960s, the anthropologist Sally Snyder's Skagit informants explained that in the past winterdancers who shared the same source of spirit power danced together as a group. [41] Today, all Stó:lō and Skagit winterdancers dance independently. The audience, who sings and drums and in other ways participates, forms the dancer's collective support group.

Additionally, outside the parameters of strict blood and in-law connections and common spirit associations, members of the winterdance community also form special 'family' ties that serve as the basis of additional smaller collective groupings. As a result of acquiring their spirit helper, new initiates (xawsó:lh, or 'babies') emerge from their initiation as new people. Henceforth, their chronological age is less important than the age of their association with their spirit helper. All winterdance 'babies' who are 'born' the same year within the same longhouse community refer to one another and treat one another as siblings. Likewise they speak

of their individual longhouse leaders as parents, and their initiators as
xólhemìlh or 'babysitters.' All winter dancers, regardless of which spirit
community or individual longhouse they belong to, consider themselves
members of a special community distinct from *st'elt'ólkwlh* (non-spirit
dancers).

The power and talent associated with dancers, Pierre explained, var-
ies in strength, depending upon how far away it is acquired. The further
away one has to travel to obtain spirit power or talent, the stronger the
power's manifestation. While all animals have power they can share with
humans, certain animals exist only in the mystic xá:xa realms, where they
reside at varying distances from humans. A person has to make the peril-
ous journey into the xá:xa dimension in order to encounter such a spirit.
Later, after a person's vitality returns from the xá:xa animal's body and
travels back to its home, the spirit's power will only be known and recognized from visions.[42] Only a person who has undergone intense and
prolonged purification, and received proper hereditary training, ever
arrives in the xá:xa realm, and it is only from this realm that one can
acquire true healing power and become a genuine shxwlá:m.

Certain other powers, Old Pierre believed, came not from these xá:xa
creatures and realms but directly from the 'Lord Above,' who bestowed
them on those Pierre referred to as 'priests,' but whom academics have
preferred to call ritualists.[43] Special powers from the Great First continue
to manifest themselves through the prayers and incantations of contemporary ritualists, who trace hereditary rights through unbroken chains
back to prominent original people like Swaniset. Such ritualists continue
to protect individuals from mysterious forces as well as wash away impuri-
ties that people acquire by going to forbidden places, or such impurity
as is associated with achieving puberty, or giving birth to twins. Ritualists
also remove malevolent shades or ghosts from people, and restore people's lost or stolen vitality. They accomplish these feats through special
prayers called *syewin* (or *yewin*). As such, today, as in Pierre's time, such
a ritual is often referred to as *syewinmet* (or *yewinmet*): 'One who knows
many prayers.' Ritualists' prayers are capable of changing the weather,
and in the past they also robbed enemy warriors of their vitality. Ritualists might also use their prayers to tame fish and animals to render them
easier to catch.

Old Pierre explained that in the past different ritualists, perhaps best
thought of as clairvoyants, possessed the power of sight. This power came
unsolicited as a gift of the 'Lord Above' and apparently was not associated with hereditary knowledge or ritual training. Such people sang

special songs, given to them by the Great First, to determine who was in danger. Once a clairvoyant ritualist identified a potential victim, he or she was bathed with water from a basin to wash away all danger.

Clearly, then, in the early contact era many of the most fundamental expressions of collective identity derived from an understanding of the workings of the spirit world, past and present. Knowledge of these matters, if not always their practice, was transmitted into the twentieth century and through to the present. Ancient mythical transformations created distinct tribal homelands, resources, and sacred rites and ceremonies, but they were also responsible for the vitally important links that bound the various tribes together. Continuing spiritual expressions, as Jay Miller recently documented for the Skagit, formed anchored radiances in which shamanic and other spirit-based power and energy were acquired from distant locales and brought back to tribal or personal homes.[44] The tribally based rites also radiated from their original homes through ties of family to form collective fraternities with supratribal expressions. These family-based cross-tribal linkages follow patterns similar to those of the more economics-based identities described below.

Taken together, from the preceding two chapters the picture that emerges of contact-era Stó:lõ society is one of overlapping networks of nested identity. Each person was simultaneously a member of more than one of the various expressions of group affiliation, some of which were set at odds with one another. People deployed a variety of systems to meet perceived needs through models provided by past precedent and illustrated through ancient narratives. Status and gender were powerful factors in shaping people's decisions about affiliation. Hereditary names, knowledge, resources, and special myth-age gifts anchored people to their tribal homes, as did the mysterious powers of local shamans and ritualists.

Supratribal identity was the result of the numerous linkages that radiated from tribal centres. The work of the transformers joined regionally diverse tribal communities through mythical stories that were intelligible only with reference to happenings far beyond any single tribe's territory. Likewise, shamans and others seeking the strength and assistance of the spirits from the xá:xa realm were required to travel far beyond their tribal territory through a dimension invisible to untrained or unworthy humans. Through these spiritual connections communities of people from various tribal homelands were connected as members of spirit-based fraternities, the most prominent of which today are the masked sxwó:yxwey dancers or the collectives of people with shared spirit helpers in the winterdance. Constant movements and visits by affines between tribal communities and the massive convergence of people in the Fraser Canyon meant that the strong sense of supratribal identity also had a strong secular economic basis. The smallest of the formal collective affiliations (extended families bound by blood and in-law connections) were often the most interested in promoting supratribal Stó:lō identity. Moreover, generally, patrilocal patterns of residence meant that women were especially interested in the familial connections that linked communities, for it was they who left their birth home to live elsewhere. Maintaining ties to their place of birth, as well as to those places where their sisters had moved to reside, likely had personal meaning that transcended or at least supplemented the more official and strategic social, economic, and political rationale their male family members had for building and maintaining such linkages.

Throughout the late eighteenth and nineteenth centuries, as we shall see, these cross-tribal linkages and supratribal identifications played a central role in shaping the way Stó:lō people adjusted to a series of externally produced pressures and crises. The various expressions of collective identity came under great strain, and often the system was unable to adjust to the changes quickly enough to prevent overt fractures and increased tensions between the various expressions of identity and the justifications behind them. The role of movement, that is, the ability to relocate on the landscape and, so important to the traditional functioning of Coast Salish collective identity, came to be increasingly important in determining which expressions of identity would dominate in light of external pressures and strains. Over time, certain aspects of the internal flexibility of the Coast Salish system became more rigid, while others grew so flexible as to become all but impossible to distinguish, as the following chapters will demonstrate.

SECTION THREE
Movements and Identities across Time and Space

Chapter Four

From the Great Flood to Smallpox

The Lord Above looked down and saw how they crowded upon the land, and one summer, after the Indians had dried their salmon, He sent the rain.[1] It rained and rained without ceasing until the rivers overflowed their banks, the plains flooded and the people fled for shelter to the mountains, where they anchored their canoes to the summits with long ropes of twisted cedar-boughs. Still it rained until every mountain-top was covered except Mount Golden-Ears, on which the Indians of the lower Fraser had taken refuge, and even on this mountain many Indians drowned when their canoes crashed into one another and upset. Higher up the Fraser River, Mount Cheam also rose above the flood and sheltered many Indians on its summit, while on Vancouver Island Mount Tzuhalem, near Cowichan, floated upward on the rising waters.

The Lower Fraser Indians riding the flood on Mount Golden-Ears lived on their stores of dried salmon until the water subsided. Several canoes, however, broke away and were carried by the swiftly flowing current far to the southward. The Kwikwitlam Indians in Washington are descendants of the Coquitlam Indians who drifted away from Golden-Ears, the Nooksack are descendants of Squamish Indians, and the Cowlitz are some Cowichan natives who were swept away from Mount Cowichan.

– Old Pierre, February, 1936[2]

As Old Pierre's story reveals, within the historical narratives of the lower Fraser River Aboriginal people, big events have big consequences: floods destroy communities and survivors relocate on a depopulated landscape. Such stories do much more than help contemporary Coast Salish generations come to appreciate what their ancestors experienced in the

distant past. Equally important is the role they play in guiding successive generations in negotiating responses to new events and happenings.
The first smallpox epidemic, for instance, was a devastating event that
many have identified as having triggered a precipitous break with tradition. Yet, while there can be no denying the extent of the human suffering and associated social disruption that accompanied the introduced
disease, what has been overlooked is the extent to which survivors' responses were shaped by their ancestors' precedents. By resituating our
analysis of Aboriginal history to enable us to simultaneously appreciate
the extent to which events alter the way communities are structured, and
the degree to which social structures necessarily shape the way events are
interpreted, we are offered the opportunity of reframing Native–newcomer relations. Perceived through local Indigenous modes of history
we catch glimpses of the continuity in change, as well as the causes of
change in continuity, and in this way Aboriginal history need no longer
be burdened with questions of cultural authenticity.

   The Stó:lō discuss certain historical events and happenings within the
context of major upheavals – upheavals that cause genuine changes in
the way people organize themselves and think about themselves in relation to others and their resources and territories: stories of the great
flood, the work of the transformers, the earliest smallpox epidemics, and
the impacts of the fur trade all fit into this model. It is the medium – the
narratives – as opposed to messages, the stories' descriptive contents,
that provide the Indigenous historiographical context that Stó:lō people
themselves have used to interpret and understand a never-ending series
of events. In this way the remembered history becomes a sequence of
organic living accounts not only of past happenings, but of emerging
and evolving paradigms and world views. Subsequent interpretations of
the world and people are shaped by the meaning imbedded in the narratives, and as such, the content of each successive narrative is informed by
the narratives that have come before. The historical consciousness is, in
this sense, genuinely historiographical: it builds upon itself and informs
itself as it adjusts to new knowledge and new ways of knowing.

The Great Flood(s)

Old Pierre's 1936 description of the fate of Stó:lō people swept away
from their Fraser River–nested homelands by the Great Flood is not
the only account of flood-induced relocation. Ethnographers working
among the Coast Salish in the late nineteenth through the mid-twentieth

century collected several such accounts. (See Map 9.) In 1902 early local ethnographer Charles Hill-Tout reported that one of his Kwantlen
consultants had described a 'great flood [that] overwhelmed the people
and scattered the tribes. Then it was that the Nooksack tribe was parted
from the Squamish, to whom they are regarded as belonging.'[3] Hill-Tout
learned that a branch of the Kwantlen became the northernmost Coast
Salish speakers, the linguistically isolated Bella Coola (Nuxalk). Elder
Bob Joe at Chilliwack described to the mid-twentieth century anthropologist Wilson Duff how 'rafts holding people from Chehalis and Scowlitz
on the Harrison River were tied to a peak on Sumas Mountain that broke
off. The rafts floated southward, and the people became the Chehalis
and Scowlitz tribes of Washington.'[4] Yet another version, provided by
Cornelius Kelleher to folklorist Norman Lerman in 1950, describes how
upper-class members of the Chehalis Tribe were able to return to their
home after the flood, whereas the people on the other raft were swept
away and 'never heard of again.'[5] Lerman also heard from Harry Uslick
a more detailed version of the flood story that had been related through
the generations from at least as far back as Harry Uslick's great-great-
great-grandfather. The story spoke of people being swept away and never
heard from again while others found themselves stranded in different
parts of the broader territory, struggling to return to their decimated
homes after the waters receded. Uslick began:

> Long ago … the people were nearly all drowned in a big, big water which
> flooded this country. It rained such a big rain that time. The people didn't
> care at first because they had seen big rains before. But this time the riv-
> ers and creeks could not take it away, so the water rose up and up until it
> reached our houses. We[6] took our dried salmon and berries and moved to
> the mountains, but the water kept following us. We climbed higher and
> higher up the mountain but still the water kept coming after us.
>
> So the greatest leaders called a council of the warriors and doctors on
> the highest hill beyond our village. The council could see that if the water
> kept coming as it had this hill wouldn't be dry [for] very long. Everything
> kept drifting past, even the great cedar planks that we used to build the
> walls of the smoke houses [longhouses]. The leaders ordered the young-
> est man to swim out and gather all the cedar planks so to make two rafts
> from the house boards and piled all their provisions on it. Then they got
> on themselves.

Uslick then described how the water continued to rise until it eventu-

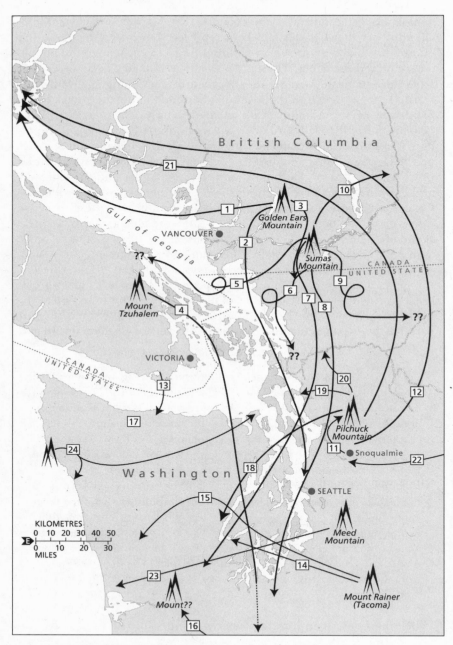

Map 9. Flood stories creating kinship across Cost Salish geographies.

Legend

1   Kwantlen to Bella Coola (Hill-Tout's consultant)

2   Coquitlam to Kwokwitlam (Old Pierre)

3   Squamish to Nooksack (Old Pierre) (Hill-Tout's consultant)

4   Cowichan to Cowlitz (Old Pierre)

5   Sumas to unknown (Harry Uslick)

6   Sumas to unknown (Dan Milo)

7   Chehalis (Can) to Chehalis (USA) (Bob Joe)

8   Scowlitz (Can) to Scowlitz (USA) (Bob Joe)

9   Chehalis to unknown (Cornelius Kolleher)

10   Sumas to Yale (Harry Uslick)

11   Snoqualmie to Pilchuck Mountain

12   Snoqualmie to Bella Coola (Hill-Tout's consultant)

13   Klallam to Olympic Peninsula (Hill-Tout's consultant)

14   Twana from Mt. Rainier to Skokomish River (Hill-Tout's consultant)

15   Twana to west side of Olympic Mountains (Hill-Tout's consultant)

16   Tsitsapam, Quileate and Chimakum to mountains at the head of Chehalis & Willapa rivers (Hill-Tout's consultant)

17   Quileate from the head of Chehalis & Willapa Rivers to Quillayte River (Hill-Tout's consultant)

18   Snokomish to Skokomish (Hill-Tout's consultant)

19   Snokomish to Stillagamish (Hill-Tout's consultant)

20   Snokomish to Skagit (Hill-Tout's consultant)

21   Snokomish to Bella Coola (Hill-Tout's consultant)

22   East Cascades to Snoqualmie Falls (Hill-Tout's consultant)

23   Chehalis from Mud Mountain to Chehalis (USA) (Hill-Tout's consultant)

24   Quileate to Hoh and Chimakum (Albert Reagan's consultant)

ally engulfed the local area: '[It was] over the top of the place where they were on the highest hill behind the village. So we drifted around. Then a big wind came up washing a lot of the provisions away. Now for food we had to catch some of the animals that swam to the raft, looking to be saved. The two rafts got separated then, one of them drifted far until the leader saw a peak still out of the water, and the wind blew the raft straight to that peak.' The Uslick narrative goes on to describe how a traveller today passing through the Fraser Canyon will notice a big mountain behind the town of Yale that looks like a 'pointing thumb.' It was on Pointing Thumb Mountain, Uslick explained, that the one raft eventually landed. There, the survivors took up residence in a cave:

> The people lived in a cave there and whenever they ate the dried salmon they took the sticks out and laid them on the side near the fire. Now, when you go to that place, you can see those sticks but you can't pick them up because they've gone to dust.
>
> It's been a long time, you see, since those people went up there to live, to get away from the rising waters.

Next, Uslick talked about the environmental devastation that occurred and the suffering of the people when they returned:

> They had a hard time getting down and nearly starved. They ate the skins that they wore and what little fish they could get in the small pools. When they got back, there was nothing left of their homes. Even the house posts had fallen down in the mud. There was no sign of life and the people on the other raft were never heard of again.
>
> Everything had changed. Some of the creeks that had been there were no more, and there were new lakes and creeks in different places. The people were pretty weak before the salmon came again but that year there was lots of salmon and the people were saved.[7]

Collectively, the Great Flood narratives complement the stories of the sky-born heroes like Swaniset and of the transformers, X̱ex̱á:ls. They explain how certain clusters of affiliated people came to be where they are. Moreover, given the attributed social characteristics of the various tribal groups, and the strict inherited distinctions that are believed to divide the 'worthless' class from the noble 'worthy' class, people today still commonly use these stories to explain why certain clusters of people are the way they are.

Perhaps most importantly, the narratives provide the basis for shared collective identities over vast geographical distances. The people who floated away from the mountains during the floods are not regarded as being lost and in need of repatriation. Rather, within the Indigenous historiography they are recognized as distinct and separate people, but people with connections to the place where their ancestors lived prior to the flood.

For contemporary Coast Salish people it does not seem to matter that the current descendants of people allegedly swept away by the rising waters might not recognize their alleged role in the flood story, or that they might have origin stories of their own locating them in their current homeland since the beginning of time. Nor does it matter that in the stories those who were washed away were usually described as having been less worthy than those who managed to stay. Rather, the principal purpose of relating a story seems to be to identify distant relations and open lines of communication. Indeed, in these contexts, such aspects of the story are generally not shared publicly.

Among contemporary Coast Salish, what matters is that the story exists, and if necessary it can be referred to by anyone seeking to open a line of communication or build a relationship with the other group. The Coast Salish acceptance of variation in different family-based versions of ancient stories easily allows members from the supposed relocated community to hear a story describing their alleged movement without insult being taken. Instead, Coast Salish take it as a compliment – a statement of shared ancestry and common interest – and recognize it as an invitation to build (or rebuild) stronger connections based on a common identity derived from history.

At a fundamental level, therefore, the flood narratives provide a basis for shared collective identities over vast geographical distances. That some versions of the flood story do not identify all the groups who were swept away, or where they landed (such as the one Dan Milo shared: 'There's three canoes went lost from there; that broked [sic] off and nobody knows where they went to'[8]) is not considered a problem. Rather, what matters is that the stories open a door for acknowledging collective identity with practically any distant group with whom one has an interest. Indeed, within the Halkomelem languages there exists the term *siyá:ye* which is often translated simply as 'friend or relative' but more accurately means 'someone to whom I feel very close, and yet with whom I am unable to demonstrate any direct blood or marriage tie.'[9] It is someone outside the standard kin and affine system with whom one wishes to establish and cement a relationship. In the current politically charged climate of Native–newcomer relations, such words, coupled with vague versions of the flood story such as Milo's, have been referred to by Stó:lō politicians while speaking to their colleagues on Vancouver Island or in the U.S. territories of Puget Sound to rationalize and validate the construction of modern political alliances. In this context, the people who floated away from the mountains during the floods are regarded less as being lost and in need of repatriation and more as potential family who can be drawn on when collective action is regarded to be useful against an external threat.

Even Earlier Calamities

But the migrations inspired by the Great Flood constitute just one chapter in a long history of population movements and collective identity reformations. The Great Flood stories provide a context for explaining the even earlier migrations associated with the transformers, and through them, the process of reducing the population generally. They also create the context that facilitated post-flood movements. A century ago Charles Hill-Tout's Kwantlen consultants, August Sqtcten, Jason Allard, and Mrs Elkins, explained that while the sky-born hero Swaniset was their tribe's first person, they also recognized certain earth-born ancestors as other legitimate First People. One of these earthly men was called Skwelselem.

Skwelselem the First lived during the time of the Great Transformations. The Creator provided Skwelselem with all the tools and utensils required for living. Kwantlen people living near Fort Langley in the early twentieth century cited an unbroken genealogical chain that stretched back nine generations to Skwelselem. It was through Skwelselem that hereditary Kwantlen leadership was traced. During the lives of Skwelselem and his sons and grandsons, as Hill-Tout recorded, 'certain important events' occurred – events the Stó:lō people use as metaphors for a variety of purposes. According to Hill-Tout's informants, during the time of Skwelselem the Second a 'mighty conflagration' (which Hill-Tout thought might have referred to as 'some volcanic phenomenon') 'spread over the whole earth' devastating the land and killing many of its inhabitants.[10] The Great Flood occurred during the lifetime of Skwelselem the Third, causing segments of the Squamish and other tribal communities to be separated from their Fraser River homeland and to develop autonomously elsewhere. Similarly, while Skwelselem the Fourth was living a 'severe and prolonged famine, which lasted for

many weeks, decimated the tribe.' Hill-Tout recorded similar genealogical traditions and associated accounts of great calamities among the
Squamish of North Vancouver and the other Coast Salish tribes with
whom he worked.[11]

Within Stó:lō historical consciousness, accounts of such devastating
and depopulating disasters as floods, fires, and famine explain and
account for population movements and changes in group identities.
Wayne Suttles discusses how the phenomenon of occasional food shortages played a central role in shaping classic Coast Salish culture. The failure of a salmon run, or even its tardy arrival in spring after winter stores
of dried food had been exhausted, were serious matters. Storing food as
a hedge against periodic shortages (which ranged from regular seasonal
variation to devastating once-a-generation deprivations) may well have
been the catalyst behind the classic quest for prestige that distinguished
Northwest Coast potlatch society. Furthermore, as Suttles points out, surviving and thriving in the face of periodic shortages required (in addition
to sophisticated harvesting technology, ritual knowledge, an elaborate
potlatch system of redistribution, and a society built around the quest
for prestige) a method of acquiring and storing food. Moreover, thriving
through periods of shortage required the development of mechanisms
for forging social relationships through economic trade and exchange.
These intertwined social and economic systems were based largely upon
marital rights to hereditarily controlled and regulated resources located
at some distance from a person's winter settlement.[12]

Beyond emphasizing for each new generation the importance of preparing for food shortages, stories associated with famine serve to explain
for Coast Salish people how certain tribal communities came into existence, and why those communities, while distinct, can only be understood
in terms of intertribal relationships. Amy Cooper, a Stó:lō woman originally from Shxw'ōwhámél near Hope, married a Chilliwack man named
William Commodore and later, after being widowed, married another
Chilliwack man, Albert Cooper, who was a relative of her first husband.
She lived most of her adult life on the Soowahlie Reserve above Vedder Crossing. As a young woman in the early years of the twentieth century she listened to her husbands' tribal Elders and half a century later
shared those stories with local ethnographer, second-generation pioneer
resident, and friend, Oliver Wells. In 1962 Amy Cooper related to Wells
a story of a great famine of biblical proportions that simultaneously provides the context for, and accounts for, the subsequent development of
the Soowahlie community: 'There was a famine that everything there –

well, I suppose like in India and other places there – that they couldn't save anything. And they couldn't dig anything to put away, like these wild potatoes and other things that they used to dig, roots and that. All that there was died off, and what didn't die off the bugs got. They didn't say it was grasshoppers. And they said the worms ate it; and all the berries there, they were all worm-eaten. And the fish never came up.' So bad was the drought, she continued, that

> according to the Soowahlies, everyone died but a woman; and she saw them all just doubling over, she says, when they were getting too weak. There was nothing to eat; so she went and got cedar bark, and made herself a pair of corsets, like, and bound that up, and she was able to stand and breathe. And then she went down to a little creek down at South Sumas [Road] … And what did she get? Minnows! So the only thing she could do to catch them was to weave a little net and make a little scoop-net out of grass there. And she got minnows. And that's how she lived. Then, when she got stronger, and the spring came and the roots came back and the other stuff there that they eat, you know, she went back home and gathered up all the bones, skin and bones, and cleaned out the big longhouse that she lived in. She got that clean.

The surviving woman's house was clean and livable, but she was all alone. According to Mrs Cooper: '…she didn't have a dog or she didn't have a man, woman or child to talk to. And she was all by herself till one day a man showed up. And he came from Lake Whatcom [via the Nooksack Tribe just south of the Canadian border]. He was the only one that survived over at Lake Whatcom. And they say that's where the Soowahlie people came from, from the man from Lake Whatcom and this woman from Soowahlie.'[13] (See Map 10.)

In Mrs Cooper's estimation, therefore, the contemporary Soowahlie community was not a primordial creation made at the beginning of time, but rather an historical amalgam of two people originally from different places. The narrative, and by extension the resulting community described in the story, are legitimized by virtue of containing Genesis-like features. As in the standard stories of the transformers and sky-born founders of most other Coast Salish communities, the Soowahlie famine story explains an important historical event – the coming together of remnants of two older communities to create a new one – in terms that are similar to, and informed by, the historical precedent of the earlier creation stories.

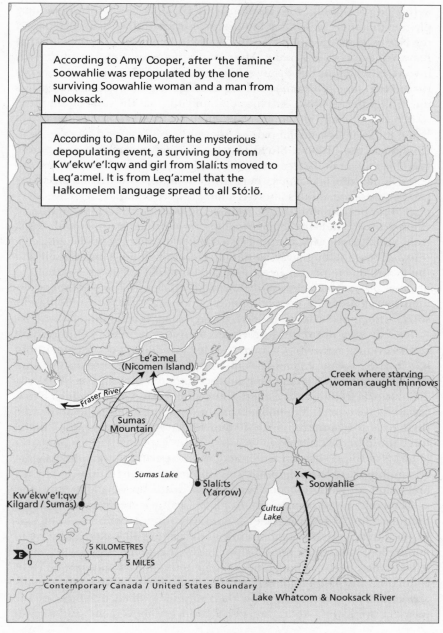

According to Amy Cooper, after 'the famine' Soowahlie was repopulated by the lone surviving Soowahlie woman and a man from Nooksack.

According to Dan Milo, after the mysterious depopulating event, a surviving boy from Kw'ekw'e'l:qw and girl from Slalí:ts moved to Leq'a:mel. It is from Leq'a:mel that the Halkomelem language spread to all Stó:lõ.

Le'a:mel
(Nicomen Island)

Fraser River

Creek where starving woman caught minnows

Sumas Mountain

Sumas Lake

Slalí:ts
(Yarrow)

X ← Soowahlie

Kw'ekw'e'l:qw
Kilgard / Sumas)

Cultus Lake

0   5 KILOMETRES
0   5 MILES

Contemporary Canada / United States Boundary

Lake Whatcom & Nooksack River

Map 10. Catastrophe creates community.

In her continuing conversation with Oliver Wells, Mrs Cooper explained that there was at that time, in the winter of 1962, a dispute among the Nooksack people as to who among their community should carry the Lake Whatcom man's name. Mrs Cooper had no intention of directly involving herself in this dispute; however, she did demonstrate her conviction that the man's name belonged to the 'new' Soowahlie people as much as to the 'old' Nooksack, and, implicitly, that the two communities were really one and the same. With the threatened return of the man's name to Nooksack, a vital part of Soowahlie history (and by extension, Chilliwack and broader Stó:lō history) was being removed and potentially lost: the man had 'come to Soowahlie, and he died and he was buried in Soowahlie, and that's where the generation comes from.'[14] As Amy Cooper's story illustrates, there is a long history of Stó:lō collective identities disappearing and then others being born or reborn in new form. Prior to the Great Famine a Soowahlie community already existed – or at least a settlement with people existed on that spot. The name *Soowahlie* translates as 'melting away,' a direct reference to the famine itself and the fact that 'the people here once died in great numbers.'[15] What the original pre-famine community was, and its relationship to other settlements and clusters of people, remains uncertain now, but undoubtedly such history once existed. Indeed, it may still exist in Chilliwack oral histories that have not yet been revealed to outsiders. What was important to Mrs Cooper's generation, or at least for the elderly people from whom she learned the story, was that the new Soowahlie community was an amalgamation of an older resident stock and new blood from Nooksack.

Some oral traditions explain that the Chilliwack Tribe, of which Soowahlie is a part, were originally endogamous, preferring to marry within their own community.[16] Within the Indigenous historiography, therefore, the precipitating event of the famine explains and accounts for changes in social customs and practices, and perhaps more importantly, sets an historical precedent allowing subsequent generations to change and adapt to new circumstances. Massive death, survivor dispersal, and assistance received from a distant place together created a context for the formation of a new identity stemming from intercommunity amalgamation. In this way, identity, history, and place are all linked and serve to continually inform one another.

Dan Milo, at the age of ninety-five in 1962, shared with Oliver Wells a story similar to the one related by Amy Cooper. Milo's narrative describes not only an unidentified calamity that wiped out most of the lower Fraser River's Aboriginal population, but movements and a series of community amalgamations and subsequent fractures that account for the existence of the linguistic unity among the Stó:lō people and, by way of extension, all the factors of pan-tribal unity stemming from a common language. Dan Milo recalled:

> Well, there was a boy from Kilgard.[17] In them days they used to call that place Semá:th. That means[18] 'Sumas.' Well, that one boy was left by himself. All his people died. So he went home. And the next morning he made up his mind to come over there and see who was living at Yarrow,[19] where he saw that smoke was coming out of a big house where there was a lot of Indians living. When he came there, he went right into the house there. There was just one girl that was left, after she had all the bodies put away. So that is the first time he ever saw this girl. So he got acquainted with her. So he got real acquainted, and they got married right there. So they stayed together. And that's where the language that the Indians are using started from. They went over to Nicomen [Leq'á:mel],[20] where there's a lot of Indians there. That was the only people that used that language that the Indians are using now, today … They come home. They raised children, and that's how the people began to speak that Halq'eméylem language.[21]

Dan Milo's story refers to the Indigenous etymological understanding of the word *Halq'eméylem*, which he and others have translated as the 'language of Leq'á:mel'[22] (refer back to Map 10). Implicit in the story is the knowledge that it was not only the two Sumas settlements that experienced the sudden depopulation, but all Stó:lō communities along the lower Fraser River. Following the mysterious depopulating event, people from the previously more distinct Stó:lō tribal groups, with their individual languages, came together at Leq'á:mel, in the geographical centre of Stó:lō territory. There, they amalgamated to become a single people speaking a single language. They subsequently refractured to re-establish distinct tribal communities that remained linked in a manner previously impossible by virtue of a shared language and the common experience of surviving the depopulation.

Smallpox

The existence of flood stories, along with narratives like Amy Cooper's famine chronicle and Dan Milo's account of the unidentified calamity that wiped out most of the region's population, have collectively created a historical consciousness through which Stó:lō people have been prepared for similar experiences within their own lives. Events and the recorded responses of people to them provide successive generations of Stó:lō with a series of precedents and/or historical examples and human responses upon which they base their own behaviour. Perhaps this is what Marshall Sahlins meant when he wrote: 'History is ordered by significance; people's' response to and interpretation of events are governed by the logic of the structures they unwittingly reproduce; and in so doing, transform.'[23] Thus, the devastating smallpox epidemic of the late eighteenth century, arriving through Native trade networks at least a decade in advance of actual European visitors and therefore completely unprecedented in terms of its biological nature, was not incomprehensible in terms of its demographic effects, nor was the social response without Indigenous precedent.

Most of the scholarly discussion concerning smallpox epidemics on the northwest coast has focused on the question of time (When did the epidemics occur?) and demographic effect (What was the fatality rate?).[24] Less attention has been directed towards assessing the cultural responses and social effects.[25] Robert Boyd maintains that the first virgin-soil smallpox epidemic probably reached the Coast Salish in the late 1770s via either European ships visiting the western coast of Vancouver Island in the wake of Juan Perez' and James Cook's expeditions, or possibly (though less likely) through Indigenous trade networks from Kamchatka and Alaska, where Russian fur traders had introduced the disease in 1769. Based largely on Wilson Duff's reading of Old Pierre's conversations with Diamond Jenness, Boyd maintains that a second smallpox epidemic probably struck the region around 1801[26] (a view that appears to have been accepted by Wayne Suttles[27]).

Historical geographer Cole Harris's review of the extant European explorers' accounts and Coast Salish oral histories led him to conclude that the evidence better supports a single epidemic in 1782. Having reviewed the same literature and documents, I am inclined to agree with Harris,[28] although I am willing to accept the possibility that a second, less virulent epidemic (variola minor or perhaps measles) may have followed in the wake of the 1782 epidemic with less devastating effects. For my purposes, however, the precise timing of the epidemic is less important than its impact on Aboriginal concepts of self, as reflected in reshaped collective identities resulting from depopulation and the consolidation of what were previously more scattered settlements. Within Stó:lō historiography, the arrival of smallpox was an historic event with profound effects.

Significantly, it has been a common practice of many of those studying introduced disease and depopulation to interpret 'mythic' accounts
of devastating historical events (such as famine stories and accounts of
supernatural monsters) as being Indigenous accounts of what were most
likely early epidemics. It is, of course, reasonable to expect people to
interpret new things within existing paradigms;[29] however, it is important to consider that within the Indigenous discourse the *sxwōxwiyám*,
or miraculous transformation stories, are generally distinguished from
the historical accounts of the arrival of smallpox – even accounts that
describe smallpox as arriving prior to the physical visitation of Europeans. This suggests that while the Aboriginal population initially interpreted the disease as something else (as either a disruption in the spirit
world, or within the context of ancient metaphysical transformations),
their subsequent experience with identifiable epidemics and the Europeans who carried the diseases enabled them to reconsider and adjust
earlier interpretations within their own historical record. Alternatively,
it is reasonable to think that by 1782 the Indigenous people would have
acquired sufficient information about Europeans and their diseases
through intertribal communication networks to allow them to have adequate knowledge to distinguish between smallpox and earlier 'natural'
calamities. Certainly this is what a close reading of the oral historiography suggests.

Old Pierre, Jenness's consultant, and each of Hill-Tout's Fraser River
Salish consultants clearly distinguished the first smallpox epidemic from
earlier disasters, providing historical narratives that unfolded within a
strict chronology that, contrary to many popular beliefs about the non-
linear nature of Aboriginal historical consciousness, was sequentially
developed.[30] Old Pierre related how human history was divided into a
series of eras, each punctuated by significant historical happenings or
events. In Old Pierre's rendition of history, the Lord Above first created
an imperfect, incomplete, world; then came the ages of the sky-born
transformers, like Swaniset, followed by the second generation of transformers, principally the siblings Xexá:ls, who 'made the world right.' It
was many generations later that the Great Flood occurred, and then,
many generations after the flood, that 'the Indians multiplied again,' becoming 'too numerous in the land.' It was at this point, 'during a certain
year' that the snow began to fall so steadily that for three months people
were trapped in their longhouses, living exclusively on their dwindling
stores of dried food. When they were finally able to dig themselves free,
they were compelled to scavenge dead birds and animals for sustenance

while they awaited the return of the eulachon to the river. All told, Old
Pierre explained, it was 'nine months before the snow melted completely
from the house tops,' during which time 'half the Indians died of starvation.' It was many generations after this great snow that 'the people
again multiplied for a third time.' Then it was that the smallpox swept
into their territory and killed off the majority of the people:

> News reached them from the east that a great sickness was travelling over
> the land, a sickness that no medicine could cure, and no person escape.
> Terrified, they held council with one another and decided to send their
> wives, with half the children, to their parents' homes, so that every adult
> might die in the place where he or she was raised. Then the wind carried
> the smallpox sickness among them. Some crawled away into the woods to
> die; many died in their homes. Altogether about three-quarters of the In-
> dians perished …
>   If you dig to-day on the site of any of the old villages you will uncover
> countless bones, the remains of the Indians who perished during this epi-
> demic of smallpox. Not many years later Europeans appeared on the Fra-
> ser, and their coming ushered in a new era.[31]

Unknown to Old Pierre, evidence of the precipitous event that ushered in the new era was also observed and described by the officers and
men on board HMS *Discovery* and HMS *Chatham,* as they sailed through
the Coast Salish waters of Puget Sound and the Strait of Georgia in 1792
under the command of Captain George Vancouver. The British sailors
described numerous abandoned Coast Salish settlements that were lit-
tered with the bones of smallpox victims:

> In all our excursions, particularly those in the neighbourhood of Port Dis-
> covery, the skulls, limbs, ribs, and backbones or some other vestige of the
> human body were found in many places promiscuously scattered about the
> beach, in great numbers. Similar relics were also frequently met with during
> our surveys with the boats. And I was informed by the officers that in their
> several perambulations, the like appearances had presented themselves so
> repeatedly, and in such abundance, as to produce an idea that the environs
> of Port Discovery were a general cemetery for the whole of the surrounding
> country.[32]

Captain Vancouver described Coast Salish territory as 'nearly destitute
of inhabitants,'[33] though he astutely recognized that it had recently 'been

infinitely more populous.' Throughout Puget Sound and Georgia Strait he encountered numerous abandoned settlements, 'each of [which] ... was nearly, if not quite, equal to contain all the scattered inhabitants we saw [in Puget Sound].' The cause of this massive depopulation (calculated to have swept through the region only a few years earlier[34]) Vancouver judged to have been smallpox rather than warfare on account of so few men having battle scars, and so many people suffering the permanent disfigurement of the pox: 'Several of their stoutest men having been observed perfectly naked, and contrary to what might have been expected of rude nations habituated to warfare, their skins were mostly unblemished by scars, excepting such as the small pox seemed to have occasioned; a disease which there is great reason to believe is very fatal amongst them.'[35] Indeed, in a later journal entry he recorded that 'this deplorable disease is not only very common, but it is greatly to be apprehended is very fatal amongst them, as its indelible marks were seen on many, and several had lost the sight of one eye, which was remarked to be generally the left, owing most likely to the virulent effects of this baneful disorder.'[36]

Other accounts of the epidemic, remembered through oral traditions, are just as horrific. Charles Hill-Tout, interviewing an aged Squamish historian at the close of the nineteenth century, learned that many generations after the Great Glood, and the great winter, a new 'dreadful misfortune befell' the Coast Salish people, ushering in a 'time of sickness and distress': 'A dreadful skin disease, loathsome to look upon, broke out upon all alike. None were spared. Men, women and children sickened, took the disease and died in agony by the hundreds so that when the spring arrived and fresh food was procurable, there was scarcely a person left of all their numbers to get it. Camp after camp, village after village, was left desolate. The remains of which, said the old man, in answer to my queries on his head, are found today in the old camp sites or midden-heaps over which the forest has been growing for so many generations.'[37] Hill-Tout himself subsequently conducted the first methodical archaeological examinations of some of these forest-covered ancient burials.[38]

Along the same lines, Albert Louie, an Elder living in the central Fraser Valley in the 1960s, explained to Oliver Wells that when the first smallpox epidemic reached the Stó:lō, 'it killed, oh, half the Indians all around the Fraser River there.'[39] Stó:lō Nation's Cultural Adviser Albert 'Sonny' McHalsie has often told me how he remembers his Elder, Evangeline Pete, explaining to him that when smallpox struck a community near Hope it killed at least twenty-five people each day; the bodies were placed inside pithouses and set on fire. From that time onward, McHalsie learned, the site was known as *Sxwóxwiymelh*, which translates as 'a lot of people died at once.'[40] In 1993 my good friend and teacher Jimmie Charlie of Chehalis, then ninety-one years old, explained to me that a site near the junction of the Chehalis and Harrison rivers is known as *Smimstiyexwála* ('people container') because it was there that people interred the bodies of relatives and neighbours during the first smallpox epidemic.[41] At the entrance to the Fraser Canyon, near the town of Yale, are other sites where smallpox victims were buried in their pithouses.[42] Similar stories exist throughout the broader region.[43]

Migration through Precedence

Nothing illustrates the consequences of Coast Salish people's induction global system of communication and exchange as clearly as the demographic catastrophe associated with smallpox. The oral traditions and associated explorers' accounts speak most forcefully perhaps of the human losses, but they also tell of the actions of survivors who struggled to rebuild an ordered society. For guidance, people turned to the wisdom of their ancestors. Within the remembered ancient narratives the pox-scarred generation of the late eighteenth century found solace in the accounts of their predecessors' migratory responses to floods, famines, and deadly snows. Indeed, as Old Pierre's narrative demonstrates, movements across the Coast Salish geography actually began immediately prior to the large-scale deaths, when married women left their pox-infected husbands' settlements to return to the place of their birth to die. Jay Miller suggests that in the face of illness Coast Salish people sought the safety of their home communities and the associated spirit forces who resided there.[44]

Western scholars have long been aware of the prominence of migration stories within northwest coast Indigenous oral histories, but until recently little energy has been directed towards understanding their social and cultural import or their historical significance. Among the first to identify the movement of people as an ethnographic/historical issue was geologist and early B.C. ethnographer George Dawson. In 1885, upon visiting the Coast Salish's northern neighbours, the Kwakwaka'wakw, he noted: 'When small-pox first ravaged the coast, after the coming of whites,[45] the Indians were not only much reduced in numbers, but became scattered, and new combinations were probably formed subsequently; while tribes and portions of tribes, once forming distinct village communities, drew together for mutual protection, when their numbers became small.'[46]

Robert Boyd has documented the process of village abandonment and survivor consolidation following early contact era epidemics among the Haida on the Queen Charlotte Islands, the Dakelhne-Nukalk of the mid-B.C. coast, and the Chinook along the lower Columbia River.[47] What remains unexplored are the implications of such migrations for changes in Indigenous social structures and the formation or reformation of collective identities, as well as the role such population movements have played in Aboriginal understandings of their own history. Boyd's analysis of the abandonment of settlements, however, never includes the Coast Salish.

Stó:lō oral history is rife with accounts of smallpox-induced population movements similar to those mentioned over a century ago by Dawson for the Kwakwaka'wakw. Old Pierre relates how his great-grandfather happened to be roaming in the mountains when the epidemic broke out: 'For his wife had recently given birth to twins, and, according to custom, both parents and children had to remain in isolation for several months. The children were just beginning to walk when he returned to his village at the entrance to Pitt Lake, knowing nothing of the calamity that had overtaken its inhabitants. All his kinsmen and relatives lay dead inside their homes; only in one house did there survive a baby boy, who was vainly sucking at its dead mother's breast. They rescued the child, burned all the houses, together with the corpses that lay inside them, and *built a new home for themselves several miles away.*'[48]

Old Pierre's son Simon, working with the anthropologist Wayne Suttles in 1952, explained that several settlements and at least two complete tribal groups had been 'wiped out, or nearly so, by smallpox before Fort Langley was founded [in 1827].'[49] These included the settlements of 'Snakwaya at Derby ... Skweelic on Bedford Channel north of the mouth of the Salmon River [which were the main settlements of the Snokomish Tribe], the Q'ó:leq' [Whonnock Tribe] at the mouth of the Whonnock River, the sxa'yeqs [tribe] at Ruskin at the mouth of the Stave River, and the Xat'seq [Tribe] at Hatzic.'[50] From a Semiahmoo consultant at Lummi, Suttles also learned that a tribe called Snokomish, who occupied Mud Bay and the Nicomekl-Salmon River portage system leading to the village of Snakwaya on the Fraser River at Derby Reach, had also been 'wiped out by smallpox.'[51] Old Pierre listed for Jenness an additional place, called 'Hazelberries' in English, just north of Townsend Station near the mouth of the Fraser River, as still another settlement 'whose inhabitants perished in the great smallpox epidemic.[52] The disappearance of people from these and other sites, either through mass death or resulting from women and half their children fleeing to the settlement of the mother's birth, created vacuums within the Stó:lō universe.

Initially, it appears, survivors gathered primarily at what had previously been the most densely populated settlement sites at or near the junctions of the Fraser River and its tribal tributaries. Smaller outlying villages and camps or hamlets located up the tributary watersheds were largely abandoned. The Stó:lō world thus changed from one in which each tribe was characterized by a fairly populous central town (potlatch centre) surrounded by a series of smaller affiliated outlying villages and hamlets, to one where most of the smaller settlements were abandoned and survivors clustered in what had been the tribal core settlements. Smaller tribes, unable to sustain themselves, often disappeared altogether with whatever survivors might remain seeking refuge with relatives in neighbouring centres – and they did so by taking advantage of various kinds of social networks. Later, as the demographics stabilized, and possibly even began to temporarily rebound, people took advantage of the opportunities the depopulation presented to migrate and establish themselves in places formerly occupied by others.

The consolidation of survivors happened first. While detailed information is not available for all regions of Stó:lō territory, the evidence that does exist for certain areas paints a vivid picture of settlement and collective identity reformulation. For example, as Old Pierre explained, 'several small settlements at the mouth of the Fraser River merged with the Musqueam, but in earlier times they were quite separate.'[53] Previously, these separate communities may have been considered distinct tribes, for each had received a special and distinct ritual from the Creator.[54] On the Alouette River the survivors of another community under the hereditary leadership of Cilecten were so reduced in numbers that both they and their funerary ritual 'merged with the Katzie.'[55] What had been southern Snokomish territory around Boundary Bay was, according to Suttles' Lummi consultant, subsequently occupied by the Semiahmoo 'who had intermarried with them.'[56] Northern Snokomish lands at Derby Reach on the Fraser River eventually fell under the influence of the Kwantlen, and ultimately became the site where the Hudson's Bay Company established the first Fort Langley in 1827.[57]

Farther upriver, Charles Hill-Tout recorded from his Lilloet consultant, the headwaters of Harrison Lake and the lower reaches of the Lilloet River were formerly occupied by Halq'eméylem speakers. The Lilloet,

who occupied the area after the mid-nineteenth century, had moved
into the region to take advantage of opportunities presented by the 1858
gold rush and the establishment of a European transportation centre
at Port Douglas. Corroborating this interpretation of migratory history
are the Halq'eméylem place names Hill-Tout recorded for the region.[58]
Living Stó:lō, such as Matilda Guiterrez, who was trained as a young girl
to become an historian[59] and who in May 2009 was the last remaining
fluent Halq'eméylem speaker to have been raised with Halq'eméylem as
her first language,[60] remembers being told that the region was formerly
occupied by the St'qwó:mpth people ('those who speak our language')
but that they were all killed by the smallpox.[61] Whether the St'qwó:mpth
were a separate tribe or a settlement affiliated with the Chehalis tribe
is unclear; regardless, survivors of the epidemic undoubtedly travelled
downriver to relocate among their Chehalis relatives.[62] Incursions by Lilloet people into land that had formerly been held by the Halq'eméylem
speakers affected settlement patterns and precipitated population migrations many kilometres south of the area that was eventually consolidated
as Lilloet territory in the 1860s. During the previous generation (circa
1820 to 1845) the Lilloet embarked on a series of violent raids down Harrison Lake against the inhabitants of a settlement on the northern end of
Seabird Island known as Sq'ewqéyl. To protect themselves, the Sq'ewqéyl
residents moved across and slightly down the Fraser River to Skw'átets,
a site safe from northern raiders, who would have had to leave their canoes on the other side of the Hick's Lake portage on Harrison Lake or
run the gauntlet of Halq'eméylem settlements along the Harrison River
before reaching the Fraser.[63]

The region still farther up the Fraser River, between what is now Agassiz and Hope, appears to have followed the same pattern of depopulation and emigration. In addition to Sxwóxwiymelh ('a lot of people died
at once'), other settlements, such as the one now referred to as Ruby
Creek, were likewise abandoned by whatever survivors lived through the
horror of the smallpox epidemic.[64] In 1952 Wilson Duff interpreted this
particular stretch of the river as having been 'characterized by an internal
fluidity of population ... in pre-white times,'[65] and while I agree this was
generally true during the early nineteenth century, the recorded mobility of residents clearly had much less to do with a natural state of affairs,
as Duff implies, than with adjustments being worked out in the wake
of smallpox-induced depopulation. Indeed, Duff's consultants Edmund
Lorenzetto and August Jim both claimed that the sites of Shxw'ōwhámél
and Skw'átets were vacant prior to the early to mid-nineteenth century,
when the emigrants from Alámex and Sq'ewqéyl occupied them.[66]

In a similar vein, Wilson Duff learned from a Musqueam consultant that the original inhabitants of Indian Arm Inlet (at the head of Burrard Inlet immediately north of the Fraser River near present-day Vancouver) had been Halkomelem speakers known by the name Tamtami'uxwtan. These people, distinct from the contemporary Squamish occupants of the central and lower reaches of Burrard Inlet, were 'closely allied with the Musqueam' but, like so many of the small tribal communities along the lower Fraser River, appear to have been wiped out by the earliest smallpox epidemic.[67] What was formerly Tamtami'uxwtan territory is now known as the homeland of the Tseil-Waututh Tribe, who maintain a historical narrative of their contemporary community being an amalgamation of an original remnant population (possibly the Tamtami'uxwtan) supplemented by new blood from afar. In a history of tribal origins provided by Tseil-Waututh Chief Dan George,[68] we learn that great misfortune befell the original community resulting in the chief's son, Wautsauk, being orphaned and raised by a female wolf. Ultimately, as a young man Wautsauk wanted to find a 'mate of his own kind.' To accomplish this he made an arduous journey to a distant land: 'Travelling up the Indian River, over the mountains to the canyon of the Fraser River, he found a bride among the people there. They came back to the Inlet and started to build our tribe.'[69] In this way, the Tseil-Waututh, like so many other Salish communities, trace their origins to the coming together of what had been two distinct communities following a crisis. In this case, the communities appear to have been a remnant resident Halkomelem group and Interior Salish Lilloet people from the middle Fraser River region.

According to traditions, Wautsauk was still chief of his community when Captain Vancouver sailed into Indian Arm a decade after the first smallpox epidemic.[70] At that time, according to Chief Dan George, the main Tseil-Waututh settlement was near the present site of Belcarra, and smaller camps were situated near the mouths of streams draining into Indian Arm. After Wautsauk's death in the 'late 1700's,' his son inherited his name, becoming Wautauk the Second. This second-generation Tseil-Waututh leader is supposed to have died about 1840,[71] which would date his life to the second decade of HBC fur trade operations.

Kwantlen – the 'Tireless Runners'

The snippets of oral histories recorded by Westerners in the twentieth century provide only glimpses of the total picture of resettlement after the smallpox era. As a result, many of the early migrations have been misunderstood and wrongly or excessively attributed to the economic incentives associated with the establishment of Hudson's Bay Company forts.[72] This is not to deny that posts like Fort Langley and Fort Yale acted as magnets and drew certain Stó:lō settlements more closely into their economic orbit (the Kwantlen in particular), but it is important to realize that the migrations previously attributed to the establishment of the forts were, in fact, well under way before the arrival of the Hudson's Bay Company, and largely the result of earlier disease-induced depopulation. Global market economies simply accelerated the resettlement process. (See Map 11.)

The Kwantlen, whose name according to an etymology shared by Old Pierre connotes 'Tireless Legs' or 'Tireless Runners' have a history appropriately replete with relocation and population movement.[73] They also have a history of tribal fracture and amalgamation making theirs among the most interesting discussed in the oral histories and early fur trade records. As mentioned, Hill-Tout's consultants explained that the original Kwantlen person was the sky-born hero Swaniset,[74] who as Old Pierre explained to Diamond Jenness, originally dropped from the sky at Sheridan Hill near the eastern shore of Pitt Lake. According to Old Pierre, Swaniset (the 'Supernatural Benefactor') was the greatest of the lower Fraser River's First People, for he 'accomplished even greater miracles than the other leaders of his generation,' including the first ancestor, Thelhatsstan, of the Katzie people.[75] In the earliest histories, as related by Old Pierre, Swaniset played the predominant role not only in facilitating physical and metaphysical transformations, but also in providing the region's populace and the other tribal leaders with supratribal leadership. As Jenness learned, among other great feats, Swaniset created the network of sloughs connecting the various waterways of the Fraser Delta. The last (and therefore the most important) slough Swaniset created stretched from the Alouette River southward, terminating at a point about 300 yards north of the Fraser River. Although the village at the end of the slough was named 'Katzie,' a geographical reference to the fact that a spongy moss called Katzie (Q'eytsi'i) in Halq'eméylem, grew in abundance there, the slough itself was known as the 'River of the Kwantlen People,' for it was at Katzie that the Kwantlen people lived.[76]

The Kwantlen, however, were not to remain the sole occupants of what was then a seasonally flooded settlement site, or even its most permanent residents, for as Old Pierre explained, Swaniset subsequently 'ordered' the rest of 'his people to accompany him to Katzie on the Fraser River,

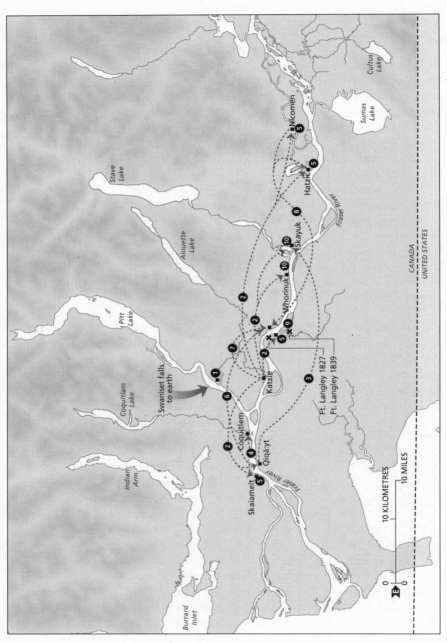

Map 11. Kwantlen – 'The Tireless Runners.'

Summary of Kwantlen movements:

1 After completing many great deeds, Swaniset moves from where he fell from the sky (near Sheridian Hill) to the village of Katzie (moss) on the Kwantlen River (a slough running southward from Alouette River). He gathers his people there with him, including the Kwantlen and the Katzie of Pitt Lake.

2 Katzie becomes overpopulated. Some Kwantlen move to Skaiamelt and Qiqá:yt (New Westminster), other Kwantlen go elsewhere (likely including Hatzic and/or Nicomen slough, the mouth of the Salmon River, and sites at Whonnock and on the Stave River). Some, under the leadership of Whittlekanim, appear to remain at the settlement of Katzie.

3 Xex̱:las the transformers turn some Kwantlen living at New Westminster into wolves and they become wanderers; others into ravens. Some of the remaining Kwantlen eventually relocate to Skayuk on the Stave River.

4 Descendents of Kwantlen elite males and their female slaves (stéxem) leave New Westminster and establish themselves at the mouth of the Coquitlam River.

5 J. McMillan visits Kwantlen settlements at mouth of Salmon River, at Hatzic and/or Nicomen slough, and at New Westminster in 1824.

6 Kwantlen from New Westminster under Tsi-ta-sil-ten move upriver to be across the Fraser River from Fort Langley (Derby Reach) in 1827.

7 Remaining Kwantlen under Whittlekanim living at the settlement of Katzie (on the Kwantlen River/slough) move to be beside Fort Langley.

8 Kwantlen under Nicamous move from Hatzic/Nicomen villages to be adjacent to Fort Langley.

9 Kwantlen at Derby relocate with the HBC adjacent to the second Fort Langley site (current site).

10 Some Kwantlen remain at Whonnock and Skayuk.

and to make homes for themselves at that place.'[77] The modern Katzie tribe, as Jenness learned, was therefore 'an amalgamation of at least two, and perhaps several, communities that claim separate eponyms. Only one community inhabited the vicinity in early times, and its village was not at Katzie itself, but at Port Hammond, a mile away. Another Katzie community occupied the district around Pitt Lake, 10 miles to the north, and did not move permanently to Port Hammond until the latter half of the nineteenth century.'[78] Thus, according to the Indigenous history, the people ultimately and officially identified by fur traders and later government officials as 'the Katzie' appear to have been the formerly more distinct community from the settlement on Pitt Lake.[79]

Once the Katzie and Kwantlen winter homes were unified on the Kwantlen River at Katzie, Swaniset set about making the site an important seasonal gathering place for other more distant people. Shortly after the amalgamation, Swaniset's wife shared the contents of a special box with the people gathered at Katzie, thus introducing eulachon to the Fraser River system. Swaniset then 'traveled around the country inviting the more distant people to come and share their good fortune.' Those who accepted the invitation came to benefit from their relationship with the growing and wealthy community at Katzie, while those who refused to make the journey and partake of the eulachon gift were chastised as 'senseless.'[80]

So powerful and influential was Swaniset, and so intent his desire to create supratribal social and economic relationships, that he even ventured with canoes of dried eulachon to distant salt water settlements in Puget Sound where he engaged in trade and gambling games. After visiting several human communities he eventually travelled so far to the south that he reached the homes of the various salmon species. Within Stó:lō history, great things are usually only achieved after heroes complete arduous journeys to distant places, and so it was with Swaniset, who upon visiting the southern settlements of the various species of salmon people, ultimately reached the home settlement of the great sockeye salmon people. It was among the sockeye that Swaniset announced his intention to take yet another wife – the leader's daughter. Sometime after the marriage union was achieved, Swaniset declared his desire to bring his new sockeye wife back to the Fraser River with him, thus establishing the precedent of patrilocal marriages among the upper class and instituting the practice of regular visits of affines to their in-laws' residences, as demonstrated by the regular return of the sockeye woman's family to her new home on the Fraser.[81]

The amalgamated Kwantlen and Katzie tribe's settlement at Katzie, however, had now become too crowded, and so, following Swaniset's lead, many of the people dispersed to other locations. Swaniset himself 'moved his home a mile farther up the river.' Later, at an unspecified time, other of Swaniset's Kwantlen people (who continued to recognize Swaniset as their first leader, but henceforth appear to have traced their leadership through another 'first man' named Skwelselem, who was not sky-born but a 'descendant of the earth') 'moved away from Katzie and occupied the site now covered by the Penitentiary at New Westminster' (just southwest of the mouth of the Burnette River.[82] These New Westminster vicinity Kwantlen settlements were called Qiqá:yt and Skaiametl.[83] It was after this migration (and after Swaniset himself along with a select few Kwantlen had moved roughly two kilometres upriver from Katzie to Hammond Mills) that X̱exá:ls the transformers arrived to finish the Creator's work. How long Kwantlen people lived at New Westminster is uncertain. What is remembered is that the eventful arrival of the X̱exá:ls set in motion a series of new transformations which led to yet additional movements. On land that would later become the capital of the future colony of British Columbia, X̱exá:ls met a Kwantlen family who listened to the transformers' words 'in secret mockery.' This was a family that 'never worked for its livelihood, but always begged from others.' Perceiving their thoughts, X̱exá:ls transformed these lazy indolent people into ravens and decreed that from that point onward they would visit other people's camps and beg for food. Here too X̱exá:ls met a man who, the Kwantlen leader explained, 'wandered in the woods all the time.' This apparently kept the man from being a good father and husband and so X̱exá:ls punished him and his family by transforming them into wolves who would continue their wandering ways. Henceforth, the wolf people would make available to other Kwantlen special spirit power to assist young men in hunting and women in mat-making and the weaving of woolen garments. The remaining Kwantlen people X̱exá:ls recognized as wise, and so did not transform them.[84]

In the summer of 2000 one of the few remaining fluent Halq'eméylem-speaking elders, Rosaleen George, explained to me that some of the close relatives of the Kwantlen who had been turned into ravens later migrated upriver to the territory around Stave River and Lake occupying lands left vacant by earlier residents who had been wiped out by the smallpox epidemic.[85] The Kwantlen migrants appear to have commemorated the earlier residents by referring to the territory as *Sxwòyeqs*, literally 'all dead' or 'tribe dead.'[86]

Along similar lines, according to oral tranditons collected by Wilson Duff, Charles Hill-Tout, and amateur historian B.A. McKelvie, when the Hudson's Bay Company arrived on the Fraser River and established Fort Langley in 1827, the Kwantlen and certain other lower Stó:lō communities moved upriver to be near the fort on lands that had formerly been occupied by the Snokomish – another small tribe that, like the people of the Stave watershed, had fallen victim to smallpox.[87] Old Pierre explained that the New Westminster Kwantlen ultimately made their home on the north side of the Fraser River across from the fort.[88] Today, the branch of Kwantlen tribe living on that site is known as the Thomas family.[89] When I interviewed Robert Thomas Sr in 1992 he explained that his son Robert Jr carried the name of the hereditary Kwantlen earth-born leader Tsi-ta-sil-ten (or as Hill-Tout recorded the name, Sqtcten).[90] Robert Jr had been given the name by his grandfather Francis Thomas when just a boy. By the late-nineteenth century the Kwantlen tribe as a whole had come to be commonly and legally referred to as the 'Langley Indians,' though in 1994, under the leadership of Chief Marilyn Gabriel, the tribe officially changed its name back to Kwantlen. Significantly, Gabriel had inherited her 'Indian name' and position from her father Joe Gabriel and through him from his father Alfred Gabriel, who in turn, received it from the leader prominent at the turn of the century, Chief Casimir (aka Strkakel).[91]

The 1820s Kwantlen migration to Fort Langley was, therefore, an aspect or extension of a much earlier process of movement that dated back to the ancient myth-age but that had been accelerated by the rapid depopulation associated with smallpox (and associated trauma among the epidemic's survivors), all accentuated by a desire to access new economic opportunities (and consolidate control over the same) while securing military protection from the 'Coastal Raiders.'[92] Its expression was, therefore, more complicated than a binary or reductionist portrayal of indigeneity as a state frozen in either time or geography would allow.[93]

If the oral histories of Kwantlen collective identity and population movement leading up to the eve of European contact is rich, the early historical documentation of regional Stó:lō migration and identity is, unfortunately, rather sketchy. The European explorers and fur traders, while keen observers and experienced students of Aboriginal culture, were motivated to record different information from what a contemporary audience might ask for. During his brief sojourn in Stó:lō territory in 1808, Simon Fraser, for example, recorded little that assists in locating or identifying Aboriginal communities. He refers to all the lower

Fraser Aboriginal people collectively by the name 'Sachinco,' which is the term used by Fraser's up-river Nlakapamux (aka Thompson Indian) interpreter and guide. It is still widely in use by Nlakapamux people today. Indeed, the only Halkomelem-speaking tribe identified by name in Fraser's journal is Musqueam, located at the Fraser's mouth.

In December of 1824, however, clerks working under James McMillan, who had been sent north from Fort George on the Columbia River to scout for a site for the future Fort Langley, recorded information indicating that the Kwantlen had already firmly established themselves in a series of winter villages stretching over thirty kilometres upriver from New Westminster.[94] Upon entering the Fraser via the Nicomekl-Salmon River portage route from Boundary Bay, McMillan's party encountered a people who identified themselves as members of what clerk John Work recorded as the 'Cahoutetts Nation.' Later, they travelled upriver and camped adjacent to a lodge the HBC men considered to be of the same 'Cahantitt' tribe near Hatzic slough. The following morning dozens of other members of this tribe visited them from a settlement 'a short distance upriver' (apparently from Nicomen slough). Upon their descent, the HBC party encountered more members of the 'Cahotitt' tribe near present-day New Westminster. Wayne Suttles has interpreted these names as variations of Kwantlen,[95] which would mean that the Kwantlen had already established themselves as far as what Charles Hill-Tout's Kwantlen consultants of half a century later identified as the uppermost extent of their post-migration territory.[96]

Significantly, in Fort Langley's early years, its journal writers frequently mention at least two major Kwantlen settlements with separate leaders who appear to have been brothers.[97] The first, located on what the traders referred to as 'the Quoitle [Kwantlen] River' (which most likely was the same slough Old Pierre described as having been made by Swaniset and which emptied into the Allouette River and from there into the Pitt River), 'where the chief of the Quoitlans, Whittlekanim, has his residence.'[98] The second under a leader called Nicamous was at a site an unspecified distance upriver from the fort. The name of this second Kwantlen leader (variously rendered by the journals' three authors as Nicamuns, Nicamous, Nicameus, Nicamoos, Nic,ca,ueus, Ni,cam.meus, Ni,ca.mous, etc.) is suggestive, as it appears to be a downriver Halkomelem dialect speaker's attempt to render the upriver dialect name Leq'á:mel. Leq'á:mel, as discussed earlier, is the name of the place where the survivors gathered in Dan Milo's story of the mysterious depopulating event, and the birthplace of the Stó:lō Halkomelem language. The

most obvious distinction between upriver and downriver Halkomelem is
the substitution of 'n' for 'l.' Leq'á:mel in the downriver dialect, therefore, becomes Neq'á:men, or expressed in common English, Nicomen.
Thus, while the exact location of Nicamous' settlement is never specified, it would appear that the second most prominent Kwantlen leader of
the early nineteenth century may have been residing at, and bearing the
name of, a site known among Stó:lō people as the birthplace of the modern Stó:lō people. By 1839, following Whittlekanim's death, Nicamous
became the entire Kwantlen tribe's most prominent leader. By this time
he had also taken up permanent residence on McMillan Island, adjacent to Fort Langley where, through his sister, daughters (and nieces?)
who had married employees of the fort, he strove to regulate trade and
(much to the chagrin of the HBC) extract payment as a middleman from
those of other tribes without marriage ties to the post's resources.[99] As
early as June 1829 many of the Kwantlen had taken up residence directly
outside the Fort's palisade, and references to the 'Quoitle River' settlement disappear from the journal, although a Kwantlen settlement 'a few
miles higher up' the Fraser (likely at Whonock or Sxayuks) continued to
be mentioned.[100] Likewise, the Musqueam, whose tribal core was on the
north arm of the Fraser near the river's mouth, are reported to have had
a fairly permanent settlement at the mouth of Kanaka Creek – across the
river from the fort's first site.[101]

Repeated early references to the main Kwantlen settlement being
on the Pitt River and to the Katzie as 'a weak tribe [further] up Pitt's
River'[102] suggest that when Fort Langley was established Old Pierre's
Katzie ancestors had not yet made the move[103] to the Fraser proper – the
site where they would ultimately have their major settlement site secured
as a reserve by the Royal Engineers in 1861.[104]

For all its strengths as an ethnographic document, *The Fort Langley
Journals* present certain challenges in terms of their usefulness in plotting early nineteenth-century settlement locations, and for assessing the
historical expressions of collective identities. This stems largely from the
fact that, as the post's second chief trader (and the journals' third author)
Archibald McDonald acknowledged, both the interconnections and the
distinctiveness of the various Stó:lō groups were sometimes difficult for
outsiders to comprehend: 'When we say the Quaitlines [Kwantlens] we
very often mean anyone of the distant Tribes called among themselves –
Quaitlains, Musquams [Musqueams], Kitchis [Katzie], and at a distance
even the whole collectivity are better known by the appellation of the
Cawaitchens [Cowichans] as that Tribe is the leading nation in this quar-
ter.' By 'the whole collectivity' McDonald likely was referring to all of the

Coast Salish people living within the region serviced by Fort Langley.[105]
This reference, however, calls into question what otherwise appear to be
the identities of distinct tribes. It likely reflects in part McDonald's nascent familiarity with the region's power structures as well as the reality
of interpenetrating Aboriginal collective groupings, especially of those
traced through elite male bloodlines and those created through marriage and the relocation of women to their husbands' homes. The latter,
or course, cut across tribal lines in the first generation while they served
to integrate tribal identities in the next (affinal ties in the first generation necessarily became consanguinial in the second).

Earlier scholars took the *Journals'* ambiguity about tribal nomenclature to be an indication that the Kwantlen had somehow amalgamated
with what were formerly more distinct tribal entities around them: 'an
aggregation that probably included the Kwantlen, Whonock, Sxayuks,
Matsqui, Hatzic, Nicomen, Qeqayt, and Coquitlam.'[106] But this explains
only part of the process. Clearly the Kwantlen did amalgamate with
some people, the Whonock (Qō:leq), for example, whose name has
been translated as 'two tribes coming together' in commemoration of
this act.[107] And clearly, as discussed above, the Kwantlen themselves have
oral histories that describe a much earlier time when they themselves
for a while became closely affiliated with what would become the Katzie
tribe, and when heroic sky-born and earth-born community founders
came together to create a larger whole. But in other cases, as with the
occupation of the Snokomish lands anchored around the junction of
the Salmon and Fraser rivers, or the resettlement of the lands associated with the Stave watershed, the evidence more clearly indicates that
Kwantlen people occupied territory left vacant by others who had either
been eliminated by smallpox, or whose numbers had been so reduced
that whatever survivors remained were absorbed into the Kwantlen body
politic. Certainly the absence of the above-mentioned seven other names
within both the 1830 and the 1839 HBC censuses suggests a pattern of
takeover.[108] As quoted previously, George Gibbs documented more
than a century ago that it was a tradition among Coast Salish people
that a tribe's title continued only until such time as the tribe became
extinct.[109] Among the Salish, as elsewhere in human history and geography, the dictum *natura abhorret a vacuo* applied.[110] Coupled with Gibb's
interpretation is Suttles' observation that Coast Salish tribal territory is
better conceived not as an area confined by specific borders, but as an
ever-decreasing interest in lands as one moves farther from the core of
tribal lands. This might best be conceived as a series of diminishing rings
emanating from a cluster of tribally affiliated settlements within a dis-

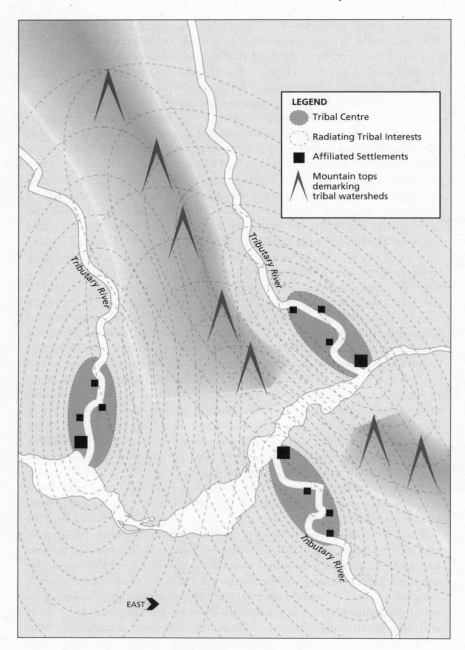

LEGEND

Tribal Centre

Radiating Tribal Interests

Affiliated Settlements

Mountain tops demarking tribal watersheds

Tributary River

Tributary River

Tributary River

EAST

Map 12. Hypothetical depiction of tribal territories and interests.

crete watershed (see Map 12). People of one tribe, in this system, have interests in the lands and resources that are generally regarded as being principally within the territory of another tribe. While such overlaps can be the cause of tensions, they are also the marrow that sustains the flexible structures of broad regional identity affiliations.

What emerges, then, is a picture of the leaders of the Kwantlen tribe asserting ownership rights to land and resources that had previously been considered by them as peripheral sites where they had most likely formerly held only access privileges forged through marriage alliances and blood relatives. The fact that certain names that earlier ethnographers had assumed to be the tribal names of the region's pre-smallpox inhabitants are, instead, sometimes names commemorating an earlier resident community's demise (recall, e.g., that *Sxwòyeqs*, meaning 'all dead' or 'tribe dead'), or names commemorating the process through which survivors amalgamating with the Kwantlen (note, e.g., that Whonock means 'two tribes come together'), suggests that the Kwantlen never intended to erase the history and identity of the previous occupants. These were strategic moves aimed at accessing valued resources that were built upon a web of kinship and hereditary power that took advantage of opportunities. The diverse expressions of these moves indicates the power that historical events can have in transforming identities, and the role that settlement names can play as cross-tribal unifying forces. The history of Kwantlen population movements suggests that often group identities were broader than a single settlement or even tribal unit. Indeed, even though the subsequent arrival of non-Native settlers and associated transformations of land tenure systems through the creation of Crown Land, fee simple title, and Indian Reserves served to render population movements much more difficult, the process of identity negotiation and identity boundary maintenance continued throughout Kwantlen territory, and throughout Kwantlen history.[111]

Though devastating, the lower Fraser River people's first engagement with disruptive global pathogens and the global market economy, as represented by smallpox and then the arrival of the Hudson's Bay Company, did not result in a sudden transformative break with pre-contact history and identity. Within the collective historical consciousness of the various lower Fraser River communities were rich storehouses of ancient narratives describing not only ancestral responses to similar cataclysmic events, but early cross-pollinating tales of tribal ethnogenesis. These stories provided precedents that sustained survivors through the immediate crisis and then guided them as they forged new collective affiliations within what was in many ways a post-smallpox vacuum. Reduced in number and dispersed, survivors relocated to build new tribal identities that would have been recognizable to their ancestors in form and substance because they were built upon existing social, economic, and storied foundations. The process was dynamic and jarring, but never chaotic.

In light of Indigenous understandings of the historical expressions of their collective identity, the scholarly interpretation of early contact-era history requires rethinking. Taking Indigenous historical sources seriously – even if, as in the case of myth-like stories, they cannot be corroborated by archival documents or Western science – not only leads to scholarship that is inclusive and meaningful to Indigenous people, it also helps us create new, and hopefully more accurate histories. For, as Julie Cruikshank's artful discussion of Aboriginal people's relationship with the natural environment in a northern context reveals in her book *Do Glaciers Listen?* it does not necessarily matter whether a Coast Salish myth-like story describes a real event though often they likely do. That is to say our focus cannot only be on trying to determine if stories of the Great Flood, for example, can be linked to a geological reality; what matters more is appreciating how belief in the historical legitimacy of the contents of such stories shapes people's subsequent historical behavior.[112]

Situating history within a context created by Indigenous historical consciousness, therefore, provides a means of highlighting what Marshall Sahlins refers to as the 'systematic ordering of contingent circumstances.'[113] Just as the subsequent non-Native re-settlement of British Columbia, so aptly described by Cole Harris (1997), was predicated on smallpox-induced Native depopulation, so too was the earlier smallpox-induced Salish re-settlement contingent upon circumstances whose significance lay in the 'structure of the conjuncture.'[114] In other words, individuals such as those genealogical founders named in the oral traditions made choices and steered Aboriginal history forward by interpreting the smallpox epidemic within the context of earlier ancestral stories describing people's responses to similar disasters – and they chose migration as a core component of their response. Moreover, as the next chapter demonstrates, these smallpox and economically induced migrations were not only not the first in Stó:lō history, they also were not the last. Much of the nineteenth century was also characterized by a series of identity-shaping migrations that, through the power of place and the problem of time, did as much to undermine certain tribally based affiliations as they did in other instances to enhance tribal cohesiveness while simultaneously promoting competing notions of supra-tribal identity.

Chapter Five

Events, Migrations, and Affiliations in the 'Post-Contact' World

With that [land]slide, that's where the main history starts.
— Bob Joe, 1962[1]

Between 1945 and 1972 Robert 'Bob' Joe spoke frequently with non-Native interviewers about the origins and history of his tribal community, the Chilliwack. Like most Coast Salish origin stories, Joe's accounts included discussions of heroic ancestors with marvellous powers. But for Joe, these were not necessarily the most important components of the narratives, let alone the most significant forces in the history of his people's collective identity. From his perspective, what most shaped and gave meaning to contemporary Chilliwack identity was a relatively recent historical migration that resulted in the transformation of his ancestors from high-elevation Nooksack speakers to Fraser Valley–dwelling, Halq'eméylem-speaking Stó:lō, or 'River People.'

Stories of population movements and large-scale migrations feature prominently in many eras of Stó:lō history and historical understanding. Some tend to place greater emphasis on the different social processes that moulded certain tribal communities into their currently recognizable forms or, as the case may be, literally caused certain other tribal communities to cease to exist. Although related within the context of event-inspired migration, these stories are as much about social dynamics as they are about the physical movement of people. They describe the relationship between social and physical displacement or relocation, and the association between collective identity and such matters as Native efforts at resolving disputes, internal conflicts over status, and external colonial manipulation. These Indigenous processes functioned through-

out the contact era and later served as precedents for colonial-era identity reformations.

An examination of those post-contact migrations associated with tribal
ethnogenesis inevitably casts Coast Salish cultural identity and history in
a new light. Moreover, such analysis provides historical context for certain contemporary tensions – tensions that exist not only between Coast
Salish First Nations and the Canadian state but also among and between
variously constituted Coast Salish communities themselves, as they struggle to establish viable economies and governing systems within a system
of global capitalism and Indian Affairs administration.

What follows is inevitably informed by a contemporary Indigenous political discourse that is often heated. Among the Coast Salish people of
the lower Fraser River watershed, various conflicts exist over who has
the right to regulate and benefit from a limited and rapidly dwindling
supply of land and resources. These tensions are typically portrayed in
the media as 'intertribal' in nature; however, in reality, the expression
and composition of the collective units remains largely undefined and
debated. At their core, these disputes engage a fundamental question:
where do Aboriginal rights reside and at what level are they operationalized? What collective unit holds Aboriginal title and has the right to
regulate and benefit from a region's (or location's) natural resources:
the band (First Nation), the tribe, the nation (supertribal affiliates), or
the smaller extended family groupings? Where, within these groupings,
does political authority reside?

At the local level, contemporary Indigenous conflicts over land and
resources tend to be cast within a historical discourse where invocations
of 'tradition' imply much more than simply continuity. For example, a
group will often assert that its claim to a particular resource is superior
to another group's claim because it is more 'traditional.' Tradition and
historical knowledge are invoked to mark authority.[2] Both the validity of
the collective group's make-up, as well as the validity of its relationship
to resources, are substantiated through historical arguments: my band/
tribe/nation/family's claim is more legitimate than yours because it is
more traditional. History, therefore, is regarded by Coast Salish people
as an important arbiter of both identity and political authority.[3]

European contact and colonialism, broadly defined, have been in-
credibly disruptive forces acting both upon, and within, Coast Salish society. Together, they have created situations rife with the potential for
sociopolitical change. The direction of these changes, and their expressions, however, has seldom been what European observers anticipated.

Even within academia, interpretive models and methodologies have obscured as much as they have revealed about the nature of post-contact identity reformations. By alternatively assessing post-contact change in terms of either the benefits of European technology to Indigenous cultural expressions or against a balance sheet of demographic decline, the adherents of the 'enrichment' thesis and its counterpart the 'culture of terror' thesis (a contemporary manifestation of the old 'degeneration' thesis) have focused primarily on the impacts of newcomers on Natives and have overlooked the dynamics sparked within Indigenous societies. Likewise, structural functionalism and the legacy of ahistorical salvage ethnography are largely responsible for the inordinate attention the process of assimilation has been given in relation to adaptation. Taken together, such factors have largely prevented scholars from looking for significant examples of early contact-era shifts in Coast Salish collective identity and political authority.[4]

This chapter examines the Indigenous histories describing five significant changes within Coast Salish collective groupings in the first century following the smallpox epidemic of circa 1782. These stories have been largely ignored, despite their centrality to Coast Salish concepts of their collective self. An analysis of the content and structure of these stories demonstrates that the nature of change within Coast Salish collective authority and political identity was driven by Indigenous concerns and agendas, even on those occasions when it was precipitated by outside colonial forces. What is more, such analysis contributes to an old academic debate over whether European contact led inevitably to a consolidation or to an atomization of Indigenous political authority and collective identity.[5] It is argued here that contact could and did have different results on Indigenous identity and authority even within a single cultural group and that such changes were not necessarily unidirectional.

The first change involves the origins of the modern central Fraser Valley Chilliwack Tribe. This story is particularly indicative of the role pivotal punctuating forces played in setting in motion the phenomenon of identity reformation. The accounts of this community's arduous migrations from mountainous uplands to the valley lowlands, and its establishment as a genuine Fraser River–oriented collective, illustrate the many complicated social mechanisms a Salish people employed to facilitate a new community's integration into existing social and physical geographies.

The second example discusses the abandonment of settlements at Alámex and analogous tribal clusters along the Fraser River near present-day Agassiz, and the subsequent geographical readjustments to new tribally defined spaces. These stories are indicative of the complex nature of identity politics in the early post–smallpox era, for they document the process through which the participants in these migrations struggled to reconcile tensions that emerged between the pull of their older identities, which were nested in their former homelands, and the need to establish and legitimize their claims to the land and resources of their new territories.

A third case study is especially useful in revealing that the process of collective identity readjustment was neither swift nor a one-time event. As recently as the late nineteenth century, Coast Salish people seeking to maximize the benefits of a new colonial economy reconstituted their tribal affiliations following a series of migrations designed to allow Fraser Canyon people to gain access to Fraser Valley farmlands. The oral history describing the emergence of the rather loosely defined and somewhat enigmatic Tait (or 'Upriver') Tribe is particularly useful in demonstrating the extent to which external colonial initiatives assumed a life of their own within Aboriginal society and how the Aboriginal responses were not necessarily what the colonial architects desired or anticipated. Moreover, the emergence of the Tait Tribe represents the first modern expression of a supra-tribal political identity of a sort that helps explain the forces behind such broad contemporary identities as those associated with the Stó:lō Nation and Stó:lō Tribal Council.

Not all of the population movements and collective identity reformations occurred within established tribal systems, however. Stories of class mobility and the establishment of independent, though stigmatized, tribal communities consisting of people who were formerly of the lower and slave classes constitute an important chapter in the history of post-contact Coast Salish identity reformations. Following the first smallpox epidemic in the late eighteenth century, the established elite experienced difficulty regulating the behaviour, as well as the identities, of their former subordinates. Ancient oral histories illustrate that class tensions have a long history among the Coast Salish that pre-date the arrival of Europeans and smallpox. Accounts of the social and political readjustments within Coast Salish society following the first epidemic have provided subsequent generations of Coast Salish people of all classes with precedents to follow as they adjusted to change. In many instances slaves and serfs alike took advantage of the pockets of unoccupied space left between newly reconfigured tribal cores to forge increasingly autonomous collective affiliations of their own. Nevertheless, the stigma of lower-class ancestry continues to plague the modern-day descendants of these people.

The Chilliwack Tribe

Robert 'Bob' Joe is widely regarded as the foremost mid-twentieth-century Stó:lō tribal historian. His various recorded accounts of the Chilliwack Tribe's origin story, in particular, stand apart from the stories shared by other lower Fraser River informants of his generation, in terms of their comprehensiveness and detail, as well as for the sheer extent of their coverage. Fortunately, Joe was interviewed a number of times over a period of more than twenty years, and so multiple accounts of particular narratives of his are available for review. He cooperated first with the anthropologist Marian Smith in the mid-1940s and then with folklorist Norman Lerman and anthropologist Wilson Duff in 1950. During the 1960s he was repeatedly tape-recorded by his friend and local ethnographer Oliver Wells. In addition, during that same decade, he shared aspects of his traditional knowledge with linguist Jimmy Gene Harris and a number of radio and print journalists. Regardless of what topic his interviewers wanted to discuss, Bob Joe always ensured that they heard the story of the migration of the Chilliwack people from the upper regions of Chilliwack Lake down to the Fraser Valley.

Through the story of the development of modern Chilliwack tribal identity, Bob Joe provided the details of Coast Salish social-political structures and functions. Moreover, as with so many other stories concerning Coast Salish collective identity, this one, too, involves a migration facilitated by a historical event (in this case a landslide on the upper reaches of the Chilliwack River) and, implicitly, a coinciding smallpox epidemic along the river's lower courses. Following these events, the narrative documents the reluctant merging of two distinct tribal communities and the emergence of the Chilliwack collective as an accepted member of the Fraser River–oriented community of Stó:lō tribes.

Reflecting the divergence of interests between informant and ethnographers, Bob Joe's accounts of the mountain-to-Fraser Valley migration have never featured prominently in the publications resulting from his interviews, and as such they have not been permitted to contribute to our understanding of the historical dimensions of Coast Salish consciousness – let alone of the role of migration in Coast Salish history.[6]

As Bob Joe explained, the Chilliwack people formerly lived in a series of settlements along the upper reaches of the Chilliwack River and at Chilliwack Lake. The tribe was led by four brothers, the most prominent and influential being Wileliq, whose ancient origins, as Bob Joe's contemporary, Dan Milo, also related, involved the transformation of a black bear with a white spot on its chest.[7] The Chilliwack settlements were not equal. Wileliq and his influential brothers originally conducted and coordinated the tribe's political and social activities from Sxóchaqel, a settlement Joe referred to as the group's 'main headquarters' on the northern shore of Chilliwack Lake near the river's entrance. The word 'Chilliwack' (*Ts'elxweyéqw*) literally translates as 'head,' meaning either the headwaters of a river or the head of a person or group of people.[8] One day, while traversing the series of trails that ran along the ridges of the region's mountains, a young hunter noticed a crack in the rocks. When he returned to the site sometime later, the crack had grown wider. Fearing that there was 'going to be great trouble, or disaster,' he warned the people living in the settlement below the fissure that they were in imminent danger of a landslide.[9] However, instead of thanking the hunter, the people 'started razzing and laughing at him, saying "where did you ever hear of a mountain cracking in two?"'[10] The next morning, people living in the neighbouring settlements heard a 'rumble.' As a result, as Joe explained, 'When daylight came, the families that were warned were no more. They were all buried under half of the mountain-slide.'[11] (See Map 13.)

While Bob Joe's narratives do not detail the social and emotional reaction of the remaining Chilliwack people to the tragedy, it is clear that the avalanche became the pivotal event in their modern collective history. With the landslide, Joe asserts, 'the main history starts,' for it was then that Wileliq and his brothers began moving the Chilliwack Tribe 'farther down' the river, embarking on a process of migration and, ultimately, the displacement and slow integration with a number of neighbouring groups.[12] In addition to burying the village near Centre Creek, the landslide also likely temporarily blocked the river's main channels, severing the migration route of salmon trying to reach their spawning grounds near the tribal headquarters, a few kilometres upriver on the shores of Chilliwack Lake. Without salmon, and suffering the grief associated with the loss of their kinspeople and the spiritual dangers inherent in living near the site of such massive human tragedy, the Chilliwack Tribe could do little else but begin the process of relocation.

According to Bob Joe, after the landslide, Wileliq and his brothers moved the tribal 'headquarters' twenty-four kilometres downstream from Chilliwack Lake to *Iy'othel*, a settlement straddling both sides of the Chilliwack River. Over time, as the population grew, Iy'othel became crowded, and so the headquarters was again shifted approximately twelve kilometres farther downstream to the open prairie at *Xéyles*,

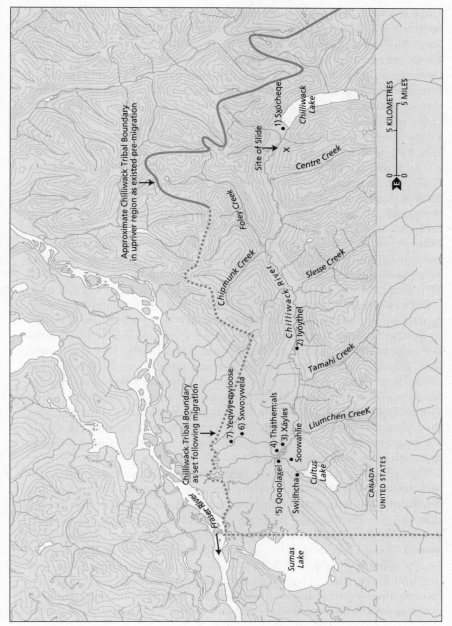

Map 13. The Chilliwack migration and their transformation into a Stó:lō tribe.

located a little less than one kilometre upstream of Vedder Crossing. Each time the headquarters moved, the satellite villages followed. By the time Wileliq established himself at Xéyles, other Chilliwack were living in the adjacent settlements around what is now the Soowahlie Indian Reserve. Not too long after their arrival at Xéyles, the brothers decided to move the headquarters again, this time a mere couple of hundred metres farther downstream to *Tháthem:als*. Bob Joe points to the significance of the move: 'At Tháthem:als was born a man who was to become a great leader of the Chilliwacks and to bear the name Wileliq – the fifth man to bear that name since time began.'[13]

The fifth Wileliq was destined to become a notable leader not only because of his noble bloodline but also because of the remarkable circumstances associated with his birth: A full month after Wileliq the Fifth was born, and during a great thunderstorm, his mother gave birth to his twin sister called *Lumlamelut* 'Lightning.' Moreover, Wileliq the Fifth's birth occurred at the climax of the era of Chilliwack migration, and he was therefore apparently regarded as special by virtue of his being a product of his antecedents' excursion to a distant location. His birth might best be considered within the context of the Coast Salish spirit quest. Just as prominent individuals ritualistically travel to remote places to acquire spirit helpers, the people of Chilliwack Lake had collectively travelled to Vedder Crossing and acquired a new hereditary leader. Thus, it is not surprising that, under the leadership of Wileliq the Fifth, the Chilliwack consolidated their position as a community no longer oriented to the mountainous upper reaches of the Chilliwack River and adjacent Nooksack and Skagit watersheds to the south and east but, rather, to the mighty Fraser River itself. Indeed, until their appearance on the Fraser floodplain, Halq'eméylem was not even the mother tongue of the Chilliwack people; rather, according to tribal traditions, they spoke a dialect of the Nooksack language called *'Kluh Ch ihl ihs ehm.'*[14]

The arrival of the Chilliwack was a disconcerting development for those already living at and near the junction of the Chilliwack and Fraser rivers. Oral narratives collected in the mid-twentieth century record that, prior to the Chilliwack people's downriver migration, the territory drained by the streams flowing into and out of the body of water now known by the Chinook jargon name of Cultus Lake was occupied by the now 'forgotten tribe' of *Swí:lhcha* people. Like their upstream Chilliwack neighbours, the Swí:lhcha spoke a dialect of the Nooksack language, reflecting that their social orientation was primarily southward, through the network of trails connecting Cultus Lake to the upper reaches of the northern fork of the Nooksack River, and not through what was then the boggy marshland leading from Vedder Crossing to the Fraser River. Another version of the Swí:lhcha people's story, related by Chilliwack Elder John Wallace in 1967, explains that the Swí:lhcha were nearly wiped out by smallpox. According to Wallace, and others, the settlements at the southern end of Cultus Lake and on the flat near Xéyles 'sidehill' were completely depopulated by the virus, and the few survivors consolidated themselves in a village at the entrance of Sweltzer (Swí:lhcha) Creek.[15]

The arrival of the Chilliwack people in Swí:lhcha territory did not result in the immediate merging of the remnant population with the new. In 1858 one of the earliest Europeans to visit the area, Lieutenant Charles Wilson of the British Boundary Commission, still described the Swí:lhcha as a separate community.[16] A century later, Mrs Amy Cooper remembered that, during her childhood in the early twentieth century, though by then united on the single Indian reserve called Soowahlie, the remnants of the Swí:lhcha population retained a collective identity that was sustained by both physical and social isolation from the Chilliwack: 'Those people never associated with the Soowahlie [Chilliwack]. They were Swí:lhcha. They were a separate people. There was a line there that they couldn't cross; and these people never talked to them ... Not unless they had to. And you couldn't go and hunt on their side, and they couldn't hunt on your side ... They kept to themselves and there's very few of them left that belonged there ... See the Band of Soowahlie [Chilliwack people] is different from the Swí:lhcha. They were different people all together.'[17]

So entrenched was the feeling of distinctiveness between the two groups occupying the single reserve, and so bitter the animosity between them, that as recently as the 1920s, the descendants of the original Swí:lhcha and Chilliwack communities refused to collect drinking water from the same spring – the Swí:lhcha of west Soowahlie preferring (or being compelled?) to walk a considerable distance and take their water from an inferior location rather than drink from the main Soowahlie source with the Chilliwack people. So deep were the animosities that friendly fraternization between members of the younger generation often provoked a violent physical reaction from adults.[18]

While relations between the recently arrived Chilliwack and the displaced Swí:lhcha took a long time to harmonize, those between the Chilliwack and the various Fraser River Stó:lō tribes proper, though initially often violent, were more quickly rationalized. Albert Louie, an old man in the 1960s, had learned from his Elders that the Chilliwack advance to the Fraser River had not been entirely peaceful. Reportedly, as they edged ever nearer the Fraser River, the Chilliwack warriors engaged in a series of largely successful conflicts with the Pilalt Tribe over territory and resources considered of central significance to the latter group.[19] The *Fort Langley Journals* corroborate that, at least during the late 1820s, violent clashes more frequently occurred between the Chilliwack and the older Fraser River (or Stó:lō) resident communities than among the established Stó:lō themselves.[20]

This suggests that, during the early Hudson's Bay Company fur trade era, the Chilliwack presence on the Fraser was not yet fully solidified or accepted by neighbouring communities. Indeed, Chilliwack visitors to Fort Langley made known to the HBC traders that their homeland was in the upper reaches of a 'river that comes in from Mt Baker' – that is, along the upper Chilliwack River – and an exploration team from Fort Langley that ascended the lower 'ten miles' of the Chilliwack River in the winter of 1828 mentioned seeing cached canoes but no people or settlements.[21]

Violence, of course, was not the only tool available to the Chilliwack. Wileliq the Fifth, in particular, was especially adept at consolidating both his own personal position and that of his tribe among the Fraser River communities. One of the continuing characteristics of Coast Salish society is that interpersonal relationships operate within a range of possibilities rather than according to a series of fixed rules. Put another way, in a society where authority was not backed by a permanent professional military or judiciary, cultural options existed. These options enabled leaders to choose from among a series of potentially applicable rules, thus enabling them to behave in different legitimate ways. The point was not to pick the correct rule as opposed to an incorrect rule but, rather, to be able to convince others within one's own variously defined communities or groups that the rule one chose to follow and apply was the best and most appropriate for the given circumstance. Historical contact and precedent, of which genealogy was a central component, provided additional legitimacy to any interpretation.

Wileliq the Fifth chose as one means of gaining acceptance of his leadership and his community's place on the Fraser floodplain the forging of marriage alliances with some of the more prominent of the established Fraser River Stó:lō families. On one occasion, an important family from the Katzie Tribe near what is now Maple Ridge invited Wileliq the Fifth and his brothers to a young girl's puberty ceremony. During the celebration, the Katzie hosts, impressed with Wileliq, suggested that he 'should take' the girl as a wife. Wileliq already had a wife and child waiting for him back at Vedder Crossing, likely a Swí:lhcha woman from an earlier diplomatic marriage, but polygamy was common at the time and so he accepted the offer. What is perhaps more significant is that Wileliq chose to remain at Katzie with his new in-laws until his second wife had a child – a daughter. By living in his newest in-laws' home, Wileliq publicly demonstrated the paramount situational importance of his Katzie connections, and although he ultimately lost his first wife and child (they eventually grew tired of waiting for him and moved back to the Swí:lhcha settlement at Cultus Lake), his new alliance resulted in his acquiring ownership of certain resource sites within his second wife's family's territory.[22] Wileliq the Fifth is undoubtedly one of the 'two men from other tribes' that Wayne Suttles learned 'had married Katzie women' and who came to be the recognized owners (sxwsiyá:m) of valuable sites and 'their neighbouring streams, berry bogs, etc.'[23]

With his regional status much enhanced, Wileliq the Fifth eventually returned to Tháthem:als, where he gathered his people and again moved the headquarters of the Chilliwack Tribe, this time a few hundred metres downriver to a small flat area immediately upstream from Vedder Crossing.[24] At this site, he began construction of a remarkable longhouse that was to secure for him immediate recognition and lasting fame. The edifice that Wileliq the Fifth built was unique in that it had an inverted gabled roof. Perhaps the best way to visualize the structure is to imagine two classic Coast Salish shed-roofed longhouses butted up back-to-back. The building and the settlement where it stood came to be known as Qoqolaxel, or 'Watery Eaves,' for running down the centre of the inverted gable was a massive hollowed-log ridge pole designed to catch rainwater like a giant eavestrough. Through an ingenious system of gates and levers, the log could be manipulated during ceremonies, causing hundreds of litres of stored water to burst through an ornately carved opening at the back of the building.[25] 'The walls were made of carved and chiselled cedar, and every pillar that was in the house was carved, polished, and painted.'[26] (See Figure 4.)

This tremendous structure – which, according to Bob Joe, required a pole that could reach ten fathoms (roughly eighteen metres) to lift the roof planks to allow smoke to escape – became a focal point for central Fraser Valley ceremonial life. As a reflection of Wileliq's growing stature, the building was constructed through the cooperation and with the assistance of prominent families from the neighbouring communities of Katzie, Kwantlen, Whonnock, Sumas, Matsqui, Leq'á:mel, Pilalt, Cheha-

4. Wileliq the Fifth's settlement of Qoqolaxel ('Watery Eaves'). Courtesy of Chilliwack Museum and Archives, P5806, Acrylic painting of an Indian village scene c.1960–1980. Artist unknown.

lis, and Scowlitz.[27] The participation of such a broad spectrum of the region's elite undoubtedly sent a clear message that the Chilliwack Tribe was an established presence in the area.

At some point, Bob Joe explained, not too long before the construction of Qoqolaxel, the Chilliwack River changed its course. Instead of running west after passing through Vedder Crossing and flowing into Sumas Lake, it swung east and then north, running along the base of the mountain and then out to the Fraser River. Branches of this river slowly emerged to the west, and as a result, the marshy land between Vedder Crossing and the Fraser River rapidly became dryer and thus suitable for year-long habitation. Onto this land Wileliq the Fifth, as an old man, moved the majority of the Chilliwack people to a settlement called *Sxwó:yxwela*, and there he constructed a second, less distinctive house, with fewer carvings on the interior house posts. After the death of Wileliq the Fifth, his relatives established further settlements at Yeqwyeqwioose, Sq'ewqeyl, Athelets, and a few other downriver sites.[28]

Before his death, Wileliq the Fifth chose to pass the name and all its invested prestige and power to his grandson[29] (who came to be known in English as Jack Wealick), though the heir was only a boy of ten to fifteen years at the time.[30] Jack's uncle, Siemches, who as an adult also acquired the additional ancient name Tixwelatsa, actually exercised leadership until his nephew came of age and had demonstrated his worth and ability.[31] Wileliq the Fifth gave Siemches '$20.00, the acceptance of which was [a] sign he'd accept [the] responsibility of leadership.' The agreement also included acceptance that the line of leadership would remain with the Wileliq boy's descendants.[32] In 1900, at the age of seventy, Jack died and the Wileliq name appears to have been transferred to his grandson George Wealick, who died at age sixty-one in 1951.[33] In the 1970s the Wileliq name was transferred to Ken Malloway (born in 1953), who has carried it ever since.[34]

This genealogical evidence, coupled with a reference by Bob Joe[35] in which he stated that he knew an old woman who died about 1925 who told him that she remembered seeing the 'Watery Eaves' building still standing when she was a girl, suggests that Wileliq the Fifth built the inverted-gable home about 1800. This date is consistent with a Chilliwack migration associated with the smallpox epidemic of 1782. That the HBC expedition of 1828 makes no reference to the structure can be explained if the traders turned back at the rapids approximately three-quarters of a kilometre downriver from the settlement of the inverted-gable home. Corroboration of a circa 1800 date is also provided in the oral history passed to Bob Joe from his Elders, who explained to him that Tixwelatsa was the acting chief at the time the first Europeans arrived in Stó:lō territory. The date Tixwelatsa assumed this role is relatively easy to calculate, given that Jack Wealick was an adolescent at the time. Given Wealick's death in 1900 at the age of seventy, Tixwelatsa must have taken over the leadership of the Chilliwack Tribe in the 1820s, just as the HBC was establishing Fort Langley.[36]

Significantly, none of the narratives about the Chilliwack migration makes reference to sudden depopulation other than that associated with the Centre Creek landslide. Possibly, aspects of the story have been neglected, or perhaps the avalanche is meant as a metaphor for smallpox. If, however, the oral tradition is accepted at face value, then, with the exception of the Chilliwack settlement crushed by falling rocks, the majority of that tribe escaped the demographic disaster that so affected their neighbours. Given the relative isolation of Chiliwack Lake vis- à-vis other known habitation sites, and the memories emphasizing the tribe's social insularity (both Hill-Tout and Duff recorded that the Chilliwack were supposed to have been endogamous prior to the migration to Vedder Crossing), it is not unreasonable to assume that perhaps the Chilliwack Tribe escaped the first epidemic. The time of year the epidemic reached the lower Fraser River would have affected its ability to spread to relatively isolated communities on the headwaters of tributary river systems like the Chilliwack, given that, at certain times of year, Coast Salish people spend less time travelling and visiting neighbours. The Chilliwack Tribe's resulting numerical superiority, and the fact that they would not have been suffering the same psychological stress as smallpox survivors throughout the rest of the Lower Fraser River watershed, would undoubtedly have facilitated their migration and territorial expansion.

Bob Joe reports that, during the time of Wileliq the Sixth and Seventh (ca. 1830s and 1840s), the Chilliwack Tribe 'split up,' that is, certain families moved to different camps and came to be associated with particular settlements along the lower Chilliwack River and Luckakuk Creek, where the two waterways run through the Fraser Valley floodplain. This physical separation appears to have been accompanied by a degree of sociopolitical atomization among the Chilliwack Tribe, a process no doubt further accentuated by the colonial government's subsequent efforts to transform each settlement into an autonomous administrative community under the auspices of the British, and then later Canadian, government. According to Bob Joe, this diffusion did not happen all at once: the 'scattering had been slow; took years.'[37] Meanwhile, under the leadership of Wileliq the Sixth, the tribal headquarters moved a short distance downstream to Yeqwyeqwioose.

While this long series of relocations was clearly important to Bob Joe's sense of Chilliwack collective history, perhaps the more important development in terms of significance to the creation of spheres of exclusion and the shaping of collective identity was the establishment of a clearly demarcated and strictly enforced boundary between the Chilliwack and their Stó:lō neighbours from the Pilalt, Scowlitz, Leq'á:mel, and Sumas tribes. It was during Wileliq the Sixth's leadership that 'the [tribal] boundary lines were set,' as Joe explained. 'Before that, lines [which had previously been] only back in mountains now extended to what had been wasteland'[38] (refer back to Map 13).

The demarcation of these boundary lines represents a significant development in Coast Salish political history. As Wayne Suttles has explained, the standard Coast Salish concept of tribal territories appears to have conceived of jurisdictions not as areas of distinct delineated space but, rather, as an ever-decreasing interest in lands the farther one moved from the core of a tribe's territory. My own research confirms that people from one tribe did not typically claim exclusive territory; rather, the tribal elites' sense of control of a territory gradually diminished the farther one moved from the tribe's principal settlement and resource sites. Under this system, people from a variety of tribes felt varying degrees of intensity of interest in vast expanses of overlapping territory. Elite polygamous males, for example, felt especially strong proprietary interest over resources near their home settlement, while they retained an active interest in the resources associated with their wives' parents' territory. This system of recognized shared interest, however, appears to have applied only to Xwélmexw ('People of Life,' whose lives centred around, although they did not necessarily permanently live along, the Fraser River). Outsiders, 'Different People' (*Lats'umexw*), who lacked sacred histories linking them to the region, or who had not developed sufficient or appropriate economic and political relationships to allow them access to the same, were simply outside the system.

Fortunately for groups like the Chilliwack, being Xwélmexw was somewhat fluidly defined. In the eyes of the Fraser River–oriented Stó:lō tribes, the Chilliwack had not been Xwélmexw prior to their migration, but they did become so subsequently. Previously, their lives had centred around the upriver transitional zone between the Chilliwack and the Skagit watersheds. Their movement down to the Fraser Valley and into core Xwélmexw, or Stó:lō, space required an adjustment and clarification of their place in the Xwélmexw universe. In practical terms, the migration meant the establishment of formal alliances with the older

Fraser River elite as well as the adoption of the Halq'eméylem language. Once established, the Chilliwack Tribe, under the leadership of Wileliq the Fifth, were keen to consolidate and protect their position along the lower Fraser. To accomplish this, the Chilliwack – or, more likely, the Chilliwack in concert with their new neighbours – carefully defined their territorial boundaries to ensure that they included the lands adjoining the recently diverted Chilliwack River through to where that water system joined the mighty Fraser. Once defined, the Chilliwack fiercely protected their newly consolidated territory. According to oral traditions still circulating, other Stó:lō people caught trespassing in Chilliwack hunting territory were summarily executed.[39]

Thus, through a shrewd combination of violence, strategic marriage alliances, and astute political manoeuvring, all precipitated by a devastating epidemic among their neighbours and a landslide among themselves, the Chilliwack established themselves as the occupants and regulators of a large tract of land and resources stretching from Chilliwack Lake to the Fraser River. Their newly defined tribal territory, as reported by Bob Joe, ultimately included an important communication centre, fishing and salmon-processing sites, and even a profit-generating local Hudson's Bay Company fish weir and salmon saltery.

The Abandonment of Alámex

Within Stó:lō history, epic movements loom large not only as a means of forging new collective identities but also as ways of severing existing ones. Not all disputes could be resolved through increased community integration and amalgamation or the strict definition of boundaries. Sometimes the cultural obligation to reduce conflict and restore balance could only be discharged by community fracture, or what has been more commonly referred to in the academic literature as 'fission' or 'diaspora.'[40] Such was the case for the families of the Stó:lō tribe formerly living on the flatlands known as Alámex (the present-day town of Agassiz).

Interviewed by Oliver Wells in the autumn of 1964, Chief Harry Edwards of Cheam explained that, within this tribe, a dispute arose over the appropriate placement of a house post within a longhouse. In the early nineteenth century, Coast Salish settlements often consisted of a series of interconnected longhouses, stretching together as a single structure sometimes for hundreds of metres along a river's bank or ocean shoreline. In 1808 Simon Fraser observed one such house in the central Fraser Valley that was 210 metres long and others at Musqueam behind what appears to have been a half-kilometre-long palisade.[41] Within these structures, place and space were apportioned according to status, the most prestigious families (or segments of families, given that extended families were not homogeneous by class) occupying the largest and most defensible quarters. Carved house posts depicting family leaders' spirit helpers or the heroic deeds of prominent ancestors anchored certain individuals and families to designated places within the longhouse. Moving a house post was not only a laborious task but it also signalled a change in the status of the family living beneath such monumental carvings. According to Chief Edwards, among the families living at Alámex, 'One party was always moving the posts. Well the other party, the other party would move it back again. So they split up, they split up without getting into a fight, you know; they just split up. Part of them went to Ohamil, and the other party moved over to what you call Cheam now. They split up without any quarrel [violence].'[42]

Fourteen years earlier, Wilson Duff recorded from August Jim, a descendant of the people who relocated to Ohamil, a more detailed version of the story of the abandonment of Alámex. His version provides an explanation as to why a certain man's house post might have been unwelcome within the communal longhouse: 'One day the women and children of *Siyita* [Sí:yita, a village in Alámex] went to a camp 3 or 4 miles north of the village at the foot of a mountain to dig roots. The women went out to dig, leaving the children in camp. One woman had left her baby in the care of her small brother. The baby cried and cried despite all the boy's attempts to quieten it, and finally ... [the boy] got angry, made the fire bigger and pushed the baby into the fire. The other children ran to get the mother, but when she returned, baby and cradle had been reduced to ashes.' The unacceptable violence and aggression demonstrated when the boy killed his younger sister only continued to grow as he matured, until ultimately it became more than the settlement's inhabitants could effectively manage and mitigate (see Map 14):

The boy grew up to become a large strong man, but a troublemaker. Several times, in fits of anger, he killed people, even visitors from salt water. The people of Alámex (Agassiz, the whole area) got tired of him and wouldn't speak to him. Finally, in fear of reprisal raids from down-river, and to get away from this man, they decided to move away.

All of the people from the village of Pilalt [Peló:lhxw, adjacent to Sí:yita] moved across the river to Cheam [Cheyó:m]; the rest moved up-river. Some went to Popkum; the Siyita people, led by Edmund Lorenzetto's great-

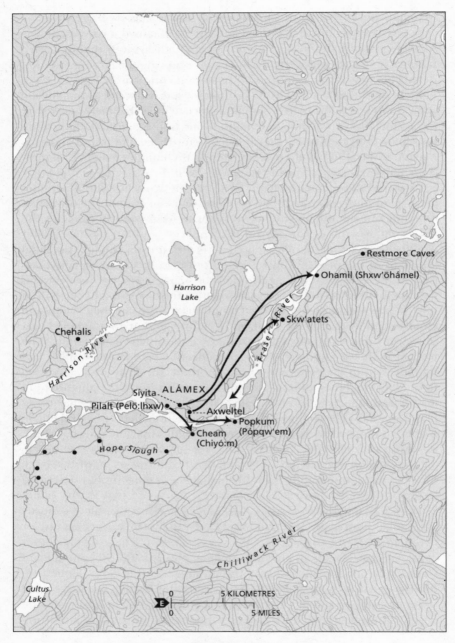

Map 14. The abandonment of Alámex.

grandfather, moved upriver to Ohamil; Old Louie's people from Axwetel moved up to Skw'atets. The troublemaker himself moved up-river to Restmore Caves near the mouth of Hunter Creek,[43] and living there alone continued his murderous deeds.[44]

Thus, it came to pass that what had once been a densely populated region of the central Fraser Valley quickly came to be abandoned. The abandonment, however, was not the result of disease or natural disaster but, rather, the concerted efforts of people seeking to both socially and physically distance themselves from a psychopathic member of their community.

While disease may not have caused the residents of Alámex to leave the site, sickness may have indirectly facilitated the move. Contemporary oral histories date the abandonment of Alámex at shortly after the HBC established Fort Langley (in 1827). Three years later, Chief Trader Archibald McDonald conducted an informal census of the Aboriginal population. Analysis of McDonald's report suggests that, in 1830, approximately 1,100 people lived at Alámex.[45] In 1839 a second census compiled by McDonald's successor, James Murray Yale, records that only 427 people were living in the same region. In assessing the ethnographic significance of the HBC records, Wayne Suttles concluded that such inconsistencies were indicative of flaws in the census. As such, he was 'strongly inclined not to take McDonald's figures seriously.'[46] But perhaps Suttles was too hasty in his dismissal. In his accompanying report, McDonald noted his own concerns over the population figures and distribution pattern but assured his superiors that 'it is however the fact proved by the repeated examination of the Indians themselves and in particular ... [Sopitchin] who is mostly a resident here, and on whose acct. of the lower Indians we knew to be correct.'[47] As no evidence exists for an epidemic in the intervening years, the most likely cause of this large depopulation is migration. It is likely that the abandonment described in the oral histories was well under way by the time Chief Trader James Murray Yale took his census in 1839 and that it was completed shortly thereafter, leaving the settlement sites throughout Alámex empty, or nearly so, by about 1840.

August Jim explained that the people who left the village of Pilalt resettled largely in Cheam near the entrance to the Hope Slough on the Fraser's adjoining southern bank. From there they later dispersed to occupy additional sites along the Hope Slough system leading to the mouth of the Chilliwack River. These people's descendants, still living primarily in the two sites at either end of the Hope Slough, regard themselves as the modern 'Pilalt Tribe' and as rightful inheritors of the earlier Alámex occupants' property rights. Those who left the settlements of Sí:yita and Axwetel and relocated to Shxw'ōwhámél and Skw'atets, respectively, had, by the mid-twentieth century, largely transferred their former identity affiliation from the Alámex area to the new region in which they lived. As Duff learned in 1949, they considered themselves, and were regarded by others, not as Pilalt or Alámex, but as Tait or 'up-river' people.[48] These attitudes have proven rather intransigent.[49]

Do the contemporary people of Shxw'ōwhámél and Skwa'tets, who so clearly acknowledge their migration, feel that they themselves, or at least their ancestors, were interlopers in another's territory? Such does not appear to be the case. Indeed, in addition to recognizing the role of migration in establishing the Shxw'ōwhámél community where it is, the Shxw'ōwhámél people also cite ancient stories of transformation as justifying and explaining how and why they are where they are. In the 1980s, Agnes Kelly explained that it was winter when Xexá:ls, the transformers, visited the village where the Shxw'ōwhámél people lived. There they found the people starving because it was too difficult to find food in the freezing weather. What made life especially difficult for the people of Shxw'ōwhámél, she explained, was the fact that the salmon and eulachon only came into the river in the spring and summer. In the winter, the Fraser 'was empty.' Mrs Kelly's narrative, as remembered by Sonny McHalsie, describes how 'Xá:ls the Transformer [the youngest of the Xexá:ls siblings] wanted to help the people so he transformed one of the village men into a sturgeon. The man's wife was very lonely without her husband, and so was told to stand by the edge of the river. She carried her lunch – a small piece of deer meat tied in a pouch – on her wrist. As she stood there in the snow, her husband called her to join him. She dove into the ice-cold river. She was suddenly transformed into a sturgeon herself. Because she had lunch tied to her wrist, all sturgeon today have dark tasty meat right behind their gills.'[50]

Though the sturgeon transformation story ostensibly refers to the current location of the Shxw'ōwhámél settlement, Franz Boas learned a slightly different version of the story more than a hundred years ago from the chief of the Chehalis. According to Chief George, the transformation narrative described events that occurred prior to the migration of the people of Alámex early in the nineteenth century. Moreover, in this version, although Sí:yita was still located at Alámex, the name was not used to describe a single village; rather, Sí:yita was used to describe the collective tribal grouping of associated settlements. According to Chief George, the primary Sí:yita village was *Squha'men*, which, significantly, is the downriver Halkomelem dialect pronunciation of the word '*Ohamil*,' or as it is known in its fuller form, 'Shxw'ōhámél.' Boas learned that at Squha'men there lived a bear who had been transformed into a man and had assumed the name Autle'n. This man had a daughter who was receiving mysterious erotic nocturnal visits from unknown strangers. News of his daughter's multiple anonymous relationships threatened to bring disgrace on the good name of Autle'n's family. After due investigation the father and daughter together discovered to both their shame that one of the visitors was the father's own dog. The second was Sturgeon, who, when confronted, insisted that he had been having relations with the girl for a longer time than dog and, that if she were pregnant, surely the child was his:

> Antle'n [the girl's father] remained completely silent, but the girl was very much ashamed. When she gave birth to a boy, Sturgeon took him and carried him to the water. He threw him into the river and he was at once transformed into a small sturgeon. Old Sturgeon caught him, killed him and cut him up. Then he served him to the people saying, 'Don't throw away any of the bones, but give them all to me.' This they did. Then he placed the bones in a bowl and carried them into the water. They came to life immediately and the boy stepped unharmed from the water. He grew up and became the ancestor of the Siyi't'a [Sí:yita].[51]

Chief George's narrative goes on to explain that, subsequent to these events, Autle'n eventually ran afoul of the transformers and was turned into a rock resembling a bear lying on its back. In Boas' time, as today, that rock was still visible on the outskirts of the town of Agassiz. That the Sí:yita people considered the Sturgeon their legitimate ancestor and not Autle'n the Bear, who was forever fixed in a permanent location, is significant. Sturgeon fish were found in abundance throughout all of the lower Fraser River's lower reaches, meaning that the subsequent high-status men carrying the sturgeon name were not restricted to living at a specific place. Just as sturgeon roamed the 'River of Rivers' freely, so too could their human relatives and descendants.

The Sí:yita people, led by August Jim's ancestor, were doing nothing exceptional in relocating their settlement. Following the precedent of their Sturgeon ancestor they simply relocated their home to another part of their Stó:lō ('River') territory. What might appear to outsiders as discrepancies between the Agnes Kelly version of the story and that provided by Chief George do not appear important to Stó:lō people. For the Shxw'ōwhámél people's collective identity, what matters is not so much the original, or 'correct,' location of Shxw'ōwhámél but that their ancestor was Sturgeon.

Class Tensions and Tribal Identity: St'éxem

The decision to resolve tension within a collective group by way of community fracture was not unique to the people living at Alámex, nor are narratives explaining how certain people chose, or were forced, to assume new identities as a result of social tensions and through the process of relocation. References to settlement fractures as a result of what were portrayed largely as personality clashes among elite males are found in many standard Coast Salish ethnographies. What have been less well documented and interpreted are the fissions and migrations that occurred as a result of tensions between different social and economic classes among the Coast Salish – as a result of internal Indigenous efforts at boundary maintenance – and yet, these form a significant chapter in the story of how many Coast Salish people constructed and discussed their own historical narratives and identity.

Within Coast Salish historical memory, class tension is a common and prominent theme, yet it is one to which scholars have devoted but scant attention.[52] Academic analysis of the question of Coast Salish class has revolved around three issues: documenting and analysing the nature of the three-tiered Coast Salish socioeconomic structures; differentiating the Coast Salish 'class-based' system from the 'ranked' strategy of their northern Wakashan neighbours; and, especially, explaining the function of the rhetoric of class within contemporary Coast Salish status maintenance.[53] In addition, some recent archaeological analysis explores the question of the antiquity of Coast Salish class divisions.[54] Thus far little effort has gone into appreciating the role of class tension in the unfolding of Coast Salish history and historiographical developments over the past two and a half centuries.

While the subject of slavery is a delicate one, because of the stigma still attached to people of slave ancestry, Coast Salish historical narratives contain many references to slavery and the tension between slaves and free people. Among the stories circulating among the people of the lower Fraser River watershed the most detailed involve movements of people that signify changes in status and collective identity. Interestingly, one such story involves the repopulating of a portion of Alámex by slaves after the desertion of the region, as described in the narratives above. This account, and other ones likely referring to somewhat earlier times, explains how certain groups of disadvantaged and exploited people were, through a process of event-facilitated migration, able to begin the process of securing greater personal and collective autonomy and freedom, as well as land and resource rights, while forging new collective identities and acquiring land and resource bases.

The Katzie Elder known as 'Old Pierre' described to Diamond Jenness how his original Halkomelem namesake, Thelhatsstan ('clothed with power'), performed many wonderful deeds of transformation, improving the world and helping put it in the order it assumes today. An important aspect of this work involved transforming people into forms for which they were most suited, that is, assigning them identities appropriate to their nature. Some of these transformations were targeted at individuals, while others affected groups of people collectively. Thelhatsstan transformed his own daughter, for example, into a sturgeon because, despite her father's admonitions, she spent all of her days playing in the water and at night rested by the shore. Likewise, Thelhatsstan transformed his son, who mourned inconsolably for his sister, into a special white owl-like bird, stating: 'Hereafter the man who wishes to capture your sister the sturgeon, shall seek power from you.' This bird, Old Pierre explained, was visible only to Thelhatsstan and his descendants. In terms of collective transformations, Pierre explained that some of the people who lived around Thelhatsstan 'were so stupid that he made them serfs (st'éxem) and divided them into three groups.' The first he settled at a site called *Hweik* on Fox Creek (Reach). A second group he placed at *Xwla'lseptan* on Silver (Widgeon) Creek, and a third at Kiloelle on the western side of Pitt Lake at its mouth.[55] These people were separated both physically and socially from the other Katzie, at least until the late nineteenth century, when the combined forces of declining numbers, a shrinking Aboriginal land base, and pressure from Western missionaries and government agents compelled higher-status people to marry people with 'tainted' pasts.

In addition to the three st'éxem sites associated with the Katzie Tribe, Old Pierre listed other st'éxem settlements that also functioned as 'tributaries' of other tribes. These included the Coquitlam people, who were subjects of the Kwantlen Tribe; the village at Ioco near Port Moody, which was tributary to the Squamish of North Vancouver; and the settlement of Nanoose on Vancouver Island, whose residents were serfs of the

Nanaimo; another of Jenness' consultants from Nanaimo on Vancouver Island added the Sechelt and the Kuper Island settlements to the list of Coast Salish settlements considered st'éxem.[56]

The term *st'éxem*, which Old Pierre used to describe these 'stupid' people, is significant for it is distinct from the Halkomelem word for slaves, *skw'iyéth*.[57] Slaves proper were women or children captured in raids (or purchased thereafter) and their male and female descendants. While many slaves were treated kindly, they and their descendants were nonetheless generally not considered fully human, that is, they were not considered to be *Xwélmexw* – 'People of Life.' Slaves were property in the strictest sense and, as such, could be treated or disposed of as their owner saw fit: exploited, sold, or even killed.[58] St'éxem people, on the other hand, were indeed humans, but humans who suffered from a severe stigma.

The term fluent Halkomelem speakers use for high-status people is *smelá:lh*. They explain that the word translates as 'worthy people.' When asked what they mean by 'worthy' they have explained that worthy people 'know their history.' Low-class st'éxem people, similarly, are considered to have 'lost' or 'forgotten their history' and, as such, to have become 'worthless.' The choice of the verbs 'lost' and 'forgotten' is significant, for they imply a historical process of change: people become st'éxem after they have become disassociated from their history. Thus, theirs is a history of losing their history; and, in lacking history, st'éxem people had neither claim to descent from prestigious sky-born or transformed First People nor the ability to trace ownership rights or affinal access privileges to productive property sites. In this regard, Old Pierre's use of the term 'serfs' to describe st'éxem people is rather appropriate for, as Jenness learned, st'éxem villages 'enjoyed their own communal lives without interference, but the overlord villages could requisition from them supplies of firewood, salmon, deer-meat, or whatever else they required ... Apparently the tributary villages accepted their position and obeyed their overlords without question.'[59] St'éxem people were, in the strictest sense, 'worthless.' (See Map 15.)

Given that the historical narratives of st'éxem people always place them in separate settlements, or in separate dwellings within the settlements of high-status people, it is clear that, within Coast Salish society, status and identity have long been intimately and inescapably linked to spaces and places. While Old Pierre explained the permanent status of st'éxem communities generally as the work of the transformers, X̱exá:ls, who at the dawn of time elevated the humble and reduced the haughty

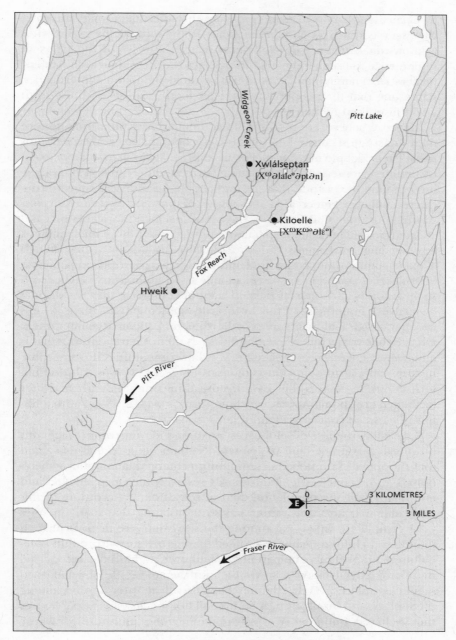

Map 15. Class and identity among the Katzie.

to permanent subordination (implying that there is a long history of class segregation and mobility in Coast Salish society), he nonetheless acknowledged distinct developments in the histories of the st'éxem settlements. As 'semi-independent' villages they had their own leaders, healers, and family names; as well, they held their own winterdances, suggesting that the people could at least forge relations with the spirit world distinct from their overlords.[60]

Indeed, I believe, Jenness' and his contemporaries' interpretations of their Coast Salish consultants' discussions about the dawn-of-time origins for st'éxem people are not meant to imply that the particular st'éxem communities described in the narratives were all created at the beginning of time but, rather, that st'éxem people (as individuals) were considered to have been created at the dawn of time and continued to exist throughout time. Only later, as a result of specific historical events, did st'éxem people consolidate, somewhat independently of their masters, into separate settlements to form collective affiliations. Thus, though st'éxem communities could not legitimately claim descent from ancient First People, and were therefore unable to forge links to families with such histories and their associated natural resources, they (as distinct collectives) nonetheless lived historically subsequent to their genesis as separate (though tributary or subordinate) settlement communities. Put another way, while st'éxem individuals do not have a history that is culturally recognized as legitimate, st'éxem communities do, and those histories appear to be products of relatively recent (post-smallpox) historical events – events that have historical meaning only because they facilitated group migrations, which, in turn, provided people with a historically nested collective identity.

References to these developments are found in numerous Indigenous historical narratives. One of Jenness' Nanaimo consultants explained that the above-listed st'éxem communities emerged 'about four generations ago ... [after] an extraordinarily severe winter gripped the land and nearly half the population died of starvation.'[61] According to this particular narrative, the winter was so devastating that many families were completely wiped out. Among the survivors were many orphaned infants and children, who were raised among the surviving adults' own children. But without true parents of their own, and without recognized or acknowledged blood relatives to train them, 'people of established families would not marry them': 'They therefore intermarried among themselves, and for protection built small houses close to the big houses that sheltered a number of closely related families, in return for whose protection they assisted in various tasks such as hunting and the gathering of berries and firewood. They received the name st'éxem (low people) because they could not marry into established families, yet they were not slaves; they could not be bought and sold, but were as integral a part of the community as the families they served.'[62] St'éxem people were, therefore, creating separate community histories outside of the dominant paradigm of ethnogenesis metanarratives used by the hereditary elite, who justified their status in terms of claims of direct descent from heroic ancestors.

Assuming Jenness' unnamed Nanaimo consultant was at least seventy years old in 1936 (placing his birth around 1865), assuming twenty years between generations, and also assuming that the people discussed in the story who lived four generations earlier were in the prime of their lives (their mid-twenties), we can roughly date the devastating winter of starvation to sometime in the late eighteenth century, or to approximately 1785. It is likely, therefore, that the devastating winter that caused the creation of entire communities of st'éxem people was associated with the smallpox epidemic of the same era. Even if the devastating winter is not a metaphor for smallpox itself, it is reasonable to assume that the smallpox survivors would have faced a series of harrowing winters as they struggled to cope with the physical and social ramifications of the disease. It is probable, in other words, that smallpox survivors may have faced winter starvation as a result of not being physically, socially, or psychologically capable of gathering and preserving adequate winter food supplies.

Charles Hill-Tout's Kwantlen consultants likewise linked the emergence of the st'éxem communities, and especially the Coquitlam tribe (located just upriver of New Westminster), directly to the calamity of a devastating winter. It was during the time when Skwelselem IV was leader of the Kwantlen Tribe (four generations before the siya:m-ship of Chief Casimir, who was chief when Hill-Tout conducted his investigations) that 'a severe and prolonged famine ... caused by a great snowstorm of unusual duration ... decimated the tribe.' At that time the Coquitlam, who had apparently up until then been living in separate houses within the main Kwantlen village at New Westminster, 'were sent away ... to the marshy flats opposite, across the river,' where they were compelled to fill the marsh with stones and gravel and convert the site into a fishing ground.[63]

Franz Boas' consultant Chief George also related the story of the Coquitlam servitude to the Kwantlen Tribe in terms of forced movement across the river to prepare fishing grounds and in terms of their subsequent freedom. What is more, he, too, dated this change in st'éxem status to roughly the end of the eighteenth century, saying that the Coquitlam gained their autonomy 'five generations ago, when wars were raging on this part of the coast.'[64] Perhaps most significantly of all, Chief George also explained that the Coquitlam were originally subordinate people because they were descendants of the Kwantlen chief's slaves. Based upon a relatively early and obscure piece of linguistic analysis conducted by Hill-Tout,[65] we learn that the literal meaning of *st'éxem* is 'offspring of female slaves sired by their masters.' If this is the more accurate description of the Coquitlam people's history, then we can perhaps best understand st'éxem people's' otherwise odd status as neither free-born people of wealth nor slaves but as a product of their being illegitimate children of high-status men who were denied the right to claim hereditary prerogatives and privileges through their father due to their mother's slave ancestry. Coast Salish extended families, as a rule, were not homogeneous by class. But st'éxem people could neither claim their father's noble birthright nor gain access to the specialized training of the upper classes, both of which were required to demonstrate good pedigree. As such, they were people without history for their father's history was *lost* to them and their mother's (as that of girls typically captured in raids as children) *forgotten.*

It appears, therefore, that within immediate pre-contact Coast Salish society a distinction existed between (1) people who traced slave descent through both the maternal and paternal lines and (2) those who traced descent through slave mothers but noble men. This is significant, for if it is correct, it explains, and goes a long way towards historicizing, the class distinctions documented and discussed by Wayne Suttles and Homer Barnett, among others, who identified a three-tiered social structure that was demographically weighted to an upper class but who do not fully explain the rationale behind people of lower (non-slave) status.[66] Suttles described the demographic expression of Coast Salish social classes as resembling an inverted pear, with a great number of upper class and a smaller number of lower class and slaves. From Hill-Tout's analysis it appears that the lower-class people, whom my own consultants also identified by the term *st'éxem*, were likely people of mixed slave and master ancestry. They constituted, therefore, a social middle ground: free but simultaneously subordinate and dependent. Perhaps these make up the majority of the 30 per cent of Coast Salish people listed as 'followers' in James Murray Yale's 1839 Hudson's Bay Company census, a portion no doubt also being full slaves.[67]

What emerges is a picture of long-term pre-contact class tension resulting from the growth of a lower class of people made up of the children of slave-and-master unions (and undoubtedly those offspring's own children) being suddenly augmented by the influx of orphans ('historyless' people) from the first smallpox epidemic. Literally overnight, the proportion of historyless, or 'worthless,' people to free people reached an unprecedented imbalance, while the region's smallpox-induced depopulation resulted in fewer people overall to fill the Stó:lō physical universe and, therefore, fewer people to compete for plentiful resources. This created a situation rife with the possibility of social change, for the upper-class leadership was undoubtedly less organized than at any time before, and it was faced with the daunting task of re-establishing a degree of societal stability and normalcy. Under these circumstances st'éxem people found themselves with an unprecedented degree of freedom, and yet they were frustrated by the continued stigmatization applied by the population of free people. It is reasonable to assume, therefore, that a solution was reached whereby these st'éxem were permitted to move out on their own into separate villages, where they asserted progressively more and more autonomy until, by the mid-nineteenth century (when the British Crown unilaterally assumed for itself fiduciary responsibility for Indian people), they no longer paid formal homage to their former overlords. Moreover, the overlords were no longer able or willing to try to assert their control.

Class Tensions and Tribal Identity: Freedom Village

If the late eighteenth century witnessed the social, political, and economic advancement of st'éxem people, there is evidence to suggest that, by the mid-nineteenth century, similar opportunities were presenting themselves to the lowest-status members of Coast Salish society – the skw'iyéth, or slaves.

In 1949 Bob Joe told Wilson Duff a fascinating story of the separation and subsequent migration of slaves from a community on an island near present-day Hope. According to Joe, the island's occupants had accumulated a relatively large number of slaves through raids against various coastal and interior communities.[68] The population of slaves was also continually augmented by births until it became so large that the slaveowners 'wouldn't let them live in [their] houses,' and they were compelled to build and 'live in their own houses on this little island.' It would appear that, over time, the 'slave village grew, multiplied and mixed,' and the slaveowners found it increasingly difficult to compel obedience and servitude from the increasingly autonomous slaves. Rather than try to impose their will through violence, the owners 'held a council over it and decided to leave them alone on the island.' In fact, the owners determined to abandon their settlement and leave their slaves behind on the island while they 'moved across [the river] to our own home.' The slaves, now effectively without masters but living within the gaze of their former overlords, decided to migrate themselves. By joining canoes together with planks from the walls of their cedar long-houses, they created catamarans upon which they loaded their posses-sions, including (according to the version of the story shared by Mrs and Mr Edmund Lorenzetto) a copy of the sacred high-status *sxwóyxwey* mask, which they stole from their former owners.[69] As the slaves under-took this historic action, their 'owners ... just watched' and sent word to the downriver tribes, 'not to interfere.' The former slaves then permit-ted the currents of the mighty Fraser River to sweep their makeshift rafts more than forty kilometres downstream until they reached the flats at Alámex, immediately downriver from the abandoned villages of Axwetel, Sí:yita, and Peló:lhxw. There they landed and 'rebuilt' a home for themselves at a settlement they called *Chi'ckem*, but which is more commonly referred to by the English name 'Freedom Village.' Finally, 'from there they scattered through relocation and marriage.'[70] (See Map 16.)

Bob Joe insisted that, subsequent to their migration, the slaves not only became free but they, like the community of st'éxem people known as Coquitlam farther downriver, acquired the status of an independ-ent 'tribe.' Even more than the Coquitlam, however, their territory was very restricted, stretching only a few kilometres 'along the bank [of the Fraser River] from Mountain Slough, which skirts the mountain west of Agassiz, to Haha'm, a rock in the river a short distance above Scowl-itz.'[71] Significantly, their territory, carved out of what had formerly been considered the lands of the *Steaten* (who were wiped out by smallpox) and the Siyita (who had migrated both upriver and across the river as described earlier) did not include any of the valuable berry-picking sites in the mountains behind Freedom Village, nor did it include any of the productive marshlands of Alámex. Its extent, interestingly, much more closely resembled the sort of land base the B.C. colonial government later assigned as reserve lands to all lower Fraser Coast Salish settlement communities: a small tract of land immediately adjacent to a settlement site.

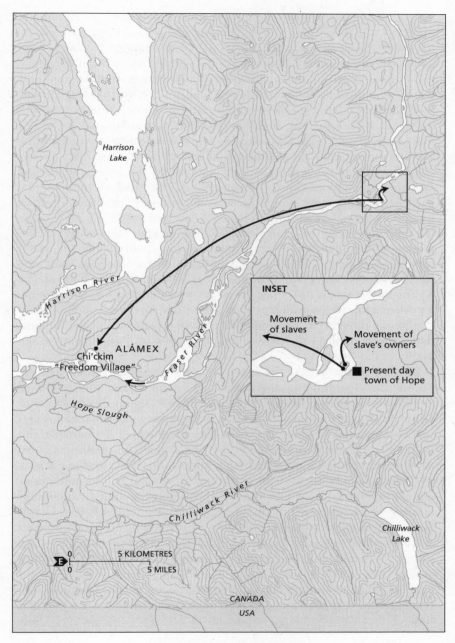

Map 16. Freedom Village.

Agriculture and the Creation of the 'Tait'

Of all the Stó:lō tribes, the Tait stand out as somewhat of an ethnographic enigma. Wilson Duff was unsure whether to even call the Tait a tribe for they appeared to lack some of the fundamental traits associated with that class of collective grouping. Unlike other Stó:lō tribes, whose settlements tended to be clustered in tight geographical proximity, the Tait were scattered along the Fraser River from Popkum all the way to Yale. In Duff's eyes, the Tait 'could be considered either as one tribe, or as a large group of Upper Stalo who had no tribal concept. They had no real feeling of internal unity, nor did they have a mythological basis for unity as had some of the downriver groups.'[72] It was for these reasons, he concluded, that the Tait felt free to move about into the territory of neighbouring tribes 'with no thought of tribal identity.'[73]

While I question Duff's assertion that the Tait lacked traditions of descent from mythical ancestors (indeed, his own fieldnotes as well as the published reports of both Franz Boas and Charles Hill-Tout reference sxwōxwiyám narratives of miraculous First Ancestors from within what is known as the Tait region), he was quite correct in asserting that there is something unique and distinct about Tait tribal identity. The Tait riddle can, however, be answered when one ceases to seek solely geographical and cultural explanations to the exclusion of temporal factors for the causes of the special nature of Tait identity.

It bears restating that the upper reaches of Stó:lō territory, where salmon can be caught and processed with greater speed and ease than anywhere else on the northwest Pacific coast, has contributed much to the general social cohesion felt by all Indigenous people whose lives revolve around the lower Fraser River and its resources. So valuable and important was the salmon fishery that it resulted in a modification of what is generally the standard Coast Salish practice of clustering the largest population centres at the mouths of rivers emptying into saltwater or main tributaries. Given that the Fraser River below Yale was generally considered an extension of the open travel routes of the Pacific Ocean (as opposed to the tribally claimed rivers flowing into Puget Sound or the Strait of Georgia), this is perhaps less surprising than it might otherwise be. Nonetheless, the population density of the Fraser Canyon was remarkable.

According to the 1830 Hudon's Bay Company census, slightly more than one-third of the total Aboriginal population residing along the lower Fraser River lived in a cluster of settlements along the seven-kilometre stretch of river between Lady Franklin Rock and Sailor Bar Rapids (approximately 2,574 people in the canyon compared with roughly 4,928 along the river's lower reaches).[74] (See Map 17.) Nevertheless, by 1878, the federal Department of Indian Affairs listed only 267 Stó:lō living in the Fraser Canyon,[75] and by 1882 there were a mere 222 (compared with 2,276 living between Yale and the Pacific Ocean).[76] Who were these canyon people, and where did they go? Clearly, something was happening to seriously alter the geographical expression of Stó:lō demographics.

According to Franz Boas' informants, when ascending the Fraser River the last Coast Salish tribe one encountered before reaching Nlaka'pamux territory at Spuzzum was the now all but forgotten Ts'okwám ('skunk cabbage') people. It was from a member of the Ts'okwám Tribe that HBC trader Joseph Mckay acquired a marvellous ornately designed woven goat's-hair blanket in the decade prior to the 1858 gold rush.[77] Yet, a generation later, nobody lived permanently in the heart of Ts'okwám territory. The unique canyon geography occupied by the Ts'okwám facilitated not only the economic prestige derived from the salmon fishery but also the ability for effective multisettlement military defence. As Stó:lō Nation archaeologist David Schaepe has documented, each settlement site within the seven-kilometre-long river frontage of Ts'okwám river territory was defended by a massive rock wall.[78] These stone palisades, apparently unique on the northwest coast, were more than just extremely effective defensive fortifications: preliminary analysis suggests that they were also connected by a line of sight, making this a truly integrated sociopolitical region. Though by eighteenth-century Indigenous standards, the Ts'okwám real estate was among the most coveted in Coast Salish territory, it lacked one feature that Native people had come to consider essential to their survival in the rapidly changing colonial world of the late nineteenth century: flat, irrigable agricultural land.

The fact that the region between present-day Agassiz and Hope was abandoned by the survivors of the late eighteenth-century smallpox epidemic suggests that this stretch of the Fraser, with its relatively small and non-navigable tributary rivers, limited slough and side channel system, and relatively mediocre fishing opportunities, was not especially coveted in pre-smallpox times. That is not to say that this stretch of the Fraser was undesirable, except in strictly relative terms. The archaeological record clearly demonstrates that the area was densely occupied throughout antiquity. Indeed, the people living there were quite possibly divided into as many as eight small tribal communities, likely similar in scale to the

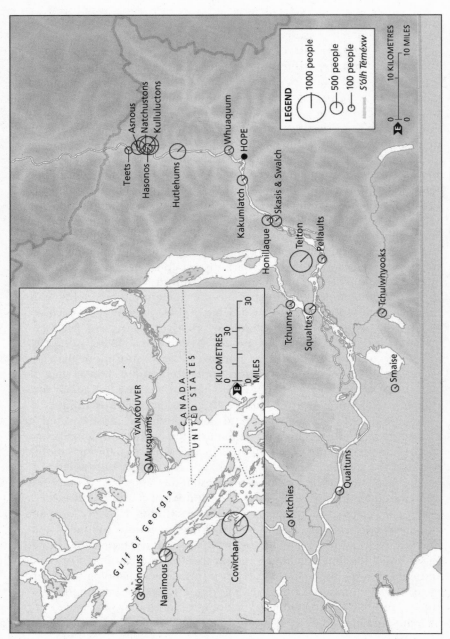

Teets
Asnous
Hasonos
Natchustons
Kulluluctons
Hutlehums
Whuaquum
HOPE
Kakumlatch
Honillaque
Skasis & Swalch
Teiton
Pellaults
Tchunns
Squaltes
Tchulwhyooks
Smaise
Kitchies
Quaituns

Gulf of Georgia
VANCOUVER
Musquams
Nonouss
Nanimous
Cowichan

CANADA
UNITED STATES

Map 17. Lower Fraser River population distribution, 1830 (per HBC census).

1830 Census Figures

Hudson's Bay Company Orthography	Halq'eméylem Orthography	Contemporary English Spelling	1830 Population
Musquams	Xwméthkwiyem	Musqueam	220
Kitchies	Q'éyts'i	Katzie	88
Quaituns	Qwó:ntl'an	Kwantlen	264
Smaise	Semá:th	Sumas	176
Tchulwhyooks	Ts'elxwéyeqw	Chilliwack	264
Peliauts	Peló:lhxw	Pilalt	220
Squaltes	Sq'éwlets	Scowlitz	440
Tchunns	Sts'a'íles	Chehalis	220
Teiton	Tsítsqem	"McCallum Site"	880
Skasis & Swalch	Skw'átets & Wolich	Sqwahtits (Peters) and Waleach	440
Honillaque	Lhelxwáyeleq	N/A	396
Kakamlatch	Sqemélwelh	N/A	352
Whuaquum	Xwyoqwem	N/A	308
Hutlehums	Sxwótl'áqwems	N/A	660
Kulluluctons	Q'alelíktel	N/A	748
Hasonos	Sxwesálh	N/A	308
Natchustons	Lexwth'istel	N/A	770
Asnous	Aseláw	Eslaio	572
Teets	Tít or Lahits	Tait or N/A	176
Cowichan	Quwutsun'	Cowichan	880
Nanimous	Snanéymexw	Nanaimo	440
Nonouss	N/A	Nanoose	132

Total mainland Halq'eméylem population = 7,502   Total Vancouver Island Halq'eméylem population = 2,574

Population of cany on dwellers (Ts'okwám tribe) = 1,452

In 1830 Archibald McDonald, chief trader at Fort Langley, compiled an estimate of the number of local Aboriginal "Men" on a community-by-community basis. McDonald derived his figures from information provided by prominent Native leaders visiting Fort Langley, which he then measured against his personal knowledge of village sizes along the lower Fraser River. His estimates were always multiples of 10 – suggestive of the speculative nature of his study – and here they are multiplied by 4.4 (the average family size as detailed in the later 1839 HBC census) to approximate total community populations. McDonald provided only vague descriptions of village locations, a problem reflected in subsequent efforts to map his data. (Harris (1994) and Suttles (1998).)

downriver community of Whonnock. If this was the case, the first (in ascending order) was likely clustered around the present-day site of Popkum and around the southern passage between Herrling Island and the mainland. The second would have been centred around a main settlement at the northwestern corner of Seabird Island. The third, centred at the mouth of Ruby Creek, might have had satellite hamlets along the upper reaches of both Ruby Creek and Garnet Creek, as well as across the Fraser River at the mouth of Jones Creek (although the latter may have been yet another separate tribe). Archaeological sites near the mouths of Silverhope Creek and the Coquihalla River indicate large pre-contact settlements, and both Emory Creek and American Creek are prime locations for similar finds.[79] Whatever the make-up of this region's immediate pre-contact population, oral histories explain that whoever survived the 1782 epidemic probably abandoned the region in favour of taking up residence with relatives living either farther up or down the Fraser River. By the end of the eighteenth century, the region was all but vacant of permanent human occupants.

Thus, while the area between Agassiz and Yale had been partially repopulated by the mid-nineteenth century with emigrants from Alámex, the area above Yale remained the most densely populated in Coast Salish territory. However, as Wilson Duff noted, and as other historians have commented elsewhere, the establishment of Fort Hope and Fort Yale in 1846 'acted like magnets to the Indians, [and] at Fort Yale, which the Indians pronounced *Puci'l*, a large Indian population gathered, and the canyon villages came to be abandoned in winter.'[80] The 1858 gold rush and subsequent construction of the Cariboo Wagon Road and the Canadian Pacific Railroad, accelerated this process, providing canyon fishers with new wage-earning employment and other economic opportunities.[81] Even more important was the government's process of allocating reserves, coupled with Western society's general insistence that Native people adopt European-style agricultural pursuits as evidence of their advancement in civilization. These pressures both drove and attracted the canyon people to seek permanent new settlements in the Fraser Valley below.

Within the mid- to late nineteenth-century Western mind, agriculture and concepts of European civilization were tightly interwoven. Certainly this was the case with those devising and implementing Canadian Indian policy in Ottawa. In 1898 Deputy Superintendent General James A. Smart spelled out clearly the Department of Indian Affairs' position when he specified that the adoption of fixed residency and Western-style agricultural pursuits were prerequisites to taking further steps in the evolutionary process from savage to civilized citizen:

> Increasing acquaintance with Indian affairs can hardly fail to strengthen the conviction that *the initial step towards the civilization of our Indians should be their adoption of agricultural pursuits,* and that if the red man is to take his place and keep pace with the white in other directions, he will be best fitted to do so after a more or less prolonged experience of such deliberate methods of providing for his wants. For the transition of nomadic denizens of the forest or prairie, or of such of them as under changed conditions have become vagrant hangers on about the outskirts of settlement, *the first essential is fixity of residence,* and the formation of the idea of a home. Without that neither churches nor schools nor any other educational influence can be established and applied. *Cultivation of the soil necessitates remaining in one spot, and then exerts an educational influence of a general character.* It keeps prominently before the mind the relation of cause and effect, together with the dependence upon a higher power. It teaches moreover the necessity for systematic work at the proper season, for giving attention to detail, and patience in waiting for results. It inculcates furthermore the idea of individual proprietorship, habits of thrift, a due sense of the value of money, and the importance of its investment in useful directions.[82]

Deputy Superintendent Smart's statement illustrates that fixed residency and agricultural pursuits were regarded as essential prerequisites to becoming 'civilized.' But as historian Sarah Carter has demonstrated in her examination of the way these attitudes were applied to the Aboriginal peoples of the Canadian Prairies, evolutionary models of development could be used to justify holding enterprising Native farmers back from engaging in what was regarded as the more advanced form of profitable commercial agriculture.[83] Popular theories of social evolution demanded that people pass through each evolutionary stage in due course. Adopting fixed residency followed by subsistence farming was equated with proof of Indian people's progress towards being civilized, which, in turn, was seen as essential to surviving in the new world order ushered in by the arrival of European settlers.

As early as the late 1860s, responding to the Western rhetoric and the economic opportunities that agriculture provided, many Ts'okwám had taken up private farms near the mouths of creeks between Hope and Yale[84] and at the junction of other major tributaries below Hope, especially at the mouth of Ruby Creek across the Fraser from the Alámex migrants at Shxw'ōwhámél. Five brothers from the canyon settlement of Xelhálh, whose mother's ancestral ties linked them to Shxw'ōwhámél, relocated there and became neighbours with the recently arrived Alámex group. The majority of the so-called Hope Indians similarly left their settlements near the mouth of the Coquahalla River and adjacent to old Fort Hope to establish themselves on fertile farmland three kilometres down the Fraser at Chawathil.[85]

In 1878 and 1879 all of these sites were designated reserve lands, but the government agent responsible for setting the land aside recognized their physical inadequacy as productive farms for the local Native population: 'Between Popkum and above Yale there is scarcely any area of suitable land for Indian reserves. The reserves they have are of thin poor soil easily spoiled by cropping and are really more residential or timber or poor stock runs than anything else, except in patches here and there.' The 'Yale Indians in particular,' he observed, 'had no good land [suitable for cultivation] and I had to find them some.'[86]

The replacement land that the agent found was Seabird Island,[87] just upriver from Agassiz. It was allocated not to the residents of a specific settlement, as was the government's usual practice, but collectively 'for the Yale Indians Proper and other tribes down to, but not including Cheam.'[88] This is significant in a number of ways. First of all, Seabird Island had not been the site of an Aboriginal settlement since its residents abandoned the village of Sq'ewqeyl near the island's northern tip sometime between 1820 and 1845. Raids by Lillooet people down Harrison Lake and across the portage to Seabird Island had driven them to seek refuge across the Fraser at Skw'atets.[89] Second, and more importantly, for the purpose of this study, the government agent learned of Seabird Island from a committee of six prominent Coast Salish chiefs led by the renowned Liquitem of Yale.[90] Finally, and perhaps most importantly, the reserve was to exclude non-Tait tribal groups, in particular people from Cheam (Cheam being the settlement site just east of Chilliwack where the Peló:lhxw people relocated after the abandonment of the Alámex region). (See Map 18.)

It is clear that the high-ranking Ts'okwám people considered their future intertwined with the more recently arrived Alámex immigrants at Shxw'ōwhámél, the 'Hope Indians,' and the Popkum and Skwa'tets community. Why Cheam was specifically excluded is not clear. In subsequent years the residents of Cheam played a central role in defending

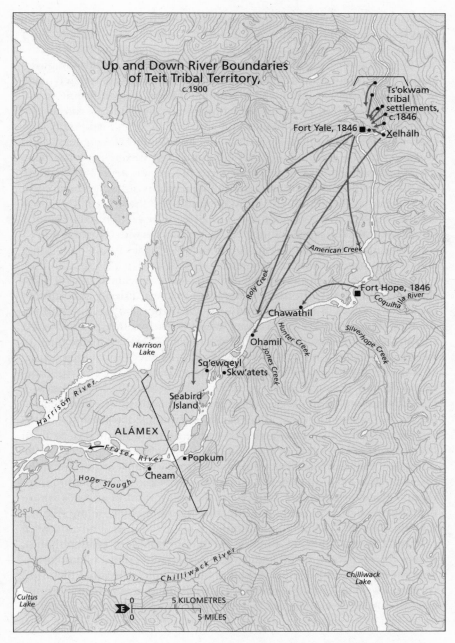

Up and Down River Boundaries
of Teit Tribal Territory,
c.1900

Ts'okwam
tribal
settlements,
c.1846

Fort Yale, 1846
Xelhálh

American Creek

Roly Creek

Fort Hope, 1846
Coquihalla River

Chawathil

Hunter Creek

Silverhope Creek

Ohamil

Harrison
Lake

Sq'ewqeyl
Skw'atets

Jones Creek

Seabird
Island

Harrison River

ALÁMEX

Fraser River

Popkum

Cheam

Hope Slough

Chilliwack River

Cultus
Lake

Chilliwack
Lake

0   5 KILOMETRES
0   5 MILES

Map 18. From the canyon to the valley: Government agricultural policy and the
emergence of the Tait 'tribe.'

the island from non-Native squatters.[91] Nevertheless, the new Tait Tribe
worked consistently as a group to protect its collective interest in Seabird
Island from both outside whites and other downriver Coast Salish.[92]

The migration to Seabird Island of the lower Fraser River's highest-
ranking individual, Yale's Chief Liquitem, signalled an important change
in regional identity politics. (See Figure 5.) This is because Liquitim and
other prominent Ts'okwám personalities who chose to relocate to the
Fraser Valley brought with them the sense of tightly knit identity that
their ancestors had nurtured in the confined Fraser Canyon geography
and superimposed it on the dispersed and tribally mixed settlements between Yale and Popkum. For these 'upriver' Tait people, collective identity became a product of supra-tribal amalgamation rather than exclusive
site-specific mythical genesis. Thus, as the Fraser River tribe whose collective origins are most extensively caught up in post-contact colonial
developments, Tait tribal identity has, as Duff observed, often assumed a
less-defined expression than that of other older tribes.

The migrating Ts'okwám people brought with them a sense of unique
canyon identity as well as a certain notion of economic and cultural pride
derived from their ownership of the river's richest fishing and salmon-
processing sites. Their upriver canyon identity was superimposed on
the various and diverse community identities below. Among the newly
merged upper class, which included not only the Ts'okwám elite but also
ranking families among the previous generation's Alámex immigrants, a
nascent sense of broader collective 'upriver' Tait identity emerged that
was modelled, it would seem, on other older tribal collectives, but with
even greater emphasis on the forces of regional social cohesion that cut
across localizing nodes of collective identity. This Tait identity, when
conceived within the cumulative context created by the migration from
the uplands to the valley of the formerly more remote Chilliwack Tribe
ultimately did much to foster the maturation of an even broader sense
of Stó:lō collective identity – an identity that encompassed the entire
lower Fraser River system. This trend was reinforced by the disruption
of status boundaries associated with the increased independence of the
various st'éxem and slave communities, who likewise took advantage of
open spaces created by smallpox-induced depopulation. Thus, although
a shared Fraser River Stó:lō identity has been couched in a historical discourse of even older economic and mythic (or metaphysical) historical
relationships,[93] in truth, it assumed a socially meaningful form largely as
a result of specific contact-era historical events. Although Stó:lō communities had been linked through shared ownership of regional resources

5. Chief Liquitem. From a post card in the author's possession.

and access protocols and overlapping stories of ancient tribal creation long before European contact, it was the post-smallpox migrations that ultimately tipped the balance and resulted in the broader identity eclipsing the more local ones.

Within Coast Salish society, collective identity, like political authority, is situationally constructed. Thus collective identity has a history. Coast Salish collective identity is neither frozen in time nor a passive passenger on a journey whose trajectory was firmly set by non-Native agents. Each time it was buffeted by an outside force (be it smallpox depopulation, the introduction of a new economic opportunity associated with the fur trade, or government policy designed to facilitate a Western agricultural agenda), Coast Salish people were compelled to relegitimize their collective affiliations. Many, as we know from the extant scholarship, found ways to re-establish existing affiliations. Others, as we have seen, seized the opportunity to recast their identity in a new mould. Historical events caused the deck to be reshuffled, and from this state of flux, migration appears to have been the preferred means of facilitating changes in identity. Migrations, and the events that inspired them, provided Coast Salish people with opportunities for adjusting to and redesigning social-political relations and, through them, collective identity and affiliation. Migrations precipitated amalgamations as well as fractures; they disrupted deeply entrenched class and status structures, providing opportunities for social mobility as well as for the consolidation of political authority. Knowledge about migrations provides us with insights into the way history occurred, was internalized, and subsequently used by Aboriginal peoples and suggests an event-centred Indigenous historiography where identity is fluid, though anchored.

By the mid-nineteenth century, a host of factors were placing stresses of various kinds on the different expressions of Stó:lō identity. What had previously been relatively easily defined tribal and class divisions were being blurred and replaced by newly constituted collective identities. Migrations played a pivotal role in facilitating these changes, but the migrations were themselves the results of other factors that were generally triggered by older pre-existing tensions. To appreciate their modern significance, these tensions need to be examined in light of the history of the wars that emerged on the new battlefields of cross-racial boundary maintenance and identity politics. By that time, colonial interests had restricted full-scale Indigenous migrations and replaced them with more temporary, constrained, but equally influential, movements of other kinds.

SECTION FOUR
Constricted Movement and Fractured Identity

Chapter Six

Identity in the Emerging Colonial Order

It's one of those kind-of-like-a-hand-shake rules of the Natives long time ago ... They didn't like to write it down ... it went by what we call 'The Indians Like It To Be Known'... The white people they didn't want that to be known because they wanted to use that land after they developed it. So they never put it down in book form, whatever you want to call it, document.

– Wes Sam, 1992[1]

If the Stó:lō were largely unaware of the colonial nature of some of the forces acting upon them throughout the late-eighteenth and early-nineteenth centuries, this changed after 1858. It was then, in the wake of the Fraser River gold rush, that the effects of anonymous and new disease-causing viral microorganisms and the readjustments associated with the spread of the European fur trade were compounded by the emergence of overt human efforts to shape their society.

Prior to the arrival of thousands of gold miners in their territory in 1858 the Stó:lō had responded to change, whatever its origin, on their own terms; thereafter, their responses were to a significant degree limited and shaped by the coercive nature of the changes. After the Fraser gold rush the migration-inspired identity reformations of the preceding decades had serendipitously and effectively remodelled Stó:lō society. Numerous tribal communities, previously without formal political linkages, were now fewer in number and often entirely reconstituted. Moreover, the collective experience of having survived smallpox epidemics and accommodated the arrival of European fur traders meant that Stó:lō people now had a better appreciation of the role of European newcomers as agents of change. This knowledge and experience, coupled with the increasingly greater threat Westerners posed to Stó:lō ways of life, encouraged Stó:lō people to think laterally outside of their tribal clusters and to forge innovative affiliations built upon the range of networks that had previously served other purposes and needs.

Some colonial initiatives were designed to foster, and indeed did foster (not always the same thing), a more localized collective identity and political authority. These actions might ultimately be seen as having established conditions that privileged an enhanced geographically nested form of tribally and settlement-based collective identity similar to the identities that would have resonated with elite males in the generation immediately preceding the first smallpox epidemic. That is, these identities encouraged a world view where identity and authority were connected to place (i.e., to local spiritual sites such as the stone remains of transformed ancestors). Different countervailing colonial initiatives or actions often inadvertently created a context whereby Indigenous regional connections became of principal importance. Such developments provided increased momentum towards the supratribal concept of collective identity that had previously been more intimately associated with elite women (and, likely, lower-status men and women), who as adults often lived away from their childhood homes and, as such, retained special personal affinities with people and places farther afield. Whether the more geographically localized expression or the more expansive manifestation prevailed depended to a significant degree upon which concept better facilitated effective responses and counter-initiatives to colonial authority.

Assessing this matter involves answering a series of more specific questions. What was the nature and effect of colonial identity politics, and how did the Indigenous community understand and respond to these initiatives? Did colonial actions ultimately alter or contribute to the process of increased supratribal collective identity that had been under way since at least the late eighteenth century? Boundary maintenance in the colonial era assumed a number of expressions. Likewise, identity-altering events assumed a number of guises. In addition to being a significant event in Stó:lō history in and of itself, the 1858 gold rush also established the context of subsequent colonial Indian policy, and dictated the haste with which that policy was conceived and implemented. An examination of the immediate effects of the gold rush provides a method for assessing the nature of the colonial Indian policy that followed and its Indigenous import. Early on, the government of British Columbia decided on a policy of 'forming settlements of natives'[2] – a process as much concerned with social identity as with physical geography. White-painted wooden posts demarcating the perimeters of Indian reserves were only the most obvious boundaries erected to separate Native and newcomer societies. Indian band membership lists that fixed Aboriginal people's residences were a less apparent but equally intrusive marker of government initiatives designed to reify local settlement-based collective identity.

The main studies of Canadian west coast Native–newcomer relations, from Joyce Wike and Wilson Duff through to Robin Fisher and Cole Harris, describe the 1858 gold rush as the event that transformed forever the cooperative, mutually beneficial (even enriching) contact-era association between Natives and newcomers into a relationship characterized by racial conflict. According to this argument, with the dawning of the settlement era, Aboriginal people shifted from being major players in a drama that was largely of their own creation, to bit players in a theatrical production that was directed by white men who generally regarded Natives as actors unfit for speaking parts.[3]

While it is true that the gold rush ushered in forces of colonial change that, though probably unavoidable, might otherwise have occurred later and at a slower rate, the distinction between contact-era cooperation and settlement-era conflict, given the discussion of the previous chapters, is better conceived as blended shades of grey rather than as crisp lines separating black from white.[4] What is more, while B.C. colonial Indian policies were ultimately too rigidly conceived to result in anything other than the wholesale marginalization of Indigenous people, the way Aboriginal people responded did hold the possibility of multiple historical outcomes. Considered in this light, the history of colonial-era Stó:lō–newcomer relations assumes a grander significance. The colonywide Indian policy that emerged in the wake of the gold rush was in large part a product of the Stó:lō context in which it was principally developed, that is, Native–newcomer relations in Stó:lō territory were the crucible for B.C. Indian policy generally. Therefore, to understand such seemingly unrelated matters as why the Okanagan people had their original reserves reduced, why the Sechelt Band pursued municipal-style self-governance, or why the Nisga'a Tribe were not able to secure a comprehensive treaty until the end of the twentieth century, one must first understand the largely Stó:lō circumstances in which B.C. Indian policy was created.

Otherness

As discussed earlier, among the Indigenous population of the lower Fraser River watershed there has long existed a concept of 'otherness.' This idea, in turn, has informed the corresponding and contrasting abstraction of 'sameness,' felt to varying degrees by all those who collectively regard themselves as somewhat distinct from others. In the generation prior to contact, not all people were considered *Xwélmexw*, that is, 'People of Life,' whose lives revolved around the resources of the Fraser. 'Different People' – people who behaved in a 'strange manner' and were not considered legitimate members of the Fraser River (Stó:lō) social and economic network – were referred to collectively, regardless of their place and culture of origin, as *Lats'umexw*. These people served as critical counterpoints to the concept of sameness derived from being Xwélmexw. This is not to say that there necessarily existed any formal political unity among Xwélmexw, but rather that Xwélmexw operated within a system that was known and understood by one another and that formed a cohesive social continuum. Within this network existed a plethora of social, economic, and political relationships, not all of which were amicable or stable. Violent conflicts and raids were common among and between variously constituted Xwélmexw groups. But, even violent relationships were conducted if not according to strict rules at least along lines that were fully understood by those concerned, involved, and impacted.[5]

Some groups of Lats'umexw were so notoriously different that they were known by additional separate names. Today, in the early years of the twenty-first century, 'Coastal Raiders' is the English term most commonly used by Stó:lō when referring to *the* Indigenous 'bad guys' of the eighteenth and nineteenth centuries. During the early days of the Hudson's Bay Company operations, it was the cry of *'Yukletaw'* (*Lekwiltok*, literally 'Unkillable Things') – announcing the arrival of a southern *Kwakwaka'wakw* raiding party – that threw the lower Fraser River inhabitants as far upriver as Sailor Bar Rapids, seven kilometres above Yale, into mass panic (and not without good cause).[6] In 1828, the *Fort Langley Journals* report, and not altogether atypically, on a single raid the Lekwiltok killed more than thirty Musqueam men and captured six young girls as slaves.[7] On at least one occasion the Xwélmexw, under the general leadership of a Cowichan man from Vancouver Island, collectively embarked on a massive retaliatory attack against the Lekwiltok.[8] In later years, after the establishment of Fort Victoria as the northwest coast's major cross-cultural trade and communication centre, the distant Haida of the Queen Charlotte Islands joined the dreaded Yukletaw as annual intruders venturing into the lower Fraser River.

These aggressors provided a context through which the Stó:lō were prepared for the arrival of bellicose non-Native strangers. The first non-

Natives to arrive at Fort Langley integrated themselves somewhat into the Xwélmexw social continuum by forging marriage alliances. The subsequent influx of non-Natives associated with the 1858 gold rush and its aftermath remained for the most part outside of Stó:lō society. As with the Lekwiltok and the other more generic Coastal Raiders, these foreigners also came to be known by a specific term, *Xwelítem*, that identified them as special strangers with particular and unique characteristics and attributes that would forever mark them as 'different.' For the Stó:lō, this new generation of European visitor was remarkable because it was 'hungry to the point of starving' (in a sense that refers to much more than gastronomics). To this day the Stó:lō refer to non-Natives as Xwelítem ('the starving ones').[9] If the term originated as a reference to physical hunger it lasted because of its applicability to non-Native appetites for natural resources, land, and even children (as federal mandatory school legislation and subsequent provincial adoption policies through to the 1980s demonstrate). To ensure the European penchant for consumption was gratified, colonial officials strove to mitigate potential Indigenous opposition. This launched colonial officials into a process of developing Indian policy that was remarkable for its overwhelming concern with identity politics.

Gold and Miners

The 1858 Fraser River gold rush constitutes a particularly violent moment in Canadian history. Given the speed of the event, the number of people involved, the size of the Indigenous population affected, and the extent to which the latter held firm concepts of property ownership, violence was inevitable. In the summer of 1857 less than a hundred non-Native men (almost all of whom were associated with the Hudson's Bay Company) lived along the lower Fraser River. Then, between April and July 1858, no less than 30,000 'Starving Ones' arrived in Stó:lō territory seeking the 'New El Dorado.'[10] Stó:lō prophets of the previous generation had foretold the coming of the white men, but no one seems to have anticipated that the whites would all arrive en masse, converging on the lower Fraser Canyon from every conceivable direction.[11]

Almost immediately, aspects of the relations between the miners and the Stó:lō turned hostile. When the veteran California '49ers arrived, the Fraser River was in freshet; the gravel bars where the miners hoped to establish their placer operations were inaccessible under several metres of surging, muddy, debris-filled water and for the next few months the water was only going to rise further. Initially small groups of miners clustered about the mouths of Emory Creek and American Creek and at Hill's Bar. But within weeks their population swelled so quickly that almost overnight hastily erected camps were transformed into small cities supporting substantial corporate and then even government infrastructures. While the gold rush environs ultimately encouraged miners to band together for security and to increase productivity, each new arrival was nonetheless a competitor to those who preceded him. Those first on the scene watched the river's relatively rapid rise and subsequent gradual descent with mounting anxiety, for so long as the gravel bars were submerged it was impossible to stake a claim. What is more, registering a claim required a visit to the government offices in New Westminster – a canoe journey taking a minimum of four days for the round trip. Moreover, untended claims, as the California experience showed, had a tendency to 'get jumped.' By late July more than 10,000 miners were huddled side by side along the narrow stretch of river between Fort Hope and Fort Yale, waiting for the waters to drop and expose what would ultimately turn out to be a mere thirty-five gravel bars containing no more than 173 hectares (428 acres) of land, or less than 1.8 m^2 (0.04 acres) per miner.[12]

Though the proclamation James Douglas read at Fort Langley in November 1858 providing for the government of British Columbia officially referred to the region as 'wild and unoccupied,' the miners certainly appreciated that they were not arriving in an empty, unused, *terra nullius*.[13] The most recent Hudson's Bay Company census showed the Fort Hope to Sailor Bar stretch of river (the area of most intense mining activities) was the summer residence of thousands of Stó:lõ, whose settlements were grouped primarily along the river frontage adjacent to creek mouths – the very sites the miners wanted to excavate.[14] One particularly revealing gold rush story, shared with me by Stó:lõ Elder Harold Wells in 1995, relates how Chinese miners arrived, probably just after the initial wave of goldseekers, and started sluicing the gravel on the river bank at what had become known as American Bar. They arrived just as Wells' ancestors were leaving to visit relatives at the Fraser's mouth. Upon their return the Stó:lõ found that the mining operation had expanded, 'back 200 feet [from the river] onto a flat field,' leaving a permanent twelve-foot-deep quarry scar where the family longhouse had been.[15]

The Stó:lõ, however, should not be construed simply as primitive residents who opposed the industrial development of their neighbourhood.

Indeed, as academic research has made increasingly clear, initially Native people did not try to avoid European-based economic development. If anything, as labour historian Rolf Knight suggests, 'Indian people did not merely take up defensive positions around their villages and camps. In many cases they reached out to meet the dangers, but also whatever opportunities existed in the new situation.'[16] As Arthur Ray has demonstrated with respect to Native people encountering Western economic systems elsewhere in Canada, Aboriginal people generally only opposed change and development when they were denied the ability to benefit from it, or when they were forced to react to it in ways that ran contrary to or challenged their world view.[17] John Lutz has invited us to think of the Aboriginal response to Western economic opportunities as 'moditional' – that is, as being a mixture of modern and traditional in that Native people often engaged in new economic activities for traditional purposes (such as working as miners in order to accumulate wealth for a future potlatch).[18]

In 1858 the Stó:lõ were less opposed to mining than they were to sharing the spoils of mining with the newcomers. It was, after all, the publicity concerning the active Aboriginal gold trade with the HBC that had precipitated the Rush of '58 in the first place. In the early summer of that year, Stó:lõ miners were themselves standing along the river banks awaiting the river's drop and suspiciously eyeing the growing immigrant mining population. As Daniel Marshall has revealed through his review of hitherto ignored American records pertaining to the Fraser River gold rush, the miners were keenly aware of the vigorous Native mining activities. One American miner recorded, 'the Indians [were] very industriously employed, and all along the river, from Fort Hope up, engaged in washing out the ore.'[19]

The Stó:lõ and their upriver Nlakapamux neighbours, however, were quite prepared to assert pre-emptory rights to the gold when they regarded the foreign miners' activities to be excessively injurious to their own economic enterprises. Throughout the spring and summer of 1858, Native miners made concerted efforts to derive as much benefit from the gold discoveries as possible. Marshall's research demonstrates that part of their strategy involved finding ways to prevent the foreign miners from monopolizing the economic opportunities.[20] Reporting to officials in Great Britain, Governor James Douglas noted that the 'Native Indian population, who are extremely jealous of the whites and strongly opposed to their digging the soil for gold ... have expressed a determination to reserve the gold for their own benefit.'[21]

Stó:lō participation in mining, no matter how important it became, did not signal an end to Stó:lō salmon fishing.[22] The same stretch of the Fraser River offering the most lucrative mining profits also constituted the most productive Aboriginal salmon fishery on the entire northwest coast. Indigenous fishing in this region consisted largely of men standing on rock outcroppings and scooping salmon from the river in specially designed 'dip-nets.'[23] Stó:lō women and their slaves, meanwhile, butchered and then wind-dried the fish on 'dry-racks' immediately above the dipping sites. These 'spots,' as they are called by the Stó:lō, were among the most prestigious of hereditary properties and were accessed and used by large networks of extended families, who did not necessarily live in adjacent settlements during the non-fishing season. Each spring, as the river's water level changed, Stó:lō families conducted sacred 'first salmon ceremonies' to welcome the arriving salmon and to ensure their future return. The arrival of the sockeye in early July marked the beginning of the two-month period when the sun's daytime heat was sufficient to warm the canyon rocks so they would keep the air surrounding the dry-racks hot and dry twenty-four hours a day. Every July the Stó:lō and thousands of other Xwélmexw gathered in the lower Fraser Canyon to wind-dry salmon and conduct trade to ensure a diversity of winter supplies. In 1858, however, the Indigenous populace was competing for space with the thousands of armed non-Native miners who were encamped on their fishing grounds. A Hollywood scriptwriter could not have invented a more potentially explosive situation.

Into this powder keg a match was thrown when, following the miners, came the usual complement of opportunists who sought to profit from the miners' vulnerability. Stó:lō people, government officials, and indeed a good number of the miners all became increasingly concerned over the copious amounts of a noxious substance popularly known as 'whiskey' (but more accurately described by Oblate missionaries in the 1860s as a mixture of fermented 'alcohol mixed with camphor and tobacco juice') that was being illicitly supplied to both the new miners and the Stó:lō in the summer of 1858.[24] For miners watching the freshet waters rise and then slowly recede, whiskey provided a distraction and bolstered fortitude. For the Sto:lo, who had never before encountered alcohol as a trade commodity, and who were experiencing unprecedented changes in their society, the whiskey likewise proved a powerful and addictive attraction. The following excerpt from the 19 June 1858 edition of the *Times of London* suggests that alcohol impaired judgment and intensified interracial aggression: 'A "difficulty" occurred between a white man and

an Indian chief on the river 2 1/2 miles below Fort Hope, in which the
Indian was shot through the body; whether killed or not I don't know.
The Indians returned the fire and killed a white man, – not the aggres-
sor, or rather not the same man who shot the Indian; this caused a great
commotion, but the [HBC] company's agent at Fort Hope pacified the
Indians.'[25]

By mid-July such isolated acts of violence were giving way to larger-
scale coordinated conflicts. Governor Douglas gave an indication of the
extent of the tensions when he described for officials in London how
'the white miners [at Hill's Bar] were in a state of great alarm on account
of a serious affray which had just occurred with the native Indians, who
mustered under arms in a tumultuous manner, and threatened to make
a clean sweep of the whole body of miners assembled there.'[26]

Following the Hill's Bar incident a delegation of Stó:lō leaders approached Douglas at Fort Hope and 'made no secret of their dislike of
the white visitors ... and complain[ed] of maltreatment.' Douglas later
reported that 'in all cases where redress was possible it was granted without delay. One small party of those natives laid claim to a particular part
of the river, which they wished to be reserved for their own purposes, a
request which was immediately granted, the space staked off, and the
miners who had made the claims were immediately removed, and public notice given that the place was reserved for the Indians, and that
no one would be allowed to occupy it without their consent.[27] Though
no official government maps or documents describe where this, the de
facto first Indian Reserve in what is now mainland British Columbia, was
located, the action had the desired effect of easing tensions.

Such stopgap measures, however, ultimately proved inadequate to
stem the rapidly deteriorating situation. California and Vancouver Island
newspapers reported a crescendo of violence in the weeks leading up to
August 1858, and a growing sense among the miners that 'war must naturally follow the emigration of white men thither.'[28] According to media
reports, shootings and stabbings were an almost daily occurrence, while
less violent but still highly provocative actions such as miners trying to
drive Natives from mining and fishing grounds and Aboriginals in turn
commandeering miners' canoes and boats and freely availing themselves
of miners' provisions when opportunities arose, worked to divide Natives
and newcomers into increasingly suspicious and resentful camps.[29] A letter from a miner working the gravel at Sailor Bar (the boundary between
Stó:lō and Nlakapamux territories) was typical in reporting 'the Indians
are very saucy, and in no fear of the whites, whom they look upon as in-

truders while on the other hand, many of our people are quite too ready to shoot, or resort to other harsh measures for retaliation whenever the Indian commits a trifling offense. Several whites have lost their lives on the river, in attempting to recover a blanket or shovel, or punish an Indian for stealing it.'[30]

It came as a surprise to no one, then, when on a hot day in mid-July the naked and decapitated body of a French miner was found swirling in the river adjacent to New York Bar (a place still commonly referred to by Stó:lō and non-Natives alike as 'Deadman's Eddy'). According to the *Times* correspondent, the killing represented an act of 'retaliation' against a man who had 'stole away and deforced an Indian girl,' and was designed to serve as an 'example, perhaps, to all poachers on other men's manors.'[31] Within a few days the 'headless trunks' of three other white miners were 'picked from the waters between Fort Yale and Fort Hope.' The journalist noted that beyond these particular incidents, the 'Indians complain that the whites abuse them sadly, take their squaws away, shoot their children, and take their salmon by force.' In the reporter's opinion, 'some of the "whites" are sad dogs.'[32]

While disjointed tales of escalating inter-racial violence along the lower Fraser River appeared in major papers like the *Times of London* and the *New York Times* as well as in regional presses in California, Washington, and Vancouver Island, giving the outside world glimpses of the conflicts erupting in British Columbia, official British government records are generally silent about the wide-scale clashes that followed the Deadman's Eddy incident. However, relying on unpublished British sources and previously ignored documentation left by the American miners, historian Daniel Marshall has reconstructed how, in response to the death of the Frenchman, well-armed bodies of American miners organized themselves into militia forces and embarked on a desperate campaign to either subjugate or exterminate the upper Stó:lō and their Nlakapamux neighbours. What followed was a series of coordinated deadly skirmishes in which dozens of American combatants and an even greater number of Indigenous men, women, and children appear to have lost their lives. American records reveal that militia under the command of a Captain Charles Rouse razed five Aboriginal settlements, destroying entire winter stores of berries and salmon at Spuzzum near the Stó:lō-Nlakapamux border. In the associated battles, Rouse's men killed up to thirty-one Natives and six chiefs.[33] Somewhat muted media accounts of this clash drew the attention of Britain's influential Aborigines Protection Society which (rather belatedly, given the extent of the violence to date) lobbied the

Colonial Office to adopt mitigative measures lest the 'present danger of a collision between the settlers and the natives will ripen into a deadly war of the races.'[34]

According to Stó:lō oral accounts, reported here for the first time, by the time London learned of the true nature of the situation a race war had already occurred. Stó:lō Elder Patrick Charlie, speaking in 1950, described how the prominent Stó:lō chief, Liquitem, was largely responsible for bringing a peaceful resolution to the rising hostilities.[35] Liquitem apparently 'held council' with a faction of the more liberal-minded miners under the command of Major Snyder, who presented the Stó:lō chief with a white flag symbolizing the Indigenous population's acceptance of peaceful alternatives. Chief Liquitem himself then travelled upriver to Spences Bridge, bringing his considerable influence to bear on the people of that settlement in the interest of non-violence.[36] American records describe the situation as well. According to a report in the *San Francisco Bulletin*,

> This morning some five or six companies met and enrolled into companies of about 30 men each. About 10 o'clock, two old chiefs of the tribe living at the head of the lower Canyon, about seven miles above here, came down. Mr Allard [of the HBC] came forward, and the chiefs, through his desire, addressed the men, he interpreting for them. The chiefs were both old men, and were eloquent in their gestures and address. They said 'that their tribe was not the one that had troubled the whites; that they had often had the white man to eat with them, and none could say that they had either killed or maltreated the white man …The Indians above were their enemies, and always had been. They were always at war with each other, and it was they who had been robbing and murdering the whites. The great God above would be sorry if he were to see his children killing one another, and would hide his face from them.' In conclusion, he said that his young men would either go with the white men and help them to fight the other Indians, or they would pack their provisions. Several men spoke up and corroborated the old man's story, relating how he had given them food when on the trail.
>
> The upshot was that two white flags were given to them to attach to staffs at their ranch up the river, and they went away in their canoes, with a cheer from the miners, who agreed not to molest them.[37]

As a result of Liquitem's diplomacy with Snyder the majority of the campaign's subsequent violence was restricted principally to the Nlakapamux Native communities in the vicinity of Boston Bar and Lytton, and by the time the Colonial Office's concerns were relayed to Governor Douglas the warring Nlakapamux and American miners (under Chief David Spintlem and Major Snyder respectively) had concluded a succession of hastily conceived 'peace treaties,' bringing a tenuous end to the bloodshed and facilitating non-Native access to Fraser River gold.[38] Thereafter, however, the tone and tenor of Douglas' dispatches shifted from being primarily concerned with protecting Aboriginal rights to ensuring compliance with London officials' desire that Indian policies 'in no way interfere with the progress of the white settlers.'[39] From 1858 onward, Stó:lō people were widely viewed as anachronistic impediments to non-Native industrial, pastoral, agricultural, and urban development schemes. Racial boundary maintenance became a pre-eminent colonial concern.

Nomads and Civilization

Over the past forty years historical enquiry into Indian policy in colonial British Columbia has generally revolved around the question of reserve size and the debate over whether Governor Douglas ever intended to negotiate treaties and compensate Natives for lost land and resources. Lost in the layers of this debate is an appreciation of other factors important to understanding colonial Indian policy, especially the desire to curtail Aboriginal mobility and to reform Aboriginal collective identity. The pattern in British Columbia reflected aspects of that in eastern and central Canada and elsewhere in the British Empire as white settlement began to spread.

The issue of addressing Aboriginal people's allegedly nomadic nature in order to recast their identity on a more European-style agriculturalist model permeated the correspondence regarding Indian policy. Writing to Douglas at the height of the 1858 racial tensions, Secretary of State for the Colonies Edward B. Lytton clarified that it was the British government's desire that 'attention be given to the best means of diffusing the blessings of the Christian Religion and civilization among the natives.'[40] To expedite the Stó:lō people's 'entrance into the pale of civilization,'[41] Lytton considered it necessary to eliminate those things in the Native character that made them different: in particular, their assumed unsettled nature and propensity for movement. He proposed, therefore, a policy that would fix the lower Fraser Indigenous people 'permanently in villages,' thereby reducing their opportunity for coming into conflict with the new settler element, while simultaneously increasing the opportunity for positive social manipulation.[42]

If Native people's assumed migratory nature could be curbed, the reasoning went, it followed that Aboriginal society could be more easily controlled and shaped – and once remodelled, it would become compatible with development interests. For both Douglas and Lytton, Indian identity was conceived as a product of an unanchored relationship with geography, an outgrowth of an errant migratory existence. In an ironic move, given the movements described in the previous chapters that had already actually facilitated a series of transformations in Coast Salish identity over the previous century, Governor Douglas embarked on a policy initiative predicated on the assumption that Native people's 'wandering' nature had placed them in a timeless and unchanging state of primitive existence. The key to thawing Aboriginal social identity, it was thought, lay in freezing their physical movements.

Although its manifestation and consequences were specific and local, the B.C. plan was neither unique, nor original. The plan was derived from a firmly established intellectual tradition, the origins of which in British thought could be traced back at least as far as the writings of John Locke, wherein the world's population is divided into two groups: 'civilized' and 'natural.' Locke regarded Aboriginals (as natural people) to be living in a disorganized, savage state of nature, without the benefit of organized government. Aboriginal people's only property rights were to products of their own labour. To vast tracks of land, they had no rights for the simple reason that Locke considered them not to have invested their labour in the soil. [43] Participating in Western-style agriculture was, therefore, regarded as symbolic of an Aboriginal people's decision to embark on the path to civilization, the benefits of which included property rights. But before natural people could become farmers they first had to associate themselves permanently with a particular piece of land.

A prominent theme within recent Canadian historical literature examines nineteenth- and twentieth-century efforts by Ottawa, and earlier colonial authorities, to devise policies aimed at preventing Native people from following traditional seasonal cycles of migration in order to transform them from hunters and gatherers into farmers. As Henry Reynolds has demonstrated for Australia, and Cole Harris for British Columbia and Canada, Locke's ideas about property, labour, and agriculture meant that 'labour established its right without any need of consent.'[44] Indeed, Barbara Arneil shows how Locke rejected conquest as a legitimate means of acquiring property rights. It was only through the investment of labour in the soil that settled and civilized Europeans could be justified in alienating land that Aboriginal people occupied but did not properly use.[45] Put another way, within the British colonial context, European agriculturalists had pre-emptive rights over Native hunters and gatherers. Accordingly, once Westerners arrived and invested their labour in the land they acquired property rights. At that point, the onus fell on the Native population to demonstrate to colonial authorities that they, too, should be entitled to a piece of the Crown's land. The only way to legitimately accomplish this, from a European perspective, was to settle on a farm and begin farming.[46]

Considered in this light, is not surprising that Governor Douglas reacted enthusiastically to Secretary Lytton's suggestion of settling Indians permanently into villages. Lockean principals continued to drive British North American colonial policy regarding Indigenous people. In the nineteenth century this was most vividly expressed in the Judicial Committee of the Privy Council's 1888 ruling in *St Catherine's Milling*, where it was determined that while Canadian Aboriginal people possessed a 'usufructory' right to hunt and gather, they did not hold property rights by virtue of their failure to cultivate the soil. *St Catherine's Milling* has proved tenacious in judicial rulings down to the modern era.[47]

Douglas regarded Lytton's 'simple plan' as 'feasible' because, in contrast to the dependency-spawning policies pursued by the Spanish in South America, and the costly and ineffective U.S. system, it appeared 'the only plan which promises to result in the moral elevation of Native Indian races; in rescuing them from degradation and protecting them from oppression and rapid decay.' Douglas was convinced the scheme would be successful so long as the newly settled Indian could be made as 'comfortable and independent in regard to physical wants in his improved condition as he was *when a wandering denizen of the forest*'[48] Douglas therefore quickly embarked on a strategy that he described as '*forming settlements of natives*.'[49]

The colonial process of forming new Indian communities necessarily involves the dismantling of previous systems. Douglas and his successors were determined that the ties linking various Native settlements be severed. This was implicit in all dealings with the Indigenous population, and occasionally stated explicitly. Whenever Indigenous populations began making active use of the social, economic, and spiritual networks connecting them together to act as a suprasettlement community, the government responded quickly to discourage it. This is perhaps best illustrated in the historical reflections of the 'Concerned Citizens Committee' struck in the late 1870s to oppose a move to amalgamate Coast Salish people from multiple settlements into single language-based self-governing bodies. This committee, composed in large part of prominent retired HBC fur traders and leading lights of B.C.'s colonial society, recounted for the new provincial government the virtues of the previous decade's policy of divide and rule: 'The past safety and security we have enjoyed in the Province is owing to the fact that the large Indian population of the Country has been divided into small bands without a head Chief possessing general authority or influence, and without the ability to unite and constitute themselves a powerful and formidable force.'[50] Upon reading the petition from the Concerned Citizens Committee, Superintendent of Indian Affairs for British Columbia Dr Israel Wood Powell stated that he 'fully endorsed every statement contained in the protest.'[51]

Systems of Surveillance and Control

By the summer of 1859 the colonial government had cobbled together the framework of a comprehensive Indian policy centred around the complementary aims of curtailing Aboriginal mobility while geographically restricting Indigenous activities. As the non-Native population grew and urban/industrial development expanded outward from the metropolitan hubs of Victoria and New Westminster, the colonial government sent military surveyors to work with affected Native leaders to demarcate Indian settlement land from territory open to settlers. They accomplished this by hammering white stakes into the ground around Stó:lō settlements: 'The extent of the Indian Reserves to be defined as they may be severally pointed out by the Natives themselves.'[52] Initially, the reserves included only village sites, burial grounds, and cultivated potato patches, but by 1862, owing to mounting Stó:lō–immigrant tensions, the criteria were expanded to include 'isolated provisioning grounds.'[53] This resulted in the protection of some of the fishing sites most valued by men, but little else. Despite at least one Stó:lō petition requesting that cranberry patches be set aside as Indian reserves, none of the countless berry sites prized by women were ever reserved).[54]

In addition, that same spring, in what a top colonial authority regarded as 'an interesting turning point in the history of the Indians of British Columbia,'[55] lower Fraser River Indigenous people requested and were granted the right to pre-empt private land 'on the same terms as they are disposed of to any purchaser in the Colony, whether British subjects or aliens.'[56] Within two months Stó:lō were reported to be 'pre-empting lands precisely as a white man could ... in "extended order" along the [lower Fraser] River.'[57]

A key component of the system of creating reserves, and one that was to fracture the links between Stó:lō extended families in a profound and lasting manner, involved the creation of lists of people who 'belonged' to particular settlements or reserves. By the end of the nineteenth century, these lists had become known as band membership lists, and were governed by the federal Indian Act.[58]

The procedure for generating membership lists emerged out of the process of creating reserves. While Governor Douglas had instructed surveyors to mark off reserves to dimensions specified by Aboriginal leaders, many of his subordinates, and certainly his successors, were concerned that the size of reserves identified in that manner were beyond Aboriginal 'requirements.' The means used to assess the adequacy of a reserve quickly came to involve assessing the ratio between residents and acreage. Thus, by 1863, reserve surveys involved the collection of census data and, increasingly thereafter, information that could be used to assess a Native community's ability to 'make adequate use of the land,' that is, information on livestock as well as occupation.[59]

Douglas himself was the first to raise the question of the people-to-land ratio. In April 1863, in response to Indigenous protests, the governor accused his Lands and Works Department of creating an Indian reserve at Coquitlam that was 'insufficient' to meet the settlement's vegetable production requirements. Heretofore, surveyors had included only existing cultivated fields within the reserve boundaries, but as historical geographer Cole Harris has documented, for Douglas' intentions to be fulfilled, that is, to make 'Native settlements ... self-supporting, adequate resources had to be secured them. This implied fairly large reserves.'[60] Henceforth, Douglas made clear that he wanted reserves to include sufficient lands to ensure agriculturally based self-sufficiency, and that if the Natives themselves did not request sufficient land for this purpose the officer concerned was to take it upon himself to set apart a larger area.[61] Under Douglas' system, Indians who remained committed to collective life on the reserve (as opposed to becoming individual farmers through private pre-emption) were not to expect to be able to access agricultural produce beyond their borders. Stated succinctly, they were not to come to expect government handouts. As such, they required sufficient land to be agriculturally self-supporting.

Responding to Douglas' reiteration and clarification of the reserve system, Chief Commissioner of Land and Works R.C. Moody wrote to the governor, explaining that without the services of someone who was sufficiently versed in the local Native language it was unrealistic to think that confusion over what was actually required by the Natives would not continue to characterize the reserve creation process. He proposed as a means of eliminating such ambiguity that a competent non-Native translator assist his men to better demarcate reserve boundaries by providing lists of the total number of villages in the region, 'the number of population in each, and extent of land wished for *or requisite*' – a task Moody thought perhaps best suited to the activist missionaries.[62]

Following this high-level exchange the next surveyor to attempt the creation of new reserves along the lower Fraser judiciously decided to meet with Douglas personally prior to embarking on his mission. Sargeant William McColl, therefore, heard first-hand the governor's instructions to identify an adequate agricultural land base for each reserve, as did two senior government officials and a delegation of central Fraser Valley Stó:lō leaders, who were present when Douglas gave McColl his instructions.[63] In May 1864 McColl produced a remarkably detailed and artistically beautiful watercolour map of the central Fraser Valley Stó:lō settlements which in addition to plotting out reserve boundaries included a table with population data and commentary on the value of the land's agricultural potential.[64] (See Map 19 and Figure 6.)

This document ultimately caused a great stir within the colonial administration and remains a focus of Native–newcomer disharmony in the Fraser Valley, and indeed all of British Columbia to this day.[65] By the time the map was completed, Douglas had retired and Frederick Seymour had taken over as governor. With Seymour's ascension, de facto control of Indian affairs had transferred to the new Chief Commissioner of Lands and Works Joseph Trutch. As the voice of B.C. capitalist development interests, Trutch complained bitterly about McColl's work, arguing that the reserves were of 'most unreasonable extent, amounting, as estimated by himself [McColl], to 50, 60, 69, 109, and even to as much in one case as 200 acres for each grown man of the tribe.'[66] The fact that Douglas was no longer in office and that McColl had likewise died shortly after producing the map no doubt encouraged Trutch to devise the strategy of publicly dismissing what he knew to be McColl's authorized actions as the improper activities of a rogue surveyor operating under dubious instructions from an aging and anachronistic governor.[67]

Aboriginal people and scholars alike have subsequently made much of

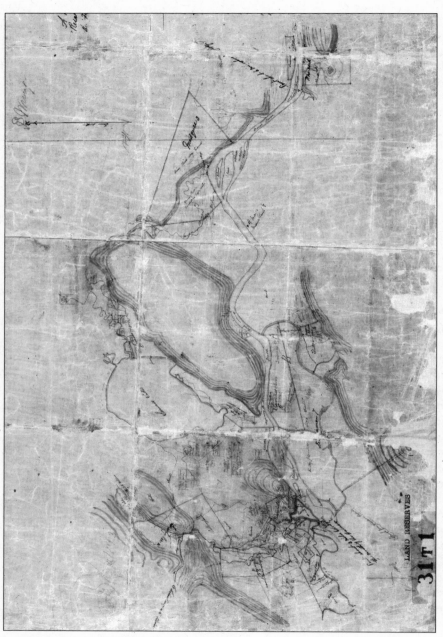

Map 19. William McColl's May 1864 map of Central Fraser Valley Indian Reserves. 'A rough Diagram shewing the position of the Reserves laid off for Government purposes on the Fraser, Chillukweyak, Sumass and Masquei Rivers,' W. McColl, 16 May 1864, 31 Tray 1, Land. Reserves, Office of the Surveyor General, Victoria, B.C.: Land Title and Survey Authority of British Columbia

the inequity between even these ratios and the 160 acres of land available to each adult white male, to say nothing of the fact that upon Trutch's direction the colonial government soon succeeded in implementing a 92 per cent reduction of the reserves mapped by McColl.[68] What has received less attention is the impact that this colonial discord has had on the Stó:lō people's sense of collective identity. After the reversal of McColl's work, all subsequent colonial surveys followed a formula of assigning a maximum of ten acres per adult Stó:lō male, along with 'a moderate amount of grazing land for those tribes which possess cattle and horses.'[69] The chart (reproduced here as Figure 7), produced by Joseph Trutch and Captain Ball after personally visiting most of the Stó:lō reserve communities originally demarcated by McColl, is the first of what were to become increasingly standardized settlement membership lists.[70] These lists included not only human census data, but also livestock statistics. Together, such information was used to justify the reduction of earlier larger reserves and to rationalize subsequent land distribution activities. That is, Trutch's work was used to make sure Indians did not have more land than they could be expected to make immediate European-style agricultural use of.

To facilitate colonial land development schemes, it became imperative to determine how many Stó:lō were associated with each Native settlement, and additionally, to formally and permanently associate certain Stó:lō people with various settlements. The government, in other words, was engaging in a process of creating communities. Moreover, Native people's ability to relocate to the settlements of relatives and friends was curtailed not only by government discouragement, but by the strain such emigration placed on the receiving community's collective land resources as defined by government reserve boundaries. By the time Ottawa assumed responsibility for Indian affairs, in 1871, the anonymous lists of people included in the colonial-era documents were being replaced by official census records that identified by name all the adult male members of each Stó:lō reserve. Once a name was registered on the official reserve census a person ceased, in official eyes, to be a part of any other Indian community. Herein lie the origins of the notion of village communities equating with what a century later would be called First Nations. This was especially true in the sense that such membership related to the distribution of government resources, the most important being reserve land, for by 1867 the colonial government had repealed its earlier policy of allowing Native people to pre-empt private land off-reserve.

Initial letter on the plan	Name of Tribe	No. of Acres laid off by Mr. McColl	No. of men in the tribe	No. of women in the tribe	No. of children in the tribe	No. of cattle, horses, pigs, etc., belonging to the tribe
A	Whonock	2,000	13	14	9	3 cattle, 12 pigs
B	Saamoqua	500	9	5		6 cattle, 3 horses, 5 pigs
C	Matzqui	9,600	22	25	24	12 pigs
D	Tlalt-whaas	2,000	Not visited			
E	Sumass (Upper)	1,200	8	12	14	21 horses, 12 pigs
F	Sumass (Lower)	6,400	22	39	39	1 cow, 3 horses, 16 pigs
G	Nickaamen	6,400	Not visited			
H	Iswhy	3,200	13	11	15	Some pigs
I	Isquhay	3,200	33	23	33	5 cattle and some pigs
J	Koquaa-pilt	400	8	8	7	8 cattle, 1 horse, & some pigs
K	Iswaya-aayla	1,000	11	12	11	9 cattle, 1 horse, & some pigs
L	Assay-litch	400	4	4	2	Some pigs
M	Yukeyouqua	2,500	Not visited			yoosesockale
N	So-why-lee	4,000	Not visited			

7. Trutch's enumeration of band membership and indicators of 'civilization' used to justify reduction of reserves earlier laid out by McColl with Aboriginal participation.

To access 'off-reserve' land, a Stó:lō man[71] first needed to prove that he had become 'civilized' and in other ways ceased to be an Indian (i.e., that he had become a brown-skinned British subject). After British Columbia entered Confederation in 1871 this was made more formal through the application of the Gradual Enfranchisement Act (later the Indian Act), which specified a procedure whereby 'civilized' Aboriginals could cease to be 'Indian' and become citizens with voting rights.[72] To the extent that becoming a Canadian citizen meant a termination to Indian status, it was genuinely impossible for a Stó:lō person to acquire (i.e., receive external recognition of ownership of) land off-reserve.

The social effects of government membership lists on Aboriginal people were enormous. In addition to preventing Stó:lō and other Native people from being able to freely relocate to the settlements of relatives to take advantage of better economic opportunities, it also meant that the extended family ties that had facilitated the movement of people to access geographically diverse, hereditarily owned properties were officially severed and replaced by 'communal band lands.' This new category of lands could be accessed and used only by officially recognized members of the local resident group. This had a particularly profound effect on the Stó:lō. Discussing this point with anthropologist Marian Smith in 1945, Seabird Island Band member Harry Edwards decried the artificial divisions the lists had created for Stó:lō people: 'We can't go to Cheam now because we don't belong there. No forefathers [live] there. Can't go to Popkum. We can't go to Puchil [Yale], Hwiaukum, Iwawas [Iwówes near Hope], Iyem [I:yem above Yale], K'alsiln'p, Thla'mzx ... People say Vincent [Harris] don't belong here [at Seabird Island], but his grandfather lived here at Kaltsialp when he was a young man. His grandfather on his mother's side was from Sq'ewlets and so he could go there if it was in the olden days.'[73]

By the end of their interview, Harry Edwards had provided Smith with a long list detailing exactly 'who could have gone where,' had the membership lists not been imposed and had people remained free to relocate to where they had familial or ancestral ties.[74] Under the government's system of creating local band governments on specific tracts of reserve land, the cross-tribal social networks that had been so important to earlier generations were effectively outlawed so far as residency was concerned. From the perspective of colonial society, Indian people living on one reserve simply had no rights in another.

Though perhaps the most explicit, Mr Edwards was certainly not the first Stó:lō to publicly express his dissatisfaction with the way colonial membership lists had linked Stó:lō people to particular tracts of land. Stó:lō first publicly raised concerns in the early 1870s. In 1874, for example, twenty-five Stó:lō chiefs, along with a number of their Aboriginal colleagues from coastal and interior communities, petitioned the federal government, protesting a number of pressing concerns. This document has previously been interpreted within the academic literature as referring principally to the inadequate sizes of reserves.[75] The contents, when read in light of the crisis regarding restriction of movement for the Stó:lō, suggest that the assigning of particular lands to particular groups of people and the inability of people to take advantage of traditional intercommunity opportunities for relocation were at least as much a concern as the simple question of quantity of land. The 1874 petition demonstrates that the Stó:lō recognized that new circumstances had arisen restricting their freedom of movement. What is more, according to a notation on the document made by a colonial official, it was a young female residential school alumna who penned the petition. Her choice of words suggests that recent exposure to representatives of Western society had enabled the Stó:lō leadership to understand that European notions concerning the supposed non-settled nature of Native existence were being used to justify the denial of Aboriginal title to land and resources. 'We are not roaming-about people, as we used to be,' she wrote on behalf of the Fraser River Chiefs.[76]

Because band membership had restricted their ability to relocate residences and their ability to seasonally visit an extensive and geographically diverse range of resource sites, the Stó:lō demanded a more equitable and sustainable land-to-people ratio for their new reserve-based communities. In other words, it was restricted mobility that subsequently made the question of reserve size so important. With mobility curtailed the Stó:lō leadership did not in 1874 simply ask for larger reserve land, they demanded it in considerable detail and through thinly veiled threats of violence:

Our hearts have been wounded by the arbitrary way the local government of British Columbia has dealt with us *in locating and dividing our reserves.* Shxw'ōwhámél, ten miles below Hope, is allowed 488 acres of good land for the use of twenty families; at a rate of 24 acres per family; Popkum, eighteen miles below Hope, is allowed 369 acres of good land for the use of four families, at the rate of 90 acres per family; Cheam, twenty miles below Hope, is allotted 375 acres of bad, dry and mountainous land for the use of twenty-seven families, at the rate of thirteen acres per family; Yuk-yuk-yoose, on Chilliwack River, with a population of seven families, is allowed 42 acres: 5 acres per family; Sumas, at the junction of Sumas River and Fraser, with a population of seventeen families, is allowed 43 acres of meadow for their hay, and 32 acres of dry land; Keatsy, numbering more than one hundred inhabitants, is allowed 108 acres of land. Langley and Hope have not yet got land secured to them, and white men are encroaching on them on all sides …

We consider that 80 acres per family is absolutely necessary for our support, and the future welfare of our children. We declare that 20 or 30 acres of land per family will not give satisfaction, but will create ill feelings, irritation amongst our people and we cannot say what will be the consequence.[77]

Nevertheless, as Chief Alexis and the other Lower Fraser Indian chiefs discovered, it was difficult in Coast Salish and other territories to orchestrate a coordinated Indigenous response to colonial injustice. Part of the problem, as we will see, stemmed from the difficulty Stó:lō people experienced in the 1870s in trying to reconcile their generally positive relationship with Christian missionaries with the proselytizers' own visions of a reshaped Indigenous society. The Catholic missionaries – the very people the early Stó:lō converts to Christianity like Chief Alexis regarded as allies – were actively pursuing policies of their own. These Catholic policies, like the government initiatives, sought to fragment older cross-settlement associations and replace them with collective identities that fixed Coast Salish people onto what were increasingly isolated social and geographical landscapes.

While Oblate missionaries actively supported Native efforts to secure larger reserves, and even provided sophisticated arguments to rebut the Lockean denial of Aboriginal property rights based on invested labour,[78] the Church simultaneously assisted the state with its own initiatives to undermine those structures that fostered a sense of shared identity across reserve boundaries. The banning of the potlatch in 1885, in particular, contributed to this process. Although ostensibly designed to undermine Aboriginal religious beliefs and what were deemed offensive cultural expressions, the various state and Church anti-potlatch initiatives directly affected the functioning of Indigenous government and the operations of intersettlement property management protocols and extraterritorial property laws. Thus, while scholarly analysis has treated colonial reserve policies and missionary actions largely as separate matters, or in terms of their cumulative effect in marginalizing Aboriginal people from the perceived benefits of colonial development, their greater importance for Indigenous people lies in their combined impact on Indigenous people's sense of shared identity. It could be said that at the dawn of the fight for Indigenous land rights the missionaries had turned the Coast Salish world upside down in more ways than one.

Chapter Seven

Identity in the Face of Missionaries and the Anti-Potlatch Law

Colonial land and reserve policies played a central role in the solidifying of localized settlement-based collective identities, but they were not the only forces at play, nor were they necessarily always the most important. Other government policies, and indeed other players, also contributed to this process – though the former did not always have this as a stated objective, and the latter as often as not developed their tactics in isolation of state authorities. Apart from designating reserve boundaries and establishing membership lists, colonial authorities largely delegated the responsibility for forming new Native settlements to Christian missionaries. The first on the scene and ultimately the most successful missionaries in Coast Salish territory were the Roman Catholics. The 'Durieu system' of ecclesiastical community building advanced by the missionaries of the order of Oblates of Mary Immaculate in all regions deemed suitable for European-style agriculture, as well as the complimentary Church- and state-sponsored process of 'creating' Aboriginal leaders, had profound effects on Aboriginal collective identity in Stó:lō territory. Likewise, the passing of the federal anti-potlatch law significantly altered the manner in which Indigenous people, including the Stó:lō, transmitted and publicly professed notions of collective self, an aspect of the prohibition's impact that has not been previously considered.

Roman Catholic Communities

Catholic evangelists first began making sporadic forays into Stó:lō territory in 1840.[1] By the late 1850s they had established a permanent headquarters in Victoria, on Vancouver Island, and in the wake of the 1858 gold rush, and at Governor Douglas' invitation, they had expanded their proselytizing activities to the B.C. mainland at New Westminster. A permanent mission and residential school were established soon thereafter at what would become Mission City on the central Fraser Valley's northern shore.

For the Oblates, conversion was predicated on escaping older pagan beliefs and practices, but also, and perhaps more importantly, on rejecting the less savoury elements of Western society. In the early 1860s the Stó:lō were exposed to and drawn into many of the worst aspects of frontier society. Thus, as Father Fouquet explained, 'We had to not only uproot their deep-rooted savage vices, but also to attack the new ones that came along with drunkenness.'[2] With this view in mind, the Oblates under Bishop D'Herbomez set about creating a 'model reduction' – a series of archetypal Church-centred villages where converted pius Stó:lō could be separated from the debauched elements of European settler society while simultaneously remaining isolated from the reactionary and corrosive influences of their traditional Indigenous culture.[3] 'Reduction,' therefore, was a Catholic euphemism for social laboratory.

Jesuit missionaries in Paraguay originally pioneered the reduction model in the sixteenth and seventeenth centuries. While the South American experiment ultimately failed, D'Herbomez, and his successor, the flamboyant Bishop Paul Durieu, were convinced of the system's potential. They determined that it was not that the philosophy behind the system was flawed, but that the Jesuits had neglected to cultivate a sufficient degree of autonomy and self-governing authority among the Indigenous populace to allow them to continue to function after Paraguay's secular authorities had expelled the missionaries. In other words, the Jesuit reduction had systematically dissolved because of the vacuum of Indigenous leadership created by excessively paternalistic Jesuit policies of priestly control.[4] Under the Oblates, the B. C. incarnation of the reduction model emphasized a significant degree of local Aboriginal self-governance, economic self-sufficiency, and autonomy from secular state interference or, as the Oblates themselves described it, 'an Indian state ruled by the Indians, for the Indians, with the Indians, under the directive authority of the bishop and the local priests as supervisors.'[5]

As the Catholic priest and historian Vincent McNally recently pointed out, the 'Durieu system,' as it came to be known, aimed largely at creating a new category of Stó:lō identity: the 'good' Native Catholic. Ideally, the Oblates hoped to establish entirely new Indian communities on fertile agricultural lands away from the sites of older Native settlements.

Until measures could be put into place to facilitate this, the short-term preoccupation was to recast existing Stó:lō settlements on the reduction model through a two-fold process of internal and external isolation.

Recasting communities so as to isolate Native people from perceived external evils was the first and greatest priority in the Oblates' strategy for promoting 'civilization.' Despite the temptation the Oblates undoubtedly felt to depict pre-missionary (but post–gold rush) Aboriginal circumstances in the starkest and darkest of terms in order to accentuate any subsequent 'improvements,' the Oblate descriptions of a Stó:lō society reeling under the effects of alcohol were quite accurate. The picture the Oblates painted of a generation of Stó:lō among whom alcohol was wreaking havoc is largely corroborated by contemporaneous colonial records as well as the Stó:lō's own oral histories.[6] In 1898 the prominent Stó:lō chief and steamboat pilot Captain John (also known as Swalis, which means 'getting rich') explained that he had been introduced to alcohol during the 1858 gold rush and that almost immediately he had 'became very fond of whiskey,' that it was 'fast obtaining such a hold' on him, and that soon 'it was becoming impossible' for him to resist it, and that when he tried to 'break himself away from the habit' all his efforts 'proved unavailing.'[7] Thus, in order to save Stó:lō souls the priests determined it necessary first to eradicate the demon rum for, after being introduced during the gold rush, these particular spirits proved especially difficult to exorcise.

Describing the state of Stó:lō society in the wake of the gold rush as one where alcohol had 'spread the most terrifying corruption,' the zealous and dramatic Father Fouquet reported:

> Their immorality would have made Sodom and Gomorrah, pagan Rome, and Turkish Constantinople blush; they were infected with dreadful/ghastly/horrible corruption. These unfortunate people had combined their own crude vices with the foul trappings of the disgusting scum of a corrupt civilization. That is not all: in spite of the laws of the country, shameless men were trafficking poisons they call *liqueurs*: which was really alcohol mixed with camphor and tobacco juice. At that time, one met none but drunken Indians everywhere. From what I saw during five or six months, it seems that fewer than one hundred of a thousand were not usually drunk, and there were many who were never sober. They were seen in groups around and even in places where the whites were, fighting and killing each other, screaming like ferocious beasts. In one night alone, two were killed in New Westminster ... In their camps, where they had nothing to fear from the

whites, it was even more horrible: that relatives, even friends should fight
and kill each other was nothing unusual; we saw drunken fathers stab their
innocent children.[8]

According to Bishop D'Herbomez's report of May 1861, 'the abuse
of liquor among [the Stó:lō] has caused terrible ravages. Nearly all the
Chiefs have been victims of this corrosive destroyer of civilization. A
great number of youngsters have disappeared due to this abuse.'[9] While
contemporary Stó:lō people generally do not like to talk about this sad
aspect of their history, there is a general agreement that such descriptions as Chirouse and D'Herbomez provide are largely accurate.[10]

To assist the Stó:lō in counteracting the whiskey, the Oblates set about
establishing 'temperance' or 'sobriety' societies in every Stó:lō community where they could identify sympathetic followers. Each society,
though under the supreme direction of the Church, was designed to
operate autonomously for the months on end when no priest could
be present.[11] Locally, the temperance societies were led by Church-
appointed 'watchmen,' 'captains,' and 'catechists.' (See Figure 8.) The
gold rush, however, had caused the Stó:lō to be suspicious of newcomers.
Throughout their 'first five or six months' of proselytizing the Oblates la-
mented that the Stó:lō 'would not even approach the missionaries.' But
if we can judge by the writings of Father Chirouse, by the end of the first
year, 'everywhere, the Indians *en masse*, [had] enrolled under the Banner
of Temperance ... With the Chiefs at the head, captains and watchmen
were organized in every camp.'[12]

After overcoming the initial Native misgiving, the Oblates found that
their primary opposition stemmed less from Stó:lō traditionalists than
from the non-Native whiskey bootleggers who had established themselves among the Stó:lō. The first in what would become a series of direct clashes between the Oblates and the temperate Stó:lō community,
on the one side, and the 'peddlers of poison liqueurs' and their Native
supporters, on the other, occurred at the settlement of Cheam, midway
between Fort Langley and Fort Hope.[13] There, on one particular day, Father Fouquet and a prominent local figure and early convert to Catholicism known as Alexis, together challenged three whiskey pedlars who
had established a presence by building a storage and distribution shed
for their product right among the Stó:lō longhouses. At the end of a prolonged sermon, nearly two hundred Stó:lō reportedly gathered around
Alexis and Fouquet showing their support for sobriety and civilization,
while only fifteen remained with the white purveyors of alcohol. Under

8. Oblate Temperance Society flag. City of Vancouver Archives, Photo number IN P47.

Alexis' charismatic leadership the majority then threatened to burn the 'rum merchant's house' and were only dissuaded by Father Fouquet's caution that the matter might be better dealt with by the colonial authorities, who could put the offenders in jail. Following this pivotal incident, Father Fouquet claims the Oblates 'received many requests to visit other camps and establish "sobriety societies."'[14]

The effects of alcohol reinforced for the Oblates the importance of boundary maintenance and provided a focus to their missionary activities. If the devil was at work among the Stó:lō, his influence was perceived as emanating at least in equal parts from the non-Native whiskey pedlar and his alcohol, as from the Stó:lō shaman and his magic. Indeed, for the Oblate observers, evil emanated from multiple sources. Boundaries were therefore needed internally as well as externally. Internally, the watchmen and other Indigenous Church-appointed and -sanctioned officials were assigned the duty of directing local religious instruction, monitoring community activities, and reporting moral violations to the priest – a responsibility many fulfilled with vigour. Within each settlement at least two catechists were appointed to lead the community in religious instruction: a man to teach the boys and a woman to instruct the girls. On those Sundays when a priest could not be present,[15] the catechists were expected to lead the faithful in communal morning and evening prayers, recitation of the rosary, catechism classes, vespers, and the Stations of the Cross. When a priest was available, they acted as lay deacons assisting with the Mass and ensuring people attended confession.[16]

Watchmen, as the name suggests, were the village's monitors – the eyes and ears of the Oblate fathers – the de facto leaders of the powerful temperance societies. Late twentieth-century Elders carried oral traditions describing watchmen of the mid- to late nineteenth century as men who were both respected and feared. They 'looked in on everything; kept tabs on people, and reported to the priest people who were doing bad things, like drinking or beating their wives and children.'[17] Church records corroborate such descriptions. Under the Durieu system, watchmen reported to chiefs 'not only on the important violations of important laws, but on family quarrels between husbands and wives, on neglect of children by parents, on the disobedience of children, on rowdyism of some men, etc., etc.'[18] Of course, they also monitored the activities of the shaman and his clientele. As agents of the Church, watchmen were the point men in establishing and maintaining a new set of internal social divisions.

'Indian courts' were central features of the Durieu system and contributed directly, if inadvertently, to the fragmentation of Stó:lō society into two new identifiable groups. These tribunals concerned themselves primarily with issues of morality and tried to keep a degree of boundary maintenance through the regulation of membership in the temperance societies. All those who 'converted' to temperance were required to make a 'communal pledge' before being admitted as full members of the society. Upon becoming members, initiates received a 'ticket' as an external sign or token of their commitment to Catholicism and 'civilization.' If, upon charges brought forth by a watchman, a temperance society member was found guilty by the local Indian tribunal of immoral conduct, the presiding chief and Oblate father confiscated his ticket and expelled the offender from the new community.[19] As a result, throughout the latter decades of the nineteenth century the Oblates tried to inculcate within the Stó:lō population the importance of being identified with the 'good' Catholic Indian community, rather than with those who had retained their superstitious traditional culture and/or had been corrupted by the vices of Western society.

While expelled former members of the temperance societies could in theory regain their membership, as time advanced it became increasingly clear to the Oblates and to the temperance societies' Indigenous leaders that to allow what were considered incorrigible personalities to remain within the settlements risked enticing others to fall away as well. At Chehalis, where the Harrison and Chehalis rivers meet, the Oblates strove to make the distinction between good and bad Indians something more tangible than mere boundaries of the mind. From Father Edward MacGugein's 1886 annual report we learn that some years earlier, 'in order to separate the good from the bad,' Bishop Durieu had physically 'divided' the 127 inhabitants of Chehalis 'into two camps.' Those deemed 'bad' (adherents to traditional spirituality as well as those who drank) were essentially abandoned and rejected by the 'good' temperate Catholic people who relocated a few hundred metres from the old settlement to live in new Western-style homes in immediate proximity to the new Catholic church.

Chehalis is the tribal community described in Stó:lō *sxwōxwiyám* as having formerly been separate mountain and lowland people, who united following the resolution of a dispute brought about by the lowland people's construction of a weir that blocked the path of migrating salmon. One cannot help but wonder the extent to which this older division was perhaps reborn through the work of the Oblate priests. Significantly, while the two new adjacent settlements retained somewhat distinct identities until the beginning of the twentieth century, when they again 'merged,' the Oblate visitor of 1886 could not help but ruminate over the fact that the supposed black and white division between Durieu's good and bad Indians was actually rather blurred: 'The majority of these self-called good Indians leave a lot to be desired. The good settlement has as yet many deplorable cases of drunks and superstition. The Chief is too inconsistent in his ideas and his conduct, and so carries the principal responsibility for this state of affairs.'[20] The chief, of course, was George Chehalis, a man whose ability to describe Stó:lō cultural traditions, communicate ancient narratives, and recall the details of nine generations of genealogy so greatly impressed Franz Boas (the father of North American anthropology) that he referred to him as 'a prize.'[21]

The divisions at Chehalis clearly never produced the results the Oblates desired. Indeed, they had been nothing more than ad hoc adaptations of the Oblates' older and grander scheme of creating a genuinely new model reduction built not upon the foundations of an ancient established Indigenous settlement, but rather, upon the virgin agricultural fields of Matsqui prairie. There, directly across the river from St Mary's Mission, the Oblates aspired to build a community where, instead of struggling for conversion and against vices old and new, already converted members of their temperance societies could live in isolation from corrupting influences and direct their energies towards achieving ever-higher expressions of civilization.

Ultimately, the rapid pace of non-Native settlement and the shift in colonial attitudes marked by Governor Douglas' retirement in the spring of 1864 prevented the Oblates from securing an adequate land base (and forced them to try experiments such as the Chehalis division).[22] The massive 9,600-acre Matsqui reserve demarcated by Saregeant McColl in May 1864 appears to have been intended by the cooperating Stó:lō and Oblate leadership precisely for this purpose. Indeed, by the mid-1860s plans were well under way to substitute the upper-class Stó:lō tradition of arranged marriages with new Church-orchestrated matrimonial unions between the male and female graduates of St Mary's residential school.[23] Together, the leaders of the temperance societies and the Oblate clergy planned to turn Matsqui prairie into the destination of the residential schools' brightest alumni. The Matsqui reduction would become a model town surrounded by thousands of acres of cultivated fields, and what was most important, separated and isolated from the uncivilized elements of Indigenous and Western society.[24] These plans were thwarted, however, when in 1868 Chief Commisioner of Lands and Works Joseph Trutch reduced the Stó:lō reserve base at Matsqui to a mere eighty acres

– an action that 'caused great dissatisfaction' among the Indigenous population.[25]

As the era of colonial settlement progressed, one thing was becoming clear: state and Church authorities were collaborating to undermine the social and familial linkages between communities upon which supratribal identity was based. Under the combined systems of Department of Indian Affairs band governments and Oblate reductions, settlements were intended to be autonomous of one another. Leadership was to be expressed through Western-style institutions and conducted under the supervision of non-Native individuals rather than through the extended family connections that bound people of different settlements together under variously ranked family and tribal leaders. As Elder Patrick Charlie explained in 1950, in the nineteenth century the 'priest came, and said each village [was] to boss themselves.'[26]

Not all the divisions that resulted from the Oblates' efforts at separating Aboriginal Christians from those who retained older belief structures were geographical. Among the most profound and disruptive were those that were generational. A cornerstone of the missionary platform was the development of initiatives designed to convert children. In the mid-1860s at St Mary's residential school this process was facilitated in part by taking children on late spring field trips to sacred sites their parents had forbidden them to visit because of their spiritual potency and danger. After ten months of tutelage these excursions were the last official school functions children participated in before returning to their parents for two months of summer vacations.

The power of these excursions as tools for community fracture and a new form of boundary maintenance are vividly portrayed in Father Gendre's report describing the Oblate's field trip to the 'Devil's mountain' in 1864: 'Before sending my dear children off on vacation, I had them go for a long walk on the mountain known as "The Devil's." Tradition maintained that whosoever should challenge that fearsome mountain would pay for his foolhardiness with his life. All of the Savages sought to frighten me with ever more sombre and dramatic tales. Thus, my students, who are as superstitious as their fathers, trembled in fear when I proposed we climb the mountain.'[27]

The fearful field trip was not a spontaneous event. Rather, it was planned and announced to the children months in advance. According to the priest, this enabled the children to become accustomed to the idea. One can imagine that it would have also created a focal point of anxiety over a prolonged period of time, and likely led to tensions be-

tween students, as they wrestled with the idea of proving their individual
bravery within a context of rejecting the teachings of their parents:

> Nearly every day for three months, I attacked their ridiculous superstition
> and gradually, they grew accustomed to the idea of attempting this endeav-
> our, which could not possibly present any danger, with me. I succeeded
> in conquering their hereditary superstition. Towards the evening of the
> 31st of May, we all set off in canoes, with the necessary provisions and we
> camped that night at the foot of the dreaded mountain on the shores of a
> magnificent lake. Early the following day, after prayers, we ascended the
> slope and towards noon we arrived, without a single mishap, at the summit,
> where none had ever stood before. There, we sang out our triumph and our
> victory. I was pleased to show these children to what extent their traditions
> were lies and that only the priest could speak the truth, which he receives
> from the Great Chief from above.[28]

We should not assume, however, that the children regarded the field
trip and its significance in terms identical to those of the priest. Pulled
between the alleged 'lies' of their parents' traditions, and the teachings
of the Church, the children may well have understood the event as an
example of the potency of one particular shaman's power (the priest's)
over that of whichever Stó:lō shaman had earlier identified the site as
dangerous. More to the point, however, the children who participated in
this allegedly transformative event were forever distinguished from their
parents and all others who had avoided the site by the fact that the priest
left a lasting reminder of the identities of his followers on the mountain
as proof of their separateness: 'We amused ourselves and afterwards, I
wrote a list of the names of all of the brave (children) who had climbed
the Devil's Mountain. I placed the list beneath the bark of a cedar tree,
where it will remain until next year when we return to this summit which
is now the "Mountain of God." On the eve of that very pleasant day, we
returned to Sainte-Marie [school] singing the Litanies of the Most Holy
Virgin.'[29]

If the trip to the forbidden mountain had been traumatic for the
children, one can imagine how news of the outing must have genuinely
terrified their parents. That the children's names had been written on
paper and then stored beneath the bark of the sacred cedar tree would
have been especially distressing, given the Coast Salish belief in residual
spirit power and the understanding that even the utterance of a person's
name, let alone its encryption, necessarily carried spirit power with it.

Their children would not have been regarded simply as lucky to return from a dangerous site without harm. Rather, if one can take contemporary attitudes towards x̱á:x̱a (taboo) spiritual places as indicative of past behaviour, families would have been terrified that aspects of their children's spiritual being would have been stolen from them and left at the site. The priest had, in other words, not only taken them to a dangerous spot, he had ensured their spiritual misfortune by leaving aspects of the children's identity in physical form at a place where their parents feared to tread.

Given that it is still common for contemporary Stó:lō parents to take children who have been exposed to similar, but much milder, x̱á:x̱a situations to visit shamans for the purpose of having them 'brushed off' and 'fixed-up,' we can assume that many children must have gone through similar ritualistic cleansing ceremonies upon their return from Devil's Mountain at the end of the 1864 school year. Those who received treatment and did not subsequently experience profound spirit loss and death would likely have been considered saved by the shaman. On the other hand, any child who either refused to receive shamanic treatment, or whose parents did not compel it, and who still did not get sick and die must have shaken the very foundations of the Stó:lō belief systems. Not only was the physical world rapidly changing, but the spirit forces that provided the world with life and order were being presented to some Stó:lō as having been falsehoods. A more profound division within a community than a generational divide between believers of the old tenets and the new is difficult to imagine.

Protestant and Catholic Divisions

As the colonial era progressed and it became increasingly apparent that sufficient land would not be secured for even one single 'new' Catholic community, divisions of different sorts came to influence Stó:lō senses of self within their existing settlements. Of increasing importance were interdenominational conflicts among the emerging Stó:lō Christian population. While the Oblates were the first missionaries to arrive on the scene, they did not have to wait long for competition. During the generation following the gold rush, the Methodists and to a lesser extent the Anglicans challenged the emerging Catholic hegemony in the Fraser Valley.

Judging from their writings, both Protestant and Catholic missionaries preferred paganism to the heresy of conversion to the wrong form of

Christianity – at least one could then be considered to have not yet made a choice, rather than having made the wrong choice. Commenting on the 1871 activities of the Methodist missionary at Chilliwack, the Oblate priest Father Charles Marchal proudly reported that the Wesleyan Reverend Thomas Crosby found himself 'established in the centre of these [Catholic] villages unable to spread his work.' However, Father Marchal noted that according to his Catholic supporters, the Protestant cleric was attempting to intimidate Stó:lō into becoming Methodists by preaching that those who rejected the Protestant faith in favour of the 'Rome-ish' doctrine 'would be chased from this land and transported along with the Catholic priest to an island in the ocean where there is no sweet water, no drink and no food of any kind; where he would soon die of misery.'[30]

In his autobiography, *Among the An-ko-me-nums [Halkomelems]*, however, Reverend Crosby paints the picture in reverse, stating that it was the Oblates who subjected those Stó:lō who had shown interest in Methodism to 'the most bitter persecution.' According to Crosby, at least one circulating version of the Oblate's 'Catholic Ladder' mnemonic pictorial teaching device depicted Catholic Indians going to Heaven, while 'Crosby and his friends went head first into the flames of hell-fire.'[31] Not to be outdone, the Methodists soon devised their own retaliatory 'Protestant Ladders' depicting the history of the world from creation to the apocalypse through Reformation eyes. In the Methodist version history ended with Protestants being allowed access into Heaven, while the Pope himself tipped headlong into Hell's torturous flames.[32] (See Figure 9.)

Competition dividing the Stó:lō into increasingly polarized camps remained a feature of missionary activity throughout the nineteenth century. In 1886 the Oblate priest Father Edward Peytavin described the interdenominational rivalry at the Stó:lō community of *Skw'átets* in terms reminiscent of the European-age of Counter-Reformation. Of a total population of only fifty-one people, thirty-six were Catholic, the remainder Protestant. The man claiming ancient hereditary prerogatives of leadership was reportedly an Episcopalian Anglican, and the Methodist families allegedly 'refused to recognize an Anglican Chief.' In response, the Methodist parson had appointed a 'Methodist Chief.' However, according to the Oblate author, this action was unacceptable to the remaining Catholic population. Therefore, in order to 'maintain peace and discipline among the Catholics,' Peytavin 'chose' a 'Catechist or Zealator' for the Catholic majority. Once appointed, this individual was allegedly given by his 'co-religionaries' the 'title of Chief': 'There are now three [chiefs] in this little village. It is the Catholic who has the most subjects, the Methodist is in control of thirteen, and the Episcopalian

9. The Pope falls headlong into Hell's tortuous flames in a 'Protestant Ladder.'
Henry and Eliza Spalding, 'Protestant Ladder,' c. 1846, Oregon Historical
Society, Hi631, 632, Portland, Oregon.

has only his wife to govern. This situation causes much laughter among whites and Indians.'[33] That it was not the priest but the Stó:lō Catholics themselves who ultimately anointed the Catholic chief is significant, and goes a long way to illuminating the degree to which internal boundaries were being created by Indigenous people along lines that were ostensibly controlled by outsiders – a process that has recently been the subject of growing academic enquiry.[34]

Significantly, the composition of the competing religious camps was at least occasionally subject to sudden shifts. Slightly upriver from Skw'átets, at the settlement of Shxw'ōwhámél, Father Peytavin reported that while fifty-one people were Catholic and only four or five Anglican (and not a single Methodist), a few years earlier the situation had been drastically different, and the 'three different parties were in a dispute over pre-eminence, with the Catholics losing ground.'[35]

Such swings in denominational allegiance suggest that conversions were at least in some instances less profound than any of the missionaries cared to admit, and likely followed older patterns of people allying themselves with the shaman who showed the greatest power and ability. Indeed, they appear to share features with those disputes documented within contemporary Tlingit culture in Alaska by Kirk Dombrowski.[36] Occasionally, relatively disadvantaged members of particular Aboriginal communities used Christian religions as a way of rejecting distinctions, including traditional class distinctions, which had served to oppress them. That those nineteenth-century Stó:lō who participated in these inter-Christian affiliation struggles apparently took their denominational identities seriously, despite their sometimes ephemeral nature, suggests that they carried considerable Indigenous import regardless of whether they served as vehicles for other older identity divisions that the non-Native observers could not perceive.

Creating or Recognizing Chiefs?

Government and Church officials together were keen to exploit every opportunity for transforming the previously associated Native settlements into autonomous political entities. The process of reserve reduction in 1868 provided ample opportunities, for not only did this cause the Indigenous land base to become abridged, but more importantly in terms of its effect on Indigenous governance, it resulted in small disconnected islands of Aboriginal space being created within a sea of white farmlands.

Under the emerging colonial system, Indian chiefs, as spokesmen and representatives of their settlements, became key figures through whom government resources – not the least important of which were reserve lands and agricultural implements – were distributed. Thus, obtaining and retaining government-sponsored symbols of chiefly authority quickly assumed practical as well as symbolic significance in Stó:lõ society. Understandably, therefore, we learn that in 1868 competing claimants had almost 'come to blows' over the question of who was more legitimately entitled to have their name 'inserted ... in the duly authorized [reserve] map of the District as the real Chiefs.'[37] (See Map 20.)

When J.B. Launders arrived in Chilliwack in October 1868 to begin anew the process of surveying Stó:lõ reserves (i.e., reducing those created by Sgt McColl under Governor Douglas' authority in 1864), he was directed by local white settlers to the house of Captain John Swalis, a recent convert to Methodism who piously rejected shamanism and strove to abolish its practice among his friends and family.[38] Together with Captain John, Launders walked the perimeter of the small cultivated fields, houses, and cemetery sites, and in the process redrew the map of the Soowahlie Reserve. In so doing, the two men effectively erased the original 4,000-acre reserve and replaced it with one of just 600 acres. Afterward, Captain John's name appeared on the resulting map as 'Chief,' and in Launder's report 'Chief Captain John, was reportedly "satisfied" with the results of the reduction.[39] (See Figure 10.)

If Captain John was satisfied with the smaller land base, other claimants to the title of community leader certainly were not. Launders' surveys effectively divided the Chilliwack Tribe into nine small and distinct settlement-based political entities. The chiefs of three of these reserves, including Chief Captain John, were Methodists who, according to their detractors, did not trace their ancestry back to an immortal founding father from the legendary myth-age time. The following spring, on the occasion of the annual Queen's birthday celebrations in New Westminster, those with counter-claims to leadership manoeuvred to displace Captain John and transform their hereditary status into government-recognized chieftainships. The Catholic priests worked with those who identified themselves as the hereditary elite in their efforts to consolidate political power. It was at the priest's behest that a senior official in the Lands and Works Department took the maps away from Captain John and his fellow Methodist chiefs, and gave them to those men the Catholic priests identified as the true hereditary chiefs – though what process or criteria the priests used is unclear. Before the transfer, the official altered the maps

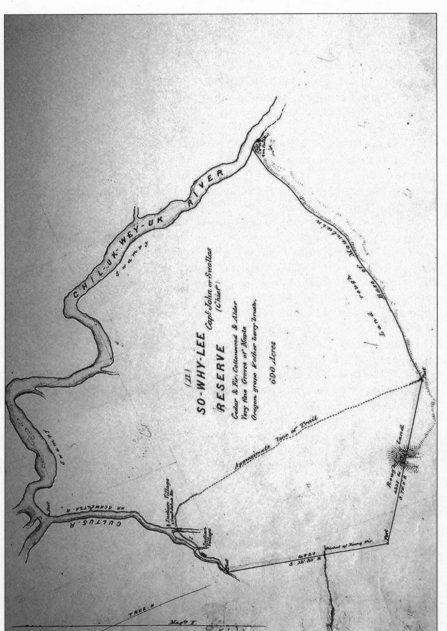

Map 20. Detail of official map of Soowahlie Reserve showing name of government appointed (recognized?) Chief, Captain John. 12 Tray 1A, Indian Reserves, Office of the Surveyor General, Victoria, B.C.: Land Title and Survey Authority of British Columbia.

10. Captain John of Soowahlie. Chilliwack Museum and Archives, AM 362, file 126, Edenbank Farm Fonds, photograph series.

so they contained only the Catholic chiefs' names. As a concerned Wesleyan minister astutely observed, the Methodists, or 'real Chiefs,' found themselves 'in the position of being, in the eyes of the Government, no Chiefs at all.'[40]

The dispute did not fade quickly. The Methodists appealed the change and demanded that the 'papers' containing the names of the originally listed chiefs be restored to their earlier possessors.[41] After considerable haranguing (at one point the government agent accused Reverend A. Browning of interfering in government business and of trying to 'make chiefs') the Lands and Works Department decided to produce a second set of maps that included the names of each and every one of the various claimants, only with the Methodists apparently listed as 'second' or subchiefs. Each new Native official was then provided a copy of the same.[42]

Ultimately, this compromise proved unsustainable. Aboriginal representatives from each camp reported to the government that white missionaries associated with their adversary's candidacy threatened that unless everyone supported their choice for chief the government ultimately would reduce their reserve lands even further.[43] In response, at the two settlements where tensions were the greatest, the government conducted the first municipal-style democratic elections for Indian chief in the history of British Columbia. At Squiala, the adult male population 'selected their hereditary chief (and not the [Methodist] one who had represented himself to … [the government agent] as chief) to receive the map by a majority of three, 9 to 6.' At Soowahlie, meanwhile, twenty-four adult males voted in an election that rejected Captain John 'by a majority of fourteen, 19 to 5.'

Despite the electoral endorsement for the hereditary leadership, the government ultimately reversed even this decision and recognized Captain John as chief. The reasons for this final switch are not explained in the government records, but sufficient context exists in other sources for us to glean insights into the officials' motives. Oral histories, for example, reveal that the financial fortunes and political careers of Chief Commissioner of Lands and Works Joseph Trutch and Captain John Swalis were intertwined. Three years earlier Trutch had been awarded the contract to build the colony's first bridge across the Fraser River at a site in the Fraser Canyon to connect the new Cariboo Road and facilitate the movement of people and commodities to and from the colony's interior. Initial construction of the Alexandra Suspension Bridge proceeded smoothly until Trutch's engineer became stymied by the problem of transporting the giant spool of cable from the riverboat landing at Yale along the narrow twisting road to the construction site, twelve kilometres farther upriver. The situation apparently looked hopeless, Stó:lō Elder Andy Commodore related in 1993, until Commodore's great grandfather Captain John Swalis approached Joseph Trutch with a solution. For a lucrative subcontract, Captian John arranged for his family and friends to unwind the cable, hoist it to their shoulders, and then snake it along the Carriboo Road.[44] It was Captain John's innovative plan for transporting steel cable that salvaged the Alexandra bridge project and which, in turn, catapulted Trutch to the office of Chief Commissioner of Lands and Works. Moreover, it was Trutch to whom Captain John owed a favour for enabling him to live up to his name Swalis – literally, 'getting rich.' Thus, when Trutch needed an Indigenous voice to give his policy of reducing the original Douglas reserves some legitimacy it was to Captain John that he turned. Now, in the wake of his electoral defeat, it was Captain John's turn to call in a favour. Moreover, he did so with the added weight of a petition from twenty-eight non-Native Protestant settlers (whose farms and pre-emptions happened to fall either in part or in whole within the original 1864 reserve boundaries that Captain John helped reduce) asking the government to annul the Indian elections and appoint John as Chief of Soowahlie. To give their message added clout, Captain John's suppporters warned that unless the government took quick and decisive action along these lines 'serious troubles will arise, involving, perhaps, the whites as well as the Indians.'[45]

With Trutch as an ally, and the threat of violence backing his candidacy, it is not surprising that Captian John and the other electorally defeated Methodist claimants to the title of chief soon found themselves the recipients of a new government-produced maps inscribed with their names as official chiefs of their communities.[46] Nevertheless, a subsequent report from the local government agent in the Fraser Valley explained that Captain John and the other non-Catholic aspirants referred to in the settlers' petition 'were not the hereditary Chiefs of their tribes, and not the Indians to whom the majority of their respective tribes wish the maps to be given.'[47] (See Map 20.)

Despite the actions of Captain John and his many non-Native supporters, and despite what may well have been their long-term intentions, in most subsequent cases the government preferred to acknowledge leaders who were already recognized as such by their fellow Stó:lō residents. Generally this meant providing those men referred to as 'hereditary'

leaders with government recognition of their role as settlement spokesmen and advocates.[48] Over the following decades the Methodist and Anglican missionaries largely abandoned the Fraser Valley, and so, with the
exception of Captain John's Soowahlie Reserve, internal contests over
leadership gradually ceased to assume denominational expressions. But
even when this was not the case, the Catholic temperance societies' hierarchy of chiefs, watchmen, and captains tended to be able to accommodate the government requirements without shifting authority too far
from the Church's own chain of command. In the circumstances, determining where political agency lay more than a century after the fact is a
difficult task.

In cases where the government and the Catholic Church disagreed,
certain compromises were made so as to avoid open conflicts. In the
early years of the Durieu system, for example, many Stó:lō reserves often
had two or more chiefs: an 'honorary' figurehead elected by the local
populace and then appointed and recognized by the government, and
what was considered by the Church to be the 'real' one (popularly referred to as 'Church Chief'), appointed by the priest and who served at
the Church's sufferance.[49]

By the last decades of the nineteenth century most of the chiefs recognized by the Canadian state were also Catholic Church chiefs, but more
importantly, they were also men who were able to demonstrate blood
ties to prominent hereditary leaders of the past.[50] In this context, there
was general continuity in leadership from past generations, but the roles
leaders played within Stó:lō society assumed new and important, if sometimes nebulous, expressions and significance. 'Chiefs' were considered
necessary by the government and the Church. Indeed, after British Col-
mbia joined Canada, Stó:lō chiefs officially became part of the structure
of both the Canadian government as defined by the nascent Indian Act[51]
and the Catholic Church as defined in the reduction model. Thus, as
time progressed, Stó:lō chiefs increasingly came to serve the dual and
often contradictory and awkward functions of being the primary DIA/
Church officials in the reserve as well as the principle Indigenous spokesmen against DIA and the Church – clashing roles that continue to compromise Native leaders to this day. Moreover, as chiefs under the Indian
Act, they came to increasingly see themselves as leaders of autonomous
communities disconnected from their relatives in adjacent settlements –
a development that hinders the re-establishment of a meaningful revival
of family-based leadership that recognizes the familial linkages that cut
across bands and bind nations together.

Potlatch Governance

Clearly, Indigenous leadership and governance were severely compromised in the late nineteenth century. In addition to developing policies that targeted patterns of residence and processes of leadership selection, the government and churches also cooperated to dismantle the fundamental governing structures of Indigenous society through their opposition to the ubiquitous northwest coast tradition of the potlatch. Although this interpretation has not previously received much scholarly attention, the 1885 amendment to the Indian Act making the potlatch illegal directly and profoundly affected Stó:lō mechanisms and protocols regulating property ownership in such a manner as to influence mobility and by extenson collective identity – although, in fairness, this was seldom explicitly articulated as a goal of the prohibition.

In Victorian B.C. society the potlatch was condemned as a major impediment to Aboriginal people successfully achieving a state of Western civilization. According to historians Douglas Cole and Ira Chaikin, non-Natives cited three main reasons for wanting to see the potlatch eradicated. The first was health related. In an era of growing awareness of the workings of infectious diseases, paternalistic missionaries and government agents alike regarded the large number of people gathered closely together participating in a potlatch in what were perceived to be unsanitary conditions as a contributing factor to continuing Aboriginal demographic decline. Second, 'respectable' Victorian society was aghast at rumours of ambitious Aboriginal men prostituting their wives and daughters to raise money to host potlatches and repay old potlatch debts. The third, and most effective and serious objections to the potlatch, however, concerned the institution's incompatibility with Western-style industry and labour. Natives participating in the elaborate series of autumn potlatches were unable to commit themselves to year-round employment. This is not to say that significant numbers of Native people, or non-Natives for that matter, were engaging in year-round employment (as Rolf Knight has shown, this did not occur until after the Second World War[52]), but that missionaries and government officials held this out to be the goal and saw the potlatch as an important impediment to the fulfilment of this vision. What is more, even those who participated in the wage labour economy were largely electing to hoard and then extravagantly distribute their hard-earned wealth rather than accumulating it for the purpose of private, individual material progress.[53] Relatedly, Native parents attending and participating in a series of autumn potlatches (and then winter season spirit dances – popularly known as Tamanawas dances – which were banned along with the potlatch) brought their children with them, meaning that for months on end these children were unable to attend missionary-run schools.

Thus, whatever the reasons behind Aboriginal people's participation in the potlatch, and whatever its function or functions within Aboriginal society, by the 1880s a prominent segment of the non-Native community had determined that the potlatch was anathema to civilized society. The Oblates had begun to dissuade people from participating in the potlatch shortly after the establishment of St Mary's Mission in 1862, when they attempted to make it one of the things that watchmen kept track of as something that could be cited as cause for expulsion from the temperance societies. It was not until the 1870s, however, that a coalition of social crusaders, consisting primarily of government agents and missionaries, began to seriously lobby the federal government to assume a more proactive role in establishing fertile grounds for economic advancement and religious enlightenment by outlawing the potlatch.[54] In the summer of 1883, at the urging of Joint Indian Reserve Commissioner Gilbert Malcolm Sproat (who otherwise was one of the staunchest and most influential non-Native supporters of Aboriginal land and governance rights),[55] Prime Minister John A. Macdonald, in his capacity as Superintendent General of Indian Affairs, advised his Cabinet that he intended to introduce measures to suppress the potlatch. In April of the following year an amendment to the Indian Act announced that, as of 1 January 1885, participating in a potlatch would be a criminal offence.

Within the anthropological literature the traditional potlatch has been studied primarily with an eye to understanding the meaning and function of exchange.[56] Analysis of historical change in the purpose and expression of the potlatch was first attempted by Helen Codere who, in 1950, argued that contact and colonialism caused Kwakiutl potlatching to greatly expand and ultimately to function as a replacement for warfare.[57] Since Codere's groundbreaking work, historical analysis has focused almost exclusively on the European side of the equation, exploring the causes and expressions of the ecclesiastical and then government prohibitions of the potlatch. While this has greatly expanded our understandings of the nature of colonial society and authority, it has done relatively little to illuminate the effects and consequences of the banning of the potlatch on Indigenous societies.[58] Indeed, within the historical literature the potlatch largely remains a captive of both Codere's study and the enrichment thesis first advanced by Joyce Wike and still most strongly associated with Wilson Duff and Robin Fisher.[59]

Assessing the social and political effects of the potlatch prohibition on Stó:lō society is difficult. Few contemporaneous records discuss such ceremonies, and those that do tend to describe the way potlatches were conducted rather than explain why they were occurring or the purposes they served. Moreover, despite all the energy that has gone into trying to understand the potlatch, nobody appears to have bothered to ask the Stó:lō what effect the banning actually had, other than in ad hoc attempts to elicit stories about attempts at holding covert potlatches. Indeed, the entire matter is significantly complicated by the fact that the Chinook trade jargon term potlatch has no exact Halq'eméylem translation. The term potlatch has been applied indiscriminately to any large gathering where gifts are exchanged. Even among the contemporary generation of Stó:lō who speak English as their first language the word potlatch remains largely meaningless. Instead, a host of different gatherings involving the exchange of wealth are referred to and distinguished by their purposes (i.e., naming ceremony, puberty ceremony, wedding, memorial, winterdance, sweep-up, etc.).[60]

Fortunately, oral traditions exist (both frozen on paper and living among families) that describe the purposes of certain nineteenth-century Stó:lō gatherings. We know that people were required to come together at ceremonies, where wealth was distributed and sometimes destroyed, to mark and celebrate any significant change in a person's status or position. We also know that the families hosting these celebrations were required to distribute items of wealth among their invited guests. All such gatherings, referred to as potlatches by non-Native observers, were vitally important if for no other reason than they allowed a non-literate society to transmit important news and information to as broad an audience as possible in as pure and unadulterated a form as possible, that is, with a minimum of interpreters.

Now, as in the past, at every Stó:lō gathering involving the distribution of wealth the host family has a hired 'speaker,' who 'calls witnesses' from among the most respected and highest-status guests. These people are charged with the responsibility of 'witnessing the work that is done here tonight,' and they are specifically obligated to describe the events and their import to family and friends who could not be in attendance. Without fail, the speaker also informs the witnesses that if any question ever arises as to the nature or validity of the work, they will be called upon to verify its form as well as content. What is more, should a controversy arise – as in someone else laying claim to a name that was bestowed or, perhaps more importantly, to the property associated with the name – a second gathering is required, after the adjudication, to allow the witnesses to be recalled as witnesses to the correction ceremony, where they receive the same charges and enter into the same obligations with regard to disseminating the news and keeping it accurate.

We can be fairly confident that the gatherings described in earlier chapters, such as occurred at the raising of Wileliq the Fifth's inverted-gable house and his subsequent marriage to the Katzie woman, were legitimized through what in the post-1885 era would have been characterized by the government as potlatch ceremonies. Indeed, it is unlikely that any of the movements and migrations described in earlier chapters could have occurred without a potlatch either clearing the way for them or ratifying and sanctifying them retrospectively.

Among the Stó:lō people interviewed by Wilson Duff in 1950, two types of status-marking exchange ceremonies (referred to in the literature as variations of the potlatch ceremony) were described as having been particularly common and important during the mid- to late nineteenth-century period: the first were ceremonies where names and associated lands were transferred to a new generation in order to facilitate change of residence among the original holders of the property; and the second were essentially one-upmanship ceremonies, similar to those Codere described among the Kwakiutil as 'fighting with property,' wherein rival families or communities attempted to outdo one another (to 'step on' one another) by hosting ever more elaborate giveaways.[61] One of the best examples of the former is the late nineteenth-century ceremony where the prominent Fraser Canyon resident Súx̱'yel (also known as Captain Charlie) transferred his name and land holdings to his youngest son Patrick Charlie.[62]

Súx̱'yel was the leader of a prominent and distinguished Stó:lō family living in the Fraser Canyon above Yale. Like his father, he possessed great wealth: he counted the snake, grizzly bear, and loon among his spirit helpers, and on behalf of his family he acted as steward of valuable hereditary lands and canyon fishing sites. Súx̱'yel was a confident man, who boldly engaged with non-Native society, ultimately securing an administrative position with the colonial government, although in what capacity it is no longer remembered among his descendants. In his middle age Súx̱'yel decided to fully avail himself of the opportunities the new colonial order presented by becoming a European-style farmer.

Accordingly, he moved to the flats across the river from Fort Yale, but insufficient irrigation stymied his agricultural ambitions. He determined that to be successful required leaving the canyon altogether. After unsuccessfully trying to establish himself at a second site farther downriver, near Fort Hope, an elderly relative at Shxw'ōwhámél suggested he try his luck on the fertile meadows surrounding the mouth of Ruby Creek, which had remained vacant since the first great smallpox epidemic. There, near to the remnants of the former villages of Spopetes, and just downriver of the settlement of Sxwoxwimelh where smallpox survivors had simultaneously cremated and interred their less fortunate relatives in their own pithouses, Súx̱'yel successfully built a farm for himself and some of his children and their spouses.

Before Súx̱'yel could make the move, however, the Elders of his family insisted that he first transfer his hereditary name and Fraser Canyon land holdings to a member of the next generation. Typically such a transfer was from father to eldest son, but in Súx̱'yel's case the decision to break with tradition appears to have been influenced by the fact that his youngest son Patrick was regarded as possessing special spiritual potential. Patrick had been born with pierced ears and a bleeding head. What is more, his head bled freshly each spring until he reached the age of twelve. This had 'scared the old people,' who had unsuccessfully hired an Indian doctor to try to unveil the secrets of Patrick's past life in an effort to explain his strange stigmata-like symptoms. Ultimately, Patrick learned the identity of his past self, and the circumstances of his previous death – knowledge that elevated rather than diminished his status. His special condition appears to have influenced his family Elders' decision to select him as the one who would remain in the canyon and carry the ancestral names and property after his father moved away.

Preparation for the name-transferring ceremony occupied Súx̱'yel's family for a full year. Taking advantage of the annual influx of people visiting the canyon fishery each summer, Súx̱'yel's family rejected the normal autumn timing for their potlatch and hosted the naming ceremony in June. Guests were invited from as far north as Sliammon, near present-day Powell River, and as far west as Vancouver Island. Hundreds of people were in attendance to witness and validate the transfer. In addition to the dozens of cattle and pigs that were butchered to feed the guests, well over $1,000 in cash and countless blankets and other items were distributed among the witnesses.

At approximately the same time that Súx̱'yel transferred his name and property to Patrick, the federal government officially banned the potlatch. Most of the academic enquiry into the potlatch prohibition has focused on those more remote Aboriginal populations where enforcement of the amended Indian Act was most difficult. The Stó:lō, located in immediate proximity to the fastest-growing non-Native urban centres in the province of British Columbia, were relatively easy targets for government agents. Indeed, the first person to be convicted for violating the anti-potlatching law was the Stó:lō man Bill Uslick.[63]

Under the anti-potlach law, high-status Stó:lō people were not merely prevented from gathering together to distribute wealth, but they were also prevented from changing residence. After the anti-potlach law came into effect those Stó:lō people with the greatest traditional wealth found themselves either unable to relocate for fear of being regarded as having either lost or abandoned their property rights in the eyes of their contemporaries, or forced to try to transfer their title to a new generation without the benefit of a public ceremony where others could witness the transmission. This, perhaps more than any of the more direct Church and government efforts to restrict movement, undoubtedly caused a reification of settlement-based collective identities among the Stó:lō population at the expense of pan-tribal associations. Certainly, it led to bitter internal twentieth-century conflicts over hereditary ownership rights among the descendants of those nineteenth-century family leaders who chose to relocate despite the ban and who had been forced to transfer their names and property at small informal gatherings where witnesses could not be called to verify proceedings. Likewise, it undermined the power of *siyá:m* and worked to reinforce the idea that political authority emanated from colonial institutions and policies rather than family networks and historical ties to the land. Perhaps more to the point, however, the banning of the potlatch simply reduced the number of opportunities for the sort of formal and ritualized intercommunity gatherings where bonds of various familial, social, economic, and political linkages were emphasized.

Throughout the colonial era the Stó:lō experienced the full thrust of external initiatives to remould their collective identities. Their proximity to major urban centres meant they were easy targets for what were as yet largely untested colonial policies. The extent to which priests and government officials concerned themselves directly with initiatives designed to regulate Indigenous movements on the landscape, while recasting Indigenous relations with the physical and social geography of their ancestors is remarkable, given the scant attention it has received from scholars. Policies ostensibly designed to facilitate the removal of Aboriginal people as obstacles to Western development have been regarded primarily in terms of their impact on Native land and resources, when, in fact, their import was much broader and struck directly at the core of Indigenous notions of collective identity and governance.

Yet, it is an ironic twist of fate, and an example of Indigenous agency and self-determination, that the increased isolation and autonomy of local Native bands that was an intended result of these colonial initiatives was simultaneously sowing the seeds for genuine expressions of supratribal collective political identity. This is not to say that the government's and Church's intentions were completely thwarted, but rather that they became immersed within an existing Indigenous tension between localized and dispersed expressions of collective identity: they became fodder for Indigenous history wars.

In the wake of the 1858 gold rush, as government and Church authorities conspired to create new geographically restricted Indigenous communities and parochial identities with indigenous leaders who owed their positions to government agents and priests, a series of countervailing colonial forces, some of them better conceived as processes than events, were subtly working to undermine the colonialists' explicit designs by enhancing and augmenting the trend towards greater supratribal identity that had been occurring independently at least since the smallpox epidemic of 1782. Frustration over their ignored overtures to develop a genuinely predictable relationship with colonial society based upon the rule of law led to increasingly bold assertions of autonomy. Ultimately, when rule of law failed to materialize, this frustration was manifested as anger and genuine military mobilization. Significantly, however, in the end it was not British actions that spawned this response, but rather, as we shall see in the next chapter, British indifference to bold-faced cross-border American aggression and vigilantism.

Together, state and ecclesiastical policies worked to promote the fragmentation of older Indigenous cross-settlement associations with the aim of fixing Coast Salish people onto what were increasingly small and foreign social and geographical landscapes. Nevertheless, while these policies were coercive, their ultimate effects were neither certain nor necessarily always imposed. As the Stó:lō engaged in the new employment opportunities provided by the canneries and other industrial enterprises, they acquired an increasingly sophisticated understanding of non-Native society. These insights were coupled with a growing appreciation of the long-term consequences of colonial actions and intentions.

Within these changed circumstances, the Stó:lō continued to respond to colonial initiatives in a manner informed by Coast Salish traditions and historiography. To a certain extent, and within certain parameters, the Stó:lō exercised agency. The Coast Salish struggled to adjust to life on geographically confined Indian reserves and in environments where their potlatch form of governance was increasingly prohibited and where new economic opportunities increasingly facilitated cross-tribal communication; at the same time, those features of their culture emphasizing the linkages between settlements worked to reinforce the importance of broadly defined collective action against colonial intrusion and aggression. Thus, despite European assumptions to the contrary, in the early colonial settlement period the fate of Aboriginal collective identity was anything but sealed.

SECTION FIVE

Expanded Movement and the Emergence of Modern Stó:lõ Collective Identity

Chapter Eight

Reservations for the Queen's Birthday Celebrations, 1864–1876

While many mid- to late nineteenth century colonial forces conspired to fix Indigenous people onto specific sites by fracturing the links between settlements and tribes, and in other ways strengthening localized collective identities nested around individual settlements, other colonial actions simultaneously gave rise to the countervailing development of the modern sense of supratribal lower Fraser watershed-wide Stó:lō collective identity. To the extent that complicated narratives emerge from any historical enquiry into identity, history is inevitably, and ironically, regarded by Stó:lō people to be as much a part of the problem as of the solution. The persistent rhetoric of the noble savage, and the current popular vogue of depicting pre-contact Indigenous society in near-utopian terms (essentially as everything Western society is not but wishes it could be) are among the many factors steering people away from studying the serious tensions that existed within Aboriginal society prior to contact. These same factors also make it difficult for some to accept that there have been historical shifts in expressions of Native collective identity despite the fact that these shifts in emphasis often reflect Indigenous agency and Native people's ability to adapt in innovative fashion to a series of rapidly changing events. Regarded in this light, it is the very power of place that, set in an ahistorical context, creates the problem of time.

Several key historical events (all associated with human movements on the landscape) served as catalysts for supratribal Stó:lō identity formation. Examined here are those associated with the common struggle for an adequate land base that were manifested through the political opportunities provided by the annual celebration of the Queen's birthday in New Westminster between 1864 and 1874, and the massive gathering associated with the visit of Governor General Lord Dufferin in 1876. To-

gether, these incidents demonstrate that while the infrastructure upon
which contemporary supratribal Stó:lō political identity is based long
predated the European settlement era, it was nonetheless particular
manipulative colonial forces that operationalized those networks and
caused them to manifest themselves as genuine political expressions.

Considered within the light of the analysis, provided in the previous
chapters, of forces contributing to a fragmentation of shared identification, the effects of the Queen's birthday celebrations and the massive
political rally associated with Dufferin's visit are probably most easily appreciated by contemporary outsiders as ironic developments set at odds
with colonial intentions. From the point of view of many lower Fraser
River Indigenous people, they are more often typically spoken about as a
natural development with roots in ancient social structures. Considered
within the context of the extant ethnohistrical literature, these overtly
political acts are indicative of the flexibility of Coast Salish leadership
and the adaptability of Coast Salish culture in the face of change.[1] Colonialism, for the Fraser River Coast Salish, was simply another factor
among many that caused their ancestors to make certain decisions. For
Indigenous people, the Queen's birthday celebrations came to epito-
mize government indifference and dismissive paternalism which, in turn,
raised among the Stó:lō issues about their place in the newly established
colonial order.

The Antiquity of Names

In 1950 Wilson Duff noted that the 'name which has been most often
applied and which the natives prefer and use themselves is Stalo.'[2]
Wayne Suttles corroborated Duff, noting that, according to his informants, 'Stalo is an ancient term.'[3] Nevertheless, one could search in vain
through the massive body of published and unpublished literature describing and discussing Pacific Coast Aboriginals in the century prior
to British Columbia's joining Confederation in 1871 and not find any
reference to a people called 'Stó:lō.' Indeed, the word apparently first
appears in print no earlier than 1882, when enthographer James Teit
assigned the title 'Dream Book of a Stalo Prophet' to a ledger he depos-
ited in the National Museum in Ottawa containing mysterious paintings
and drawings that had been left by a deceased lower Fraser Aboriginal
mystic.[4] A few years later, in 1888, a French Catholic missionary used the
word 'stalo' to describe the 'people of the Fraser,' and in 1896 the Catholic Church began publishing a translated prayer book entitled *Polyglot
Manual – Stalo Manual; or Prayers, Hymns, and the Catechism in the Stalo or*

Lower Fraser Language.[5] That same year the ethnographer Charles Hill-Tout recorded Chief Mischel[6] of Lytton referring to 'the Lower Fraser River Indians' as 'Stalo,' and in 1899 Hill-Tout again described the collective of Natives living downriver of Spuzzum in the Fraser Canyon as 'the Stalo or Lower Fraser Tribes.'[7]

It is unlikely that any of the authors of these sources invented the phrase. Rather, the uses of the term Stó:lō most likely reflect Indigenous realities as they existed at the time. Certainly, in 1938 'Stalo' was the term the Indigenous people of the region used in referring to themselves and their ancestors when they erected the 'Eayem [Iyem] Memorial' just upriver from the town of Yale. That stone marker, destroyed in 2008 by members of the Yale First Nation who opposed the downriver Stó:lō people's interpretation of the marker as a signifier of their title to the canyon fishery, commemorated a new graveyard containing the remains of people from a variety of older cemeteries – made necessary when road and railway developments destroyed older villages and their associated cemetery sites.[8] Of course, Stó:lō is also the name the majority of the lower Fraser Aboriginal people have chosen to describe themselves, as demonstrated in their membership in the Stó:lō Nation and Stó:lō Tribal Council organizations.[9]

If one thing is clear, it is that Wilson Duff cannot, as some have asserted, be credited with coining the expression Stó:lō.[10] Nineteenth-century literature proves that the word carried and conveyed an Indigenous import long before Duff arrived on the scene. But how much longer? Is its relatively recent late nineteenth-century appearance in the Western lexicon suggestive of the fact that though the term might be older than Duff's writings, it is nonetheless still a product of a colonial writer's imagination? If, as Suttles maintains, his informants of half a century ago insisted that the word Stó:lō was ancient, then why does it only make its literary debut in the 1880s? Why, in other words, did earlier explorers and fur traders not record the word? Perhaps these earlier non-Native sojourners and immigrants were less engaged with the Aboriginal people than were subsequent missionaries and ethnographers. But a potentially more satisfying explanation seems to arise when one considers that it was not until the late 1800s that it became consistently necessary for the lower Fraser Indigenous population to act collectively in the face of persistent external intrusions.

Considered in this light, and within the precedence of the identity-shaping migrations and population movements of the late eighteenth and early nineteenth centuries, one can interpret the relatively sudden appearance of the term Stó:lō as the emergent political expression of what had formerly been principally economic, social, and spiritual link-ages connecting diverse settlement groups over a broad geographical region. This nascent political consciousness emerged largely through Indigenous agency and in response to pivotal historical events that were themselves linked to processes of geographical movement.

The idea of Stó:lō identity is, therefore, indeed an ancient one. Until imperial forces threatened the very fabric of lower Fraser River Indige-nous society, however, the concept was largely social and economic, and to the extent that it was informed by ancient stories of the transformers' movements and epic floods, it was also spiritual and sacred. Moreover, it was primarily the upper-class women of a predominantly polygamous and patrilocal society who were interested in maintaining intimate so-cial connections between settlements. Likewise, lower-status men and women, by virtue of their lacking geographically anchoring hereditary rights and property, were especially vulnerable to local economic and political fluctuations and therefore dependent to a greater extent than the male elite upon maintaining intimate ties with more powerful distant relatives in other settlements for the purpose of being able to relocate to live under the sway of a more wealthy and generous leader elsewhere.

Lower Fraser River Aboriginal identity politics, therefore, were largely gender and class based in the pre–gold rush era. As such, it is not surpris-ing that the local settlement and tribal elite who supplied the explorers and fur traders with almost all their information concerning Aborigi-nal society chose to emphasize settlement and tribal political collectives and not the broader supratribal identity that would have carried greater meaning for both high-status women and lower-status men and women. This Indigenous bias is, not surprisingly, reflected in the early European documentation. Below I document those post–gold rush colonial forces that inadvertently worked against the Native upper-class males' disposi-tion to emphasize local political units, and explore the manner in which the broader Stó:lō identity that had previously been of primary interest to high-status women and lower-class males came to prominence and was, in fact, ultimately embraced by certain prominent members of the male hereditary elite.

Mapping and Politics in the Spring of 1864

One of the oldest and most contested chestnuts in west coast Native–newcomer history is the debate surrounding Governor James Douglas' intentions regarding the creation of Indian reserves on the B.C. mainland in the spring of 1864. At question is the extent to which surveyor Sargeant William McColl's actions were consistent with the governor's instructions or a serious departure – as characterized by Chief Commissioner of Lands and Works Joseph Trutch, following Douglas' retirement.[11] Earlier it was demonstrated how the process of reserve creation was a key component of Governor Douglas' plan to 'create' Indian communities. Little could Douglas have anticipated, however, that his successor's wholesale reversal of these policies would actually sow the seeds for a unified Stó:lō identity set increasingly in opposition to non-Native society.

News of James Douglas' impending retirement in the spring of 1864 caused anxiety among the Stó:lō. While his Indian policies were often frustratingly vaguely defined (a fact that ultimately caused Native people no end of problems after his retirement), Douglas was nonetheless regarded by Indigenous people as an ally and protector against the growing and increasingly demanding local settler population. His status stemmed not only from his long tenure as Chief Factor of the Hudson's Bay Company, but also from his role as representative of the Queen. Fearing the new colonial administration, which now included for the first time an elected assembly to directly represent settler interests, would abandon them, the 'Fraser River Indians uttered many lamentations over their deserted condition.'[12] Within the temperance societies, a rumour quickly passed throughout 'all the Indian tribes that all who spread the word of the Catholic priest will have misfortune: and once the big new English chief [governor] arrives, He will reject the earth and the priests and all those who pray.'[13]

Some time in late March 1864 a delegation of lower Fraser Indians travelled to New Westminster to lay their common concerns directly before the outgoing governor. This collective political action has parallels with the previous decade's large gatherings of Coast Salish people in Puget Sound, who debated how to respond to U.S. treaty offers.[14] In the pre-colonial era, a similar precedent for such extensive intertribal political cooperation has been recorded with respect to the great 1830s' Cowichan-led, Coast Salish attack against the more northern Lekwiltok ('Unkillable Things') of Johnston Strait.[15] In each case it was the incursions of an external enemy into Coast Salish territory that had inspired the Indigenous leadership to activate as political linkages those affiliations more typically deployed as intertribal social, economic, and spiritual connections.

Beginning in the 1780s the Lekwiltok began acquiring significant

American firearms from Bostonian fur traders visiting the northern coast of Vancouver Island. These weapons, and the fact that the smallpox epidemic of 1782 seems not to have affected them, provided the Lekwiltok with a military advantage that enabled them to relentlessly push southward, killing, enslaving, and permanently displacing the northern Coast Salish people. By the 1840s they had successfully occupied northern Coast Salish settlements in areas now better known as Campbell River and Comox, and assumed control of many of the adjoining resources. From their new position at the northern end of Georgia Strait, Lekwiltok raids on the central and southern Coast Salish people living in the vicinity of the Fraser River and southern Vancouver Island increased.[16] It was this development that had led Cowichan and neighbouring Coast Salish people to devise collective plans to halt the Lekwiltok's southward advance. Political and military cooperation had proven effective then – the Lekwiltok had been stopped.

In 1864, as alcoholism and disease reduced their numbers and recently arrived European farmers occupied more and more of their lands, the central Fraser Valley tribes sought to recreate something of the ephemeral political unity that had served them so well two generations earlier. This time, however, the tactic would be more diplomatic than military, for while violence was occasionally threatened and increasingly implied, it was never opted for during the early colonial era. The Stó:lō chose to walk softy and carry a big stick. But in a period where the balance of power on the northwest coast was rapidly shifting in response to the arrival of new settlers, the Stó:lō stick became ever smaller in relation to the power at the disposal of non-Native society. Indeed, by the first decade of the twentieth century the Indigenous war club had become, in the eyes of the representatives of newcomer society, little more than an annoying switch.

It is uncertain if the Stó:lō were aware of the statements James Douglas had made to the colony's first Legislative Assembly on the eve of his retirement in January 1864.[17] Likely, one of the Oblate priests conveyed the news to temperance society members. The governor chose to describe his policy of reserving 'lands embracing the Village Sites, cultivated fields, and favourite resorts of the several tribes' as having 'secur[ed] them from the encroachments of Settlers, and forever removing the fertile cause of agrarian disturbance'; no doubt this formlation was meant to soothe the settlers' own fears that B.C.'s Native population would retard the colony's economic growth. Douglas' assertion that the effects of these policies had 'been productive of the happiest effects on the minds of the Natives' is best appreciated in light of his desire to allay fears that isolated farmers on remote pre-emptions might fall prey to hostile Natives. Furthermore, in a blatant lie most likely designed to curry favour with the settler population by creating the popular impression that he was someone who had facilitated rather than hindered the colony's advancement from fur trade backwater to agricultural and industrial centre, Douglas stated that the reserves 'thus partially defined and set apart, in no case exceed the proportion of ten acres for each family concerned, and are to be held as the joint and common property of the several tribes, being intended for their exclusive use and benefit, and especially as a provision for the aged, the helpless, and the infirm.'[18] The fact remains, however, that reserves significantly larger than ten acres per family had been created, and that when on occasion they had been created smaller, Douglas had regularly intervened to make them larger.

It is the concluding section of the outgoing governor's speech that provides the clearest indication of his true intentions towards the Aboriginal population, for there he explained the limits of his reserve policies, noting that they were 'not intended to interfere with the private rights of individuals of the Native Tribes, or to incapacitate them, as such, from holding land; on the contrary, they have precisely the same rights of acquiring and possessing land in their individual capacity, either by purchase or by occupation under the Preemption Law, as other classes of Her Majesty's subjects; provided they in all respects comply with the legal conditions of tenure by which land is held in this Colony.'[19]

These measures, he clarified, were designed with an eye to 'averting evils pregnant with danger to the peace and safety of the Colony, and of confirming by those acts of justice and humanity, the fidelity and attachment of the Native Tribes to Her Majesty's rule.'[20] In other words, Douglas was clinging to the hope that the Aboriginal population, and in particular the Stó:lō of the fertile lands along the lower Fraser River, would continue making 'progress,' as he saw it, along the path to civilization and integration; that like his own Aboriginal wife, perhaps, they would within a single generation cease to require large communal reserves and become, for all intents and purposes, British subjects living on individual plots of private land, indistinguishable from the recently arrived English farmers except for the colour of their skin.

For the Aboriginal population, this vision was at best only partially appealing. For those Fraser Valley Natives still lacking reserves, as well as those who had encountered the racism that characterized the new settler communities off-reserve, change was occurring too rapidly, and in too many instances, at the discretion of people other than themselves. Even if the Lower Fraser Natives had wanted to become assimilated, the non-Native population was making it abundantly clear that Natives were not welcome in their society. It was within this context that the Stó:lõ delegation met with Governor Douglas on the lawn of the government building on a cool March morning in 1864. Their arrival made apparent to Douglas that his dream of quick integration was not coming to fruition; that the Natives were not necessarily as 'quiet and well disposed' as he had characterized them to the Legislative Assembly.

Calling a number of prominent government officials as witnesses, as well as the surveyor assigned to demarcate their reserve boundaries, Douglas, speaking in Chinook and then English, assured the Stó:lõ chiefs and instructed his staff that 'all lands claimed by the Indians were to be included in the reserve; the Indians were to have as much land as they wished, and in no case to lay off a reserve under 100 acres.'[21] The Stó:lõ left well satisfied, and within a few short days William McColl arrived in the central Fraser Valley and began the job of marking off the reserves. By mid-May he reported that he had 'laid [them] off accordingly'[22] (refer to Map 19).

For the Stó:lõ, this was a major political victory. Collective action had worked for the them: their concerns had been addressed, and they were publicly given the governor's assurance that the land demarcated for each reserve community would be secured through a consistent and equitable system that would ensure that each settlement had the resource base to achieve self-sufficiency in the emerging new economy. Quickly the chiefs began working with McColl to identify as reserve land not only the small cultivated potato patches associated with every settlement, but also thousands of acres of as yet uncultivated meadow and pasture land, as well as forests, adjacent to their settlements.

But what was regarded by Natives to be securing a future was interpreted by settlers to be the thwarting of dreams. Literally within days of McColl beginning his work some of the most recently arrived immigrants began complaining to their legislative representatives that the land they had intended to pre-empt, indeed the land that some of them had already begun clearing and cultivating and in some cases had constructed homes on, fell within the newly identified Indian reserves.[23] The local media picked up the story and decried Douglas' March address to the Stó:lõ delegates on the Government House lawn as a 'grand potlatch' at which the outgoing governor had 'given away... to the Indians... seven or eight miles square' of land in the central Fraser Valley. As far as the paper's editor was concerned, Douglas' promise to the Stó:lō leadership was indicative of the extent to which the governor had failed to establish policies that would elevate Natives into European-style civilization. They were, instead, proof that Douglas himself had regressed and fallen into a savage state of being; that 'in one fell swoop' his Indian-like actions had 'throw[n] so large a tract of settled country into the hands of the Indians' that it was almost certain that the effect would be 'trouble between the white settlers and the natives.'[24]

The following week, in an unrelated incident far to the north on a trail at the head of distant Bute Inlet, Tsilhqot'in (Chilcotin) Natives killed a party of road construction workers.[25] The Legislative Assembly simply linked the two events as proof that the retiring governor had left the colony in an untenable situation: local Fraser Valley agricultural land was being denied to loyal British settlers and provided to Indians who were not necessarily farming it, while farther north Indians were killing white men who were involved in trying to facilitate the development of the colony's mineral wealth.

It was within this climate of racial tension that, on 14 May 1864, the new governor, Frederick Seymour, contacted the priests at St Mary's Mission and informed them of his desire 'to reunite all of the savage chiefs and their subjects for the 24th of May, The Queen's birthday.' He then 'ordered' the priests to 'inform the Indians and ... [to] help in the organization of this event,' a task the Oblates 'happily consented to.'[26] According to non-Native observers, ten days later, on the muddy grounds outside Government House in New Westminster, between 3,500 and 6,000 Aboriginals gathered, most of whom were Lower Fraser River residents.[27] Governor Seymour described the assemblage as 'probably the largest Native gathering ever seen on this side of the Rocky Mountains.'[28] Various observers recorded their impressions, but none in such detail as Father Gendre, OMI, who actually accompanied the Salish flotilla as the canoes travelled downriver from St Mary's Mission to the governor's residence in New Westminster. His account portrays vividly the extent to which boundaries had been created separating Natives from newcomers, and the growing effects that that realization had on an Indigenous sense of shared identity, or nation building. Because of its richness, and despite its length, Father Gendre's account is presented here almost verbatim:

> There was little time to lose in informing the tribes, even those in the farthest distances, of this news, I sent a chief travelling throughout the camps in a distance covering over one hundred miles. In four or five days all those

who could respond to the calling had been notified; and in order not to miss their chance, they came and reunited immediately at St Marie, where we were given the opportunity to educate and strengthen them ...

The 22nd of May, prior to the eve of the big day, was for us a day of hard work and preoccupation. It was not an easy task for us to manoeuvre three thousand natives, to prepare them to meet at a designated area, not far from New Westminster, in order to form one compact mass on the Fraser river and to land near the governor's house, to compose three speeches that the chiefs of the main tribes were to recite to His Excellency, etc.[29]

It is unclear to what extent the three speeches conveyed three different messages from three different Indigenous constituencies, or a single message in three languages. Certainly the governor's brief response, as described below, was aimed at a single Indigenous audience. That such a large grouping of Native people could be organized so quickly speaks to the Oblate's organizational skills and the sense of urgency Aboriginal people felt regarding their collective future vis-à-vis newcomer society. The collective nature of the event was demonstrated not merely in the political messages, but also in the very nature of the coordinated movement of people Father Gendre described from St Mary's Mission downriver to the governor's residence in New Westminster:

In the afternoon the weather cleared after a long bout of rain. I gave the signal to leave and we embarked, singing, on the short waves of the Fraser. We raised our elegant flags, as did all the chiefs; our fleet resembled a triumphant parade. A few miles from the designated encampment, a steamboat passed traveling from Fort-Yale en route to New Westminster. On board were the governor, the colonial secretary, and the ship captain. These three men, charmed by the looks we bestowed upon them, turned toward my canoe and saluted our flags by waving their hats. We returned the gesture in the native fashion. This salutation dissipated any past worries we had anticipated about the governor's intentions.

Upon arrival at two miles from New Westminster we pulled ashore and camped in the forest for the night. How I would have loved to describe to our dear inexperienced and scholastic brothers the wonders of this night spent under the stars, under the great trees of the forest, in the company of close to three thousand natives! Brothers of Breton and the South (of France) believe me, it was pure poetry!

Impressive indeed. Moreover, as the priest goes on to explain, the awesome spectacle of the first day's events were exceeded by the pageantry, pregnant with political significance, of the following day's activities:

> Early the following morning the whole party was on its feet. The bells of each chief could be heard through the thick of the woods, instantly five or six savages fell to their knees on the moss to worship the one the angels love in the heavens in indelible beauty. O religion! Thou art so beautiful! How you help the poor child of the rallied forest grow around your immortal flag!
>
> At nine o'clock, I received from New Westminster the order to organize our naval army; but all our men were already in their vessels with flags flying. Soon the R.P. Fouquet arrived, accompanied by R.P. Grandidier, at the head of five hundred natives that expanded our rows. The R.P. Fouquet held a large white paper, wrapped in a magnificent red ribbon, in his right hand, that was quite intriguing to our natives. He travels through the rows to give his orders, and at his command all the vessels moved off shore; six to seven hundred ships slide into the current of the Fraser. Sixty flags, on which shines the symbol of redemption, wave in the free will of the wind; fifty-five native chiefs lead the first line; the students of St Mary's hold a place of honor. They break into the song of the oar, and three thousand five hundred mouths hold the mountains and the forests at bay. What a panorama! What enthusiasm! As for me, it was difficult to hold back shouts of admiration.

When the Native flotilla arrived in New Westminster a large crowd of nervous, and rather awestruck, settlers greeted it. (See Figure 11.) From that point onward, all those celebrating the Queen's birthday, and participating in the associated politicking, would be in the same location but occupying distinct racially designated spaces. The Native community assumed positions appropriate to conveying their message(s) to the government, while the non-Natives looked on as though the politics was itself a feature of the birthday celebrations:

> A few moments later, we arrived at our landing stage, quite close to the governor's house. A large number of whites, friends or enemies, were present at the landing stage and assisted in the spectacle of disembarkation. The reunion took place a few feet away from the residence. The R.P. Fouquet thus opened his grand paper wrapped in red ribbon, he pronounces all the native chiefs, and carefully, in order not to insult their vanity, places them in a half circumference so that no one comes last. The school children of

St Marie formed two rows above the chiefs, and our three or four thousand natives grouped themselves around the semi-circle. All the colonists of New Westminster contemplated the *Indian meeting*. Finally, at noon, the R.P. Fouquet, who had been assigned a place of honor, arrives at the residence of His Excellency. The Governor thus emerges from his lodgings with his first officers in full dress; he is accompanied by his guards and led by a musical band. Upon arrival, all heads turned and a thunder of twenty thousand cheers for His Excellency could be heard far in the distance. What a dignified moment for our dear natives![30]

Governor Seymour's arrival on the muddy lawn in front of his official residence has to be considered in the context of the meeting Douglas had held at the same location a few short weeks earlier. Prior to Douglas' meeting with the central Fraser Valley chiefs to address their concerns over the size of reserves, official Indian policy in the broad sense had never been conveyed directly from the Crown's representative to Indigenous people. Certainly Governor Douglas had on a number of occasions in the past resolved disputes and clarified his position 'on the spot.' But before 1864 Native people had not collectively approached the government's top official demanding that government policy be applied equally to all Native communities. Following the meeting with Douglas, William McColl had been immediately sent to demarcate Stó:lō reserves according to Stó:lō specifications.

Thus, as the 24 May Queen's birthday celebrations unfolded, Governor Seymour was presented with a series of speeches by Native leaders who had either just had their new reserves demarcated, or who had within the past couple of days heard about such activities from their neighbours and relatives:

When there was silence, the first chief, who had been given orders to speak first, presented himself to His Excellency, gave a grand salute and proceeded to recite imperturbably his short speech given in his native language, interpreted in Chinook by another native, and finally translated into English by the R.P. Fouquet. The first speech followed by the second, followed by a third. The governor responded to the three speeches with one. The R.P. Fouquet translated the words of the governor into Chinook, and three good interpreters would then translate these words into their own language, with loud bellowing voices in order to be heard by the people far in the distance. This truly unusual scene brought smiles to the lips of the spectators.

11. Indian canoe races on occasion of Queen's birthday and meeting Governor Seymour, 1867. Courtesy of B.C. Archives, PDP00252.

The speeches were thus followed by the distribution of presents. Each chief presented himself before His Excellency to receive a gift reflective of his royalty: a pretty cap laced with a gold braid that dazzles, like the sun's rays, the joys of the day; fifty five chiefs, fifty five royal caps. The little school children of St Marie all took turns in front of the governor to receive promises, a handshake and a complimentary tie. With the completion of the gift distribution the governor left the chair and reentered his dwelling among loud and dizzying cheers.

A joyous meal was offered to our dear Indians. They were lavished by bread, cookies, molasses and tobacco, their appetites satisfied with delight because for them, molasses is a food that was for the Gods of a fable.[31]

While the impressive gathering was ostensibly a celebration of Queen Victoria's birthday, Governor Seymour had other, more politic reasons for desiring to meet with the Aboriginal populace. (See Figures 12 and 13.) In a letter to London, he explained that in truth he had originally conceived of the gathering primarily as an opportunity to soothe the Lower Fraser Indians' fears over Douglas' departure and to ingratiate himself in their minds: 'It became desirable for me to make myself known to the natives and show them that I had succeeded to all the power of my predecessor and to his solicitude for their welfare.' Yet, it was the intervening 'recent intelligence of the terrible massacre of our Countrymen at Bute Inlet, and vague rumours ... of a general insurrection of the Indians being imminent' that set the tone for the massive get-together.[32] While the Stó:lõ and their immediate neighbours feasted on the governor's biscuits and molasses the Tsilhqot'in of Bute Inlet retreated before an advancing retaliatory military expedition.

Reflecting upon the Queen's birthday celebrations in a letter to the Colonial Office three months after the gathering, Seymour drew obvious pleasure in contrasting the written petition from the Lower Fraser Natives with the violent methods employed by the Tsilhqot'in. For the Stó:lõ, however, the non-violent nature of their political expression was less significant than the experience of having spoken with a united voice and through the newcomers' written medium. They came away from the gathering with a new sense of their collective power and influence. To the extent that it was impossible not to notice that following the delivery of the speeches the Indigenous leadership were relegated to eating biscuits and molasses at the river's bank while the 'whites repaired to the Legislative Hall where they partook of a sumptuous dejeuner provided by His Excellency,' the Stó:lõ also became increasingly aware of the ra-

12. Stó:lō gathered to express to Governor Seymour their satisfaction with Reserves recently created under James Douglas' tenure as Governor, 24 May 1864. Note Union Jacks and Catholic Temperance flags. Courtesy of B.C. Archives, PN 8947_AA-00013_BCNATIVES_GS300.

13. Coast Salish leaders gathered to dialogue with Governor Seymour, May 1867. Courtesy of B.C. Archives, PN 8949.

cial boundary and its maintenance that was coming to shape their collective Aboriginal identity.[33]

Queen Victoria's 1864 birthday celebration in New Westminster represents a genuinely pivotal moment in northwest coast Indigenous history. The gathering was of unprecedented scope and rife with pageantry, but more importantly, it involved the movement of Coast Salish people from diverse, scattered, and increasingly isolated settlements to a single site for a concentrated political purpose. To be sure, large intertribal gatherings were nothing new to the Coast Salish, and especially the lower Fraser Stó:lō. The annual summer migration of thousands of coastal people to the lower Fraser Canyon for the purpose of procuring salmon to be wind dried there provides perhaps the best example of such 'traditional' opportunities for gatherings. In addition, in the early years of the twentieth century Chief William 'Billy' Sepass of Skowkale related to a non-Native friend that Chilliwack had formerly been the site of great intertribal gatherings that were held every fourth year to 'celebrate the sun ceremony.'[34] Contemporary Elders such as Jeff Point of Skowkale still carry and share oral traditions of these events.[35]

All of these pre-colonial gatherings, however, appear to have been held principally for either social reasons, or for focused economic or spiritual reasons. The 1864 Queen's birthday celebration may well have built upon such Indigenous precedent, but ultimately, as the celebration turned into an annual event, it came to be regarded by the Aboriginal participants as a primarily political occasion where shared visions were presented and defended, and where shared collective identity was nurtured and strengthened. The roughly 4,000 Natives in attendance each year between 1864 and 1874 were provided only brief opportunities to publicly address the governor. As such, the pre-birthday gatherings at St Mary's Mission hosted by the Oblate priests assumed even greater importance, as they provided opportunities for the leaders of roughly fifty regional settlements comprising at least three distinct language groups to compose a single coordinated political statement or at the least a series of them.[36]

Thus, it was as a single body that the lower Fraser Natives and some of their neighbours made known to the colonial and later federal Canadian authorities their collective concerns, hopes, and wishes. In particular, at the first Queen's birthday celebration in 1864 they attempted to explain that those who had only days before had their reserves created by William McColl were well satisfied with their land, and that those still lacking a reserve wanted the same; that they expected Governor Seymour to protect and honour their land base, and to provide them with compensation for lost resources outside of the reserves. Thus what was to become known as the 'Indian land question' came to lie at the heart of the movement towards modern collective Stó:lō political identity: 'Please to protect our land, that it will not be small for us; many are well pleased with their reservations, and many wish that their reservations be marked out for them. Please to give us good things as to make us become as the good white man, as an exchange for our land occupied by white men.'[37]

This message, composed in the wake of Douglas' promise and Mc-Coll's surveys, was to be repeated annually over the ensuing years with only slight modification in wording. What would eventually change were the government's responses. So long as incidents like the Bute Inlet conflict raised the spectre of Indian violence, the government was willing to engage in meaningful discussions with Native people to avoid open conflict. As legal scholar Douglas Harris has observed, in nineteenth-century British Columbia it was the government, and not the Aboriginal people, whose actions concerning Aboriginal land policy were unpredictable and outside the rule of law.[38] Indeed, as Seymour's correspondence to the Colonial Office in the summer of 1864 makes clear, an inverse relation existed between the degree to which Indians behaved in a civilized manner and the extent to which the government addressed their concerns. The greater the perceived threat of violence from supposed savages, the more the government strove to encourage progress in civilization. But the more a Native community demonstrated that its members were civilized (i.e., the more they acted peacefully, used written petitions, and sent their children to residential schools, etc.), the less the government considered them worthy of consideration and the more the government saw fit to ignore their own established laws and protocols for dealing with Natives.

In his 1864 Queen's birthday speech, Governor Seymour announced to the assembled Natives: 'As you say, there is plenty of land here, for both White men and Indians. You shall not be disturbed in your reserves. I shall protect you from both bad White men and from bad Indians. I am glad you want to be civilized and raised to an equality with the White Men. Cultivate your Lands; send your children to school; listen to what the clergymen tell you, and believe in it.'[39]

Within a few years Seymour's promises that the Stó:lō would not be disturbed in their reserves and, more specifically, that their reserves 'shall not be reduced without my personal inspection,'[40] were broken, and reserves laid out under Douglas' directions reduced by over 90 per cent.[41] Moreover, the 'good things' that the Stó:lō had asked for in 'exchange for our land occupied by white men' were never provided. A treaty was never negotiated, and compensation never provided.

Among members of colonial society, the peaceful nature of the first Queen's birthday gathering caused non-Natives to view the subsequent gatherings not as political events where through the process of racial boundary maintenance two distinct groups negotiated their relationship, but as festivals, or 'celebrations' with ample opportunities to observe exotic others behaving exotically. Whites gathered not to hear the Aboriginal political speeches and to engage in cross-racial political dialogues, but to listen to Native music, marvel at Native costumes, and be thrilled by Native canoe races.[42] (See Figure 14). For the Stó:lō, by way of contrast, who regard all gatherings, especially those associated with music, drumming, singing, and eating, and in particular, any event associated with human movement over great physical space, to be spiritually charged, the birthday celebrations were powerful events in other ways as well. As such, they were inherently political.

At the Queen's birthday gatherings geographically fixed tribal and settlement-based collective identities were momentarily subsumed in a supratribal identity cast in opposition to the political power of colonial society. With each passing year Aboriginal leaders more fully appreciated that whatever distinctions existed between themselves and their variously defined communities, a more meaningful division as concerned their ability to govern land and resources existed between Indians generally and the white hosts of the Queen's birthday celebrations. Identities cast in relation to tribally based watersheds (as discussed in Chapter 2) and transformed ancestors remained meaningful, but in the face of mounting non-Native competition over land and resources Native people recognized the value of a united voice. Non-Natives' claims to land were not based on ancestral references to place, and non-Natives did not employ the potlatch to assert property ownership. To use a modern metaphor, the Western and Aboriginal systems of governance and resource management simply could not interface.

Henceforth, despite the government's best efforts to promote the contrary, the Lower Fraser River Indians acted increasingly as a single unit. The urgency of a rapidly diminishing land base remained at the heart of their shared vision and their shared identity. As such, in 1867, when Governor Seymour's lieutenant Joseph Trutch reduced the Indian reserves established under Douglas' directions, it became suddenly clear

14. Queen's birthday celebration, New Westminster, 1867. Courtesy of B.C. Archives, D-07233.

that even the Queen's representative could not necessarily be trusted to respect Stó:lō interests or to uphold the British rule of law.[43] The government simply did not fulfil promises; and the Crown's honour was severely undermined. As a result, the Stó:lō, like some other Indigenous communities in British Columbia, increasingly focused their energies on achieving a means to become more independent of government control through the implementation of new systems of Aboriginal self-government. As Douglas Harris has documented for the Stó:lō's upriver Nlakapamux neighbours, Indigenous people sought to create a system that would establish predictable rule-based relationships between Indigenous and newcomer society.[44] But to be meaningful, the new Native government initiatives needed more than predictable rules. They also needed to be crafted in such a way as to not directly challenge or undermine existing expressions of Indigenous governance and identity. The option that emerged for the Salish of the lower Fraser River was a model of supratribal collective governance built upon the existing network of family connections that would ensure consistent protection of resources and standardized political experiences throughout the broadest territory.

Chapter Nine

Collective Governance and the Lynching
of Louie Sam

While the annual Queen's birthday gatherings steadily enhanced a sense
of Stó:lō collective identity, they ultimately proved unsuccessful in affecting government policy or non-Native public opinion. Indeed, it was the
failure of the gatherings to cause real change in either colonial or later
federal/provincial government policy that provided the subsequent impetus to try to create mulisettlement collective governance to advance
and protect shared Aboriginal interests. These developments had two
key expressions. The first was in the Stó:lō people's autonomous 1879
attempt to establish a genuine supratribal political body that would provide local self-governance under the rubric of the British Crown and
Canadian federalism. The second was largely in response to the government's failure to act upon the first initiative. The Stó:lō will to operate
as a collective political unit with genuine political authority manifested
itself briefly, but poignantly, in 1884. Early that year, before the drifting
ice had disappeared from the Fraser River, hundreds of lower Fraser Aboriginal people travelled by canoe to gather in Chilliwack and contemplate a coordinated supratribal military campaign against the non-Native
civilian population of Whatcom County, Washington. Stó:lō ire had
been raised after a mob of dozens of mounted Americans had crossed
into Canada and lynched a young Stó:lō boy who was then in the custody
of Canadian police officers. It was the Canadian government's abject
failure to protect Aboriginal life and liberty that effectively operationalized Stó:lō supratribal political identity, and the explicit hypocrisy in
subsequent Canadian overtures to bring the guilty Americans to justice
that demonstrated to the Stó:lō that external governing bodies could not
and should not represent their interests.

A Community of Communities

By 1874 the Stó:lō and their neighbours had become disenchanted with both the monarch's birthday celebrations and the government's patronizing responses to their concerns. That year, during the pre-gathering meeting at St Mary's,[1] the chiefs decided that it was insufficient to simply ask for general protection of reserves and compensation for lost lands and then leave it to the government to interpret what that meant. Instead, they drafted a detailed petition outlining not only their concerns, but also what they considered just options for government redress. Local land issues were identified on a tribe-by-tribe basis, but the petition demanded that a consistent and equitable land and governance policy be applied to all lower Fraser Indians. In this way, the Stó:lō made clear that they were a community of communities. An equitable share of resources between Native settlements and consistent access to government services were crucial. At the heart of the petition lay the statement that reserves needed to include a minimum of eighty acres per nuclear family. The chiefs explained that they were frustrated with the government's inconsistent treatment and unpredictable behaviour: 'We are commencing to believe that the aim of the white men is to exterminate us as soon as they can, although we have always been quiet, obedient, kind and friendly to the whites.' Clearly recognizing that their efforts to behave in a civilized fashion had actually worked against them with the government, they put the government on notice that their tactics might soon change, that failure to give them 'satisfaction' would 'create ill feelings, irritation among our people, and we cannot say what will be the consequence.'[2]

The government's failure to respond to the 1874 petition caused the Stó:lō leadership in mid-May 1875 to write to Superintendant Powell stating that they would not participate in that year's Queen's birthday celebration, that through her agents, Queen Victoria had 'not been a good mother and Queen to us, she has not watched over us that we should have enough land for the support of our families.'[3] The time was fast approaching to take matters into their own hands – to create a government that would be responsive to their cultural traditions and particular needs, but also established in a form and style that the European newcomers could relate to and understand.

A New Generation of Leadership

Within the colonial-era historical record describing the Stó:lō, the ma-

jority of people referred to as 'chiefs' or 'headmen' are associated with
individual settlement-based communities. As was demonstrated, state or
ecclesiastical authorities created a good portion of these authority positions. Certain leaders, however, are described as 'hereditary.' Within this
same period, a few names also begin to be associated with some form of
supratribal leadership. In particular Alexis Squiteelanoo[4] of Cheam and
Liquitim of Yale, but Casmir of Langley, William Sepass of Skowkale, and
Pierre Ayessik of Hope are also periodically referred to in terms such as
'Head Chief of the Lower Fraser Indians.'[5] In 1950 Wilson Duff reported
that all his informants 'were clear there had been no chiefs – in the sense
of men chosen to fill an office of leadership – in former times,' that is,
prior to the colonial era there had been no one 'appointed by the Indian
Superintendent to conduct the affairs of a reserve.'[6]

The Elders Duff worked with explained that while there were no
'chiefs,' 'there had been 'leaders' and 'main leaders.'[7] In Halq'eméylem,
a leader was referred to as *siyá:m*. Edmund Lorenzetto explained to Duff
that 'a siyá:m was a good man who talked to his people to keep them
straight and to settle rows. He didn't really boss the people around, that
is why they liked him, but all the people would take his advice.'[8] Three
generations earlier Charles Hill-Tout described Coast Salish leadership
in similar terms: 'The power and influence of a chief in any given tribe
would seem to have depended upon his personal qualities and character, the more able and intelligent he was the greater and wider his influence; and one might lay it down as a general rule that the office of
headman in a Salish tribe was held by the ablest, most intelligent and
therefore wealthiest man in the tribe.' As such, 'a Salish chief was rather
a patriarch than a ruler. He was essentially the tribal father and stood to
the tribe as a whole on much the same footing as did the several elder-
men to their individual families.'[9]

Persuasive, charismatic Stó:lō siyá:m were, as Duff learned, 'ranked
in an ascending scale regardless of place of residence, but this was a
social ranking and only incidentally and to a limited degree a political
one.'[10] According to Duff's informant Edmund Lorenzetto, 'The two
most highly respected by the Stalo have always been the heads of permanent family lines at Yale and Langley.'[11] Hill-Tout referred to such Coast
Salish leaders as 'divisional heads,' noting 'in many groups or divisions
these heads received scant recognition … [They] had nothing to do with
the local affairs of the other villages. Their function seems to be to represent the group or division as a whole and look after its interests.'[12] Given
that the hallmarks of a good 'traditional' siyá:m were 'wisdom, ability, in-

dustry, generosity, humility, and pacifism,' and that the most respected and therefore influential leaders were able to demonstrate 'the marks of wealth,'[13] we can safely assume that the most respected leaders were not only experts in dispute resolution, but also controllers or regulators of important resources. They were, in other words, the ones who took care of people and communities.

It is not surprising, therefore, that Wilson Duff's informants identified the two most prominent pre-colonial leaders as having always come from Yale and Langley. Yale was at the entrance of the region's most important fishing and fish-processing sites, and, prior to the 1858 gold rush, Langley was the only place where coveted European trade goods could be readily accessed. Both locations were scenes of massive gatherings where not only important financial transactions occurred, but where information could be shared and social or diplomatic relationships arranged and maintained. Moreover, as was discussed earlier, the resources of both sites were, much to the chagrin of the Hudson's Bay Company traders at Langley, strictly regulated through Indigenous hereditary access protocols.

By the 1860s farmland was fast becoming the resource that people most needed to access, and the disputes siyá:m were asked to resolve increasingly involved interpersonal and interracial violence and tension surrounding the land issue. Given that in the absence of adequate reserve lands, and with the banning of the potlatch, the canyon fishery retained its social and economic significance long after other retail outlets presented themselves as alternatives to Fort Langley, it is understandable that the Yale chief retained a prominent status well into the settlement era. It also explains, however, why a new cadre of leaders arose – leaders who were equipped to best look after the people by advocating for them in their relations with the colonial and then federal and provincial regimes.

Alexis Squiteelanoo of Cheam and Pierre Ayessik of Hope increasingly assumed roles as supratribal leaders throughout the 1860s and 1870s. They do not, however, appear to have done this in opposition to more traditional leaders such as Yale's Liquitim or Langley's Casmir, but rather more as protégés of the older elite. In fact, both Alexis and Pierre were related to Liquitim. Indeed, while many Elders today remember Pierre Ayessik of Hope as having been a prominent 'Church chief,' his authority was not based entirely upon his relationship with colonial authorities. Later generations argued that proof that 'he was a real siyá:m' was illustrated by the fact that he had been born with pierced ears and

nasal septum – clear indications of upper-class status and the endorsement of prominent ancestor spirits.[14]

Alexis' and Pierre's names also appear alongside Liquitim's on petitions to the government.[15] Unlike Liquitim, however, these new regional
leaders increasingly communicated in English.[16] Additionally, through
their involvement in the temperance societies, they had close relations
with the influential Roman Catholic missionaries at St Mary's. By the
time British Columbia joined Confederation in 1871, Alexis and Pierre
had together assumed the role of primary political spokesmen for the
Stó:lō collective (with Soowahlie's Methodist chief, Captain John, retaining a distinct though somewhat marginalized regional voice). From
these positions they provided broad guidance and leadership, as the Indigenous people of the lower Fraser River adjusted to what Old Pierre
of Katzie would later refer to as 'a new era.'[17] Ultimately, the perceived
roles of the two generations of leaders were the same: look after community interests as best they could. It was the definition of what constituted
both *community* and *community interests* that was changing.

Dialogues with the Crown

In the decade following the 1858 gold rush the lower Fraser Aboriginal
population retained an immense, if ultimately unfounded, trust in the
honour of the British Crown. The first formal associations established
with white society were, as per Indigenous custom, honour based, and
built upon personal relationships. Indigenous people's petitions demonstrate a persistent faith that the British Crown would eventually honour its personal commitment to providing adequate reserve acreage to
facilitate farming around existing Native settlement sites. By the 1870s
this faith was being seriously questioned, and Aboriginal people were
looking for new and better ways of creating binding relations with the
representatives of settler society. By far the greatest concern was the omnipresent fear that in meeting their persistent demands for a more equitable ratio of people to acres the Crown might abandon the practice of
making existing Native settlements the core of new agriculturally based
Indian reserves, and instead forcibly uproot Aboriginal people and compel them to live on a singe giant reserve far removed from their ancestral
homes. This concern was neither irrational nor groundless. The U.S.
government's policy in adjacent Washington Territory had been precisely this. As early as 1860 the Coast Salish living on the British side of
the 49th parallel had sought assurances from Governor Douglas that the

same would not happen to them. Indeed, as Lieutenant R.C. Mayne of the Royal Navy learned first-hand, the Coast Salish living in British territory had developed an intense hatred of Boston Men 'owing in great measure to the system adopted by Americans of moving them away from their own village when sites became settled by whites. The Indians often express dread lest we should adopt the same course, and have lately petitioned Governor Douglas on the subject.'[18]

From a colonial administrative perspective, such reserves made sense. One of Joseph Trutch's strongest criticisms of the adjoinng village reserve system was that it separated the open farmlands from one another, making them less appealing to arriving white settlers. In places like Chilliwack, it also made it difficult for the government to establish urban township centres.[19] Although the idea of creating central reservations does not seem to have been seriously considered by Douglas, the spectre of forced resettlement on communal reserves was a constant terror for the Stó:lō.

By the time British Columbia, with its capital at Victoria, joined Confederation in 1871 support for a centralzed reserve had gained a great deal of currency among certain members of the colonial elite. Politicians and administrators in Ottawa were especially intrigued by the apparent success the Anglican missionary William Duncan had in converting and civilizing a large number of Tsimshian Indians. Duncan's technique had been to remove those Indians who followed his doctrine from their old settlements and to re-establish them on his new Christian colony of Metlakatla.[20] So impressed were both Ottawa and Victoria officials with Duncan's achievements that his advice was solicited to help resolve the intractable Indian land question confronting the rest of the province and, in particular, the lower Fraser Valley.[21]

For Duncan and many other British Columbians of his generation, the 'scattered condition of the Indians' was a problem requiring a 'remedy.' Writing to the federal minister of the interior, Duncan predicted: 'Unless they become more collected it would seem impossible that education or civilization should ever reach them as a whole.' Chief among Duncan's proposed remedies was the suggestion that the government 'lose sight of the tribal divisions of the Indians, which are so numerous and perplexing.' Instead, he proposed that they 'regard only the natural division of languages': divisions that would soon be equated in official provincial and federal documents with 'nations.'[22]

Duncan estimated that there were approximately a dozen natural linguistic divisions, each with a population of roughly 4,000 to 5,000 Natives.

He proposed that a government agent be assigned to live near the centre
of each of these language-based collectives at a remote site, as far as possible removed from existing Native and white settlements. The agent's
primary task, in Duncan's view, would be to 'encourage [the Natives]
to settle around him, without regard to tribal or sub-tribal distinctions,'
and to thereby establish a 'headquarters' around which a new civilized
'Native town' or 'Indian Settlement' would emerge.[23] Under Duncan's
proposal, the problem of 'having some ten or fifteen smaller reserves for
each language,' which inevitably resulted from the complicated village-
by-village system of reserve allocation, would be eliminated. In its place
there would be 'one Reserve for each tongue.' Though the Protestants
and Catholics never worked together and seldom agreed, what Duncan
was proposing was in large part the Durieu system of reductions writ
large.

Both federal and the provincial officials were receptive to many of
Duncan's recommendations, if for no other reason than they seemed to
confirm ideas that had been floating around rather loosely within the
halls of government for a number of years. Indeed, as early as 1872, the
Victoria office of the superintendent of Indian affairs had drafted a map
that divided the province into 'Nationalities or Dialects.' (See Map 21.)
Throughout the 1870s the provincial government found especially appealing a system consisting of a series of differentiated Indian agencies
that could accommodate themselves to the requirements of larger lan-
guage-group-based collectives. In 1875 the B.C. government passed an
Order in Council stating 'that no basis of acreage for [Indian] Reserves
be fixed for the Province as a whole, but rather that each nation [and
not tribe] of Indians [of the same language] be dealt with separately on
their respective claims.'[24] For British Columbia, this was a not so thinly
veiled attempt at ensuring that Natives who lived in agriculturally rich
regions of the province could be denied larger reserves than those in
areas deemed less desirable by European settlers.

Ottawa, too, embraced the idea of dealing separately with each nation of Indians of the same language. After receiving the Stó:lō petition
of July 1874, prominent federal officials stationed in British Columbia
briefly encouraged the Dominion government to adopt a reserve policy that established a minimum of eighty acres per family of five.[25] In
the end, because of fierce provincial opposition and an insistence that
twenty acres be the maximum allotment for each Indian family, Ottawa
capitulated and decided to work with the provincial government through
a special joint commission. The proposed Indian Reserve Commission

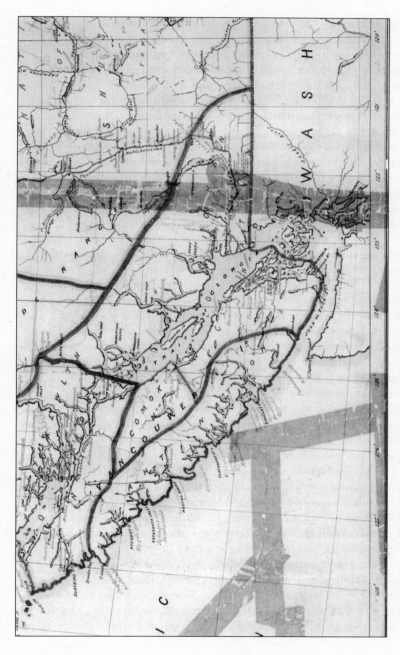

Map 21. 'Map of British Columbia – Being a Geographical Division of the Indians of the Province According to their Nationality or Dialect.' Compiled at the Office of the Superintendent of Indian Affairs, Victoria, B.C., 1872. LAC, RG 10, Black Series, 118-040075-5.

would travel the province and visit with 'each Indian nation (meaning by nation all Indian tribes speaking the same language) ... and after full enquiry on the spot into all matters affecting the [land] question ... fix and determine for each nation, separately, the number, extent and locality of the Reserve or Reserves to be allowed it.'[26]

Under Duncan's model, the existing settlement-based reserve base of the lower Fraser population would be gradually eliminated and replaced by one or two regional reserves – probably one for each of the two mainland Halq'eméylem dialects. News of the recommendation apparently spread rapidly through a receptive non-Native community, and rumours of its impending implementation were soon ringing in Aboriginal ears. Throughout the spring of 1876 the Indian superintendent at New Westminster received visits from large numbers of Natives representing 'deputations from the various Tribes of the Lower Fraser country and Burrard Inlet.' Though many in number, they presented a single message: they were concerned about reports 'that they were to be removed from their present Reserves.'[27]

Experience had taught the Aboriginal people that even well-intentioned government appointees could not be relied upon to protect their interests from the whims and abuses of the local settler population. The ever-increasing number of immigrants of European descent was a growing problem. What was needed was a return to a time when Aboriginal people could speak directly to the Crown's representative; when Douglas would meet personally with Stó:lō delegates and immediately address their concerns. Government leaders might be the settlers' representatives, but the Queen was the Indians' 'mother.' What was needed was one or two recognized Indigenous spokespersons who could dedicate themselves to understanding the issues, make recommendations, and then follow through on collective decisions on behalf of the entire Aboriginal community. The best solution seemed to be to develop a system of internal collective decision making that would facilitate the establishment of a direct relationship with the British Crown; one consistent with the familial ties the Queen professed, but that was also based on predictable rules that could be connected to existing British law. The summer of 1876 provided an opportunity for just that.

The Indian land question was the most pressing political concern for the majority of British Columbia's still predominantly Aboriginal residents. However, it was the failure of the federal government to live up to its commitment to provide a transcontinental railroad that captured the attention of the non-Native minority and therefore received the most notice in the columns of the local media and the halls of the legislative buildings. To help quell anxieties of the 'spoilt child of the Dominion' over the railroad issue,[28] Governor General Lord Dufferin was dispatched to the Pacific to remind westerners of the east's devotion to the west. He was to assess the situation, try to allay concerns, and then report back to Ottawa. For the Stó:lō and other Native people, this was regarded as a golden, and perhaps last, opportunity to have their mounting concerns addressed through the British/Canadian government system.

Dufferin arrived in Victoria via steamer from San Francisco on 15 August 1876, where the aged and long-retired Sir James Douglas officially greeted him. Together, Douglas and Dufferin travelled from Esquimalt, through the Songhees Reserve, and to the legislative buildings. En route, they passed under ornately decorated arbours and along streets lined with cheering crowds. The sight of the Queen's new representative shaking hands with the old chief factor must have lightened many Native hearts.

Three days later, the Stó:lō and many other coastal people began gathering in New Westminster at the site where twelve years earlier the first great gathering with the Crown's representative had occurred. Although Dufferin's revised agenda took him directly north to the Queen Charlotte Islands before returning to the Fraser River, thousands of Coast Salish Aboriginal leaders determinedly chose to wait. The governor general finally arrived at New Westminster on 5 September. After meeting with white politicians and discussing the railroad issue, Dufferin was confronted by the giant Aboriginal delegation (see Figure 15). The grandeur, pageantry, and symbolism of the day's event, if not the political import, were captured in the journal of the Marchioness of Dufferin and provide a sense of the importance of the affair to the Indigenous people:

> After various varieties of white men had presented addresses and been replied to, and after numbers had been shaken hands with, we looked down the hill, and saw a mass of flags marching up; the bearers of these gay banners were all Indian Chiefs, or great men, followed by a set of Indian Volunteers, who had got themselves into a very smart blue uniform, and were commanded by the owner of an old red coat and a pair of epaulets. The chiefs formed into a circle, while the army remained in a column, and stood facing the platform. D[ufferin] went down and shook hands with the chiefs, and then returned to the platform and listened to the speeches of four of them, every sentence of each being translated by an interpreter into English.

When it was his turn to reply, D[ufferin] spoke one sentence, which was taken up by five interpreters, who each, in turn put it into some new Indian tongue. The process was long, but it was interesting ...

[Later that evening] we stood on the roof of our drawing room on the steamer to see a most beautiful torch-light display by the Indians in canoes. We steamed up a little way, and then back, the canoes following, their torches looking very brilliant in the darkness and reflected in the water. Some men on foot, also with torches, ran along the banks, and then the town was illuminated. Before the lights disappeared there was cheering, and 'God save the Queen.'[29]

For people who for two years had steadfastly chosen not to participate in the celebration of the Queen's birthdays hosted by the superintendent of Indian affairs, the presence of the Crown's actual representative acted as a political lightning rod. Exactly what the various Indigenous leaders said, and what Dufferin replied, was, unfortunately, neither documented by the local newspapers nor preserved in personal papers in the archival collections left behind by the participants. All we learn from the newspapers is the following:

At the conclusion of the Indian addresses his Lordship addressed the assemblage of Indian chiefs. He told them that he had been sent by their English mother the Queen to converse with them about their affairs, and assist them when practicable. He had been told by their chief that they were ignored and weak, but this he attributed to their humility. He found them sturdy and respectable in appearance, sober and well conducted. He said there were three persons in whose eyes the Indian were always equal to the white man, they were God, the Queen and the Law. His Lordship, in conclusion, warned them against the effects of intemperance and indulgence in spirituous liquors.[30]

Some further indication of the talks, however, can be gleaned from a subsequent speech Dufferin made to the corporate and political elite in Victoria a few days later, and from the oral traditions of the Aboriginal people who attentively listened to the governor general's reply. Before leaving British Columbia Duffering stepped beyond the bounds of protocol and into the arena of provincial politics when in a speech in Victoria he stated frankly that the condition of the B.C. Aboriginal question was 'unsatisfactory'; that it had, in fact, been in 'error ever since Sir James Douglas quitted office.' In light of these bold assertions we can

15. Gathering at New Westminster to address Governor General, Lord Dufferin, 1876. Drawing by J. Davis, 'Reception of the Governor General the Earl of Dufferin and the Countess of Dufferin at the Pavilion, New Westminster.' Courtesy of B.C. Archives, PDP01792.

be fairly confident that the Aboriginal leaders at New Westminster had raised the land question. Whether or not they also addressed the inadequacy of the emerging Indian Act band governance model is less clear but certainly by 1881 Superintendent Powell was vigorously promoting municipal-style government in British Columbia, and especially among the Cowichan.[31] Whatever the specifics, however, it is clear that Dufferin had been made aware of the defectiveness of the colonial-sponsored system of Aboriginal governance and the mechanisms regulating Aboriginal–newcomer relations.

The use of four spokespersons to convey messages to Dufferin suggests that the numerous Native people gathered in New Westminster had somehow devised and agreed upon a decision-making system whereby certain people were sanctioned to speak as representatives of particular Native political groups or interests. As with the three spokespersons who communicated with Governor Seymour in 1864, it is unclear whether the decision to have four speakers address Governor General Dufferin in 1876 reflected a simple attempt to ensure that a single message was communicated in four languages that could be witnessed and understood by a diverse multilinguistic group of Natives, or whether the various speakers delivered different messages and therefore represented separate and distinct issues, or perhaps even nascent political communities that cut across language groups. Either way, the gathering represented a pivotal moment in the history of Aboriginal nation building.

Many of the Indigenous people present, likewise, saw fit to describe the gathering and its significance to their descendants, some of whom have, in turn, succeeded in transmitting that knowledge to subsequent generations. Today, for example, Rena Point-Bolton shares with her children and grandchildren what she learned of the great gathering with the Queen's representative from her father-in-law Dan Milo. As a young boy, Milo had been present when Dufferin spoke in New Westminster. According to Mrs Point-Bolton, the Queen's representative was informed of the inequitable way Aboriginal people had been treated by first the colonial and then the federal and provincial governments. The Native spokespersons reminded Dufferin that his friend James Douglas had promised the Stó:lō people compensation for land and resources alienated from their control through the process of creating reserves, and they asked that this promise be honoured. According to the oral tradition, Dufferin acknowledged that such was the British practice and stated that the proceeds collected by the Crown from private interests for the lands outside of reserves within the Fraser Valley would be divided three ways: one-third to the federal government, one-third to the provincial government, and one-third to the lower Fraser people so they could govern themselves. The government's failure to live up to the Crown's promise has been a sore spot in Stó:lō–newcomer relations ever since. The ironic fact that the current Lieutenant Governor of British Columbia (the Right Honourable Steven Point) is Mrs Point-Bolton's son, and that he carries this oral tradition and is on record stating that the Crown's honour was sullied by the breaking of the promise, raises all sorts of interesting questions about what might come of this long-ignored promise.[32]

Whatever might have been communicated verbally to Governor General Dufferin, and back from him to the Aboriginal communities, one thing is certain: the lower Fraser Valley's Indigenous inhabitants apprised Dufferin of their opposition to the proposed amalgamation of their reserves and relocation of their homes and made clear their desire to become self-supporting and self-governing.

The New Westminster gathering had been largely a Catholic affair. While Protestant Natives shared the same political concerns as their Catholic relatives, they felt it necessary to present them independently. The relatively small Methodist Aboriginal communities at Sumas and Chilliwack (concentrated at Soowahlie under Captain John Swalis) ensured that their voice was heard by hand-delivering the following written petition to Dufferin when his steamer reached Yale the following day: 'A rumour has reached us that it is probable we shall be removed from the home of our ancestors and placed with strangers upon distant reserves. We feel, therefore, very much troubled on account of this report and wish that your Excellency would intercede on our behalf that we may be allowed to remain at the reserves already allotted to us where remains of our parents and children are buried.'[33]

Likewise, in addition to the Protestant petition from Sumas and Chilliwack, the Aboriginal people living in the reserve adjacent to the town of Yale also presented Governor General Dufferin with an official address in the form of an illuminated manuscript on a large formal parchment. There, in elegant gold lettering surrounded by swirling designs and artistic borders the lower Fraser people living at the entrance of the Fraser Canyon boldly informed Dufferin: 'We wish that you would give us a present of something. We heard that you made a present to the Indians below and we wish that you would make us a present here.'[34]

Whether by 'present' the upper Stó:lō were requesting confirmation that they too would be provided with sufficient revenues to take care of themselves, or whether they were simply hoping to receive some 'trifles' of the kind that were often distributed to Aboriginal people when royals and other prominent dignitaries visited may never be known for certain. What is known is that immediately after presenting the formal written address, the chief at Yale impressed the governor general by leading an Aboriginal military honour guard, and then, with 'the timely prompt-ings and suggestions of his wife,' he spoke directly to the Crown's rep-resentative through a Native translator. What he said was not recorded on paper, but according to the *Toronto Globe* correspondent who covered Dufferin's western sojourn, the governor general's response was a simple 'exposition of the goodness of the Indian tum tum, or heart, in a few ap-propriate sentences.' The Stó:lō translator, however, in the traditional style of a good Coast Salish speaker trained to take a siyá:m's choice words and elaborate on them so as to convey the full spirit and intent behind the words in the leader's heart (thereby saving the siya:m from having to speak too much and risk appearing arrogant), engaged in what the jaundiced pen of the journalist described as 'an oration that Burke might have envied, and some even of our own time might have in vain sought to emulate. There was no prospective termination to it; sentence followed sentence, exhortation succeeded explanation, until it really be-came interesting to speculate upon what he might be putting into the mouth of the Governor-General.'[35]

But if there is ambiguity over the content of the Stó:lō chief's ex-changes with Dufferin, no such uncertainty characterizes the commu-nication of the Nlakapamux leaders Chief Spintlum and Chief Mischel, who resided immediately upriver from Yale in Lytton:

> As the strong Friend who is the same to us as our great and good Mother the Queen we hail you as our Chief and we hope you will succeed in *securing our rights so that we may be able properly to provide for our families our herds and belongings.*
>
> Your Exellency will be sorry to learn that for the last two years our Salmon and Berries have failed us and yet glad to know that by our own industry we have kept ourselves from want whilst living at peace with all: that our people are free from crime and our prison stands empty ...
>
> We desire to be good, sober and industrious; to keep our homes, to have our children educated, our sick and poor cared for; to advance in civiliza-tion: and to ever show ourselves the dutiful and obedient children of our good Mother and all in authority under her. With heart and voice upraised we one and all shout with joy – God Save the Queen.[36]

From an Indigenous perspective the process leading to the written and verbal dialogues with Governor General Dufferin were simultaneously empowering and frustrating. Following Dufferin's visit little changed in terms of government policy, and no official assurances were ever issued from federal or provincial authorities regarding Native concerns over the relocations of settlements or funding for self-governance. Ultimately, the centralized reserve option was rejected by government, not, however, because of Aboriginal protest, but rather because non-Natives ultimately thought it too dangerous to consolidate Native people. Divide and rule was the preferred option, and the military threat posed by the 'Shushwap Confederacy' in British Columbia's interior plateau region seemed to prove this point.[37] The dialogue with Dufferin had, however, reinforced in the Aboriginal mind the need for collective action to secure a more standardized and predictable system of communicating with the Queen's government. In the wake of Dufferin's visit, Coast and Interior Salish groups along the Fraser-Thompson River corridors began to organize themselves into a series of formal supratribal political bodies.

Indigenous Visions of Governance for a Colonial World

When, after spending two years demarcating reserves throughout the Okanagan and Thompson River regions, Joint Indian Reserve Commissioner Gilbert Malcolm Sproat finally returned to the lower Fraser in 1879, he was immediately confronted by an Indigenous delegation with an urgent political mission: 'All the tribes living between Yale and the mouth of the Fraser' wished to organize into a single government.[38]

Unfortunately, Sproat did not record the details of what the lower Fraser Aboriginal leaders envisioned for their government. As was so often the case when ranking federal officials visited Stó:lō settlements in the late nineteenth century, when Sproat met the chiefs from between Yale and the mouth of the Fraser on 29 July 1879 he was en route to another part of the province. As such, his schedule prevented him from stopping and discussing the matter more fully with the Stó:lō. At a similar meeting among the Nlakapamux the previous week, however, the commissioner had agreed to a request that he stop to witness and document proposals for collective Indian self-government. In his correspondence concerning the lower Fraser Stó:lō Native leader's proposal, Commissioner Sproat simply observes that they 'wished to do what the ... [Nlakapamux] have done ...to organize themselves under the Indian Act.'[39]

The lack of documentation makes it impossible to know the extent to which the Stó:lō proposal might have been derived from the previous week's Nlakapamux example, or if, indeed, the Nlakapamux had instead modelled their new government after the Stó:lō. The only chronology that is clear is the one provided by Sproat's correspondence, and that was a product of his travel itinerary. Indeed, if one Indigenous group was a leader in this regard, perhaps one needs to look beyond the Fraser corridor to find it, for the previous summer the Shushwap had been acting as a 'Confederation.' Similarly, in the 1880s the Cowichan of Vancouver Island were amalgamated into a single political body and became the first band in Canada to have adopted municipal-style governance under the Indian Advancement Act. This suggests that the move towards tribal amalgamation had earlier historical roots among the Coast Salish Cowichan, at least.[40] What is more, the man elected head chief of the Nlakapamux, Mischel of Spuzzum, is remembered by current Stó:lō as a cultural broker – one of his parents was Stó:lō and the other Nlakapamux. Europeans also regularly hired Chief Mischel when they needed a translator to communicate with Fraser River Natives.[41] The following discussion and analysis, therefore, is not necessarily exactly what the Stó:lō were contemplating. It is a description of what the Nlakapamux had proposed, as related by Sproat, and what the Stó:lō apparently requested as well.[42]

Reflecting the tension between localized and dispersed expressions of Salish collective identity, as well as the new boundaries being maintained between Natives and newcomers, the constitution adopted by the Nlakapamux on 17 July 1879 identified and codified various spheres of authority. In addition to recognizing a distinction between national and tribal spheres of authority, the Nlakapamux plan provided for a distinct judicial system, as well as a formal role for the Queen or her representative in Indigenous governance. In this way, their model provided for direct linkages with the Canadian federal government and bureaucracy. Though reminiscent of Western European governing systems, and clearly informed by the judicial processes established under the Oblate's temperance societies, Commissioner Sproat nonetheless considered their particular manifestation to be genuinely Indigenous. In fact, the reserve commissioner made clear that the idea for the government and the rules by which it was supposed to function were entirely of the Native's own making. Sproat expressed genuine surprise and, at least initially, real concern at how the system departed from one that he might have recommended. He came to appreciate, however, that such ingenuity was appropriate not only given the realities of then-current Native–newcomer relations, but also the cultural context in which the Salish people found themselves.

The Nlakapamux constitution specified that their national government was to be led by a head chief who would be assisted by an elected council. Both the head chief and the council were to be elected for three-year terms at what might best be described as a national convention. Whatever other obligations these representatives carried, they were obliged to meet as a governing body at least once per year, that is, at an annual convention they were to have the power to make laws and regulations 'over such matters as schools, medicine, fishing and hunting, and aspects of personal conduct.'[43] The system was not entirely democratic, however. In addition to restricting the vote to adult males (which was also, of course, still the norm in non-Native Canada), the constitution provided that in the event of a councillor ceasing to hold office, the head chief and a majority of the remaining councillors were empowered to appoint a replacement for the remainder of the three-year term.

Distinct from the national-level government, the constitution also recognized the authority of domestic tribal collectives. All traditional hereditary tribal chiefs were entitled to remain in office 'until their death, resignation or removal by the Queen,' after which the adult males of each tribe would elect successors for three-year terms. The tribal chiefs would presumably exercise jurisdiction over certain local tribal matters, while the head chief and his council acted nationally. The tribal chiefs' primary responsibilities, however, were judicial and not legislative or executive. This, of course, was consistent with the traditional role of Salish leaders who, as discussed above, were expected to function as dispute-resolution experts to diffuse interpersonal and interfamily tensions. Under the Nlakapamux constitution, tribal chiefs were also eligible to run for positions as national councillors, and in fact, in the first election tribal chiefs secured most of the council seats.

After forming their government the Nlakapamux Council immediately passed a series of resolutions. The first provided for the building of a school and the hiring of a teacher to instruct children in arithmetic and teach them to read and write English. The second pertained to the provision of medical services and Western medicine. Fifty per cent of these services were to be financed through separate school and medicine taxes. The balance would be made up through fines. Once these structures were in place the Nlakapamux lost no time in passing their first legislation: the banning of drunkenness, gambling, and the potlatch. In

addition, legislation declared that agricultural lands on reserves were to
be divided 'in a fair way' into individual landholdings, and that houses
and yards were to be kept tidy and fenced. Animals were to be kept cor-
ralled and fines levied for damage caused by trespassing animals. 'Idle-
ness' was not only a sin, but also a crime, and restrictions were devised
for the regulation of hunting and fishing. Those who violated the laws
faced fines of between five and fifty dollars. Those found guilty of potlatching could also be disqualified from becoming a chief, councillor, or
constable.

The Nlakapamux criminalization of the potlatch is striking, given
the attention scholars have drawn to Native opposition to the federal
government's subsequent decision to ban the potlatch, in 1884.[44] The
Nlakapamux action is indicative of the extent to which some Indigenous communities strove to demonstrate that they could survive and
even thrive in the new Western society. Moreover, many of those who
ultimately opposed the potlatch did so not because it represented In-
digenousness, but because the recent transformations in the ceremony
appeared to render it incompatible with Western society and corrosive
of all that was regarded as best in traditional society. In describing the
Nlakapamux decisions to officials in Ottawa, Commissioner Sproat explained that Native men who previously would have sought to elevate
their status through feats of hunting or as warriors were no longer able
to do so in the colonial era. As an alternative method of 'making themselves known,' some had succumbed to what he described as a 'mania,'
that is, they had taken to 'more or less lavish distributions of property,'
the initial funds sometimes being raised through the prostitution of
women.[45] The Nlakapamux hereditary elite, like Sproat, opposed such
developments.

When recently asked about the Nlakapamux banning of the potlatch,
one contemporary Aboriginal family leader, whose mother was Stó:lō
and whose father was Nlakapamux, provided an additional context for
understanding his ancestors' decision. He noted that his Elders had explained to him that elaborate potlatching of the kind practised on the
coast had only been introduced among the Nlakapamux around the
time of the fur trade. Because it was not a deeply established tradition it
was relatively easy for the Nlakapamux to abandon it. Indeed, the Nlakapamux of 1879 may have regarded the coastal-style potlatch as a foreign
influence within their culture – the sort of elaborate gift-giving ceremony
the missionaries opposed might also have been regarded as unwelcome
among Nlakapamux 'traditionalists.' The prominent act of banning the

potlatch may have been a relatively easy matter for a community seeking to protect its own traditions and distinguish itself from its downriver neighbours. Considered in this light, what may have been a traditionalist reaction to change would have served the valuable function of appearing to non-Native authorities as a strong indication of the Nlakapamux's commitment to working within the new Canadian political system.[46]

The Nlakapamux legislative body that created these laws was a thirteen-man national council. It is important to stress, however, that this number was not determined by any numerical formula. There were neither provisions for tribal representation by population nor guarantees to ensure at least one councillor per tribe (although efforts were made to ensure all groups felt included and accounted for). Rather, at the national general assembly prominent Elders, traditional tribal leaders, and other respected individuals determined how many men qualified as 'just and good,' and from among this group of 'generally younger men,' how many were willing to hold office. As such the election did not necessarily conform to democratic traditions that most non-Native Canadians living either then or now would recognize, but they did meet Salish requirements as expressed through complex webs of interrelated families.

The Nlakapamux constitution bound all its citizens to abide by the laws of the council. Enforcement was placed in the hands of a series of local 'tribal committees of council.' The various hereditary or elected tribal chiefs led these tribally based judicial committees, but the other committee members were chosen from the national council. Joint Indian Reserve Commissioner Sproat had initially objected to this model, suggesting that each tribe select from among its membership its own councillors to assist the tribal chiefs. This Western-style system of representative government, however, proved unappealing to the Aboriginal community. As they pointed out, their own system not only ensured a higher calibre of representative, but as Sproat conceded, also meant that those within the various tribes who were seeking adjudication and dispute resolution would regard the councillors sitting on these adjudicating bodies as more impartial.

Sproat also expressed concern over other features of the tribal committees of council. The Nlakapamux constitution stated that a minimum of four councillors sit on each committee. Paternalistically sensing an oversight, Sproat pointed out to the Nlakapamux community that 'a court of four would not work among white men, for 2 might think the same and the other two differently, and so there would be a deadlock.' The Nlakapamux's confident rejoinder was simply that 'this could not happen in an Indian court.' In his subsequent correspondence to Ottawa, Commissioner Sproat conceded that, indeed, 'though [the Indians] debate vehemently and at great length, the minority in the end quietly disappears.' Consensus across tribal and family divisions was therefore an integral feature of Salish government. What was important was not that there be an odd number to break an impasse, but that there be at least four people, each with a broad enough set of life experiences and family connections to ensure that justice was served and that all interests were accounted for. Perhaps the Nlakapamux also chose four as the minimum membership of a tribal committees of council because of that number's sacred significance in Salish cosmology. In Salish society the number four conveys a special spiritual significance not unlike the Holy Trinity–derived number three in European Christian society.

The tribal committees of council were required to act consistently and according to firm standardized rules in all their judicial decisions. They were required to give notice that they were going to hear a case, after which they were obligated to meet at the appropriate time, state their decisions clearly, and have them noted for future reference. What is more, council decisions could not be altered after the court had finished sitting.

Finally, to ensure sectarian differences did not weaken Indigenous national identity, the Nlakapamux constitution prohibited, with the exception of 'proposals connected with schools,' the introduction of 'church matters' before either the council or the tribal committees. This provision is less an indication of the Salish adopting a Western-style division of religion and governance (or 'the spiritual and the material'), as some have suggested,[47] than it was an innovative means of protecting communal Native interests against powerful outside forces. As Sproat learned, the goal was to provide the Nlakapamux community with stronger negotiating power vis-à-vis those churches currently working within their territory as well as any who might 'arrive in the future.' Spirituality was still considered inseparable from daily life and human existence. In short, the Nlakapamux constitution was a remarkable document. It not only established a constitution, a national government, and a locally responsive tribally based judiciary, but also two nationally funded public services, a revenue system to operate them, and a series of laws to protect the public good and regulate resource sectors such as fish and wildlife.

Interestingly, while Commissioner Sproat initially embraced the Nlakapamux proposal and promoted its virtues to Ottawa, he was much less keen on the lower Fraser Stó:lõ initiative for collective self-governance. Rather than assist in the process of constitution building, Sproat informed the lower Fraser delegates that 'they must not be in too much a hurry.'[48] This reluctance might, in part, be accounted for by the long-standing bias within colonial society that placed coastal Aboriginal fisher-people lower on the evolutionary scale than the supposedly more manly hunting societies of the interior plateau.[49] An additional cause of Sproat's reluctance was that the much larger Stó:lõ population (nearly double the Nlakapamux) was in closer proximity to the rapidly growing non-Native urban/commercial centre of New Westmister/Vancouver. In his report, Sproat nervously emphasized to his Ottawa superiors that the Natives living between Yale and the mouth of the Fraser River who were proposing a collective government 'number[ed] about 1900 Indians.'[50] By way of contrast, two years later, the official Census of Canada listed the non-Native population of New Westminster as merely 1,500 inhabitants – and this town, located in Stó:lõ territory, was the largest non-Native urban centre on the B.C. mainland.[51]

Colonial society in British Columbia was simply not ready to allow that much concentrated power to manifest itself in the hands of Indians. Six months earlier, having caught wind of the Aboriginal plans to organize, the province's largest newspaper openly expressed its opposition, arguing that 'singly the Indian tribes are easily dealt with, but once bind them together by ties, whether political or social, and they will be much more difficult to coerce or persuade.'[52] Commissioner Sproat's federal colleagues in the Department of Indian Affairs Pacific Office made no effort to distance themselves from the popular white opposition. Deputy Superintendent James Lenihan warned Ottawa that the 'new organization ... [would] be the entering of the small end of the wedge, for the promotion of [Indian] schemes and intrigue.' Meanwhile Superintendent I.W. Powell wrote that he believed Sproat had 'committed a most serious error in attempting to combine the large population of [Nlakapamux] under one head chief.' In fact, as noted in the previous chapter, Powell 'fully endorsed every statement contained in [a letter of] protest' presented by a group of prominent 'Concerned Citizens' to the provincial premier warning of the dire consequences of allowing Natives to organize into supratribal organizations.[53] In their letter, the concerned citizens explained that 'at the present time these hereditary chiefs have little authority or influence for good.'[54] They expressed fear that 'the future peace of the province is being seriously jeopardised [sic] in this proposed combination of semi-civilized natives' and that 'serious trouble and probably bloodshed' would be the result of allowing the scheme to proceed. In their opinion, the Native population was 'in a state of transition ... and unable to appreciate or properly utilize the advantages of civilized government.' Until the civilizing process was complete (and the petitioners clearly doubted that it ever would be) any large Native organization inevitably posed a security risk: 'especially just at a time when their ancient privileges are being somewhat curtailed.' Ultimately, the concerned citizens justified their opposition to supratribal Indigenous self-government with reference to historical precedent: 'We desire especially to bring to your notice, that the past safety and security which we have enjoyed in the Province is owing to the fact that the large Indian population of the Country has been divided into small bands without a head Chief possessing general authority or influence, and without the ability to unite and constitute themselves a powerful and formidable force.'

This formidable opposition to collective Indian self-government, even self-government designed to link with the federal Indian Affairs bureaucracy and explicitly subordinate to the British Crown, effectively killed any thoughts the Dominion government had of supporting either the Nlakapamux or the Lower Fraser initiative. Indeed, it became an accepted practice in Ottawa to designate all western Natives as 'less civilized' than central Canadian ones, and therefore suitable to be treated differently and even more paternalistically.[55]

The Stó:lō, however, were largely oblivious to developments in Ottawa, and their prolonged exposure to the rabidly anti-Indian expression of B.C. politics had rendered them jaded and all but numb to local political rumblings in British Columbia. Governor General Dufferin's visit was still fresh in their minds, and their proposal to Sproat was entirely consistent with what they had been led to believe the government wanted and what the Indian Act was designed to promote: self-sufficient, civilized Indian communities. It was not Sproat's subsequent unwillingness to immediately press their case in his correspondence with Ottawa, but his rather impromptu recommendations when he met with them to informally begin the process of political organization and establishing self-government that made the greatest impact and provided them with lasting encouragement. While Indian Reserve Commissioner Sproat had told the lower Fraser leaders to be patient, he had also assured them that the best way to secure Ottawa's and the Queen's recognition of their scheme was to work to 'try to abate the prevalent jealousies among themselves and limit the number of ridiculously small tribes ... [and] show ... good sense and businesslike views.' Likewise, he suggested that since de jure, Canadian-recognized, political unity was going to be slow in coming, the Stó:lō would be wise to move ahead independently with de facto organization. He noted that government agents would never be as competent in matters of Indian justice and governance as the Indians themselves, and so he encouraged the Stó:lō to get 'organized, and for their chief and a few councillors [to] form a court and settle questions [themselves].[56] The following day the Stó:lō chief returned to Sproat's tent and informed the commissioner that he had taken the advice and established a judicial committee; with his councillors, the chief had adjudicated an old dispute between two families over a piece of land. What they had done, in short, was apply a traditional potlatch-style system of governance within the framework of an Oblate temperance society-style court, all within an intertribal context and without the involvement of Church or state authorities.

Vigilante Violence, State Malfeasance, and Stó:lō Self-governance

Shortly after meeting with the Stó:lō, Sproat retired from the Joint Indian Reserve Commission. The government's failure to recognize a unified lower Fraser Aboriginal political entity did not, however, stop the momentum towards stronger collective identity and political unity. While the Stó:lō did not oppose government- and Church-sponsored initiatives designed to strengthen and fortify local band-level governance, they clearly wanted to pursue the parallel development of something bigger – a national government to deal with national issues. It quickly became apparent that collective governance required more than internal legislative and judicial mechanisms. It also required the power to compel outsiders to respect and honour Indigenous life and property; it required the power to ensure non-Natives' compliance with what were clearly emerging shared cross-cultural concepts of the rule of law and jurisprudence. When a fourteen-year-old Stó:lō boy named Louie Sam was wrongly accused of murdering an American shopkeeper in Nooksack, Washington, and then later abducted from a Canadian jail (where he was awaiting transport to New Westminster to stand trial) by a mob of American vigilantes who summarily lynched him from a giant cedar tree five hundred feet north of the Canada/U.S. border (see Figure 16), the scene was set for the enactment of Stó:lō government despite European opposition.[57]

On a cold day in February 1884 approximately two hundred lower Fraser Native men, representing all the Native settlements between the

16. Author standing at site where Louie Sam was lynched by American
vigilantes. Photo by Albert McHalsie, March 2004.

Fraser's mouth and the Fraser Canyon, travelled by canoe and trail to the central location of Chilliwack to 'consider the best means of obtaining justice.'[58] They came to decide upon a collective response to the murder of one of their youth. The intertribal gathering lasted for a more than a week. Before the gathering ended, two prominent tribal leaders and an Indian constable 'summoned' the local Indian agent and asked him to record 'on paper' the community's feelings and intentions, and to send that message to the senior official in the Department of Indian Affairs.[59] Through their spokesmen, the Stó:lō informed the Indian agent that 'some of those present objected to letting you know anything about our intentions until it was all over, but the majority have decided to tell you everything and to take your advice.' The Natives, the agent discovered, were debating not whether to take action against the Americans, but rather, the form their action should take: 'Some of the most determined men [believe we have] a perfect right to ... hang and kill sixty-five Americans' (the number reported to have been in the lynch mob). While consensus had not been achieved on the number of lives to take, the Stó:lō were 'unanimous' in feeling 'fully justified in going immediately in very large numbers across the boundary line and tak[ing] the first white man [they met] and bring[ing] him to the spot where they hung the Indian and treat[ing] him in the same manner.'[60]

It is a long-standing Coast Salish tradition that justice be informed by a notion of balance and harmony.[61] In the past, if raiders killed someone, the victim's family was under an obligation to restore balance. Typically this involved a counterattack against the collective group responsible for the first death. The revenge did not have to be against the specific individual who had committed the offence, but against someone, anyone, with whom the culprit was closely associated. For example, while family members would typically seek vengeance among those believed responsible for a particular wrongdoing (i.e., a shaman believed guilty of killing or injuring someone with bad magic), they might kill someone close to the shaman rather than the shaman himself. Balance could be restored in other ways as well. For example, members of the family guilty of the original offence could compensate the injured family with items of wealth. By washing away the offence with payments, those associated with the actual offender restored balance by mitigating a counterattack against themselves.

Oral histories also explain that the process of restoring balance did not necessarily even have to involve any determination of guilt or innocence. In one example provided to Marian Smith, her Stó:lō informant explained that it was not considered wrong or improper for parents who were grieving the loss of a child who had died of what might today be considered an accident or natural causes (fallen in the river, say) to restore balance in their life by randomly selecting and visiting a different settlement with the expressed purpose of killing a child there. The grief caused the second child's family would bring balance to the first by having someone match their own grief. Whether the second family's members would accept this rationale is doubtful. More likely, they would launch a retaliatory attack against either those responsible for their child's death or some other non-grieving family in an effort to bring balance back into their own lives. Arranged marriages were one method family leaders used to pre-empt any such aggressions. What has been referred to in anthropological literature as the 'blood balance' was, therefore, only the most sensational example of the way in which Coast Salish brought balance and harmony to their interpersonal relationships.[62]

With regard to Louie Sam's lynchers, the Indigenous desire to restore balance was mingled with the more typically British concern (also found in the temperance society court proceedings) with determining guilt and responsibility. According to the government reports, the Stó:lō were at pains to point out that Louie Sam had indeed been innocent of the shopkeeper's murder.[63] They were, in other words, seeking to meet British criteria for justice before administering their own. Significantly, the information the Stó:lō provided the Indian agent (which named the shopkeeper's actual murderer, as well as the name of the leader of the lynch mob) was later corroborated by Canadian undercover detectives, who conducted a thorough investigation within U.S. territory.[64]

If the Nlakapamux and Lower Fraser efforts to organize had caused unease in 1879, the collective Stó:lō reaction to the lynching of Louie Sam five years later caused near panic. To the settler society, whose economic and political hegemony depended in large part upon the maintenance of racial boundaries, the Stó:lō response to the illegal cross-border lynching of an Aboriginal boy raised serious problems. This was all the more the case when one considers that Louie Sam was not a prominent individual from a prestigious family. Indeed, Louie Sam's father was universally known by Natives and whites alike as Masachie Sam – Masachie being a Chinook jargon term for evil or bad. Masachie Sam was currently serving time in the provincial penitentiary, having been convicted of killing his half-brother when the latter attempted to stop Louie's father from marrying his own widowed stepmother.

The Stó:lō, in other words, were not acting savagely against non-Natives. In fact, it was Louie Sam's non-Native lynchers who had painted their faces with red and black designs intended to mimic and mock Coast Salish spirit dancers. In responding to Louie Sam's murder the Stó:lō were attempting to create predictable order out of a chaotic world. In their minds, the consistent deceit demonstrated by powerful representatives of non-Native society over the land question and other pressing Native concerns would have dwarfed many of the wicked deeds of the evil Indian doctors that Xexá:ls, the transformers, had been compelled to defeat as they turned an ancient world of disharmony into one of predictable order. The lynching of Louie Sam, perhaps, marked the moment when Stó:lō society, as a whole, came to understand that they could not leave it to others, not even the honourable Queen, to look after their interests in a rapidly changing colonial world; that they would have to take action to achieve ends, or at the very least, threaten violence to compel others to do so.

Despite the gold rush era precedent where American miners and Governor Douglas each independently established systems of Native-newcomer governance that included certain Aboriginal leaders having the authority to arrest non-Native transgressors of the peace, what frightened the government most in 1884 was the Aboriginal insistence that their own Indigenous sphere of governance (linked to concepts of justice which they had been told were not inconsistent with the Crown's) be extended to include jurisdiction over non-Natives. The worst fears of Victoria's 'concerned citizens' appeared to be coming to fruition. Lower Fraser Aboriginal self-governance appeared to be assuming a supratribal military dimension with regard to the administration of justice. The Stó:lō leadership, with the 'unanimous' support of their various constituent tribes, offered to strike a formal arrangement with the Dominion government. Speaking though the Indian agent, they asked that the Canadian federal and provincial governments be told 'how sick our hearts are.' Then they offered to hold their own governing mechanisms temporarily in abeyance while the Crown's agents worked to bring the lynch mob to justice. Canada was then granted three months to prove its honour and ability, after which the Stó:lō reserved the right to act independently.[65]

Ultimately, the good faith upon which this decision was made proved unfounded, at least as regards the immediate goal of providing justice to Louie Sam. Though investigators quickly determined that the Stó:lō had been correct – that Louie Sam apeared innocent of the original murder charges and that, in fact, the leader of the lynch mob had concocted the story of Louie Sam's guilt and then coordinated the daring cross-border lynching to hide his complicity in his brother-in-law's murder of the shopkeeper – the Canadian government chose neither to act on the information, nor to inform the Stó:lō of the investigation's results. Instead, they boldly lied time and time again to the Stó:lō delegates who visited the government offices over the ensuing year to enquire into the results of the investigation and what the Queen's government proposed to do about it. The Stó:lō, for their part, eventually grew weary of waiting for the investigations' results, and moved on to other pressing matters. They never did follow through on their threat of cross-border military retaliation.

In the end, the Stó:lō were deceived and disappointed. But the seeds of a broad regional unity and the desire for shared self-government had been sown upon a foundation of kinship ties and affiliation derived from interconnected myth-age stories. Indeed, the experience of political cooperation through shared collective identity in the face of colonial intrusions and violations had been empowering and invigorating. Henceforth, the lower Fraser River Indians came to be most commonly known among themselves as well as non-Natives, not by their various tribal affiliations, nor even as the lower Fraser Indians, but by the term they chose to reflect their own Indigenous supratribal unity: the Stó:lō.

Throughout the two decades following the lynching of Louie Sam the government and churches continued their efforts to solidify a splintered settlement-based or band-level collective identity. Nevertheless, other factors continued the trend towards strengthening supratribal Stó:lō identity. New employment opportunities in the 1870s associated with cannery work and hop yards provided renewed opportunities for inter-community gatherings, as did the popular and widely attended Easter Passion plays hosted by the Oblate fathers at St Mary's Mission. Together, all these provided opportunities for the nascent political identity emerging from the earlier Queen's birthday celebrations to be sustained, and for the political response to the lynching of Louie Sam to be reinforced on an annual basis in forums that were not recognized as threatening or subversive by either colonial or Church authorities.

The debate over whether Western academics created a fictional Stó:lō identity is in many ways really moot. The fact that people continue to engage it and that it conjures such strong emotional responses is, however, fascinating. This debate reflects a long history of tension between various expressions of collective identity, and it is a signifier of the ongoing importance of such debates to contemporary Indigenous people. It provides insights into the way in which colonialism can become a factor operating within Indigenous culture and history, and not just upon it. The debate over whether Western academics created a fictional Stó:lō identity also provides insights into the nature of Indigenous history wars and the cultural and economic import lurking behind such tensions. Finally, this debate helps clarify the multifaceted nature of various expressions of boundary maintenance existing both between ethnic class and gender groups and among them.

SECTION SIX

Conclusion

Chapter Ten

Entering the Twentieth Century

The Ancestor of Everything is an Action.
– Stó:lō Grand Chief, and B.C. Lieutenant Governor,
His Honour Steven Point[1]

The 1906 Delegation to London

On a hot day in August 1906, after travelling more than 7,000 kilometres and overcoming concerted opposition from the Canadian Dominion government, Simon Pierre of Katzie walked into Buckingham Palace in London and spoke directly with King Edward VII. Together with Squamish Chief Joe Capilano (the delegation's official leader), Chief Basil David of Bonapart, and Charlie Isipaymilt of Cowichan, Simon Pierre had completed an incredible journey that started nearly two months earlier at the Canadian Pacific train station in Vancouver, British Columbia.[2] Unlike the other members of the delegation, Pierre was not an Aboriginal politician. Rather, as a young residential school graduate, he had been chosen at a massive intertribal gathering to accompany the three senior Indigenous statesmen as translator. It was Simon Pierre, therefore, that the British journalists swarmed around immediately following the royal audience. The question they asked (in addition to 'What did the King say?') was the same one that for the previous three weeks had been inspiring headlines in London's leading daily newspapers: What was wanted by these Indians, who, though claiming to be chiefs of particular villages, had travelled across a continent and an ocean to seek redress for grievances on behalf of 'all 80,000 of British Columbia's Indians'? The British journalists were confused by the relationship between place, time, and Aboriginal collective identity.

Though Simon Pierre's voyage was undoubtedly the greatest journey undertaken by a lower Fraser River Indigenous person up to that time, other Salish people from British Columbia's interior plateau had, in fact, preceded the 1906 delegates to London by two years. In 1904 Chiefs Chilihiza of Douglas Lake and Chief Louis of Kamloops, in the company of the Oblate priest Father Le Jeune, travelled to England en route to France and then Rome, where they would participate in a missionary-organized symposium on Aboriginal literacy. However, these earlier sojourners officially represented only their home settlements – two relatively impoverished Indian reserves far from any large non-Native urban centres. Though Chief Chilihitza and Chief Louie were not part of an official political delegation, and though they made no effort to meet with King Edward, their journey and its political potential were massively inspirational to those Indigenous leaders in British Columbia who sought large-scale political reform of Canadian Indian policy, and the right to collective self-governance and identification. This was especially the case given Chilihitza's and Louie's success in securing an audience with Pope Pius X.[3]

Joe Capilano, who learned of the 1904 journey to Rome through Father Le Jeune's Chinook jargon-language newsletter, the *Kamloops Wawa*, immediately recognized the potential that a high-profile delegation to the titular head of the British Empire held. He quickly began to organize a multitribal, explicitly political, delegation consisting of himself, Chief Chilihitza, and Chief Louie. Capilano travelled throughout British Columbia meeting with like-minded Indigenous community leaders at large public gatherings, where, speaking the lingua franca Chinook jargon he was able to communicate with people from multiple language groups, garnering their political support, and securing their financial assistance. Unfortunately, by the time Capilano was ready to travel, one of the veterans of the 1904 European excursion had passed away, and the other was too ill to travel; and so alternatives were found.

Chief Capilano calculated that the leader of the world's largest empire could not ignore the 1906 delegates because they spoke on behalf of a large multitribal Indian population in an important region of the Dominion of Canada. His designs were overtly political and extremely well conceived. There was nothing naïve about the 1906 delegates' decision to bypass the British Columbian and Canadian governments in their effort to secure recognition and protection of Indigenous governance and economic security. Nothing in Capilano's or the other delegates' numerous discussions with government officials or the media suggested that

they actually expected King Edward to immediately or unilaterally re-
structure Canadian Indian policy. Chief Capilano, in particular, was skil-
ful and cagey as he teased and manipulated not only the Canadian and
British press, but also a host of political figures ranging from the mayor
of Vancouver to the minister of the interior in Ottawa, to the Canadian
high commissioner in London. It seems clear that the delegation's aim
was to draw attention to the injustice of Canadian Indian policy in British Columbia as a whole, and in so doing embarrass the Dominion into
applying the rule of law with consistency in all of its provinces.[4]

Nevertheless, being a political act did not prevent the expedition from
also assuming a deeply spiritual dimension for the Native travellers. The
1906 trip to London was a sacred journey; a spirit quest not unlike those
that Coast Salish shamans embarked upon when they travelled through
the x̱á:x̱a realm linking their homes with the metaphysical domain of
the Creator or Great First. Like shamans, the delegates sought information and power: they wanted clarification of the Crown's intentions and
proof of the government's willingness to live up to the rhetoric of the
rule of law. Thus, it was a movement across not only physical and legal
landscapes, but spiritual and racial ones as well. (See Figure 17.)

Clearly, it was a very proud moment for Simon Pierre when he translated the words of Joe Capilano and his other Elders for the king, and
then those of the British monarch back to his chiefs.[5] The audience in
Buckingham Palace represented a masterful political coup for the British Columbia Native leaders.[6] After arriving in England they had spent
three weeks trying to circumvent the Canadian high commissioner's
concerted efforts to derail their mission. Contemporary Stó:lō oral traditions relate how, as Old Pierre's son, Simon Pierre had been trained in
certain of the esoteric traditions of Coast Salish shamanism, and how, in
order to demonstrate the potency of Native spirit power, Simon Pierre
had conjured a small bird and caused it to circle repeatedly less than a
metre above his head during a dinner meeting with senior British and
Canadian government officials.[7] This feat so amazed and impressed the
Londoners, the oral history explains, that it was in large part responsible
for the delegation's success in securing respect for Indigenous political
aspirations and royal guarantees for Aboriginal rights.

British newspapers, as well as official government correspondence
documenting the 1906 delegation, also relate a complicated game of
identity politics engaged in by both the Indigenous delegates and the
Canadian Office of the High Commissioner. Each side struggled to
have contrasting interpretations of the delegates' political standing and

THE DAILY GRAPHIC, FRIDAY, AUGUST 3, 1906.

17. Simon Pierre of Katzie, Chief Charlie Isipaymilt of Cowichan, Chief Joe Capilano of Squamish, Chief Basil David of Bonapart, preparing to meet King Edward VII in London. *Daily Graphic*, 3 Aug. 1906. By permission of the British Library.

objectives recognized by British authorities, and through them, by Dominion officials in Ottawa. But, unlike the oral traditions, these Western mnemonics suggest that it was the Aboriginal leaders who were overawed and impressed by symbols and expressions of British power. As a result, the documents explain, the delegates were ultimately thwarted in their aspirations and returned home humbled and firmly aware of their subordinate position to the Canadian government.[8]

The 1906 delegation to London receives cursory attention in scholarly treatments of west coast people and history. Neither, for that matter, do standard histories of British Columbia or Canada refer to the 1906 delegation as significant to understanding regional or national political development.[9] Nevertheless, it is the first time an Aboriginal leader presented himself as the spokesperson for the entire Indigenous population of Canada's Pacific province. Following this act, a series of formal supratribal and broad regional political organizations emerged which, operating in varying degrees of formal political unity, placed and kept B.C. Aboriginal rights issues firmly on the Canadian political agenda throughout the twentieth century.[10]

That the current Indigenous memory of particular details of the 1906 delegation's actions and experiences does not perfectly coincide with the documentary observations left by contemporaneous non-Natives is unimportant. Even without the added complexity of trying to understand an occurrence across a gulf of nearly a century, it is uncommon even for people of the same gender, class, and ethnic predisposition to describe a shared experience in identical terms. Native and non-Native politicians involved in a serious contest over the definition of Aboriginal land and governance in 1906 are unlikely to have transmitted identical interpretations and memories. The important point is coming to recognize that, even if it is difficult to reconcile the various interpretations of what happened in London in 1906, it is impossible to deny any longer the significance of this event, when read in light of the history of Stó:lō-Coast Salish collective identity leading up to and following it.

'The Ancestor of Everything Is an Action'

This study concludes with an account of the 1906 delegation not because it represents the culmination of the history of Stó:lō or B.C. provincial Aboriginal collective identity, for it does not. Indeed, there have been since then numerous instances when certain groupings of Indigenous people openly rejected the idea of any meaningful collectivity beyond the local reserve-based settlement.[11] Rather, the 1906 delegation more accurately represents an important climax in a long process of collective identity reformation tending unevenly towards ever-greater supratribal association and affiliation. The converging of a generally shared appreciation that meaningful, legitimate, and real Aboriginal collective identity could simultaneously nest or reside not only at the local band level, but also at the supratribal Stó:lō, Coast Salish, Salish, and ultimately British Columbian, level is reflected publicly for the first time in the 1906 delegation. Yet, it was a realization that had been gaining currency within Indigenous society at least since the smallpox epidemic of 1782 that swept in with the first influences of Europeans. Certainly, throughout that period there had been countervailing forces emphasizing smaller, more localized expressions of collective identity, the most prominent being the settlement- and tribally based symbols of authority emphasized by the Coast Salish male elite, on the one hand, and the colonial initiatives in creating reserves and the government banning of the potlatch, on the other. But as the 1906 delegation so ably demonstrates, these trends were being constantly challenged by the perceived advantages of increased collective cooperation and group identification between Aboriginals – matters that upper-class women and non-elite males had more consistently related as important in the past.

If the move towards greater emphasis on broader regional collective identities parallels the history of European colonial penetrations into the region, it does not necessarily follow that supratribal identity is a product of colonialism. Though the public expressions of broadly based political identity increasingly assumed Western-looking appearances, they were nonetheless based upon long-established Indigenous precedence. The emerging new order had to be rationalized within the old epistemology. Ancient stories of flood-inspired migrations provided models for inter-community amalgamation in the wake of the earliest smallpox epidemics, just as the periodic and ephemeral collective supratribal Coast Salish political response to certain instances of external aggression by Coastal Raiders provided a model for collective action against American whiskey pedlars, and then later the colonial government, on the land question. Moreover, all of these expressions of shared identity were built upon a pre-contact economic and diplomatic network designed to minimize conflict while maximizing access to regionally dispersed and seasonally specific food resources.

Thus, while the process of Stó:lō supratribal collective identity formation ultimately assumed expressions that appeared to outsiders to be derivative of European ideas and institutions, they were not necessarily regarded as such by Indigenous people. Nevertheless, to earlier historians these expressions were inconsequential to the story of European expansion, and therefore ignored. Likewise, for the early ethnographers, who sought to salvage descriptions of pre-European cultural types before they were eclipsed by Western civilization, these expressions were largely dismissed as being too contaminated by Western influences. Certainly, these factors account in large part for the scant attention practitioners of either discipline have paid to the gigantic gatherings associated with the Queen's birthday celebrations in the 1860s and 1870s and Lord Dufferin's 1876 visit, or the efforts to form rule-based supratribal governments such as emerged out of these earlier intertribal gatherings, and during the time the government began inducing Fraser Canyon residents to relocate to fertile agricultural lands in the lower Fraser Valley (lands earlier depopulated because of epidemics and associated migrations). Equally, the seemingly European-like expressions of Stó:lō supratribal collective identity formation explain why scholars have overlooked the coordinated military action that the 1884 lynching of Louie Sam by American vigilantes almost provoked, or even the 1906 delegation to London.

What is significant is the following: the trend towards broader regional group affiliation developed not as a result of colonial design but, in fact, despite overt governmental objectives to atomize Aboriginal collective political consciousness. Thus, the ascendancy of Stó:lō and similar expressions of supratribal collective identity elsewhere in the province of British Columbia represent remarkable examples of Indigenous agency despite the increasingly European-like appearance of their formal organizational expressions. Considered in this light, the old ethnohistorical debate over whether contact resulted in increased fragmentation of collective identity and political authority, or in a narrowing of group identification and a reification of chiefly authority, takes on a new meaning. Indigenous communities have never been static units. The various options available at any given time have meant that collective identity has always been a somewhat contentious and negotiated matter.

Thus, it is possible to say with confidence that collective identity has long assumed a situational salience. Aboriginal people, like people everywhere, accept or adopt a form of identity (from among a number of widely recognized legitimate options) that they think provides them the greatest benefits in any given historical context. Inevitably conflict and contestation are involved in any such reorganization. Aboriginal culture has been constantly changing, and Indigenous experience has shaped the changes.

Among the people commonly identified as the Stó:lō, collective identity is an expression forged in the hearth of vigorous debate where more than one legitimate option is always available. 'Traditional' identity in this sense can never be anything more than a particular cultural expression that is informed by past experience and historical understanding. The more informed a definition is, the more likely it is to be perceived and received as legitimate. Thus, while internal tensions remain over what constitutes the most traditional definition of collective identities, it is important to remember that these strains are nothing new – this is as it has always been.

The Indigenous criteria used to assess how and why certain collective identities periodically eclipse others are not always readily apparent to us outside observers who do not share their historical experiences or cultural perspectives. The contemporary lack of Indigenous consensus over what constitutes the most important identity today can be too easily misunderstood from a modernist viewpoint as unresolved Indigenous efforts to define empirical truths, or from a postmodern perspective as proof of the absence of truth and possibly evidence of the continuing colonial state of Indigenous thought processes. When viewed across both temporal and cultural divides, the subtleties of Indigenous ways of knowing are difficult to appreciate, but this does not mean that they are impossible to discern, nor does it absolve us from the task of trying. This study does not claim to have fully achieved cross-cultural historical understanding. Still, a prolonged period of intimate professional and social interaction with the Indigenous people of the lower Fraser watershed has provided insights not readily achievable through standard ethnographic interview and archival research methods alone.

A decade ago the historical anthropologist Marshall Sahlins observed that 'if Anthropology was for too long the study of "historyless peoples," history for even longer was studying "cultureless peoples."'[12] Close ethnographic study is essential to historical analysis. Without it, modern Western sensibilities are inevitably projected onto past Native cultures.[13] The ethnographic information that late-nineteenth and early-twentieth century Stó:lō Elders provided to various anthropologists working in Coast Salish territory reveal the importance and significance of movements and migrations to Indigenous historical understandings. Coast Salish Indigenous historiography emerges through stories of human population movement. After each movement or migration, the deck was reshuffled, so to speak, and people needed to re-establish their identity in reference to new places of residence and new physical and metaphysical geographies.

Indeed, another reason the 1906 delegation represents the beginning of modern B.C. Aboriginal political identity is that by this time the population movements characteristic of an earlier age had been effectively halted. The final phase of significant reserve creation in Stó:lō territory occurred in 1904, when the last of the Fraser Canyon reserves were surveyed and registered. Henceforth, the Indian land base was essentially fixed, and changes of residence between reserves were governed by strict rules as defined in the Indian Act.

Careful ethnographic contextualization is essential to understanding local Indigenous groups, for it also contains within it the potential to reinterpret important aspects of the histories of such non-local entities as nation states and corporate globalization. That Indigenous people did not disappear in the face of concerted government assimilation policies and the onslaught of international capitalism is significant. That Indigenous people have found new ways to be distinct, principally through complicated internal negotiations emphasizing the value of maintaining connections to the past, reveals the importance of local studies for our understanding of national and global processes.

Sustained ethnohistorical conversations and investigation also provide a foundation upon which new historical interpretive frameworks can be built to enrich the history of Native–newcomer relations: the combining of ethnographic investigation with temporal analysis holds the potential to do more than add regional flavour to what has largely been portrayed as essentially the identical story of the advance of Western colonialism across a continent that is politically and culturally diverse.

The history of Native–newcomer relations has been portrayed largely in terms that have little regional or temporal variation. What happened in British Columbia in the nineteenth century has, for all intents and purposes, been regarded as yet another expression of what had already occurred in the Maritimes in the eighteenth century, or would occur in the Yukon in the twentieth, or indeed, in any and all places where Indigenous people have encountered colonialism: Europeans arrived and engaged in an initial phase of meaningful relationships during which they were largely dependent upon Native good will. Disease reduced Aboriginal populations, unsettling their cultural anchors. Over time, the relationships inevitably soured as the Europeans came in greater numbers, settled, and promoted settlement and became increasingly exploitative of the human and natural resources they encountered. Eventually, Natives came to be perceived as impediments rather than facilitators of European aspirations and, as such, were displaced and marginalized through systematic state-sponsored assimilative initiatives. Ultimately, however, Aboriginal people avoided complete victimization and cultural extinction, and instead began a process of cultural revival and renaissance associated with court victories and direct action that led to greater economic and political clout. Within this chronological paradigm, contact inevitably becomes conflict, and resistance ultimately transforms into renewal.

Whatever its value (and undeniably it is great), this metanarrative essentially portrays the impact of Western colonialism on Aboriginal people from the colonial perspective. Within this interpretive framework, Native people are principally depicted as foils and used to critique and expose the excesses of Western colonialism and capitalism. This, unfortunately, has generally prevented Indigenous people from being regarded as much more than reactive victims in the history of Western development, and more recently as ecological prophets for a society that experiences pangs of guilt over its consumptive past and consumer-driven present. Nevertheless, accounts such as the history of the trend towards greater collective identification among the Stó:lō in the period leading up to the twentieth century illustrate that individual tribal histories, and even the history of Westerners in Native history, can also be understood as the unique products of conscious and unconscious decisions made by Indigenous people in a host of unique historical and geographical circumstances. Their history is much more than a component of our history.

The title of a popular collection of Native history essays asserts that the Aboriginal historical experience needs to be brought 'out of the background.'[14] The assumption is that Aboriginal happenings are significant to all Canadians and have been improperly and unjustly hidden in shadows. Certainly, historical events of the scale and significance of the various migrations associated with the smallpox epidemic of 1782, the establishment of Fort Langley, the abandonment of Alámex, the merging of the two Chehalis communities, the Chilliwack displacement of the Swí:lhcha people, and the abandonment of the Fraser Canyon settlements have, at least on occasion, become part of the Canadian historical consciousness when they involved non-Natives.

Of course, others would argue that these and other Stó:lō events did not impact the unfolding of Canadian history generally. Yet, it is difficult to imagine political rallies on the scale of the various Queen's birthday gatherings in New Westminster, or the coordinated Aboriginal response to Lord Dufferin's visit, or the reaction to the lynching of Louie Sam occurring anywhere in Canada by non-Natives and not receiving significant political and scholarly attention. Standard histories of British Columbia devote considerable space to the various white people and organizations that made presentations to Governor General Dufferin at New Westminster, and yet whites made up only a small fraction of the total number of people present at that event.[15] Perhaps it is indicative of the political clout the Stó:lõ and other Indigenous communities are now acquiring in Canada that works like this study are being composed. The coordinated Indigenous response to the marginalization of their land rights, their determined efforts to thwart government attempts to restrict their movements across the landscape, and their continuing spiritual connection to what are commonly dismissed by outsiders as the 'resources' of their largely alienated territory have resulted in a series of legal and political victories that have made their collective history meaningful to those non-Native individuals and interest groups who stand to lose or gain from the changes that Aboriginal self-governance and treaty settlements promise to facilitate.

Given that non-Native society is currently struggling to adjust to the new economic and political influence of Aboriginal communities, interest will no doubt turn increasingly to trying to understand within which expression of Native collective identity power nests. Among the Stó:lõ there are differing opinions as to which identity is the most legitimately empowered to represent certain Aboriginal interests. If, like the people behind the recent Trans-Canada Trail Project, one wants to do something as supposedly benign and innocuous as constructing a hiking trail across Canada, one is faced with the dilemma of trying to identify which Aboriginal political bodies to consult: each local Indian band the trail passes near? the regional tribal council? provincially derived bodies like the B.C. Summit or Union of B.C. Indian Chiefs? Furthermore, what happens when two or more Native communities assert conflicting and possibly exclusive claims to the natural or heritage resources of a particular region? Whose claim will take precedence, and who will arbitrate such a decision? Stated simply, non-Aboriginal society is suddenly being faced with the dilemma of trying to figure out how to consult, and with whom. Though no doubt disconcerting, this is a positive development.

Canada's scattered Indian reserves have contributed to the false impression among non-Natives that Indigenous collective identity is prin-

cipally settlement-based as well as primordially fixed. A short while ago,
in November 2001, members of the Stó:lõ Shxw'õwhámél First Nation
discovered that the federal Department of Indian Affairs official Reserve
Registry no longer listed the X̱elhálh Reserve in the Fraser Canyon as belonging to their band. Instead, it was shown as the property of the nearby
Yale First Nation. When Shxw'õwhámél representatives questioned and
challenged this change, the government official initially replied that it
was simply a clerical oversight created by an anonymous bureaucrat who
assumed the map had originally been made incorrectly. 'Why,' the Ot-
tawa-based civil servant supposedly asked, 'would Shxw'õwhámél have a
reserve so many kilometres away?'[16]

In a related manner, in the summer of 2001, the Department of Fisheries and Oceans issued special Aboriginal fishing licences on a band-
by-band basis that resulted in certain Native individuals attempting to
fish at sites claimed as the hereditary property of other families, ostensibly because the government gave them the right. Conversely, the U.S.-
based Seattle City Light and Authority paid annual compensation to a
single Canadian Interior Salish Indian band for damage caused by the
damming of Ross Lake simply based on the fact that a century-old ethnographer's map identified the region as the territory of the Thompson
Indians. Canadian Coast Salish people living on reserves closer to the
affected area, who also claimed the territory, were neither compensated
nor consulted.[17]

The French proverb, *l'action est fille de la pensée,* reveals a great deal
about the way Europeans conceive of human agency in the unfolding
of history. Among the Stó:lõ there is a saying: 'the ancestor of everything is an action.'[18] Actions, events, happenings, all have agency that
takes precedence over unaided human thought and reason. Important
actions are literally charged with history-shaping power. A person's journey through one of the mystical tunnels that connect various Indigenous
communities in Coast Salish territory, the transformation of a person
into a stone, the never-ending movement of the Fraser River's waters,[19]
a region's sudden depopulation by disease, a community's migration
from the mountains to the valley, a shaman's metaphysical travels into
the domain of the Great First, a group of freed slaves' journey to a territory recently abandoned by others, the surveying of Indian reserves,
the banning of the potlatch, the lynching of a young boy, etc. – these actions, these events, have consequences and results. They shape people's
relationships with the environment and with one another. Over time,
these relationships change. However, when one's status and authority

are largely dependent upon the ability to demonstrate connections between important actions and one's family's history, the relationship between place and time becomes central to maintaining shared notions of collective identity. Put another way, changing historical circumstances challenge geographically anchored power just as place-based authority mitigates and simultaneously shapes the outcomes of changing historical circumstances. Since actions and events affect people differently, history becomes the arbiter of identity. Actions, events, and places are powerful and, in turn, provide power: they are also compromised by the problems inherent in maintaining a stable and shared collective understanding and acceptance of collective identity over time.

Glossary of Halq'eméylem Terms, People, and Place Names

There are sounds in Halkomelem that are distinct from those in English. To accommodate these (in a way that would avoid the esoteric symbols used in the international phonetic alphabet and thereby allow people to type the words on a standard typewriter or with a basic word processor), the linguist Brent Galloway and elders with the Coqualeetza Centre worked together in the 1970s to devise a practical orthography for upriver Halkomelem (Halq'eméylem). This system of writing has been adopted by the Stó:lõ Nation and Stó:lõ Tribal Councils. The following pronunciation guide is an abridged version of that found in Galloway's chapter 'The Significance of the Halkomelem Language Material,' in Oliver Wells, ed., *The Chilliwacks and Their Neighbors* (Vancouver: Talonbooks, 1987), 23–7. Where possible, I have used this orthography throughout the volume.

Halq'eméylem Vowels

a   as in English 'fat,' 'bat' (when under ´ or before w or y) or as in English 'sell,' 'bet' (elsewhere)
e   as in English 'sill,' 'bill' (when between palatal sounds l, lh, x, y, s, ts, ts', k, k') or as in English 'pull,' 'bull' (when between labialized sounds m, w, kw, kw', qw, qw', xw, xw) or as in English 'mutt,' 'what' (elsewhere)
i   as in English 'antique,' 'beet,' 'eel'
o   as in Elglish 'pot,' 'mop,' 'father,' 'brother'
õ   as in English 'no,' 'go,' 'crow'
u   as in Elglish 'Sue,' 'soon,' 'moon,' 'flu'

Most vowels can be followed by [y] or [w] in the same syllable:

aw   as in English 'cow'
ay   as in some pronunciations of the English 'sang' or 'slang'
ew   as in English 'about'
ey   as in English 'bait'
iw   as in English 'peewee' minus the last 'ee'
iy   as in English 'beet'
ow   as in English 'ah well' minus the last 'ell'
oy   as in English 'bite'
ow   as in English 'bowl'

Stressed and Dragged-Out Vowels

Most Halq'eméylem words have a stressed vowel (e.g., á or í or ì). Stress marks indicate which part of the word is said louder and higher. Stress marks do not change the pronunciation of the vowel. The ´ accent indicates a high stress and is roughly four notes higher than an unstressed vowel. The ` accent indicated a mid stress – roughly two notes above an unstressed vowel. A colon ':' means that the preceding sound is dragged out twice as long as a sound without a colon.

Consonants Pronounced as in English

p   as in English 'pill'
t   as in English 'tick'
ch   as in English 'church'
ts   as in English 'rats'
k   as in English 'king'
kw   as in English 'queen' or 'inkwell'
th   as in English 'thin' (but not voiced as in 'this' or 'the')
sh   as in English 'shine'
s   as in English 'sill'
h   as in English 'hat'
m   as in English 'man'
n   as in English 'nod.' Note this sound appears in the downriver and Vancouver islands dialects of Halkomelem and not in upriver Halq'eméylem where it is replaced by 'l'
l   as in English 'land'
y   as in English 'yes' or 'say'

w   as in English 'wood' or 'how'

Consonants that Do Not Appear in English

q   made by raising the very back of the tongue to touch the soft palate
qw   made just like the q but with rounded lips
lh   made by putting the tongue in position to say an 'l' but then blow-
       ing air around the sides of the tongue as if pronouncing an 'h.' As
       in the English 'k' sound found in 'clean' or 'climb.'

Pops (Glottal Stops)

A sound followed by an apostrophe (as follows the st in the Halq'eméylem
word st'éxem) indicates a pop or what linguists refer to as a glottal stop.
It is found in a few English words such as 'mutton' or 'button.' It follows
many vowels in Halq'eméylem as well as the following ten consonants:
ch', k', kw', p', q', t', th', ts', tl'. The 'th' sound occurs in English words
such as 'width' or 'breadth.'

Blow Sounds

There are four blown 'x' sounds. These sound nothing like the 'z' sound
that 'x' sometimes makes in English words. Rather, in Halq'eméylem
these sounds are made by raising the tongue to narrow the passage of air
till the friction of the air is heard.

x   made with the middle of the tongue raised roughly in the same
       place as it is put to make a 'y' as in 'yawn.' But instead of articulat-
       ing a sound the speaker just blows air so as to produce a friction
       sound in the middle of the tongue and the front of the roof of
       the mouth. As in the first sound of the English words 'Hugh' or
       'hew.'
xw   made with the tongue raised a little further back by the middle of
       the roof of the mouth, but with rounded lips. This is similar to the
       'wh' in English but with more friction on the roof of the mouth.
x̲   made still farther back with the back of the tongue raised close to
       the roof of the mouth where the 'q' is made. German has this in
       'ach' and Scottish has it in 'lock' meaning 'lake.'
x̲w   made in the same back place as x̲, but with rounded lips. It is like a
       blown qw while x̲ is like a blown q.

Halq'eméylem Word List

cexwte'n – a rite or ceremony (sometimes referred to as 'entertainments' or 'playthings') belonging to specific tribal communities as
  gifts from the Lord Above; these have spread across tribal communities through marriages.

Chíchelh Siyá:m – literally 'Wealthy Respected One Up Above'; The
  Lord Above, God, Creator, the Great First.

Cwaietsen – a term of address for God, the Creator; parent.

Halq'eméylem – 'language of Leq'á:mel.' The upriver dialect of
  Halkomelem (the language spoken on southeast Vancouver Island,
  as well as along the lower Fraser River watershed as far upriver as
  Sawmill Creek near Yale).

hi'weqw siyá:m *or* yewal siyá:m – head chief or 'master of the whole
  country'; hereditary family leader who carried name of original community founder, or genealogical hero; thus, providing the name
  carrier with legitimate claims to tribal leadership. The entire tribe
  considered itself related to one another through transformer-era kin
  ties to a tribal founder.

lats'umexw – 'different people'; those Aboriginal people who are not
  part of the Fraser River continuum.

lumlamelut – lightning.

q'eytsi'i (*from which* 'Katzie') – a spongy moss.

qey'xene'?ten – shadow or reflection; literally the spirit associated with
  one's shadow cast by the sun or moon.

Qoqolaxel – Watery Eaves.

s'téxem – 'worthless people' who have 'forgotten or lost their history';
  lower-status/class people without hereditary rights to prominent
  food resource sites; historically, these were likely the illegitimate offspring of unions between elite males and lower-status women or slave
  women.

shxwelí – life force, spirit, soul.

shxwlá:m – healers, shamans; specially trained people (usually men)
  who have the power to heal by controlling spirit entities; some have
  the esoteric knowledge to travel through mystical tunnels to the xá:xa
  spirit realm where they receive special knowledge including details of
  sxwōxwiyám histories.

siateluq – a family member recognized as having authority to regulate
  access to an owned food resource site; task master.

siyá:m – respected leaders, tribal spokesmen.

siyá:ye – 'friend or relative,' but more accurately 'someone to whom I feel very close, and yet with whom I am unable to demonstrate any direct blood or marriage tie.'

skw'iyéth – slaves.

sle'qwem – the spirits that impregnate one's breath with power.

smelá:lh – 'worthy people' who 'know their history'; member of elite high-status/upper-class family.

smestíyexw – vitality; spirit force responsible for conscious thought, and associated with memory.

smílha – winterdance, spirit dance, smokehouse dance.

spoleqwíth'a – shade or ghost; the merging of the vitality (smestíyexw) and shadow (qey'xene'ʔten) after death, and which roams invisible in the neighbourhood of its old home, being a source of great concern among surviving relatives who fear it may entice away a living person's vitality.

sqwélqwel – true stories, real news, life history, personal history, or history that's happened to you or someone you know.

st'elt'ólkwlh – people without winterdance spirit helpers, non-spirit dancers; the uninitiated.

st'éxem – serfs.

St'qwó:mpth – 'those who speak our language.'

stó:méx – warrior spirit power, often associated with wasps; warriors.

Swalis – 'getting rich.'

Swaniset – the Supernatural Benefactor.

swia'm – talent or power; closely associated with vitality/thought (smestíyexw) and is sometimes difficult to distinguish from it, and which perishes with the physical body at death.

sxá:sls – 'one who keeps track of everything'; a respected older person recognized as a carrier of sacred stories and knowledge.

sxa'yeqs – tribe formerly living on Stave Lake.

sxwóxwiyám – stories/histories describing the activities of the Creator, the transformers, and sky-born heroes; often taking place in the distant past, but may involve recent miraculous happenings.

Sxwóxwiymelh – 'a lot of people died at once.'

sxwóyxwey – sacred mask and regalia typically worn by men but inherited through women who decide which men within a family are worthy of wearing the mask.

sxwsiyá:m – 'wealthy men with property'; family leader with recognized ownership rights over a food resource site (e.g., camus bed, salmon stream, cranberry bog); recognized owners.

syewin or syewil or yewin – prayers used to remove malevolent shades or ghosts; special prayers.

syewinmet *or* yewinmet – ritualists who 'know many prayers'; such prayers can heal, rob enemies of their vitality, tame animals, and change the weather.

syúwél *or sometimes* ó:lkwlh – guardian spirits; generally acquired from birds, animals, or natural elements and which manifest themselves during the winterdance, and which were associated with professional or vocational skills and abilities.

tel swayel – sky-born heroes and community founders sent to earth by the Creator.

Thelhatsstan – 'Clothed with Power'; Old Pierre's namesake.

Ts'elxweyéqw (*from which* 'Chilliwack') – literally 'head,' meaning either the headwaters of a river or the head of a person or group of people.

Ts'okwám – Skunk Cabbage; the name of the tribe that throughout most of the nineteenth century occupied the seven villages located between the rapids at Lady Franklin Rock and the rapids at Sailor Bar (aka the 'Five Mile Fishery').

xá:xa – sacred, taboo, spiritually potent.

xawsó:lh – 'babies'; new initiates in the winterdance community.

xelth'it – true history.

Xexá:ls – 'The Inscribers'; the powerful transformer siblings (three bear brothers and their sister) who were the children of Red-Headed Woodpecker and Black Bear; they travelled the territory 'making things right,' i.e., making them permanent and recognizable/predictable.

xólhemìlh – 'babysitters'; those who care for new winterdance initiates.

Xwelítem – literally 'hungry to the point of starving,' 'the starving ones'; the name applied to non-Natives.

Xwélmexw – human beings, or literally 'people of life'; those Aboriginal people whose lives are in some meaningful way oriented towards the Fraser Canyon fishery and connected to the lower Fraser resident population.

yewal siyá:m – most respected leader, First Chief

Yukletaw (Lekwiltok) – literally 'Unkillable Things'

Notes

1 Encountering Lower Fraser River Indigenous Identity and Historical Consciousness

1 Quoted in James Morton, *Capilano, the Story of a River* (Toronto: McClelland and Stewart, 1970), 36.
2 Benedict Anderson, *Imagined Communities: Reflections on the Origin and Spread of Nationalism* (London: Verso, 1983).
3 Keith H. Basso, *Wisdom Sits in Places: Landscape and Language among the Western Apache* (Albuquerque: University of New Mexico, 1996); Julie Cruikshank, with Angela Sidney, Kitty Smith, and Annie Ned, *Life Lived Like a Story: Life Stories of Three Yukon Native Elders* (Vancouver: UBC Press, 1990); Julie Cruikshank, *Do Glaciers Listen: Local Knowledge, Colonial Encounters, and Social Imagination* (Vancouver: UBC Press, 2005); Jay Miller, *Shamanic Odyssey: The Lushootseed Salish Journey to the Land of the Dead* (Menlo Park: Ballena Press, 1988); Brian Thom, 'Coast Salish Senses of Place: Dwelling, Meaning, Power, Property, and Territory in the Coast Salish World' (Ph.D. diss., McGill University 2004); Crisca Bierwert, *Brushed by Cedar, Living by the River: Coast Salish Figures of Power* (Tuscon: University of Arizona, 1999); Alexandra Harmon, *Indians in the Making: Ethnic Relations and Indian Identities around Puget Sound* (Berkeley: University of California Press, 1998); Aletta Biersack, ed., *Clio in Oceania: Towards a Historical Anthropology* (Washington: Smithsonian Institution, 1991); Paige Raibmon, *Authentic Indians: Episodes of Encounter from the Late-Nineteenth-Century Northwest Coast* (Durham: Duke University Press, 2005); Philip Deloria, *Indians in Unexpected Places* (Lawrence: University of Kansas Press, 2006); Gary Zellar, *African Creeks: Estlvste and the Creek Nation* (Norman: University of Oklahoma Press, 2007); Jeff Oliver, *Landscapes and Social Transformation on the Northwest Coast: Colonial Encounters in the Fraser Valley* (Tucson: University of Arizona Press, 2010); Sarah

Carter, *Capturing Women: The Manipulation of Cultural Imagery in Canada's Prairie West* (Montreal and Kingston: McGill-Queen's University Press, 1997); John Sutton Lutz, *Makuk: A New History of Aboriginal-White Relations* (Vancouver: UBC Press, 2008); Diane M. Nelson, *A Finger in the Wound: Body Politics in Quincentennial Guatemala* (Berkeley: University of California Press, 1999); Marshall Sahlins, *How 'Natives' Think: About Captain Cook for Example* (Chicago: University of Chicago Press, 1995); Marshall Sahlins, *Apologies to Thucydides: Understanding History as Culture and Vice Versa* (Chicago: University of Chicago Press, 2004); Clifford Geertz, 'Thick Descriptions: Toward an Interpretive Theory of Culture,' *The Interpretation of Cultures: Selected Essays,* ed. Clifford Geertz (New York, Basic Books, 1973).

4 *Stó:lō* is pronounced Staw-low.

5 The Indian Act (s. 74) has provisions for the appointment by the minister of Indian affairs of non-elected councils, known popularly as the 'custom system.'

6 Vincent Stogen, personal communication, Sept. 1992.

7 In subsequent years it came to be known as the Stó:lō Fishing Authority.

8 Skowkale Chief Steven Point explained at a community gathering at Soowahlie in September 1994 that he initially expected each Stó:lō tribe to individually submit 'statements of intent' to the B.C. Treaty Commission, in the hopes that these would be coordinated by the leadership of a larger Stó:lō Nation governing body.

9 The last such 'traditionally' chosen supra-tribal leader, I was told, was Liquitim who died c.1900.

10 Wayne Suttles, 'Post-contact Change among the Lummi Indians,' *BCHQ* 18/1&2 (1954): 29; Wilson Duff, *The Upper Stalo Indians of the Fraser Valley, British Columbia* (Victoria: BCPM, Anthropology in B.C., Memoir No. 1, 1952), 86.

11 Under the 1876 Indian Act, a 'band' was 'any tribe, band or body of Indians who own or are interested in a reserve or in Indian lands in common, of which the legal title is vested in the Crown ... for which the government of Canada is responsible' (s. 3.1). 'Indians' were 'any male person [and his children and spouse] reputed to belong to a particular band' (s. 3.3) and 'reserves' were lands 'held in trust for ... [the Indians'] benefit' (s. 4.1).

The act clarified that 'no person, or Indian other than an Indian of the band, shall settle, reside or hunt upon, occupy or use the land or marsh, or shall settle, reside upon or occupy any road ... belonging to or occupied by such band' (s. 11). Non-members who settled, hunted, resided, or in other ways used a part of a reserve without the approval of the superintendent general were subject to criminal charges and eviction (ss. 12–20). Only band members (originally only male band members) could vote in elections for

Chief and council (s. 61). Indian and Northern Affairs Canada, *Indian Acts and Amendments, 1868–1950* (Ottawa: Treaties and Historical Research Centre Research Branch, 2nd ed., 1981).

12 *Corbiere* v. *Canada* (Minister of Indian and Northern Affairs), [1999] 2 Supreme Court Record, 1999 CanLII 687 (Supreme Court of Canada), Docket 25708.

13 Sproat to Supt. Gen., 25 Nov. 1878. 'The Lower Fraser,' British Columbia Archives (hereafter BCA), Government Record (hereafter GR) 1965, File 2; emphasis in original.

14 See esp. Cole Harris, *Making Native Space: Colonialism, Resistance, and Reserves in British Columbia* (Vancouver: UBC Press, 2002); also Paul Tennant, *Aboriginal Peoples and Politics: The Indian Land Question in British Columbia, 1849–1989* (Vancouver: UBC Press, 1990), and Ken Brealey, 'Travels from Point Ellice: Peter O'Reilly and the Indian Reserve System in British Columbia,' *BC Studies* nos. 115&116 (1997/8): 180–242.

15 The original challenge to the classic interpretation was launched by Kenneth D. Tollefson in 'The Snoqualmie: A Puget Sound Chiefdom,' *Ethnology* 26/2 (1987): 121–36. He sustained his argument, despite concerted opposition, in his 'In Defense of a Snoqualmie Political Chiefdom Model,' *Ethnohistory* 43/1 (1996): 145–71.

Wayne Suttles led the defence of the non-centralized model he had done so much to popularize in his article '"They Recognize No Superior Chief": The Strait of Juan de Fuca in the 1790s,' in Jose Luis Peset, ed., *Culturas de la Costa Noroeste de America* (Madrid: Turner, 1989), 251–64. Suttles was supported by Bruce G. Miller and Daniel Boxberger, in 'Creating Chiefdoms: The Puget Sound Case,' *Ethnohistory* 41/2 (1994): 267–93, and 'Evolution or History? A Response to Tollefson,' *Ethnohistory* 44/1 (1996): 135–7.

Jay Miller took exception to all in his commentary 'Back to Basics: Chiefdoms in Puget Sound,' *Ethnohistory* 44/2 (1997): 375–87.

16 Chief Hope of the Yale First Nation has been quoted in local Fraser Valley newspapers as viewing the Stó:lō use of the canyon fishery as an 'invasion' of Yale's First Nation's traditional territory. See the following 1998 articles in *Chilliwack Progress*: 'Yale Territory Defended from Sto:lo Invasion,' 7 April, and an article of the same title a few days later, on 12 April; 'Family Feud: Sto:lo Say Fight over Fishing Rights with Yale Band Comes Down to Respect for Traditional Fishing Rights,' 17 April.

17 David M. Schaepe, 'Rock Fortifications: Archaeological Insights into Pre-Contact Warfare and Sociopolitical Organization among the Stó:lō of the Lower Fraser River Canyon, B.C.,' *American Antiquity* 71/4 (2006): 671–705.

18 R.G. Collingwood, *The Idea of History* (New York: Oxford University Press, 1956), 323–8.

19 Aletta Biersack, 'History and Theory in Anthropology,' in A. Biersack, ed., *Clio in Oceania: Toward a Historical Anthropology* (Washington, DC: Smithsonian Institution 1991), 12.

20 Patrick J. Geary, *The Myth of Nations:The Medieval Origins of Europe* (Princeton: Princeton University Press, 2002).

21 Suttles, 'They Recognize No Superior Chief,' 251.

22 See, e.g., Fredrik Barth, *Ethnic Groups and Boundaries* (Boston: Little Brown, 1969; Sarah Carter, *Capturing Women: The Manipulation of Cultural Imagery in Canada's Prairie West* (Montreal and Kingston: McGill-Queen's University Press, 1997); Sergei Kan, *Memory Eternal: Tlingit Culture and Russian Orthodox Christianity through Two Centuries* (Seattle: University of Washington Press, 1999); Kirk Dombrowski, *Against Culture: Development, Politics and Religion in Indian Alaska* (Lincoln: University of Nebraska Press, 2001); and Alexandra Harmon, *Indians in the Making: Ethnic Relations and Indian Identities around Puget Sound* (Berkeley: University of California Press, 1998).

23 Wendy Wickwire, 'To See Ourselves as the Other's Other: Nlakapamux Contact Narratives,' *Canadian Historical Review* 75/1 (1994): 1–20.

24 See Keith Windshuttle's *The Fabrication of Aboriginal History* (Paddington, NSW: MacLeay Press, 2002), 360. For a response, see Robert Manne, ed., *Whitewash: On Keith Windshuttle's* Fabrication of Aboriginal History (Melbourne: Black Ink Agenda, 2003).

25 Marshall David Sahlins, 'The Return of the Event, Again: With Reflections on the Beginnings of the Great Fijian War of 1855 between the Kingdoms of Bau and Rewa,' in Biersack, *Clio in Oceania*, 38–9.

26 Ibid., 40.

27 Marshall David Sahlins, *Historical Metaphor and Mythical Realities: Structure in the Early History of the Sandwich Islands Kingdom* (Ann Arbor: University of Michigan Press, 1981).

28 Fernand Braudel, *The Mediterranean and the Mediterranean World in the Age of Philip II*, 2 vols., trans. by Sian Reynolds (New York: Harper and Row, 1972–3 [1949]).

29 Raymond Fogelson, 'The Ethnohisotry of Events and Nonevents,' *Ethnohistory* 36/2 (1989): 139.

30 Sahlins, 'Return of the Event, Again,' 46.

31 Ibid., 45.

32 Marshall David Sahlins, *Islands of History* (London: Tavistock, 1985), 152.

33 Ibid., 47.

34 I am indebted to Sonny McHalsie for his steadfast dedication to, and encouragement of, historical and cultural research that, as he puts it, is simultaneously both 'respectful and accurate.'

35 *Out of the Background,* Ken Coates and Robin Fisher, eds., is the title of a
popular textbook anthology on Canadian Native history (Toronto: Irwin,
2nd ed., 1998).

2 Economics, Geography, Environment, and Historical Identity

1 John Smith, *Fifth Book of the Generall Historie of Virginia, New England, and the
Summer Islands, 1642,* 169.
2 Within the anthropological literature the Coast Salish are divided into the
following six major groupings or language families: (1) the isolated Bella
Coola (Nuxalk) of the central coast of British Columbia; (2) the Northern
Coast Salish of the northern Strait of Georgia (speakers of the Comox, Pent-
latch, Homalco, Klahoose, Sliammon, and Sechelt languages); (3) the Central Coast Salish of southern Strait of Georgia and the Strait of Juan de Fuca
(speakers of the Squamish, Halkomelem, Nooksask, Straits, and Clallam
languages); (4) the Southern Coast Salish of Puget Sound and Hood Canal
(speakers of the Lushootseed and Twana languages); (5) the Southwestern
Coast Salish of the outer coast of Washington State (speakers of Quinault,
Chehalis, and Cowlitz languages); and finally, (6) the isolated Tillamook of
the coast of central Oregon.
   For ethnographic and historical overviews of these groupings consult
Wayne Suttles, *Handbook of North American Indians,* vol. 7, *The Northwest Coast*
(Washington,DC: Smithsonian Institution, 1990), esp.: Dorothy Kennedy
and Randall T. Bouchard, 'Bella Coola,' 323–39; Kennedy and Bouchard,
'Northern Coast Salish,' 441–52; Suttles, 'Central Coast Salish,' 453–75;
Suttles and Barbara Lane, 'Southern Coast Salish,' 485–502; Yvonne Hajda,
'Southwestern Coast Salish,' 503–17; and William R. Seaburg and Jay Miller,
'Tillamook,' 560–7.
3 See David M. Schaepe, 'Stó:lō Communication and Transportation Routes,
c.1850,' in K.T. Carlson et al., eds., *A Stó:lō-Coast Salish Historical Atlas* (Vancouver: Douglas and McIntyre, and Chilliwack: Stó:lō Heritage Trust, 2001),
60–1.
4 Colin Duffield et al., eds., 'Constructing a Province, Clear-Cutting a Nation,'
in Carlson, *Atlas,* 112–13.
5 Suttles, 'They Recognize No Superior Chief,' 252.
6 Suttles reports that his informants translated *Xwélmexw* simply as 'Indian' or
used it to apply to any identifiable group of Native people. He speculated
that the older Indigenous meaning was likely restricted to a tribe. In my
own investigations Elders have consistently translated *Xwélmexw* as 'Aboriginal people' or 'First Nations people' (equivalent to Suttles' 'Indian'). How-

ever, they also point out the significance of the suffix *mexw*, which is found
in many terms associated with life such as *mexwiya* (belly-button or navel).
Hence, as one Stó:lō person who had given the matter much thought
explained, the best translation of *Xwélmexw* is probably 'People of Life,' a
concept best appreciated within the context of social and spatial distance.
Thus, I will be using *Xwélmexw* to refer to all those 'known people' whose
lives centre around the lower Fraser River. They need not be year-round
residents.

7 Franz Boas 'The Social Organization of the Haida,' in *The 68th Report of the
   British Association for the Advancement of Science for 1898*, 17–18, London, 1898.

8 See Franz Boas: 'Notes on the Ethnology of British Columbia,' *Proceedings
   of the American Philosophical Society* 24/126 (1887): 422–8; 'Indians of British
   Columbia,' *Transactions of the Royal Society of Canada for 1888* 6/2 (1888):
   47–57; 'Notes on the Snanaimuq,' *American Anthropologist* 2/4 (1889): 321–8;
   'Indian Tribes of the Lower Fraser River,' in the *The 64th Report of the British
   Association for the Advancement of Science for 1890*, 454–63, London, 1894.

     See also Thomas T. Waterman, *Notes on the Ethnology of the Indians of Puget
   Sound* (New York: Museum of the American Indian, 1973); and Lewis Henry
   Morgan, *Ancient Society: Or, Researches in the Lines of Human Progress from Sav-
   agery, through Barbarism to Civilization* (New York: H. Holt, 1877).

9 In the *Second Report to the British Association for the Advancement of Sciences*
   in 1898, the Committee on the Ethnological Survey of Canada included a
   letter from Charles Hill-Tout which promised the imminent publication of
   an article he then had 'in hand' describing 'an account of a great confederacy of tribes in the Salish region of "Chilliwack."' This report was never
   published, and no trace of the manuscript has yet been found.

10 See Charles Hill-Tout's Salish texts, collected and introduced by Ralph
   Maud, *The Salish People: The Local Contribution of Charles Hill-Tout*, vol. 3, *The
   Mainland Halkomelem*, and vol. 4, *The Sechelt and the South-Eastern Tribes of
   Vancouver Island*(Vancouver: Talonbooks, 1978).

11 The significance of the watershed-based tribal community was recognized
   by even the earliest permanent European observers, as in 1838 when Hudson's Bay Company (HBC) Chief Factor James Douglas commented that
   the Puget Sound Salish were 'without a doubt ... one and the same people,
   deriving a local designation from their place of residence.' Douglas explained that river-based 'community' or 'society' 'appellations,' corresponding with what the earlier HBC employee T.C. Elliot had described as 'tribes'
   or 'nations'('The Journal of John Work, November and December, 1824,'
   Washington Historical Quarterly 3/3 [1912]: 198–228) such as 'Squaly amish,
   Puce alap amish, Sino amish, Sina homish, Skatchet, Nowhalimeek ... were

regarded as the source of an imaginary line of demarcation, which divides the inhabitants of one petty stream, from the people living upon another, and have become the fruitful source of the intensive commotions, that so frequently disturb the tranquility of the District.' See James Douglas, Fort Vancouver, to Gov. James Simpson, 18 March, 1838, in E.E. Rich, ed., *The Letters of John McLaughlin from Fort Vancouver to the Governor and Committee, First Series*, vol. 4, *1825–38*, Appendix A (Toronto: Champlain Society, 1991), 280–1.

12 Ibid.

13 Marian Smith, *The Puyallup-Nisqually* (New York: Columbia University Press, 1940), 4.

14 Subsequently, Sally Snyder documented five distinct tribes along the Skagit River. With the exception of the lower Fraser system the Skagit drainage is home to more tribes than any other Coast Salish river. See her 'Skagit Society and Its Existential Basis: An Ethnofolkloristic Reconstruction' (doctoral dissertation, University of Washington, 1964), 63, 65.

15 Smith, *Puyallup-Nisqually*, 5.

16 Ibid., 3, 1.

17 Ibid., 3.

18 I provide a preliminary exploration of the applicability of this model to the Fraser River region in 'Expressions of Collective Identity, ' in Carlson et al., eds., *Atlas*, 24–9.

19 Charles Hill-Tout explained, during a phone conversation with Miss Annis of the Carnegie Library in Vancouver, that his informants defined the term *Stó:lō* as 'River of Rivers.' Miss Annis conveyed this information to Denys Nelson, who in turn, had the information corroborated by Jason Allard, the son of a Coast Salish woman and an HBC trader at Fort Langley. See 'Diary of a Trip up the Fraser,' in Denys Nelson's Journal, 5 March 1925, VM, Hill-Tout Collection, General Files, B.XI.

20 Suttles' writings on this topic have been gathered in his 1987 anthology, *Coast Salish Essays* (Vancouver: Talonbooks, 1987). See 'Affinal Ties: Subsistence, and Prestige among the Coast Salish,' [1960] 15–25; 'Variation in Habitat and Culture on the Northwest Coast,' [1962] 26–44; 'The Persistence of Intervillage Ties among the Coast Salish,' [1963] 209–32; 'Coping with Abundance: Subsistence on the Northwest Coast,' [1968] 45–66. More recently he has added to this corpus with 'They Recognize No Supreior Chief' and 'The Ethnographic Significance of the Fort Langley Journals,' in M. MacLachlan, ed., *The Fort Langley Journals, 1827–30* (Vancouver: UBC Press, 1998), 163–210.

21 Suttles, 'The Persistence of Intervillage Ties, ' 209–34.

22 Ibid., 210–11.

23 Suttles, 'Variation in Habitat,' 32.

24 Ibid., 36–7, 40. Suttles compared the seasonal availability of food resources within the lower Fraser River habitat region with those farther north to tentatively suggest that 'as we go northward along the coast we find less variety in types of resources, greater local and seasonal variation, and possibly less year-to-year fluctuation.' As a result, 'the more northern tribes rely on fewer kinds of plants and animals and get them at fewer places and for shorter times during the year, but in greater concentration, and with consequently greater chance for failure' (37, 40).

25 George Gibbs, 'Tribes of Western Washington and Northwestern Oregon,' in J.W. Power, ed., *Contributions to North America Ethnology* 1/2, 187 (Washington, DC: Department of the Interior, U S. Geographical and Geological Survey of the Rocky Mountain Region, 1877; repr. Seattle: Shorey, 1970).

26 Duff, *Upper Stalo*, 77.

27 See Suttles, 'Affinal Ties,' in *Coast Salish Essays*, 21, and 'Variation in Habitat,' 56–61; Duff, *Upper Stalo*, 77. See also, Karen Albers, 'Resource Sites in S'olh Temexw: Traditional Concepts of Ownership – Final Report for the Family-Owned Sites Project,' June 2000 (unpublished technical report in SNA).

28 Suttles, 'Affinal Ties,' 21.

29 Contrary to evidence presented here as collected by myself and most anthropologists, Charles Hill-Tout's investigations of the Chehalis Tribe led him to declare that the 'essentially democratic spirit' of the Salish prevented the development of individual or family-based property rights. 'Hunting, fishing, berry, and root grounds were all common to the whole tribe.' See, Hill-Tout, *Salish People*, vol. 3, 116.

30 Wayne Suttles and Diamond Jenness. *Katzie Ethnographic Notes, and the Faith of a Coast Salish Indian* (Victoria: BCPM, Anthropology in B.C., Memoir No. 2, 1955), 10, 26.

31 Duff, *Upper Stalo*, 77.

32 Rosaleen George, personal communication, Aug. 1996.

33 Smith, *Puyallup-Nisqually*, 49.

34 Miller, 'Back to Basics,' 380–1.

35 Suttles and Jenness, *Katzie Ethnographic Notes*, 10.

36 Hill-Tout, *Salish People*, vol. 3, 44.

37 Suttles and Jenness, *Katzie*, 10.

38 Hill-Tout, *Salish People*, vol. 3, 103.

39 Duff, *Upper Stalo*, 32.

40 Jay Miller, *Lushootseed Culture and the Shamanic Odyssey: Anchored Radiance* (Lincoln: University of Nebraska Press, 1999), 122–30.

41 Suttles, 'Variation in Habitat,' 42.

42 Duff, *Upper Stalo*, 76.

43 Maclachlan, *Fort Langley Journals*.

44 Bruce G. Miller, 'Centrality and Measures of Regional Structure in Aboriginal Western Washington,' *Ethnology* 28/2 (1989): 265–76.

45 Ibid., 271.

46 Keith Thor Carlson, 'Stó:lō Exchange Dynamics,' *Native Studies Review* 11/1 (1997): 30–5.

47 Ibid., 30–3.

48 Schaepe, 'Rock Fortifications.'

49 Duff states that it took four to five days to travel from Musqueam at the Fraser's mouth to Yale at the entrance to the canyon, and two to travel the reverse downriver; see his *Upper Stalo*, 16. Simon Fraser made his hasty retreat from Musqueam to Yale in four days, stopping along the way to steal a canoe and put down a threatened mutiny; see W. Kaye Lamb, *Simon Fraser: Letters and Journals, 1806–1808* (Toronto: Macmillan, 1960), 107–14.

     On numerous occasions while travelling in a small boat in the waters between Yale and Langley on the Fraser I have been impressed by how often my companions and I encountered locations where if we pulled in near to shore and shut off the boat's motor we would be drawn upstream, often for several hundred metres, by the currents of gigantic back eddies.

50 Fishing sites are owned and regulated by families during the fishing season. During other times of the year these sites are left open and others used them for purposes other than fishing (mainly travel); other uses of these sites were not contested, so long as those uses did not interfere with the owner's ability to fish during the appropriate season.

51 Gibbs, 'Tribes of Western Washington and Northwestern Oregon,' 186–7.

52 Smith, *Puyallup-Nisqually*, 3.

53 Wayne Suttles, 'Space and Time, Wind and Tide – Some Halkomelem Modes of Classification,' in *Coast Salish Essays*, 67–8.

54 Charles Hill-Tout, *The Native Races of the British Empire, British North America I, The Far West, The Home of the Salish and Dene* (Toronto: Copp Clark, 1907), 44.

55 More than one Stó:lō Elder has explained to me how the spirit songs of the Coastal Raiders hypnotized listeners and ensured safe and expeditious passage up and then back down the Fraser River.

3 Spiritual Forces of Historical Affiliation

1 Diamond Jenness, *Faith of a Coast Salish Indian*, 66, ed. by W. Duff (Victoria: BCPM, Anthropology in British Columbia, Memoir 3, 1955).

2 See Lutz, *Makuk: A New History of Aboriginal-White Relations*.

3 The early ethnographer, Charles Hill-Tout, noted that the idea of a
   Supreme Being is 'entirely foreign to the native mind, and is in direct
   conflict with the democratic genius of Salish institutions, and with the ideas
   embodied in their myths.' This interpretation was directly challenged by
   Diamond Jenness' informant Old Pierre, who insisted that the idea was ancient and Indigenous. Jenness himself, and every other anthropologist who
   followed him into Stó:lō territory asking similar questions, was very reluctant to accept Old Pierre's opinion. Suttles and Jenness, *Katzie Ethnographic
   Notes*, 6; see also Wayne Suttles, 'The Plateau Prophet Dance among the
   Coast Salish,' in *Coast Salish Essays*, 164, 178, 185–7; and Duff, *Upper Stalo*,
   119–20.
      Jay Miller's recent conclusion (*Lushootseed Culture*, 64, 50) that the 'Salish
   belief in a supreme diety ... was probably ancient, although subsequently
   influenced by beliefs about the Christian God' is in keeping with my own
   thoughts on the subject. This view appears to be in agreement with the early
   ethnographic observations of Franz Boas, who noted ('Indians of British Columbia,' 55): 'Among the Coast Salish ... [the sun] is worshiped, although
   no offerings are made to him, while it is said that the Salish of the interior
   burn food, blankets and other property as an offering to the sun ... The
   wanderer ... considered the son of the diety ... is called Qals.'
4 For an account of Indigenous Christians' opposition to social scientists' efforts to historicize belief in a Supreme Being, see Ian McIntosh, 'Anthropology, Self-determination and Aboriginal Belief in the Christian God,' *Oceania*
   67/4 (1997): 273–89.
5 Rev. Thomas Crosby, *Among the An-ko-me-nums [Halkomelems] or Flathead
   Tribes of the Pacific Coast* (Toronto: William Briggs, 1907), 112.
6 Commander R.C. Mayne, RN, FRGS, *Four Years in British Columbia and Vancouver Island: An Account of the Forests, Rivers, Coast Gold Fields, and Reasons for
   Colonization* (London: John Murray, 1862), 272.
7 As quoted in William Carew Hazlitt, *The Great Gold Fields of Cariboo: With an
   Authentic Description, Brought Down to the Latest Period, of British Columbia and
   Vancouver Island* (New York: Routledge, Warne, and Routledge, 1862), 34.
   I am grateful to Dave Robertson for drawing my attention to this source.
8 J.W. McKay, 'Indian Tribes, Correspondence 1881, Regarding Festivals,
   Traditions, etc.,' BCPA, J.W. McKay Papers, Add Mss 1917.
9 Snyder, 'Skagit Society and Its Existential Basis,' 21–2.
10 This person asked not to be identified with this particular comment.
11 Diamond Jenness, 'Chapter VII: Community Rituals,' in *Faith of a Coast Salish Indian*, 77.
12 Ibid., 78. A non-Native social scientist who altered a *sxwōxwiyám* and began

publicly telling his new version of the story quickly found himself ostracized from a portion of Stó:lō society and ultimately censured.

13 Rosaleen George and Elizabeth Herrling, personal communications, 1995–2001.

14 For an interesting discussion of the way Cree concepts of the spirit world and the relative importance of a monotheistic Creator vis-à-vis other spirit helpers and entities changed throughout the contact and colonial eras, see John Milloy, '"Our Country": The Significance of the Buffalo Resource for a Plains Cree Sense of Territory,' in K. Abel and J. Friesen, eds., *Aboriginal Resource Use in Canada: Historical and Legal Aspects* (Winnipeg: University of Manitoba Press, 1991), 51–70.

15 Crosby, *Among the An-ko-me-nums*, 112.

16 In my most recent discussions with fluent Halq'eméylem speakers a third category of historical narrative called *xelth'it,* has been mentioned, which is also translated as 'true history.' The context in which this expression is used suggests it is probably the word applied to a version of an historical narrative that has proven more true than another after a council of historical experts has assessed the merits of two competing historical discourses.

Hill-Tout, in his work among the Kwantlen Tribe near Fort Langley identified two types of Stó:lō historical narratives: 'siyis,' which his informants described as 'stories they believed to be true, in contradistinction to the term soqwiam (swoxwiyam) which signifies a "fable or myth."' See his 'Ethnological Studies of the Mainland Halkomelem, a Division of the Salish of British Columbia,' in *Salish People,* vol. 3, 416–41.

17 Jan Vansina, *Oral Tradition as History* (Madison: University of Wisconsin Press, 1985).

18 M. Teresa Carlson et al., 'Stó:lō Oral Narratives,' in K.T. Carlson et al., eds. *You Are Asked to Witness: The Stó:lō in Canada's Pacific Coast History* (Chilliwack: Stó:lō Heritage Trust, 1997), 181–96.

19 Jenness, *Faith,* 75.

20 I first heard the expression 'making the world right' used to describe the works of the transformers from Mrs Matilda 'Tilly' Gutierrez in the summer of 1992. Since then I have heard many other Elders using the same phrase.

21 Franz Boas, *Indianische Sagen von der Nordpacifischen Kuste Americas* (Berlin: A. Asher, 1895) . Now available as *Indian Myths and Legends from the North Pacific Coast,* ed. by R. Bouchard and D. Kennedy, trans. by Dietrich Bertz (Vancouver: Talonbooks, 2002). See also, Hill-Tout, *Salish People,* vol. 3, 145–8, 156. See also Franz Boas, 'Tsimshian Mythology, ' in *31st Annual Report of the Bureau of American Ethnology to the Secreatry of the Smithsonian Institution, 1909–1910* (Washington, DC: Government Printring Office, 1916), 29–1037.

In examining the role myths play in building a sense of anchored com-
minity among the Cowichan Coast Salish, Brian Thom (Ph.D. diss., 2004)
has documented similar diversity in the content of stories.

22 This synoptic description conveys the general belief of most Stó:lō people concerning the transformers. It is interesting that many Elders know
continuing stories of X̱exá:ls that occurred after their journeys had taken
them beyond Coast Salish territory into British Columbia's interior plateau,
although the characters often change identity.

Stó:lō Elders, however, prefer not to tell these stories themselves.
Instead, they simply explain that X̱exá:ls eventually 'reached the sunset.'
They explain that the transformers' activities beyond the Fraser Canyon 'are
not our stories.' This lends support to the thesis of this book that collective
identity is related to specific territories that are defined, at least in part,
through reference to sacred stories.

23 A central objective of Hill-Tout's writing and analysis was to identify evidence that could be used to demonstrate distinctions between Coast Salish
tribes. Thus, for example, he spent a great deal of time speculating, from little evidence, about the possible greater antiquity of one tribe's occupation
of a region rather than another's. Such uninformed theorizing, disregarded
and discredited by most of his peers, appears to have been a contributing
factor to Hill-Tout's academic marginalization.

24 See Hill-Tout, *Salish People*, vol. 3, 48, and 53n9. See also, Jenness, *Faith*, 39:
Healers, of course, still train and inherit powers and special incantations.
Old Pierre describes how this was true for his time as well, but he argues
these people receive weaker powers due to the less rigorous training they
undergo: 'Today there are priests who know many old prayers, but they
have little power because they did not undergo the long training and purification of their ancestors.'

Wayne Suttles reminds us that the role of gossip within Coast Salish societies serves as a powerful check on claims to greatness. It was common for
him, as it is for me today, to encounter people who claim that their power is
stronger and more legitimate than another's for a variety of reasons, whereas the belittled individual will privately say the same thing about the original
person. Moreover, not all people who learned the esoteric knowledge of the
spirit world and transformer narratives were training to be healers.

One Stó:lō Elder, Matilda Guiterrez, living today and from the community of Chawathil, was taken as a pubescent girl by her Elders and taught the
many transformation stories and was given the responsibility to 'keep these
stories and pass them down.'

25 See Hill-Tout, *Salish People*, vol. 3, 69. While I am inclined to think that both

the Katzie and Kwantlen are referring to the same myth-age individual, it is possible that they are speaking about different entities and simply using the name Swaniset as a title. Evidence for this line of thought derives from the fact that the Kwantlen translated the word Swaniset differently than the Katzie. The Kwantlen translation is 'to appear in a mysterious manner.'

26 Jenness, *Faith*, 71.

27 Certain technical knowledge was also considered specific to certain groups of people. According to oral histories, when upriver Nooksack tribal territory was over-run and occupied by coastal people, certain Nooksack community members were retained as slaves specifically to operate the great salmon weir. It was not that coastal people could not have figured out how to physically maintain and use a weir on their own, but that that particular weir functioned in part due to special Nooksack spirit power. The coastal people did not even bother to try and operate the weir, knowing full well that it would only work for those who built it and those in whose territory it resided, for only they had the appropriate spirit helpers and associated knowledge from the spirit world.

28 In the published *Faith of a Coast Salish Indian,* Jenness lists only the Musqueam as having original rights to the sx̱wōyx̱wey. In his unpublished manuscript and fieldnotes in the Canadian Museum of Civilization in Ottawa, Jenness quotes Old Pierre as listing a second unnamed community farther upriver. This was undoubtedly Ewawas near Hope, the people of whom claim that the mask reached Musqueam indirectly via marriage from them.

29 Jenness, *Faith*, 71.

30 Ibid.

31 Hill-Tout, *Salish People*, vol. 3, 150.

32 Ralph George and James Fraser, personal communications, summer 1994.

33 Periodically throughout the 1990s certain members of the Cheam Band asserted their community's inherent right to supra-tribal leadership – an assertion that was contested by some other Stó:lō.

34 Jenness, *Faith*, 71.

35 Old Pierre reported that 'the prerogative [to wear the mask] was heritable through either the male or female line' (Jenness, *Faith*, 72). Wilson Duff's informant Mrs Robert Joe corroborated that 'the right to use a sxwaixwai mask, costume and ritual was obtained from either parent and passed on to all children [exactly like the right to use a fishing-station]' (Duff, *Upper Stalo*, 78). Mrs Joe also explained that, initially, the masks were also worn by women (ibid., 124). Today, among a certain family in the Chilliwack area

the role of the special female *sxwōyxwey* dancers is being revived. Both the dance and the function they perform in the ceremony, however, differ from those of male dancers.

36 Suttles, 'Productivity and Its Constraints: A Coast Salish Case,' in *Coast Salish Essays*, 110.

37 For a slightly different description of spirit entities residing within humans, see Duff, *Upper Stalo*, 116–17. Duff, however, acknowledges that some of the knowledge of the older pre-Christian system may have been forgotten by his informants. It is also possible that some of his informants did not know the full body of knowledge because they were not entitled to know it as per Indigenous protocols. See also Homer Garner Barnett, *The Coast Salish of British Columbia* (Eugene: University of Oregon, 1955), 211, 221, and Brent Galloway, *A Grammar of Upriver Halkomelem* (Berkeley: University of California Press, 1993).

38 Jenness, *Faith*, 27, 35.

39 See Suttles, 'Spirit Dancing and the Persistence of Native Culture among the Coast Salish,' in *Coast Salish Essays*, 207–8. In 1960 Suttles observed that 'at present most songs are not associated with specific skills or professions still practiced. A great many dancers have, in fact, songs which once would have been associated with the professional warrior ... [spirits which when expressed] today ... can only mean "I am an Indian."'

My own contemporary fieldwork and observations indicated that Suttles' observations still generally hold. Many male dancers continue to acquire warrior spirit helpers, but healing helpers, or woodworking helpers are not uncommon, for example, and these expressions certainly do have modern professional application.

40 For a longer list of spirit helpers and their vocational expressions consult Jenness, *Faith*, 48–64.

41 Snyder, 'Skagit Society,' 92.

42 Most Coast Salish, Old Pierre asserted, did not know or understand the difference between travelling to seek spirit powers at physical distance and travelling to seek spiritual powers through the spiritual dimension of the xá:xa realm, as this was part of the special esoteric knowledge of properly trained and initiated healers. People without hereditary access to this special knowledge who wanted spirit helpers simply went to remote physical locations to acquire their power, power that, according to Old Pierre, was fundamentally weaker than power acquired in the xá:xa realm. Jenness, *Faith*, 90.

43 Jenness, *Faith*, 37–8.

44 Jay Miller, *Anchored Radiance*.

4 From the Great Flood to Smallpox

1 Salmon can only be effectively wind-dried in July, although the use of smudges can extend the season through September. River and lake levels peak in late June following the spring melt in the inland Rocky Mountains. Beginning in July water levels start to quickly recede. Rivers and lakes within Stó:lō territory are generally at their lowest through the fall and winter. As such, the flood Old Pierre is referring to was not simply a summer freshet, but something truly exceptional.

2 Jenness, *Faith*, 33.

3 Charles Hill-Tout, 'Ethnological Studies of the Mainland Halkomelem, A Division of the Salish of British Columbia,' in *Salish People*, vol. 3, 70.

4 Duff, *Upper Stalo*, 23.

5 Norman Hart Lerman, 'Lower Fraser Indian Folktales Collected by Norman Lerman, 1950–1951' (Chilliwack: Stó:lō Nation, SNA), 245–7.

6 Often Stó:lō people telling stories of the ancient era will speak in the present tense and use the second person personal pronoun 'we.' This may be indicative of spiritual link between people of different generations. Further research is required to determine if this is the case.

7 Norman Hart Lerman and Betty Keller, eds., *Legends of the River People* (Vancouver: November House, 1976), 23–5.

8 The flood story shared by Dan Milo does not specify exactly where people went to, but clearly emphasizes that groups of people did go somewhere. Milo is quoted verbatim in Oliver Wells, *The Chilliwacks and Their Neighbours*, 88, ed. by R. Maud and B. Galloway (Vancouver: Talonbooks, 1987). He shared the same story with CBC radio personality Imbert Orchard a few years later. See Imbert Orchard, interview, cassette tape recording and typed transcript, cassette 96-SR11, SNA.

9 Rosaleen George, personal communication, 18 May 1995. Jay Miller (*Lushootseed Culture*, 111–29) provides essentially the same definition in his discussion of Lushootseed social networks.

10 Hill-Tout, *Salish People*, vol. 3, 70.

11 Ibid.

12 Suttles, 'Coping with Abundance,' in *Coast Salish Essays*.

13 Mrs Amy Cooper, interview by Oliver Wells, 8 Feb. 1962, in Wells, Oral History Audio Collection (1959–69), CA (copies and transcripts at SNA; hereafter Wells, Audio Collection). See Wells, *The Chilliwacks and Their Neighbours*, 50.

14 Ibid.

15 Hill-Tout, *Salish People*, vol. 3, 41.

16 Bob Joe asserted that this was previously the Chilliwack custom. See Bob
     Joe, interview by Oliver Wells, 16 Jan. 1964, in Wells, Audio Collection.
     Charles Hill-Tout collected the same information over half a century earlier
     from his Chilliwack consultants; see his *Salish People*, vol. 3, 46.
17 Kw'ekw'e'i:qw, a Sumas settlement just west of Sumas Lake.
18 By 'means' Milo does not mean 'translates as' but rather 'has been ren-
     dered by Europeans as.'
19 Yarrow is the modern European name for a town built on the former site of
     Sali:ts, a Sumas settlement on the southeast side of Sumas Lake.
20 On Nicomen Island in the Fraser River immediately north of Sumas.
21 Dan Milo, interview by Oliver Wells, 8 Jan. 1962, in Wells, Audio Collection.
     See Wells, *The Chilliwacks and Their Neighbours*, 40.
22 Robert Joe provided Duff with the same translation (Wilson Duff, Unpub-
     lished Fieldnotes, Book 3, 1950, SNA, 41). Interestingly, linguist Brent
     Galloway believes the word *Leq'a:mel* translates as 'level place' or 'meeting
     place.'
        Often folk etymologies emphasize the significance of a name, that is, its
     historical meaning or significance, over what linguists feel is the genuine
     etymological root of the word. In this case, however, Galloway's second
     translation 'meeting place' would fit with the story of the locale becoming
     the place where survivors gathered after the mysterious depopulating event.
     Galloway records the word for 'visiting one another' as *la:leq'el*, which ap-
     pears to be derived from the same proto-Salish root.
23 Sahlins, 'Return of the Event, Again.'
24 The leading figures in this debate have been Robert Boyd and Cole Harris;
     however, among others, significant contributions have been made by Rob-
     ert Galois and James Gibson.
25 See George M. Guilmet et al., 'The Legacy of Introduced Disease: The
     Southern Coast Salish,' *American Indian Culture and Research Journal* 15/4
     (1991): 1–32. However, as Robert Boyd points out, in *The Coming of the Spirit
     of Pestilence: Introduced Infectious Diseases and Population Decline among Northwest
     Coast Indians, 1774–1874* (Seattle: University of Washington Press, 1999),
     276–8, what we know about the effect of introduced disease and population
     decline on northwest coast cultural systems remains largely speculative.
26 Boyd, ibid., 38–9.
27 Suttles, 'Introduction,' in *Handbook of North American Indians*; see also Sut-
     tles, 'Ethnographic Significance of the Fort Langley Journals.'
28 Carlson et al., eds., *Atlas*, 76–9.
29 Much of the most interesting analysis in this regard has focused on Aborigi-
     nal interpretations of Europeans at first contact. Marshall David Sahlins, for

example, argues that the Hawaiian people originally interpreted the British explorer Captain James Cook as the god Lono; see his *How 'Natives' Think: About Captain Cook for Example* (Chicago: University of Chicago Press, 1995).

. Wendy Wickwire has advanced essentially the same interpretation for the Nlakapamux in their initial interpretation of the Northwest Company explorer Simon Fraser as the returning transformer; see her 'To See Ourselves as the Other's Other.' I have personally encountered a number of Stó:lō oral histories that suggest that their ancestors initially also interpreted Fraser as the returning transformer X̱a:ls.

30 Most of the early Coast Salish genealogies collected by anthropologists record only eight or nine generations reaching back from the present to the beginning of time. This caused Sally Snyder ('Skagit Society,' 29) to speculate that the Coast Salish regarded history as cyclical, that every seven or eight generations history began over again with the first generation.

Hill-Tout considered the nine-generation genealogies as evidence that the Coast Salish were relatively recent immigrants to the region; that the spectacular stories of the actions of the 'first people' were really glorified accounts of the actions of the first generation of Coast Salish conquerors, who wrested the territory from its earlier inhabitants. Hill-Tout's thesis has been largely discounted by subsequent anthropologists, who argue for a great antiquity in Coast Salish occupation of the region, whereas Snyder's position remains largely unexplored. While her thesis is possible, the fact remains that neither her Aboriginal consultants, nor anyone else's have ever interpreted their history as cyclical, that is, they never discussed or described it as being a repetitive narrative that began anew each seven, eight, or nine generations. Rather, they presented it as a linear narrative with a fixed beginning and a fixed end. However, the fact that Halq'eméylem kin terms extend through time for a maximum of seven generations in either direction from the person using them, coupled with the fact that names and aspects of identity are regarded as hereditary, may be suggestive of a cyclical or repetitive view of history.

31 Jenness, *Faith of a Coast Salish Indian*, 34.

32 George Vancouver, 'Journal Entries,' in W.K. Lamb, ed., *A Voyage of Discovery to the North Pacific Ocean and around the World, 1791–1795* (London: Hakluit Society, 1984), 538.

33 Ibid., 517.

34 That the disease had decimated the population only a few years before Vancouver's arrival is evident from his observation that 'the habitations had now fallen into decay; their inside, as well as a small surrounding space that appeared to have been formerly occupied, were over-run with weeds;

amongst which were found several human skulls, and other bones, promis-
cuously scattered about' (ibid., 516–17). On other occasions he described
the extent of the vegetation that had encroached on the former living
spaces in terms that perhaps better indicate that several years had passed
since the depopulating event: 'nothing but the smaller shrubs and plants
has yet been able to rear their heads' (ibid., 538).

35 Ibid., 540.

36 Ibid., 528. A few days later, while travelling northward along the eastern
coast of Puget Sound, Vancouver recorded that among the people he
encountered 'most had lost their right eye, and were much pitted with small
pox' (ibid., 559).

37 Charles Hill-Tout, *Salish People*, vol. 2, 22.

38 Charles Hill-Tout: 'The Great Fraser Midden,' *Museum and Art Notes* 5 (Sept.
1930): 75–83, and 'Prehistoric Burial Mounds of British Columbia,' *Museum
and Art Notes* 5 (Dec. 1930): 120–6.

39 Albert Louie, interview by Oliver Wells, 28 July 1965, in Wells, Audio Collection.

40 Albert 'Sonny' McHalsie, 'Halq'eméylem Place Names in Stó:lō Territory,'
in Carlson et al., eds., *Atlas*, 150.

41 Jimmie Charlie, personal communication, 16 Jan. 1993.

42 Jimmie Peters, interview by Gordon Mohs and Sonny McHalsie, 29
Sept.1986, Tape recording, SNA.

43 Cole Harris documents the evidence of early disease extensively. See R.
Cole Harris, *The Resettlement of British Columbia: Essays on Colonialism and Geographical Change* (Vancouver: UBC Press, 1997), 3–30; see also Boyd's *Spirit of
Pestilence*, 38–58. In addition, Stó:lō Elders Elizabeth Herrling and Rosaleen
George, dedicated participants in the Halq'eméylem language revival program, regularly insist that almost every village has a story of depopulation
resulting from smallpox, but that only a few resulted in the name of a place
being changed to reflect that history.

44 Miller, *Lushootseed Culture*, 132.

45 Early explorers and fur traders' ships' logs suggest that the Kwakwaka'wakw
escaped the first smallpox epidemic. Their experience with the disease
therefore occurred within the time period when they would have known
that the Europeans were the source of their disaster.

46 George Dawson, 'Notes and Observations on the Qwakiool People of the
Northern Part of Vancouver Island and Adjacent Coasts, Made during the
Summer of 1885,' in *Transactions of the Royal Society of Canada* 11 (reprint
Fairfield, Wash.: Ye Galleon Press, 1973), 4.

47 Boyd, *Spirit of Pestilence*, Chapters 8 and 9.

48 Jenness, *Faith*, 34; emphasis added.

49 Suttles and Jenness, *Katzie Ethnographic Notes*, 12.

50 Ibid.

51 Ibid.

52 Jenness, *Faith*, 57.

53 Ibid., 72.

54 Ibid., 71.

55 Ibid.

56 Suttles and Jenness, *Katzie*, 12; also related in more detail by Boyd, who quotes Suttles' fieldnotes verbatim, in *Spirit of Pestilence*, 43.

57 MacLachlan, *Fort Langley Journals*, 28.

58 Hill-Tout, *Salish People*, vol. 2, 100.

59 Mrs Matilda 'Tilly' Gutierrez, as a young girl achieving her first menses, was taken by her Elders and instructed to spend an entire night alone sitting on a site known as Th'exelis ('gritting his teeth') located at the edge of the Fraser River near Yale. It was a site where the transformer Xa:ls had himself once sat while engaged in a spiritual confrontation with a shaman on the other side of the river. Mrs Gutierrez was instructed to contemplate the stories of the beginning of time, and thereafter received ongoing training in how to relate the various narratives of Stó:lō history. To this day, she is sought after by Stó:lō and non-Natives alike as an expert on both the content and meaning of numerous ancient historical narratives. Mrs Gutierrez first related to me the story of her training in the summer of 1992.

60 In 1993 the Stó:lō Tribal Council conducted a study which found that only eight people could fluently speak the Upriver Halkomelem dialect. Even these fluent people humbly acknowledged that their command of the language was less than that of fluent speakers of the previous generation. Over the past sixteen years, several younger and middle-aged Stó:lō have become partially fluent after taking Halq'eméylem immersion classes and night courses. However, only one of the eight fluent speakers identified in 1993 is still alive. Mrs Guitierrez, who in May 2009 was in very frail health, is the last fluent speaker who was raised with Halq'eméylem as her first language.

61 Mrs Guiterrez has told this story to the author on numerous occasions.

62 Oral history recently recorded among Chehalis elders suggest the headwaters of Hamson Lake have long been considered an integral part of Chechalis tribal territory. Chief Willie Charlie of Chehalis, personal communication, May 2009.

63 This migration is discussed in Duff, *Upper Stalo*, 40. See also, Skw'atets Indians, Chilliwack, to H. Graham, 6 Dec., 1918, LAC, RG 10, Reel C-12144, Vol. 7859, File 30165-5(1).

64 Duff, *Upper Stalo*, 41.

65 Ibid., 40.

66 Ibid.

67 Significantly, Duff discusses the Tamtami'uxwtan only in the unpublished M.A. thesis version of his *The Upper Stalo Indians*. See Duff, 'The Upper Stalo Indians: An Introductory Ethnography' (M.A. thesis, University of Washington, 1952), 37.

68 Chief Dan George is possibly best known among the non-Native population as Dustin Hoffman's Indian 'grandfather' in the movie *Little Big Man* (1970), and as Clint Eastwood's companion and comic foil in *The Outlaw Josey Wales* (1976).

69 Dawn Sparks and Martha Border, *Echoes across the Inlet* (Deep Cove, BC: Deep Cove and Area Heritage Association, 1989), 1.

70 Ibid., 6.

71 Ibid.

72 Robin Fisher, *Contact and Conflict: Indian-European Relations in British Columbia, 1774–1890* (Vancouver: UBC Press, 1977, 2nd ed., 1992); R. Cole Harris, *The Resettlement of British Columbia: Essays on Colonialism and Geographical Change* (Vancouver: UBC Press, 1997); MacLachlan, *Fort Langley Journals*.

73 Old Pierre (in Wilson Duff's fieldnotes, 'Stalo Tribes,' 8 Nov. 1952) gives 'tireless legs. Can run and never tire' as the etymology for Kwantlen. This Duff abbreviates to 'tireless runners' in his published ethnography. Duff, *Upper Stalo*, 27.

74 Hill-Tout, *Salish People*, vol. 3, 69.

75 Jenness, *Faith of a Coast Salish Indian*, 12.

76 Ibid., 13.

77 Ibid., 16.

78 Ibid., 6.

79 Ibid., 10, 12–13.

80 Ibid., 17.

81 Ibid., 17–20.

82 Ibid., 12–13. Also, Hill-Tout, *Salish People*, vol. 3, 69.

83 Duff, *Upper Stalo*, 23.

84 Jenness, *Faith*, 22, 48.

85 Rosaleen George, personal communication, July 2000.

86 McHalsie, 'Halq'eméylem Place Names in Stó:lõ Territory,' in Carlson et al., eds., *Atlas*, 150.

87 Suttles, 'Katzie Ethnographic Notes,' 12; Hill-Tout, *Salish People*, vol. 3, 68; also Duff, *Upper Stalo*, 23.

88 Jenness, *Faith*, 48n3.

89 Yet another group of New Westminster residents who X̱exa:ls supposedly
   recognized as lazy, for they never worked for their livelihood, preferring
   instead to beg from the other people. X̱exa:ls transformed these people
   into Ravens. See Jenness, *Faith*, 23. From what I was able to learn from one
   of the few remaining fluent Halq'eméylem speakers before her death, the
   close relatives of those Kwantlen people transformed into ravens migrated
   upriver to occupy the territory around Stave Lake (a region left vacant by
   the Skayuk who were decimated by the first smallpox epidemic). Rosaleen
   George, personal communication, Summer 2000.
90 Robert Thomas Sr, personal communication, July 1993.
91 I was in attendance at the naming ceremony on the Langley Indian Reserve
   on McMillan Island where Chief Marlyn Gabriel officially reassumed the
   Kwantlen name for her community.
92 MacLachlan, *Fort Langley Journals*, 107; see esp. the entry for 7 April 1829.
93 Using much the same evidence and methods Wayne Suttles (*Fort Langley
   Journals*: 170) has likewise recently expressed the opinion that the Kwantlen
   migration was already under way prior to the establishment of Fort Langley.
94 Accompanying McMillan were 37 boatmen, one French Canadian translator, and three clerks: John Work, Francois Noel Annance, and Thomas
   McKay. Of the clerk's reports only the journals of Work and Annance have
   survived. Both are available in published form with somewhat uneven and
   speculative interpretive editing. See T.C. Elliott, ed., 'The Journal of John
   Work November and December, 1824,' *Washington Historical Quarterly* 3/3
   (1912): 198–228. See also Nile Thompson, 'Journey through the Land: A
   Journal of a Voyage from Fort George Columbia River to Fraser River in the
   Winter of 1824 and 1825, by Francois N. Annance,' *Cowlitz Historical Quarterly* 32/1 (1991): 5–44.
95 Suttles, *Fort Langley Journals*, 170.
96 Hill-Tout, *Salish People*, vol. 3, 68, 69.
97 'The Quaïtlain Chief Nicamuns and his brother [Whaitlakainum] came
   in with 20 skins, small and large which they traded for blankets – these
   being the principal Indians of the neighbourhood, and who at all exert
   themselves to collect beaver, we thought it good policy in Mr Yale to form
   a Connection with that family – and accordingly he has now the Chief's
   daughter as after making them all liberal presents.' See MacLachlan, *Fort
   Langley Journals*, 13 and 25 Nov. 1828, 85, 86. Later, it turns out that What-
   likainum's daughter was already married to a Skagit man, a fact resulting
   in a great deal of tension and confusion among the Stó:lō and the HBC. In
   Halq'eméylem, siblings and cousins up to the fourth degree are called by
   the same kin term 'Qelo:qtel,' meaning that while Nicamous and Whatlikai-

num chose to emphasize the closeness of their relationship for social and
political reasons, they may have actually been rather distant blood relatives.
See Carlson et al., eds., *Atlas*, 27.

98 MacLachlan, *Fort Langley Journals*, 35. But, of course, Kwantlen River may also
have been the slough that terminated 300 yards north of the Fraser River.

99 See esp. MacLachlan, ibid., 8 Jan. 1829, 7 April and 19 May 1827, 31 July
1829, and 5 May 1830, 92, 107, 113, 122, 147.

100 Ibid., 116, 133.

101 Ibid., 136–7.

102 Ibid., 67.

103 By 'made the move' I perhaps should say 'made the *return* move' for it is
unclear whether Swaniset's call for the Katzie to relocate from Pitt Lake
to the settlement near the Fraser occurred: (a) once, at the beginning of
time; (b) is thought of as occurring at the beginning of time but actually
occurred during the early fur trade era, or (c) whether after Swaniset's
amalgamation of people the Katzie eventually returned to Pitt Lake
whence they ultimately made a second return journey to the Fraser in the
mid-nineteenth century. While the timing of these movements is of interest to historians, the more important thing for the Stó:lō is the fact that the
movements occurred, not when they occurred.

104 See Sgt. William McColl to Col. Moody, 13 May 1861, *Royal Engineers Letterbooks*, BCA C/AB/30.6J: 1–7.

105 MacLachlan, *Fort Langley Journals*, 26 Feb. 1829, 99.

106 Duff, *Upper Stalo*, 24.

107 McHalsie 'Halq'eméylem Place Names in Stó:lō Territory,' in Carlson et
al., eds., *Atlas*,145.

108 Archibald McDonald, [Census] Report to Governor and Council, 25 Feb.
1830, HBCA D.1/123:66d–72. Also, James Murray Yale, 'Census of Indian
Population [from Fort Langley] and Crossing Over to Vancouver's Island
and Coasting at About Latitude 50° from There Returning Southward
along the Mainland and up the Fraser's River to Simpson Falls,' (1839),
HBCA B.223/2/1: 30–53.

109 George Gibbs, 'Tribes of Western Washington and Northwestern Oregon,'
186–7 in John Wesley Power, ed., *Contributions to North American Ethnology*
1(2): 157–61 (Washington: Department of the Interior, U.S. Geographical and Geological Survey of the Rocky Mountain Region, 1877; reprinted
Seattle: Shorey Press, 1970).

110 Nature abhors a vacuum.

111 In 1879, for example, Indian Reserve Commissioner Gilbert Malcolm
Sproat appears to have regarded the Whonock as a village and band within
the larger Langley (Kwantlen) Tribe. Certainly, due to the extent of non-

Native land ownership in the Langley region, Sproat recorded that 'taking
the Langley and Whonock people together I did the best that I could as a
whole.' Recognizing the affiliation between the two bands, without denying their separate political identities, Sproat registered the reserves for
'these bands in common' and noted that 'Stave River is the place where
they much wished for their land.' (Gilbert Malcolm Sproat, Indian Reserve
Commissioner, Minutes of Decision, 27 June, 1879, vol. 18, 334.) Later,
however, in the early years of the twentieth century Chief Casimir of the
Langley Indian band on McMillan Island argued to federal officials that it
had never been his understanding that his band of Kwantlen on McMillan
Island was supposed to share the Stave River reserve with the Whonock
band, and indeed he stated that he had received assurances to that effect
from Commissioner Sproat. In Chief Casimir's words, 'I had foresaw ...
the evil consequences which would result in having lands in common with
other bands.' The Whonock, Casimir went on to explain, had two distinct
reserves that were theirs alone. Chief Fidelle, the Whonock leader, knew
this, Casimir asserted, for in 1880 Casimir and his Langley community had
fought alone to expel a non-Native settler from the Stave Reserve (the
Whonock apparently showing no interest), and in 1881 compensation for
a railroad right of way through the land had been paid only to Casimir's
band; further, in the 1880s Casimir's people had logged the Stave Reserve
without protest or participation from Whonock. The contestation, Casimir
asserted, had arisen only recently after Chief Fidelle had fallen under the
influence of a man Casimir described as a non-native Hawaiian half-breed
and ex-convict who was looking to benefit personally from the reserve
land. Only four people, according to Casimir, were 'legally Honocks, and
that is Phiddell, his two sons, and old Borce' (Chief Cassimere [sic] to Indian Agent R.C. McDonald, 17 Jan. 1905, RG 10, Vol. 4051, File 363, 600–1).
See J. McTiernan to Chief Casimir, 25 April 1891, ibid. Ten years later,
testifying before the Royal Commission on Indian Affairs, Chief Casimir
explained to the Commissioners that not all of his tribe lived on McMillan Island. When asked if the Chief at Whonock was a sub-chief of his,
Casimir replied, 'No, he is an independent chief' (p. 122). Chief Fidelle
of Whonock confirmed that there were two bands, Langley and Whonock,
and implied that the two were part of the same larger tribe. (See Royal
Commission on Indian Affairs for the Province of British Columbia 1915,
Meeting with the Langley Band or Tribe of Indians on Saturday, 9 Jan.
1915, B.C. Archives. GR-l965 Microfilm B-1456, 122, 126.) As such, while kin
ties, shared history, and links to myth-age heroes bound people, political
actions within the British and Canadian Indian Affairs bureaucracy were
often in large part independent.

112 Julie Cruikshank, *Do Glaciers Listen?: Local Knowledge, Colonial Encounters, and Social Imagination* (Vancouver: UBC Press, 2005).
113 Marshall Sahlins, *Islands of History* (London: Tavistock Publications, 1985), 144.
114 Marshall Sahlins, *With Apologies to Thucydides: Understanding History as Culture and Vice Versa* (Chicago: University of Chicago Press, 2005), 10.

5 Events, Migrations, and Affiliation in the Post-Contact World

1 Smith, Fieldnotes, 5:5:5.
2 The relationships between tradition and authority are examined in Mark Salber Phillips and Gordon Schochet, eds., *Questions of Tradition* (Toronto: University of Toronto Press, 2004).
3 I discuss the role of tradition and innovation within Salish conflicts over resource ownership in my article 'Innovation, Tradition, Colonialism, and Aboriginal Fishing Conflicts in the Lower Fraser Canyon,' in S. Neylan and T. Binnema, eds., *New Histories for Old* (Vancouver: UBC Press, 2007), 145–74.
4 Recently, in response to an article arguing the existence of formal pre-contact Coast Salish chiefdoms, Wayne Suttles, Bruce Miller, and Daniel Boxberger, among others, have begun creating a model of Coast Salish identity that recognizes the situational nature of political authority and the historically contingent factors shaping Coast Salish collective identity. This chapter builds directly upon these earlier studies. See Suttles, 'They Recognize No Superior Chief,' and Miller and Boxberger, 'Creating Chiefdoms: The Puget Sound Case.'
5 Charles Bishop, for example, tackled the question of whether contact had an atomizing effect on Canadian Ojibwa clan structures or whether it caused increased clan solidarity and a new sense of shared collective identity. He concluded that, while there was clear evidence of increased centralization, the inherent biases of both oral and written records could be used to support either position. See his *The Northern Ojibwa and the Fur Trade: An Historical and Ecological Study* (Toronto: Holt, Rinehart and Winston, 1974).
6 Moreover, the edited accounts of the Chilliwack migration story that have made it into print tend to be somewhat confused, a fact as likely attributable to both typographical errors and to his interviewers' lack of familiarity with the local geography. Additionally, Bob Joe's deep and soft voice – as revealed in audio recordings in the Stó:lō Oral History Project Tapes in the Stó:lō Nation Archives – made it difficult to hear exactly what he was saying. Wilson Duff, for example, in his Unpublished Fieldnotes, Book 2, clearly records the location of the village as 'Below Centre Creek.' Likewise, Norman Lerman recorded Joe as stating that the slide occurred 'just above Slesse Creek,' which

is consistent with the site also being 'below Centre Creek' as described in Duff's notes (see Lerman and Keller, *Legends of the River People*, 12). However, in the list of place names and accompanying map published in *The Upper Stalo Indians*, Duff translates Xéyles (#16 – a village three-quarters of a kilometre upriver from Vedder Crossing) as 'slide,' when in fact, as Albert Louie twice clarified to local ethnographer Oliver Wells, it means 'sidehill' (see Albert Louie, in Wells' *The Chilliwacks and Their Neighbours*, 160).

Moreover, while Duff's published list does provide the name of the village where the slide occurred, his map does not show it. Somehow, the publisher cropped the map leaving village #22 unplotted. The fact that Wells and certain Stó:lō people have become confused by the error is indicative of the problems associated with particular ethnographic accounts coming to be accepted as authoritive.

I have personally visited the area below Centre Creek on several occasions and have identified the sites of two major landslides, either large enough to bury a settlement. The first involved boulders more than three metres in diameter, whereas the second was made up of small rocks and talus debris.

7 Dan Milo, interview by Oliver Wells, July 1964, in Wells, Audio Collection.
8 Bob Joe, interview by Imbert Orchard, 2 April 1963, transcripts, CBC Archives, Toronto, copies at SNA. Linguist Jimmy Harris, who conducted re-search with Dan Milo in the early 1960s, recorded Milo providing a transla-tion of *Chilliwack* as being 'back water,' referring to the point on a river that was 'as far as you can go [in a canoe].' Milo, however, admitted to Harris that he was guessing at the meaning, whereas Bob Joe was confident of his translation. Jimmy Gene Harris, personal communication, July 1996.
9 Bob Joe, interview by Lerman, in Lerman, 'Lower Fraser Indian Folktales,' 269.
10 Bob Joe, interview by Orchard. See also Dan Milo, interview by Wells, in Wells, *The Chilliwacks*, 90.
11 Bob Joe, interview by Lerman, in Lerman, 269.
12 Bob Joe, interview by Oliver Wells, 8 Feb. 1962, CD audio copy, track 2, 4:55, in Wells, Audio Collection. SNA.
13 Duff, *Upper Stalo*, 43. While Joe describes this Wileliq as the 'fifth,' five years earlier, when speaking with Marian Smith, he provided an even greater gene-alogical history in which he explained that the Wileliq born at Thathem:als was actually the seventh man to bear the name since the beginning of time. Similarly, in his conversations with Norman Lerman, Joe is recorded as refer-ring to the twin Wileliq as the sixth in the noble line. Joe himself, however, never referred to any of the Wileliqs by numbers, instead referencing them in relation to one another, as in 'the third Wileliq since such and such.'

In this way the discrepancies in numbers between Smith's, Duff's, and

Lerman's notes reflect the emphasis assumed by the ethnographer and not that implied by the narrator. See Marian Smith, Unpublished Fieldnotes, summer 1945 (London: Royal Anthropological Institute , MS 268; microfilm copy, BCARS); Lerman and Keller, *Legends of the River People*, 15.

14 Bob Joe and Billy Sepass both provided Oliver Wells with this as the name of the language spoken by the Chilliwack people prior to their movement downriver and their adoption of the Halkomelem language.

15 John Wallace, interview by Oliver Wells, 3 Oct. 1967, audiotape and transcript, in Wells, Audio Collection.

16 Wilson refers to them as 'Schweltya.' See George F. Stanley, *Mapping the Frontier: Charles Wilson's Diary of the Survey of the 49th Parallel, 1858–1862, While Secretary of the British Boundary Commission* (Toronto: Macmillan, 1970).

17 Mrs Cooper, in Wells, *The Chilliwacks*, 106.

18 Mrs Cooper, interview by Oliver Wells, 31 March 1968, in Wells, Audio Collection.

19 Albert Louie, interview by Oliver Wells, 5 Aug. 1965, audiotape copy and transcript, in Wells, Audio Collection. See also Wells, *The Chilliwacks*, 390.

20 See Carlson et al., ed., *Atlas*, 48–9.

21 See entries for Dec. 1828 in MacLachlan, *Fort Langley Journals*, 88–91.

22 Bob Joe in Smith, Fieldnotes, 5:5:10.

23 Suttles and Jenness, *Katzie Ethnographic Notes*, 10.

24 Some accounts collected by Wells place the headquarters and principal longhouse right at Vedder Crossing, on the west side of the current bridge.

25 See Albert Louie, 5 Aug. 1965, audio copy and transcript in SNA. Also, Andy Commodore, personal communications, summer 1993.

26 Bob Joe, interview by Lerman, 13.

27 This full list of the tribes who assisted in the building of the inverted gable house is found in Duff, Fieldnotes, Book 2, 68, and differs from the shorter list found in his published material.

28 Bob Joe, in Smith, Fieldnotes, 5:5:12.

29 The various recorded genealogies are confusing on this point. The Halq'eméylem word for 'grandson' is the same as the word for 'grand nephew' (as well as grandfather and grand uncle). An account of this genealogy collected by Duff records that Wileliq the Fifth passed his name on to his grand nephew by his younger brother. Both accounts concur that Jack Wealick became Wileliq the Fifth.

30 Bob Joe, in Smith, Fieldnotes, 5:5:12. Duff's fieldnotes and published accounts do not coincide with what is found in Smith's records. Duff records that Wileliq the Fifth had no sons and so passed his name to his nephew, the son of his younger brother. This man, in turn, passed it to his grandson,

who was an old man in 1950. I believe Duff was confused on this point. See
Duff: *Upper Stalo*, 44, and Fieldnotes, Book 1, 65.

31 Again, there is some confusion here. Tixwelatsa may have been a different
uncle (another brother or possibly even a cousin of Siemches and Wileliq)
since the Halkomelem language does not distinguish between such relationships. Additionally, it is important to note that Siemches is the name
of one of the original black-bear-with-a-white-spot-on-its-chest brother who
was transformed into a founder of the Chilliwack Tribe at the beginning
of time. The name is currently carried by Chief Frank Malloway of Yeqwyeqwioose. In a potlatch naming ceremony in the late 1990s, Chief Malloway
clarified that the name and all its associated prestige and privileges will
eventually be transferred to his nephew Dalton Silver, who will 'carry it' so
long as he continues to act in a way that brings honour and not shame to
the name and his ancestors.

32 Bob Joe, in Smith, Fieldnotes, 5:5:10.

33 Joe explained to Marian Smith that his wife's oldest son by her earlier marriage to Wileliq the Sixth's son carried the Wileliq name in 1951. Wileliq
the Seventh was also known as George, who, in addition to being Bob Joe's
stepson, was also his cousin. In other words Mrs Bob Joe was the great-
great-granddaughter (niece?) of Wileliq the Fifth's second wife (the Katzie
woman). Wileliq the Sixth was Bob Joe's grandfather's older brother. See
Duff: *Upper Stalo*, 44, and Fieldnotes, Book 2, 67.

34 In 1992 Bob Joe's grandson, Wesley Sam, told me that his grandfather had
quietly and informally transferred the Wileliq name to him. Prior to his
death in 1997, Wesley Sam arranged for the name – which he pronounced
as 'Wi-ley-lug,' and which he explained was the older and more correct
Nooksack-style pronunciation of Wileliq – to be transferred to his infant
grandson. Sam's family later arranged a naming ceremony, where it was
explained that the name was to be 'shared' between the grandson and Wesley's own son Bruce. Personal communications with Wesley Sam, Myra Sam,
and Bruce Sam, May 1993.

35 Smith, Fieldnotes, 5:5:101.

36 I am grateful to genealogist Alice Marwood, who drew my attention to Jack
Wealick's grave marker, and who patiently provided guidance as I struggled
to make sense of the complicated Weliliq family tree. I am also grateful to
Sonny McHalsie, who spent at least two full days with me as I struggled to
plot and understand the information on Wileliq genealogy found in the various oral histories recorded by Oliver Wells, Wilson Duff, and Marian Smith.

37 Smith, Fieldnotes, 5:5:5.

38 Ibid.

39 Patrick Charlie and Robert Joe, in Duff, Fieldnotes, Book 4, 37. More
    recently, Ken Malloway (Weleliq) has related to audiences of Natives and
    non-Natives alike how the Chilliwack formerly killed trespassers.

40 Community fission was not an unusual process in societies with social organi-
    zation like the Coast Salish. Examples of fission, without much historical con-
    text, are described in most standard Coast Salish ethnographies. It occurred
    for a variety of reasons, some as mundane as sanitation or to gain access to
    new sources of firewood, although both these concerns were typically met by
    seasonal rounds and the steady supply of wood, which was deposited along
    the sides of the Fraser River and its tributaries in yearly floods and freshets.
        One of the most sophisticated discussions of the social tensions and
    mechanism used to facilitate community fission is found in Sally Snyder's
    unpublished doctoral dissertation ('Skagit Society and Its Existential Basis'),
    wherein she describes how new leaders occasionally arose among the Skagit
    and challenged the existing elite by forging their own settlement com-
    munity. She also documents how these new communities attempted, often
    unsuccessfully, to legitimize themselves through the hosting of potlatches
    and other ceremonial activities.

41 Lamb, *Simon Fraser: Letters and Journals*, 103, 106.

42 Chief Harry Edwards, interview by Oliver Wells, 8 Oct. 1964, CD audio copy
    and transcript, 283, in Wells, Audio Collection.

43 These caves were destroyed by the construction of the Trans-Canada High-
    way in the 1960s.

44 Duff, *Upper Stalo*, 42. Likewise, Dan Milo, in 1964, provided additional
    details about the reasons behind the abandonment of Alámex. According
    to Milo, there were 'a lot' of people living there at the time, 'and the head
    man of those people ... had a little son, a small little kid, and that kid gets
    so rough and killed other kids. And he could do nothing [to stop] this little
    child. He told his friends, "The only way we can do it is to leave my kid.
    We'll leave him. We'll move away from here."' As a result, the headman told
    the other boys to take his son behind the little mountain in the woods and
    to abandon him there. According to the story, 'He called, and they an-
    swered him at different times, then they just played dumb.' The boys came
    back and the rest of the people were 'ready to move.' 'They took off and
    came way up to Cheam ... They went to Cheam and they began to get that
    name [the people of] "Lexwchiya:m" [always strawberries].' See Dan Milo,
    interview by Oliver Wells, July 1964, in Wells, Audio Collection.

45 Archibald McDonald, '1830 Census, Fort Langley,' HBCA; Yale, 'Census of
    Indian Population.' For the 1830 and 1839 census I have combined the Pel-
    lalt and Teiton population figures as both tribes dwelled at Alámex. For the
    1830 census, McDonald only provided figures for 'men.' I have therefore

multiplied his totals by 4.4, the ratio of men to other family members found
in the 1839 census.

46 Suttles, 'Significance of the Fort Langley Journals,' 258–9n5.

47 McDonald's report is presented in full in MacLachlan, *Fort Langley Journals*,
221.

48 Duff, *Upper Stalo*, 43.

49 Indicative of this is the reaction of certain people living in Ohamil and
Skw'atets to the 'Map of Pilalt Territory' produced in 2000 by the Cheam
Band. This map included as 'Pilalt' those upriver lands associated with the
Ohamil and Skwa'tets settlements. People in these upriver communities did
not necessarily interpret the map as a gesture of their shared and common
interest in land and resources. Some saw it more as a provocative move by
the people of Cheam to assert control over 'Tait' resources. One contemporary politician of one of the upriver settlements referred to it as a 'wake-up
call that all us Taits need to start working together more.' Personal communication, May 2001, with a band councillor from Seabird Island, who asked
not to be identified by name.

50 This is a commonly told story among the people of Shxw'ōwhámél. Sonny
McHalsie recorded the version related here in Keith Thor Carlson with
Sonny McHalsie, *I Am Stó:lō: Katherine Explores Her Heritage* (Chilliwack:
Stó:lō Heritage Trust, 1999).

51 Boas, *Indianische Sagen von der Nordpacifischen Kuste Americas*, published in
English as, *Indian Legends from the North Pacific Coast of America*, 107, R. Bouchard and D. Kennedy, eds..

52 Leland Donald's excellent and provocative *Aboriginal Slavery on the Northwest
Coast of North America* (Berkeley: University of California Press, 1997) is one
of the few studies to confront the issue of class tension within northwest
coast society and history. Unfortunately, due to what he refers to as a lack of
sources, his analysis is particularly thin on the Coast Salish.

53 For an overview, see Suttles, *Handbook of North American Indians*, introduction.

54 See Brian David Thom, 'The Dead and the Living: Burial Mounds and
Cairns and the Development of Social Classes in the Gulf of Georgia
Region' (M.A. thesis, University of British Columbia, 1995); and David M.
Schaepe, 'Recycling Archaeology: Analysis of Material from the 1973 Exca-
vation of an Ancient House at the Maurier Site' (M.A. thesis, Simon Fraser
University, 1998).

55 Jenness, *Faith of a Coast Salish Indian*, 12.

56 Ibid., 86.

57 Jenness also noted the distinction between the term for serf communities
and the common word for slaves (ibid.).

58 Duff, *Upper Stalo*, 92–84; Barnett, *Coast Salish*, 136–7, 249–50; Suttles, *Hand-*

book, 465; and Leland, *Aboriginal Slavery on the Northwest Coast,* 34, 91, 126–8, 279–284, 295–8.

59 Jenness, *Faith,* 86.

60 Ibid.

61 Ibid.

62 Ibid.

63 Hill-Tout, *Salish People,* vol. 3, 70.

64 Boas, 'Indian Tribes of the Lower Fraser River,' 455.

65 Hill-Tout, *Salish People,* vol. 2, 33.

66 Suttles, *Coast Salish Essays,* 3–23; Barnett, *Coast Salish,* 239–71. Sally Snyder ('Skagit Society and Its Existential Basis,' esp. 72–100), however, does attempt to provide a more interpretive discussion of the significance of class distinctions within Coast Salish society, and she does this by looking at the symbolic associations between class, property, and gender.

67 While 30% of the total Coast Salish population are listed as 'Followers of all descriptions,' only 12% of those living along the Fraser River proper are so identified. See Yale, Census, 30–53.

68 In his fieldnotes Duff (Book 2, 56) lists Sechelt, Vancouver Island, and the B.C. interior as the sites from which the slaves were taken.

69 Ibid., Book 5, 30, 58.

70 All preceding quotes relating to the story of Freedom Village were taken from Duff, Fieldnotes, Book 2, 56–8, which provided a slightly richer account than the block quote found in Duff, *Upper Stalo,* 21.

71 Ibid.

72 Ibid., 18.

73 Ibid., 12, 19–21, 30–7, 40–3, 85–7.

74 Plottings of place names here differ slightly from those found in Harris, *Resettlement of British Columbia.* All credit for revising these locations goes to Sonny McHalsie and the Elders who translated the HBC orthography into proper Halq'eméylem.

75 Canada, Department of Indian Affairs, Annual Reports (Ottawa: Government of Canada, 1878).

76 Carlson et al., eds., *Atlas,* 80.

77 See William C. Orchard, *A Rare Coast Salish Blanket,* Leafletts of the Museum of the American Indian Heye Foundation, No 5 (New York: Vreeland Press, 1926).

78 David M. Schaepe, 'Rockwall Fortifications: Reconstructing a Fraser Canyon Defensive Network,' in Carlson et al., eds., *Atlas,* 52; also Schaepe, 'Rock Fortifications.'

79 David Schaepe, personal communication, May 2001.

80 Duff, *Upper Stalo,* 41. The phenomenon of Native people moving to live

nearer European outposts and settlements was repeated numerous times in British North America; see, e.g., Arthur J. Ray, *Indians in the Fur Trade: Their Role as Hunters, Trappers, and Middlemen in the Lands Southwest of Hudson's Bay, 1660–1870* (Toronto: University of Toronto Press, 1974), esp. Chapter 7, 125–36.

81 See Daniel P. Marshall, 'Rickard Revisited: Native "Participation" in the Gold Discoveries of British Columbia,' *Native Studies Review* 11/1 (1997): 91–108; Lutz, 'After the Fur Trade'; and Keith Thor Carlson and John Sutton Lutz, 'Stó:lō People and the Development of the B.C. Wage Labour Economy,' in Carlson, *You Are Asked to Witness*, 109–24.

82 James A. Smart, Canada, *Sessional Papers*, DINA Annual Reports (Ottawa: Government of Canada, 1898), xxi, emphasis added. I am indebted to Amber Kostuchenko for drawing my attention to this document.

83 Sarah Carter, *Lost Harvest: Prairie Indian Reserve Farmers and Government Policy* (Montreal and Kingston: McGill-Queen's University Press, 1990).

84 Duff, *Upper Stalo*, 42.

85 Smart, *Sessional Papers*, xxi, emphasis added. Oral history records that Governor James Douglas promised Chawathil to the Hope Indians as a reserve (Sonny McHalsie, personal communication, June 1993). In 1879 Reserve Commissioner G.M. Sproat reported that the move to Chawathil took place around 1858, which would be consistent with the Douglas story. Chawathil was not officially designated a reserve until 1879.

86 Sproat to Supt. Gen., 5 Aug. 1879, LAC, RG 10, LTS, Vol. 5/1:19. I am grateful to Hillary Blair for drawing my attention to this document.

87 Named after a steamboat that ran aground on the island.

88 Sproat to Supt. Gen., 5 Aug. 1879.

89 Duff, *Upper Stalo*, 40.

90 See Chief James of Yale, testimony before the 1913–1916 Royal Commission, SNA.

91 In 1891 twenty-seven white squatters built rudimentary houses on the Seabird Reserve and attempted to have their claims to the land recognized; see A.W. Vowell to the Supt. Gen., 19 May 1891, and also F. Passingham to P. McTiernan, 21 Feb. 1891, both in LAC, RG 10, Reel C-10139, Vol. 3795, File 46607-1.

92 In 1958 the various bands making up the Tait Tribe succeeded in having Seabird Island officially designated as an independent band with its own local Chief and council. See the excellent local history of Seabird Island by Hillary Kathleen Blair, 'Settling Seabird Island: Land, Resources and Ownership on a British Columbian Indian Reserve' (M.A. thesis, Simon Fraser University, 1999).

93 McHalsie, 'Halq'eméylem Place Names,' 134–53.

6 Identity in the Emerging Colonial Order

1 Personal communication.
2 Emphasis added; James Douglas to Edward B. Lytton, 14 March 1859, in
   British Columbia, in 'Executive Council Committee Report, approved by
   the Lt-Gov. on 6 Jan. 1876,' *Papers Connected with the Indian Land Question,
   1850–1875, 1877* (Victoria: Richard Wolfenden, Government Printer, 1877;
   reproduction, 1987, hereafter *Papers*), 17.
3 *Contact and Conflict,* Robin Fisher's reissued and still popular 1977 study,
   remains the most prominent work to distinguish between contact-era
   cooperation and settlement-era conflict; see also the other recently reissued
   classic, Wilson Duff, *The Indian History of British Columbia,* vol. 1, *The Impact
   of the White Man* (Victoria: RBCM, 2nd ed., 1969), 53. See also Joyce A. Wike,
   The Effect of the Maritime Fur Trade on Northwest Coast Indian Society (New York:
   Columbia University, 1951), and Harris, *Resettlement of British Columbia.*
4 Cole Harris writes that 'the cultural enrichment hypothesis needs to be approached very cautiously. Crudely applied, it quickly becomes ethnocentric
   and far too simple. It tends to measure cultural achievement against quanti-
   tative and materialistic Western values of accumulation,' 80. See his 'Social
   Power and Cultural Change in Pre-Colonial British Columbia,' *BC Studies*
   nos. 115&116 (1997/8): 45–82.
      For other works that blur the line between the eras of cooperation and
   conflict, and which find continued Aboriginal agency well into the settlement era and perhaps greater instances of colonial coercion in the pre-gold
   rush period, see: Tennant, *Aboriginal Peoples and Politics;* Rolf Knight, *Indians
   at Work: An Informal History of Native Labour in British Columbia, 1858–1930*
   (Vancouver: New Star Books, 1978; 2nd ed., 1996); Barry M. Gough, *Gunboat Frontier: British Maritime Authority and Northwest Coast Indians, 1846–90*
   (Vancouver: UBC Press, 1984); Dianne Newell, *Tangled Webs of History:
   Indians and the Law in Canada's Pacific Coast Fisheries* (Toronto: University of
   Toronto Press, 1993); Robert Galois, *Kwakwaka'wakw Settlements, 1775–1920:
   A Geographical Analysis and Gazetteer* (Vancouver: UBC Press, 1994); Carlson
   et al., eds., *Atlas;* and Harmon, *Indians in the Making.*
5 Raids against other communities occurred for a number of reasons, such
   as: to avenge an earlier raid or perceived wrong; to acquire wealth (e.g., to
   steal); to allow a new warrior to demonstrate his spirit power and prowess;
   to alleviate the suffering in one community by inflicting greater suffering
   on another and therefore transferring the grief.
6 'Lekwiltok = "unkillable thing."' Edward S. Curtis, *The North American Indian; Being a Series of Volumes Picturing and Describing the Indians of the United*

States, and Alaska, Written, Illustrated, and Published by Edward S. Curtis, vol.
10 (Norwood, Mass.: Plimpton Press, 1930; reprinted New York: Johnson
Reprint, 1970), 308.

7 For accounts of this particular Lekwiltok conflict with the Musqueam, see
various entries for June 1827, in MacLachlan, *Fort Langley Journals,* 23–8. The
ethnographic context of the conflict and raiding described in the Fort Langley Journals are discussed in detail by Suttles in 'Ethnographic Significance
of the Fort Langley Journals.'

8 The collective military response to the Yukletaw aggression is placed within
a larger context in the next chapter.

9 *Xwelitem* remains common in Stó:lō parlance. Both folk etymologies and the
work of professional linguists such as Brent Galloway state that *Xwelitem* is the
Halq'eméylem term for someone who is 'hungry to the point of starving.'

10 Between 19 May and 1 July 1858, nineteen steamships, nine sailing vessels,
and fourteen decked vessels transported 6,133 men from San Francisco to
Victoria, while thousands more trekked northward along the coast on foot
or in small private vessels. On a single day in July over 2,800 miners arrived
at Victoria Harbour on two steamers, looking for smaller vessels to take
them to the Fraser. G.P.V. Akrigg, 'The Fraser River Gold Rush,' in *The
Fraser's History, from Glaciers to Early Settlements: Papers from a Seminar Presented
at the Annual Meeting of the British Columbia Historical Association on May 27,
1977, Burnaby, British Columbia,* with a foreword by Blythe Eagles (Burnaby:
Burnaby Historical Society, 1981), 32.

According to the estimates of the American consular agent, during the
months of May, June, and July at least 23,000 men had travelled from San
Francisco to Victoria by sea and another 8,000 reached the Fraser River
through Puget Sound or overland (Elwood Evans, 'The Fraser River Excitement, 1858,' BCA, Unpublished manuscript).

11 During the 1830s a prophesy movement swept through Coast Salish territory.
Indigenous prophets acquired knowledge of the world to come and then embarked on a process of informing people how to prepare for change (Carlson
et al., eds., *Atlas,* 154–61; see also Suttles, *Coast Salish Essays,* 137–51).

Chapter 5 of Dan Marshall's doctoral dissertation, 'Claiming the Land:
Indians, Goldseekers, and the Rush to British Columbia' (University of British Columbia, 2000), documents the feverish nature of the early migration
of miners to the Fraser River gold fields. While most miners arrived in Stó:lō
territory by boat up the Fraser River via Victoria, many came in small vessels
northward through Puget Sound, and then overland along the Whatcom
Trail from what is now Bellingham, Washington. Still others reached the
gold fields from the north, having travelled through the Okanagan Valley

from Washington Territory and ultimately down the Thompson and upper
Fraser River.

12 The region between Hope and Yale, while subject to incredible annual
hydrological forces, contains a relatively stable sand and gravel profile
(each year a roughly comparable amount of gravel is both washed away and
replaced) allowing contemporary TRIM (Terrain Resource Information
Management, a data set produced by the B.C. government) data to inform
our understanding of the scope of gravel availability in 1858. I am indebted
to Leeanna Rhodes, Geogaphical Information Systems (GIS) technician at
Stó:lō Nation, for providing me with information on the size of contemporary gravel bars between Hope and Yale.

13 See preamble to *Anno Vicesimo Primo et Vicesimo Secundo,* Victoræ Regina,
CAP. XCIX. An Act to provide for the Government of British Columbia.
[2nd Aug. 1858.]

14 See Carlson et al., eds., *Atlas,* 76–83.

15 Harold Wells, in conversation with Keith Carlson and Brian Thom at Mr
Wells' home, near Hope, 21 Feb. 1995. Mr Wells explained that the story
had been told to him by his grandmother. For a discussion of the economic
and political process through which the various sites along the lower Fraser
River came to acquire gold rush names such as 'American Bar,' see Daniel
P. Marshall, 'Mapping a New Social-Political Landscape: British Columbia,
1871–1874,' *Histoire Social/Social History* 31/61 (1998): 127–53.

16 Knight, *Indians at Work,* 87.

17 Arthur J. Ray and Donald Freeman, *'Give Us Good Measure': An Economic
Analysis of Relations between the Indians and the Hudson's Bay Company before
1763* (Toronto: University of Toronto Press, 1978), 218–30.

18 Lutz, *Makuk: A New History of Aboriginal-White Relations.*

19 John K. Ledell, 'Narrative of a Miner's Trip to the Head Waters of the Gold
Region,' in *Northern Light* (Whatcom: Bellingham Bay, 13 June 1858), 78–80.
Reprinted from P.R. Jeffcott, ed., *Nooksack Tales and Trails* (Ferndale, Wash.:
Sedro-Wooley Courier Times, 1949).

20 Marshall, 'Rickard Revisited,' 94–5, 99–100.

21 James Douglas to Home Government, 6 April 1858, Fort Victoria, Correspondence Out, 1856–1858, BCA, A/C/20/Vi4.

22 Although it does seem to have usurped the salmon trade to the HBC for
the summer of 1858. In that year the HBC canneries at the mouths of the
Chilliwack and Harrison rivers sat idle as the Stó:lō pursued more lucrative
mining operations (*Times of London,* 'British Columbia,' 30 Nov. 1858, 4).
Stó:lō people, however, continued to preserve sufficient salmon for their
own needs, as well as enough surplus to allow them to trade for profit with

the foreign miners in their territory (*Times of London*, 'British Columbia,' 1 Dec. 1858, 9).

23 Sockeye was the preferred species, but Spring (Tyee, King) were also caught in this manner.

24 Fr. Leon Fouquet to Rev. Father Tempier, 8 June 1863, in Oblats de Marie Immaculée, Reports and Letters published in the annual series, *Missions de la Congrégation des Missionnaires Oblats de Marie Immaculée* (hereafter, *Missions*), *1864*.

25 *Times of London*, 'British Columbia,' 5 Aug. 1858, 8.

26 Despatch from Gov. Douglas to the Right Hon. Lord Stanley, M.P. (No. 26), Victoria, Vancouver's Island, 15 June 1858 (received 9 Aug. 1858; answered No. 8, 14 Aug. 1858, 47), in *Papers Relative to the Affairs of British Columbia, Part I*, 16–17 (London, 1859).

27 'Copy of a Despatch from Governor Douglas to the Right Honourable Sir E.B. Lytton, Bart,' Victoria, Vancouver's Island, 12 Oct. 1858 (Received 14 Dec. 1858) (Answered No. 60, 30 Dec. 1858, 74) – *Papers Relative to the Affairs of British Columbia, Part II*, 3–7, London, 1859. For a cinematographic account of this incident see the DVD production 'Canyon War: The Untold Story,' directed by Eva Wonderman, Wonderman Film Inc., 2009.

28 'Fraser River News,' *San Francisco Herald*, 4 May 1858 (reprinted editorial from *Butte Record*), quoted in Lewis J. Swindle, *The Fraser Gold Rush of 1858 as Reported by the California Newspapers of 1858: Was It a Humbug?* (Victoria, BC: Trafford Publishing, 2001), 61.

29 See Swindle, *Fraser River Gold Rush*, 78, 80, 81, 86–7, 91, 98–9, 104, 106–7, 108, 114–18, 119–20, 123, 124, 125–6, 127–8, 135–6, 138, 151–2, 156–7, 161, 170, 174–5.

30 *San Francisco Times*, 7 June 1858, quoted in Swindle, ibid., 106–7.

31 'British Columbia,' *Times of London*, 25 Dec. 1858, 7.

32 Ibid., 1 Dec. 1858, 9.

33 Marshall, 'Rickard Revisited,' 96.

34 F.W. Chessen, Secretary of the Aboriginal Protection Society, to the Right Honourable Sir Edward Bulwer Lytton, MP, Her Majesty's Principal Secretary of State for the Colonies, enclosure in Sir Edward Lytton to Governor James Douglas, Despatch No.12, 2 Sept. 1858, in *Papers Relating to the Indian Land Question*, 12–13.

35 Daniel Marshall has documented parallel diplomatic activities by the Nlakapamux Chief Spintlum just upriver of Stó:lō territory. It would appear that Liquitem and Spintlum were working in tandem, if not necessarily coordination, to find a peaceful resolution to the Native-newcomer conflicts centred in the territory between the two powerful leaders.

36 Wilson Duff, interview with Patrick Charlie, in Fieldnotes, Book 1, 1950, Royal British Columbia Museum, 80.

37 *San Francisco Bulletin*, letter dated 16 Aug. 1858, quoted in Swindle, *Fraser River Gold Rush*, 235.

38 Marshall, 'Claiming the Land.' See in particular, Chapter 6, 'Fortunes Foretold: The Fraser River War,' 199–259. Marshall transcribed and published a complete copy of H.H. Snyder's letter to Douglas describing the treaty negotiations in *Native Studies Review* 11/1 (1997): 140–5. Detailed oral traditions among the Nlakapamux describe the diplomacy of Chief David Spintlem, who like Liquitem among the Stó:lō, was the principal spokesperson and leader of the Nlakapamux in their relations with the miners. ('War Stories,' n.d. Unpublished ethnographic field notes of James Teit. Originals held by the American Philosophical Society Library, Philadelphia. Microfilm copy held by the BCARS, Victoria, Microfilms A236-A268.)

39 Governor James Douglas to Edward Lytton, 15 Aug. 1859, Dispatch No. 199, Colonial Office, 60/5, 13; also PRO, London. See also, Edward Lytton to Governor James Douglas, 20 May 1859, in *Papers*, 18.

40 Lytton to Douglas, 31 July 1858, in *Papers*, 12.

41 Chessen to Lytton, copy forwarded to Douglas, 2 Sept. 1858, in ibid., 12–13.

42 Lytton to Douglas, 30 Dec. 1858, in ibid., 15.

43 John Locke, *Two Treatises of Government* (Cambridge: Cambridge University Press, 1960), esp. Chapter V, 'On Property,' 327–44.

44 Harris, *Making Native Space*, xxiii. Henry Reynolds, *The Law of the Land* (New York: Viking Penguin, 1987). For a discussion of how these ideas ultimately played themselves out on the Canadian prairies, see Sarah Carter, *Lost Harvest*, esp. 15–20, 79–84.

45 Barbara Arneil, *John Locke and America: The Defence of English Colonialism* (Oxford: Clarendon Press, 1996).

46 Nancy M. Williams provides a succinct discussion of the way Lockean ideas concerning property and the law of nations and the four stages theory of human social development, associated with the Scottish philosopher Adam Smith, were applied to Aboriginal lands within the British Empire. See her *The Yolngu and Their Land: A System of Land Tenure and the Fight for Its Recognition* (Stanford: Stanford University Press, 1986), 109–38.

47 See discussion of Canadian court cases pertaining to Aboriginal rights through 'Resources for Aboriginal Studies,' University of Saskatchewan Native Studies portal, http:library2.usask.ca/native/cnic/vol02/541.html.

48 Emphasis added; Douglas to Lytton, 14 March 1859, in *Papers*, 16.

49 Emphasis added; ibid., 17.

50 Alexander C. Anderson, William Duncan, Rod Finlayson, W.I. Macdonald,

I.W. Mckay, Archibald McKinlay, W.F. Tolmie, Charles A. Vernon, and Admiral Provost, Petition to the Hon. G.A. Walkem, Att. Gen. and Premier of B.C., 25 Sept 1879, LAC, DINA, RG 10, Reel C-10117, Vol. 3669, File 10691. This petition and the context behind it are discussed in greater detail in Chapter 9 of this volume.

51 I.W. Powell to Supt. Gen., 29 Sept. 1879, LAC, DINA, RG 10, Reel C-10117, Vol. 3669, File 10691.

52 Charles B. Goode, for the Col. Sec., to R.C. Moody, 5 March 1861, in *Papers*, 21.

53 William Young to R.C. Moody, and Moody to Young, June 1862, in ibid., 24.

54 Fraser Valley Chiefs, 'Petition of Fraser Valley Chiefs to Gov. Musgrave Regarding Sale of Cranberry Patches,' in Holbrook to Musgrave, 7 Jan. 1870, BCA, Colonial Correspondence, F778/38, Reel B-1334; copy in Carlson et al., eds., *Atlas*, 172.

55 Moody to Young, 27 May 1862, in *Papers*, 23.

56 Young reported Douglas' instructions regarding Aboriginal pre-emption rights in, Young to Moody, 18 June 1862, in ibid., 24.

57 Moody to Young, 11 June 1862, in ibid., 24; see also Moody to Young, 2 July 1862, and Moody to Douglas, 28 April 1863, in ibid., 25.

58 Membership lists became a formal part of DINA administrative procedures in 1951.

59 Joseph Trutch, a construction contractor, became Chief Commissioner of Land and Works in 1864. The question of whether Natives 'made adequate use of the land' became particularly synonymous with Trutch and his interpretation and application of Indian policy, as it was used by him repeatedly in his colonial correspondence and subsequently, while he was Lt Gov. of the province of British Columbia, with his superiors in Ottawa.

60 Harris, *Making Native Space*, 33.

61 Douglas to Moody, 27 April 1863, in *Papers*, 26–7; Young to Moody, 11 May 1863, in ibid., 28.

62 Emphasis added; Moody to Douglas, 28 April 1863, in ibid., 27. See also R.C. Moody, Letters and Enclosures, Colonial Correspondence, Indian Reserves on the Fraser River, 1860, BCA, GR 1372.

63 William McColl's report, 16 May 1864, in ibid., 43. See also A.R. Howse, 18 Dec. 1865, Report of A.R. Howse, BCA, Colonial Correspondence, File 1030; Chartres Brew to Joseph Trutch, Chief Commissioner of Lands and Works, 26 Jan. 1866, BCA, GR 1372, File 943/13, Microfilm B-1339. Also, B.C., Colony, Lands and Works Department, 1859–1872, BCA, GR 2900, Vol. 11, Microfilm B-11044, 16.

64 William McColl's map of the 'Douglas Reserves,' as they are commonly

referred to, has been at the centre of Stó:lō specific and comprehensive
claims from the moment of their reduction in 1867 through to the present
climate of treaty negotiations and specific claims. The original is held in the
Provincial Crown Lands Vault, B.C. Surveyor General's Office, Victoria, BC,
Ref no. 31-T1.

  When I first examined this precious document in 1990 it was still in relatively good condition. The intense interest in this document has resulted in
a marked deterioration in its physical health over the intervening decade.
Bits of the map, present in 1990, have subsequently fallen off and disappeared, while portions of the pencilled comments inserted to show the
location and status of various non-Native pre-emptions have smudged and
can no longer be read.

65 While Stó:lō people have consistently protested the loss of these reserves,
the period from 1969 through to the present has seen the rise of direct
action initiatives as well as litigation to secure redress over the loss of these
lands. The reserves' status remains unsettled to this day.

66 Joseph Trutch to Acting Col. Sec., 28 Aug. 1867, in *Papers*, 41–2.

67 The deception in Trutch's public statements is revealed by his own hand
in the marginal notes he made on a series of letters discussing the conflict
between the McColl reserves and the desires of newly arriving non-Native
settlers. Also in his official memorandum of justification sent to the governor and then to federal officials after Confederation: 'There is yet an
impediment to the survey of the claims in question. All the ordinances and
Proclamations on the subject of Pre-emption have consequently required
[that] the Pre-emption claims shall be of a rectangular form and the short-
est side of the rectangle shall be about two-thirds of the long side – except
where the land is bounded in whole or in part by natural boundaries. In the
accompanying tracing [sic] in which the boundary lines of the Pre-emption
claims as recorded are indicated by dotted lines and those of the Indian
Reserves as laid off by Sarg't McColl in a blue line, it appears that the longer
side of the [pre-emption] claims are four times the length of the shorter
sides. If this departure from the strict requirement of the encroachments
on this subject should be sanctioned in these cases which do not appear
to me to offer any extraordinary grounds for compliance with the specific
wording of the law, a precedent will be established which must rule in all
other surveys. I am aware that but few records of pre-emptions will be found
to comply with the requirements above skiled [sic] when surveyed, and I
can only suggest that a provision be inserted in the said ordinance –allowing discretion to the CCr of the L&W [Chief Commissioner of Lands and
Works – i.e., Joseph Trutch] in regard as to all claims hitherto recorded –

and that all future records should comply exactly with the survey clause of the ordinance.'

68 See Carlson, *You Are Asked to Witness*, 65–79; see also Young to Trutch, 6 Nov. 1867, Trutch to Young, 19 Nov. 1867, and Young to Trutch, 4 Dec. 1867, in *Papers*, 45–7.

69 Trutch to Col. Sec., 19 Nov. 1867, in ibid., 45–6.

70 Ibid., 47.

71 Women of any race could not pre-empt land on their own, and so it is only Stó:lō men discussed here.

72 John L. Tobias, 'Protection, Civilization, Assimilation: An Outline History of Canada's Indian Policy,' *Western Canadian Journal of Anthropology* 6/2 (1976): 13–30.

73 Harry Joe, interview by Marian Smith, in Smith, Fieldnotes, 4–5.

74 Ibid., 5–7. Ironically, while the government worked so hard throughout the 1860s to replace the Stó:lō sense of collective family title with communal band title, within a generation the Dominion's Indian Affairs bureaucracy was devising new policies to break down band title and replace it with a system of private individual ownership.

75 Fisher, *Contact and Conflict*, 184; Tennant, *Aboriginal Peoples and Politics*, 53–4; Harris, *Making Native Space*, 85–6.

76 Peter Ayessik, Chief of Hope and other Chiefs, Petition to the Supt. of Indian Affairs, 14 July 1874, in *Papers*, 136–8; also in Carlson et al., eds., *Atlas*, 173.

77 Ibid.

78 Lynn A. Blake, 'Oblate Missionaries and the Indian Land Question,' *BC Studies* no. 199 (1998): 27–44. Blake shows how various Oblates, and in particular Father C.J. Grandidier, employed Thomas Aquinas' ideas about how property rights derive directly from God, and how human actions, including the investment of labour into agricultural pursuits, did not change God's will. Grandidier wrote copious letters to government officials articulating this position, at least one of which was published in the widely circulating *Victoria Standard* Newspaper.

7 Identity in the Face of Missionaries and the Anti-Potlatch Law

1 In 1838 the Jesuits, headquartered at Fort Vancouver on the lower Columbia River, became the first Catholic priests to begin active missionary work on the northwest coast since the abandonment of Nootka by the Spaniards. Father Norbert Blanchet was the first missionary to set foot in Stó:lō territory, visiting Fort Langley in 1840. Blanchet was accompanied to the west coast by Father Modeste Demers, who, in 1841, claimed to have baptized 400 chil-

dren after preaching to 1,500 Stó:lō at a summer camp near Fort Langley. In 1844 Father Peter DeSmet became the third priest to visit the Stó:lō.

2 Fr. Leon Fouquet to Rev. Fr. Tempier, 8 June 1863, *Missions (1864)*.

3 Bishop D'Herbomez, quoted in Vincent J. McNally, *The Lord's Distant Vineyard: A History of the Oblates and the Catholic Community in British Columbia* (Edmonton: University of Alberta Press, 2000), 62.

4 Ibid., 58.

5 E.M. Bunoz, Vic. Apost., 'Bishop Durieu's System,' *Etudes Oblates: Revue Trimestrielle* (Montreal: Maison Provinciale, 1942), 194. I agree with McNally that Bunoz's writing should be considered a primary source, as his descriptions of Stó:lō society and the Durieu system are based upon his personal conversations with Durieu, and his own participation in trying to implement the Durieu system among the Coast Salish people.

6 There has been no effort to formally collect oral accounts of the history of alcohol and alcoholism among the Stó:lō. Nonetheless, these are rather common topics of conversation among Stó:lō people gathered together in semiformal family settings. In addition, at least some such information has been collected inadvertently by earlier ethnographers such as Oliver Wells and Jimmie Harris while in the process of documenting folk tales or vocabulary. Wells even recorded a Stó:lō 'drinking song' entitled, 'Oh Chief, It Must Have Been Nice to Be Drunk and Have Whiskey,' which appears to date to the early settlement era. See Dan Milo, interview by Oliver Wells, Jan. 1962, in Wells, Audio Collection. Also, Wells, *The Chilliwacks and Their Neighbours*, 15.

7 Captain John, 'The Story of the Conversion and Subsequent Experiences of Captain John, as Narrated by Himself.' Translated from Chinook into English by Rev. W.H. Barraclough, B.A. (30 March 1898), Chilliwack Archives, Add Mss 253.

8 Fr. Leon Fouquet to to Rev. Father Tempier, 8 June 1863.

9 Bishop D'Herbomez, 30 May 1861, *Missions (1862)*.

10 Throughout the 1990s, as an invited speaker at a number of local First Nation-hosted 'community healing' sessions, I was repeatedly told stories of the horrible effects of alcohol on past generations of Stó:lō people. While most of the stories people shared described alcohol and drug problems among more recent generations, some explicitly identified the problems of generational alcohol addiction as beginning with the whiskey introduced during the 1858 gold rush.

11 Bunoz, 'Bishop Durieu's System,' 194, 199.

12 Fr. Chirouse, 16 July 1862, *Missions (1862)*.

13 Fr. Leon Fouquet to Rev. Fr. Tempier, 8 June 1863.

14 Ibid.

15 Many Stó:lō communities were only visited three or four times a year by the Oblates, and indeed, as historian Dianne Newell has documented (*Tangled Webs of History*, 46), after 1870 missionaries all along the B.C. coast often found it easier to conduct their proselytizing activities within the context of visiting industrial worksites, such as those associated with the commercial cannery industry. At the canneries, and later at the hop yards, missionaries essentially found the equivalent of large multitribal seasonal villages that relieved them of some of the necessity of making more frequent visits to smaller remote settlements. Methodist missionaries, lacking the numbers and institutional backing of the Catholics, appear to have been especially attentive to the opportunities the canneries provided. See, e.g., BCA, Logbooks for the Methodist missionary vessel, *Glad Tidings,* as it travelled up and down the B.C. coast in the 1880s, and Robert Clyde Scott, Scrapbook, Logbook entries for 16, 23, 24, 25, 28 July 1887, and March 24, 1887; and Second logbook entries for June and July 1884, and July 1886, BCA, Add Mss 1299, Box 2/2. I am grateful to Dianne Newell for directing me to the Scott manuscript.

16 Bunoz, 'Bishop Durieu's System,' 194–9; McNally, *Distant Vineyard*, 130–1.

17 Edna Bobb, personal communication, July 1992.

18 Bunoz, 'Bishop Durieu's System,' 195.

19 McNally, *Distant Vineyard*, 64.

20 Fr. Edward MacGugein, 'Report for 1886, Fraser Districts,' *Missions (1887).*

21 Ronald P. Rohner, ed., *The Ethnography of Franz Boas: Letters and Diaries of Franz Boas, Written on the Northwest Coast from 1886 to 1931* (Chicago: University of Chicago, 1969), 155.

22 The Oblates had much greater success among the more isolated community of Sechelt on Gibson's Peninsula, and among the Squamish of North Vancouver. The Methodists achieved even greater success with Metlakatla. See Fisher, *Contact and Conflict.*

23 Bunoz, 'Bishop Durieu's System,' 200–1; McNally, *Distant Vineyard*, 132–3. Interestingly, such democratic matrimonial unions were also advocated by the Stó:lō prophets of the previous generation. See Suttles, 'The Plateau Prophet Dance,' in *Coast Salish Essays,* 160–4.

24 In the summer of 1993 I attended a meeting of Matsqui Elders and listened as two elderly women described what they remembered about the nineteenth-century OMI plans for Matsqui prairie. This paragraph is derived from my memory of their observations. I did not record their conversation or make extensive notes, as I was there on other business and was only serendipitously privileged to hear their oral history.

25 Edward Mohun to Joseph Trutch, 3 Dec. 1868, in *Papers*, 54. A few years later two separate reserves were created on the Matsqui meadows, one 50 acres and the other 82 acres.

26 Patrick Charlie, interview with Wilson Duff, in Duff, Fieldnotes, Book 1, 47.

27 Fr. R.P. Gendre, OMI, *Missions (1865)*.

28 Ibid.

29 Ibid.

30 Rev. Father Charles Marchal to Rev. Father Durieu, 12 Feb. 1871, in *Missions (1874)*.

31 Crosby, *Among the An-ko-me-nums*, 189.

32 See Carlson, 'Prophesy,' in Carlson et al., eds., *Atlas*, 154.

33 Eduard Peytavin to MacGuckin, 'Columbie Britannique: Lettre du R.P. Ed. Peytavin au R.P. MacGuckin, New Westminster, le 21 fevrier 1887,' *Missions (1887)*, 238–51.

34 Historian Susan Neylan has recently documented how within Tsimshian communities competing families also used denominational rivalries to their advantage to the point of recruiting churches to their areas. See her *'The Heavens Are Changing': Protestant Missionization on the North Pacific Coast* (Montreal and Kingston: McGill-Queen's University Press, 2003).

35 Eduard Peytavin, 'Report of 1886,' *Missions (1887)*.

36 Dombrowski, *Against Culture*.

37 A. Browning to Officer Administering the Government, 6 July 1869, in *Papers*, 71.

38 Captain John, 'Story of the Conversion.' Additionally, in 1992 I was told by Captain John's grandson Andy Commodore that Captain John had at one time attempted to prevent winter spirit dancing from occurring on the Soowahlie Reserve. When his own mother began dancing Captain John physically attempted to stop her. However, when he touched his dancing mother he was struck and knocked back by the spirit, and himself began to dance uncontrollably. From that point onward Captain John remained opposed to spirit dancing, but never again attempted to directly intervene to stop others.

39 J.B. Launders to the Chief Commissioner of Lands and Works Joseph Trutch, 18 Dec. 1868, in *Papers*, 54–7. Also, J.B. Launders, Various Survey Maps, PCLV.

40 Browning to the Officer Administering the Government, 6 July 1869, in *Papers*, 71.

41 Ibid. See also Capt. Ball to Col. Sec., 4 Dec. 1869, BCA, GR 1372, File 397/1 B-1322.

42 Ibid.; also Capt. Ball to the Col. Sec., 14 July 1869, in *Papers*, 72.

43 Ibid.

44 Andy Commodore, personal conversation, July 1993.

45 V. Vedder and 27 others to His Excellency Anthony Musgrave, Gov. of British Columbia, 30 Nov. 1869, in *Papers,* 73.

46 Indicative of Captain John's ability to consolidate his power is the fact that ten years later, in 1880, he was still listed as Chief in the new reserve map created by W.S. Jemmett. See Jemmett, B.C. Fieldnotes Book, 31 July 1880, PCLV, B.C. Surveyor General's Office, W26.

47 Ball to the Col. Sec., 15 Dec. 1869, in *Papers,* 74.

48 For example, refer to the correspondence between A.T. Bushby and B.W. Pearse describing the confusion over government recognition of the Chehalis Chief in 1870. See, A.T. Bushby to B.W. Pearse, and Pearse to Bushby, in *Papers,* 83.

49 Bunoz, 'Durieu's System,' 196.

50 I am grateful to Sonny McHalsie who reviewed various of the Church Chiefs' genealogies with me and determined that several of them carried high-status names and were descendants and relatives of people claiming hereditary rights to leadership.

51 The Gradual Enfranchisement Act and the Assimilation Act were not combined into the single Indian Act until 1876.

52 Knight, *Indians at Work,* 120–1, 321–8.

53 Douglas Cole and Ira Chaikin, *An Iron Hand upon the People: The Law against the Potlatch on the Northwest Coast* (Vancouver: Douglas and McIntyre, and Seattle: University of Washington Press, 1990), 18–21. More recently John Sutton Lutz has confirmed and elaborated this interpretation; see his *Makuk.*

54 See Cole and Chaikin, *Iron Hand,* 15–16.

55 Gilbert Malcolm Sproat, Papers, BCA, MS 0257. Also, Field Minutes, LAC, Government of Canada, DINA, LTS, Vol. 18: 309.

56 Franz Boas concluded that the potlatch fulfilled two important goals. It was primarily a means of acquiring rank but it also served as an important 'interest-bearing investment.' See his: 'First General Report on the Indians of British Columbia,' in *The 59th Report of the British Association for the Advancement of Science for 1889,* London, 834–5; 'The Social Organization and the Secret Societies of the Kwakiutl Indians,' in *Report of the U..S National Museum for 1895* (Washington, DC: U.S. National Museum, 1895; repr. New York: Johnson Reprint, 1970), 341–3; and 'The Social Organization of the Haida,' 681–2.

Most other early twentieth-century scholars, by way of contrast, interpreted the potlatch as an expression of Indian greed; see esp. Ruth Benedict,

Patterns of Culture (Boston: Houghton Mifflin, 1934; repr. 1969). I am grateful to Wayne Suttles for drawing my attention to Benedict's work on this.

Against this intellectual and social backdrop, Edward Curtis provided a fresh and insightful interpretation that challenged all previous interpretations. Curtis was the first academic observer to recognize that people potlatched out of a sense of pride and accomplishment. His conclusions, however, were largely overlooked – perhaps obscured behind the prominence of his evocative (and ultimately controversial) photographs that for so long were deemed to speak without the need for accompanying text. See his *North American Indian*, vol. 10, 141–55.

By the mid-twentieth century, the growing body of ethnographic investigations allowed academics to apply increasingly sophisticated comparative dimensions to their study of the potlatch. George Murdock, in his article 'Rank and the Potlatch among the Haida,' *Yale University Publications in Anthropology* (1936) 13: 1–20, alerted people to the fact that potlatching had different meanings within and between various Aboriginal communities and in particular he demonstrated that (at least within the Haida context) potlatches served to elevate the status of the host's children and not those of the guests. Viola Garfield, meanwhile, argued in 'A Research Problem in Northwest Indian Economics,' *American Anthropologist* 47/4 (1945): 626–30, that among the Tsimshian the potlatch stimulated economic productivity and in so doing facilitated the redistribution of wealth.

In what remains among the most insightful revisionist challenges to the Boasian assumption that potlatches were primarily investment systems dependent on sustained competition, Homer Barnett, in 'The Nature of the Potlatch,' *American Anthropologist* 40/3 (1938): 349–58, observed that the potlatch was less about acquiring a new status than about asserting one's claim to a position that was already understood and accepted by society at large. Guests validated their host's claims by accepting gifts (as witnesses) to the transference of property and titles, and by their commitment to reciprocate. Certainly, this is the context in which the traditional Coast Salish potlatch continues to be described by such contemporary cultural experts as Albert 'Sonny' McHalsie; and this interpretation informs the discussion found in Chapter 3 of this study.

It was during the rise in environmental consciousness of the 1960s that a new generation of scholars, led by Wayne Suttles, advanced the innovative and compelling interpretation that the potlatch was largely a social response to ecological variation over time and space: a safety valve created to enable in-laws living in dispersed settlements to access a range of food wealth that was subject to geographical and temporal fluctuations in availability. See Suttles: 'Affinal Ties'; 'Variations in Habitat and Culture on the Northwest Coast,' in *Proceedings of the 34th International Congress of Americanists* (Vienna, 1960), 269–305; and 'Coping with Abundance: Subsistence on the Northwest Coast,' in R.B. Lee and I. DeVore, eds., *Man the Hunter,* 56–68 (Chicago: Aldine, 1968).

Most scholars embraced Suttles' interpretations, but some remained unconvinced. Philip Drucker, for one, saw value in defending the older interpretations, while others, especially in the late 1960s and 1970s, rejected the economic functionalist approach altogether and looked instead to the symbolic and psychological theorizings for new insights. See: Philip Drucker and Robert F. Heizer, *To Make My Name Good: A Reexamination of the Southern Kwakiutl Potlatch* (Berkeley: University of California Press, 1967); Marcel Mauss, *The Gift: Forms and Functions of Exchange in Archaic Societies,* trans. by Ian Cunnison (New York: Norton, 1967); Kaj Birket-Smith, 'An Analysis of the Potlatch Institution of North America,' *Folk* 6/2 (1964): 5–113; Kaj Birket-Smith, 'Potlatch and Feasts of Merit,' in K. Birket-Smith, ed., *Studies in Circumpacific Culture Relations* (Copenhagen: Munksgaard, 1967); Irving Goldman, *The Mouth of Heaven: An Introduction to Kwakiutl Religious Thought* (New York: Wiley, 1975); Alan Dundes, 'Heads or Tails: A Psychoanalytic Study of the Potlatch,' *Journal of Psychological Anthropology* 2/4 (1979): 395–424; and Mark S. Fleisher, 'The Potlatch: A Symbolic and Psychoanalytic View,' *Current Anthropology* 22/1 (1981): 69–71.

Most recently, the potlatch has come under the gaze of scholars inspired by the post-structural theoretical approach of literary criticism. Christopher Bracken's monograph, *The Potlatch Papers: A Colonial Case History* (Chicago and London: University of Chicago Press, 1998), presents the potlatch as a product of colonial anxiety. Without colonialism, he argues, the diverse and multifaceted Indigenous gift exchange ceremonies that characterized the northwest coast would never have been conceived as a coherent social or economic system.

57 Drucker and Heizer (*To Make My Name Good*) rejected this view. But Codere's thesis, as argued in 'Fighting with Property: A Study of Kwakiutl Potlatching and Welfare, 1792–1930,' *Monographs of the American Ethnographic Society* 18 (1950), remains influential if for no other reason than the fact that no one has seriously engaged the subject since, although Ferguson's 1984 review of northwest coast warfare essentially kept the interpretation before the public eye and probably accounted for its continuing appeal. See R. Brian Ferguson, 'A Reexamination of the Causes of Northwest Coast Warfare,' in R.B. Ferguson, ed., *Warfare, Culture, and Environment* (New York: Academic Press, 1984), 133–47. More recently Bill Angelbeck has reopened the topic

330 Notes to pages 202–3

of warfare in his archaeological study of Coast Salish defensive sites, arguing
that they are reflective of a process of decentralizing power and the establishment of a hierarchy of leadership. See W. Angelbeck, '"They Recognize
No Superior Chief": Power, Practice, Anarchism and Warfare in the Coast
Salish Past' (doctoral dissertation, University of British Columbia, 2009).

58 John Lutz has argued that the large gatherings associated with certain non-
Native economic activities such as hop picking and cannery work may have
provided Indigenous people with an opportunity to fulfil certain potlatch
obligations in a manner not regarded as threatening to colonial society; see
his 'After the Fur Trade.'

   Another largely overlooked study promoting a different view of post-
contact change in the potlatch is Daniela Weinberg, 'Models of Southern
Kwakiutl Social Organization,' in B. Cox, ed., *Cultural Ecology: Readings on
the Canadian Indians and Eskimos* (Toronto: McClelland and Stewart, 1973),
227–53.

59 Forrest LaViolette, in 1951 (the year the potlatch was decriminalized), documented the role of missionaries in late nineteenth-century public policy and
social engineering; see her 'Missionaries and the Potlatch,' *Queen's Quarterly*
58 (1951): 237–51. Later she expanded her analysis, placing the anti-potlatch law squarely within the context of the larger cultural clash between
Indigenous ideology and the Protestant work ethic; see her *The Struggle for
Survival: Indian Cultures and the Protestant Ethic in British Columbia* (Toronto:
University of Toronto Press, 1961).

   In 1977 Robin Fisher discussed (*Contact and Conflict*, 207–9) the banning
of the potlatch within the context of the consolidation of European settlement interests, linking its motives to questions of land and resources ownership and management. More recently, as already mentioned, Christopher
Bracken (*The Potlatch Papers*) has applied the theoretical methods of literary
criticism to his analysis of the colonial documents concerning the potlatch
prohibition.

   In their 1990 monograph *An Iron Hand upon the People*, Douglas Cole and
Ira Chaikin embrace Codere's view and some of the older anthropology.
Thus, they present a picture of the potlatch as competitive gift exchange
aimed at enhancing the host's status and that this got more and more
pronounced throughout the nineteenth century as Aboriginal people who
would have been formerly lower status acquired new wealth through the
opportunities of the fur trade and wage labour economy and then used this
wealth to try and augment their positions within Native society vis-à-vis the
old elite. *An Iron Hand* focuses on the repressive measures the government
used to suppress the potlatch and the debate within non-Native society over

the means and merits of these measures. The authors do not describe the Indigenous import of the prohibition in terms of how it caused alterations in Native society other than in their efforts to thwart the prohibition itself.

60 Interestingly, the federal government's own inability to define a potlatch in its legislation led to more than two decades of half-hearted and geographically imbalanced efforts at enforcing the anti-potlatch amendment to the Indian Act. The judicial response to early attempts at convictions was to call on the government to more precisely define potlatch and to articulate what it was about the potlatch that was so objectionable. See Cole and Chaiken, Chapter 3, 'The Law Is Weak as a Baby,' *Iron Hand*, 25–42.

61 See esp. Patrick Charlie, interview by Wilson Duff, in Duff, Fieldnotes, Book 1, 81.

62 The following information about Suxyel comes from Wilson Duff's Fieldnotes, Book 1, and from the oral history preserved within Suxyel's family. In particular, I am indebted to Sonny McHalsie, Suxyel's great-great-grandson, for sharing his knowledge of his ancestor. Elsewhere McHalsie and I have presented additional information on Suxyel. See Carlson, with McHalsie, *I Am Stó:lō*, 83–94.

63 Bill Uslick was arrested and convicted in 1896; see Carlson, *You Are Asked to Witness*, 99.

8 Reservations for the Queen's Birthday Celebrations, 1864–1876

1 For discussions of leadership and innovation see Wayne Suttles: *The Plateau Prophet Dance among the Coast Salish* (Albuquerque: University of New Mexico Press, 1957), and *Coast Salish Essays*; see also Miller and Boxberger, 'Creating Chiefdoms: The Puget Sound Case,' 283–4.

2 Duff, *Upper Stalo*, 11.

3 Wayne Suttles, personal communication, Feb. 1998.

4 James A. Teit, 'Dream Book of a Stalo Prophet,' Canadian Museum of Civilization, Ottawa, MS VII-G-19M, c.1882. I am grateful to Kevin Washbrook for initially drawing my attention to this remarkable document.

5 *Missions (1888)*, 79–80; also Jean Marie Raphael LaJeune, *Polyglot Manual – Stalo Manual; or Prayers, Hymns, and the Catechism in the Stalo or Lower Fraser Language* (Kamloops, BC, c. 1896).

6 Chief Mischel's father was Stó:lō from Yale.

7 Hill-Tout, *Salish People*, vol. 2, 95. See also Charles Hill-Tout, 'Report on the Ethnology of the South-Eastern Tribes of Vancouver Island, British Columbia,' *Journal of the Royal Antrhopolgical Institute of Great Britain and Ireland* (1907): 312.

8 The Iyem Memorial was erected under the organizational leadership of
   Dennis S. Peters (the first cousin of Pierre Ayesick), Isaac James, and the active support of Chief Harry Stewart of Seabird Island among others (*Chilliwack Progress*, 17 Aug. 1938; *Vancouver Sun*, 20 Aug. 1938). For a detailed
   discussion of the Iyem Memorial in its historical context, see Amanda Beth
   Fehr, 'The Relationships of Place: A Study of Change and Continuity in
   Stó:lō Understandings of I:yem' (M.A. thesis, University of Saskatchewan,
   2008).

9 Membership in the two umbrella organizations is flexible. At the time of
   writing (2008) 19 of the 29 lower Fraser River Bands were active participants
   in either Stó:lō Nation or Stó:lō Tribal Council governance, another five
   receive certain services from the Stó:lō Nation while remaining politically
   autonomous, and five other bands had no formal ties to either Stó:lō organization.

10 Chief Robert Hope of the Yale Band is one of the proponents of this position. He has recently and repeatedly asserted that 'the word "Stó:lō" or
   "Stalo" in reference to a cultural group was coined by the anthropologist
   Wilson Duff around 1950, and is only properly used as the word meaning
   "river or river people" in a local dialect.' The argument's adherents maintain that Duff manipulated the information shared with him by lower Fraser
   tribal Elders. He is accused of inventing a collective identity that had never
   really existed in either Indigenous minds or Indigenous history, ostensibly
   to advance his career. See Affidavit of Robert Hope, *Chief Robert Hope* v.
   Lower Fraser Fishing Authority and Others, File c92-4333, 8 July 1992 , B.C. Supreme Court, Vancouver Registry; *Yale Indian Band* v. *Aitchelitz Indian Band
   et al.*, Reasons for Order of Prothonotary John A. Hargrave, File T-776-98,
   24 June 1998, Federal Court, Vancouver, B.C.; *Chilliwack Progress*, 17 March
   2006, as quoted in *Fraser Valley Treaty Advisory Committee Local Media Excerpts
   to 31 March 2006*; Robert Freeman, 'Bands Feud Over Canyon Cleaning,'
   Chilliwack Progress, 18 May 1999, 1; 'Yale Territory Defended from Sto-lo
   Invasion,' *Chilliwack Progress*, 7 April 1988.
       Other Native people boldly reject this view. Some even point out the
   irony of criticizing Duff in this manner when, in fact, he never classified the
   Stó:lō as any sort of cohesive political group in any of his writings. Indeed,
   Duff went perhaps excessively far in the other direction, emphasizing the
   situational and ephemeral nature of Stó:lō leadership and the tenuous
   network connecting people across a broad and diverse landscape.
       As such, there is a body of counter-Indigenous thought that ironically
   takes issue with Duff for not fully recognizing the powerful, if largely latent,
   supra-tribal collectivity that existed in the century prior to his conducting

his fieldwork. Those defending the 'Stó:lō have always known they were Stó:lō' position like to point out that their opponents are typically male Chiefs from bands whose reserves lie adjacent to the most valuable natural resources: forest land, minerals, water, salmon, spiritual sites etc., and that by denying the historicity of the concept of shared Stó:lō identity these men simultaneously deny the broadest definitions of shared collective Aboriginal title. The significance of this position is that if the concept of the broader Stó:lō nation did not exist pre-historically, then Aboriginal title to resources, as well as the right to manage those same resources and govern the Native people who may access and benefit from them, falls by default to the next smallest cultural-political unit: the supposedly autonomous tribe or band.

11 On one side of this debate are Wilson Duff (*Indian History of British Columbia*) and Robin Fisher (*Contact and Conflict*) and, on the other, Paul Tennant (*Aboriginal Peoples and Politics*) and, to a degree, Cole Harris (*Making Native Space*, 2002). Though the debate no longer rages in academic circles, it remains a topic of great interest within Aboriginal communities.

12 Frederick Seymour to Cardwell, 31 Aug. 1864, BCA, Colonial Despatches, CO 60/19, no. 30, Microfilm B-4034, 95.

13 Gendre, *Missions (1865)*, 297–8.

14 These political gatherings, most commonly associated in the popular mind with the quixotic speech attributed to Chief Seattle, are discussed within the context of other nineteenth-century evidence for and against Coast Salish chiefdoms, in Miller and Boxberger, 'Creating Chiefdoms,' 273–7.

15 For an account of the Salish military action against the Lekwiltok, see Daniel P. Marshall, *Those Who Fell from the Sky: A History of the Cowichan Peoples* (Duncan, BC: Cowichan Tribes Cultural and Education Centre, 1999), 82; see also Curtis, *North American Indian*, vol. 9, 32–6, 76.

16 For a detailed account of the impact of Western fire arms and the aggressive southward movement of the Yukletaw, see Galois, *Kwakwaka'wakw Settlements*, 223–76.

17 *British Columbian*, 27 Jan. 1864. See also Opening Address by James Douglas to First Session of First Parliament, 21 Jan. 1864, in James E. Hendrickson, ed., *Journals of the Colonial Legislatures*, vol. 4 (Victoria, 1980), 179–82.

18 Ibid.

19 Ibid.

20 Ibid.

21 William McColl to Chief Commissioner of Lands and Works, 16 May 1864, *Papers Connected with the Indian Land Question*, 43.

22 William McColl, 'Report to Chief Commissioner of Lands and Works,' 16 May 1864, in *Papers*, 43. See also George Turner to Joseph Trutch, 20 Oct.

1865, in ibid., 45; and memorandum of A.R. Howse to Wm McColl, Colonial Correspondence, File 1030, BCA.

23 J. Hendrickson, ed., *Journals of the Colonial Legislatures of the Colonies of Vancouver Island and British Columbia, 1851–1871*, vol. 4 (Victoria: PABC, 1980), 237.

24 *British Columbian*, 'The Last Potlatch,' 27 April 1864.

25 See www.canadianmysteries.com.

26 Gendre, *Missions (1865)*, 298.

27 Ibid.

28 Seymour to Cardwell, 31 Aug. 1864, 95.

29 Emphasis in original; Gendre, *Missions (1865)*.

30 Gendre, *Missions*, 307.

31 Ibid.

32 Seymour to Cardwell, 31 Aug. 1864, 95.

33 *British Columbian*, 'The Queen's Birthday,' 26 May 1865.

34 Eloise Street, *Sepass Tales, the Songs of Y-ail-mihth* (Chilliwack: Sepass Trust, 1974), 13. These particular series of gatherings were possibly products of the prophet dance phenomenon of the early nineteenth century. See Suttles, *Plateau Prophet Dance*. Perhaps this was associated with the 'great confederacy of tribes in the Salish region of "Chilliwack"' that Charles Hill-Tout is reported to have 'in hand' in the *Second Report to the British Association for the Advancement of Sciences in 1898*, 698–9.

35 Jeff Point, personal communication, 17 May 1995.

36 Both the pre-birthday gatherings at St Mary's Mission and the New Westminster meetings provided Native people with opportunities to meet that were deemed non-threatening to government officials and settlers alike. The Treaty Day celebrations of the Puget Sound Salish were similar events that were equally palatable to American authorities. See Miller and Boxberger, 'Creating Chiefdoms,' 278; and Harmon, *Indians in the Making*, 151–2, 182.

37 Seymour to Cardwell, 31 Aug. 1864, 95; quoted in full in Carlson et al., eds., *Atlas*, 170. The following year, as the newspapers reported, the Stó:lō again emphasized the land question in their presentation to the governor: 'The prayer and hope of the Indians is that Your Excellency will constantly preserve their lands to them and protect them from bad white men and bad Indians.' See *British Columbian*, 'The Queen's Birthday,' 26 May 1865, 3.

38 Douglas Harris, 'The Nlah7kapmx Meeting at Lytton, 1879, and the Rule of Law,' in *BC Studies* no. 108 (1995/6): 15.

39 Seymour to Cardwell, 31 Aug. 1864. See also Sir Arthur Nonus, BCA, MSS 0061, Reel A00272, Vol. 2, File, 'Birch Papers.'

40 Gov. Seymour to the Earl of Carnarvon, BCA, C.O. 60/27, 237–40.
41 See Carlson, 'Indian Reservations,' in Carlson et al., eds., *Atlas,* 94–5.
42 See accounts of the Queen's birthday celebrations in successive years' editions of the *British Columbia Guardian.*
43 See B.W. Pearse to J. Trutch, 21 Oct. 1868.
44 Harris, 'The Nlha7kapmx Meeting at Lytton,' 5–25.

9 Collective Governance and the Lynching of Louie Sam

1 In *Making Native Space,* 85, Cole Harris states that the meeting took place at Hope. He apparently bases this assertion on the fact that the petition's principal Aboriginal author, Chief Pierre Ayesik, resided on a reserve adjacent to Hope. It is more likely that the political meeting actually occurred at the Oblate's mission headquarters at St Mary's during the annual pre-birthday celebration gathering. Ayesik likely coordinated or spearheaded the meeting, but there is nothing to indicate that it took place at Hope. Pierre Ayesik was a devote Catholic and is remembered to this day as a 'Church Chief.' As such, although Harris is correct to note that the 'meeting itself was an extraordinary achievement' (85), it was perhaps less extraordinary than it might otherwise have been. The significant point is that the St Mary's meeting, though designed by priests and government officials alike to be a social gathering to coordinate planning for the Queen's birthday celebration, had in fact clearly become the region's principal forum for supra-tribal political strategizing.
2 Chiefs of Douglas Portage, the Lower Fraser and other Tribes on the Seashore, Petition to Supt. of Indian Affairs I.W. Wood Powell, 14 July 1874; reproduced in Carlson et al., eds., *Atlas,* 173.
3 Chief Alexis of Cheam to James Lenihan, New Westminster, 5 Sept. 1875; reproduced in Carlson et al., eds., *Atlas,* 174.
4 Alexis' Indian name is also rendered variously: Srouechealeou, Shrouityneeoh, Rwetselalough, Srouetlanoh, and Sru-ets-lan-ough on various church records.
5 See, e.g., James Lenihan's, 'Report of Indian Commissioner James Lenihan, Mainland Division, British Columbia, 1875,' in *Report of the Deputy Superintendent General of Indian Affairs* (Ottawa: Government of Canada, 1875), 53–6.
6 Duff, *Upper Stalo,* 81.
7 Ibid.
8 Ibid., 80.
9 Charles Hill-Tout, 'Report on the Ethnology of the Stlatlumh of British

Columbia,' *Journal of the Royal Anthropological Institute* 35 (Jan.–June 1905), reprinted in *The Salish People,* vol. 2, 104.

10 Duff, *Upper Stalo,* 81.

11 Ibid.

12 Hill-Tout, *Salish People,* vol. 2, 105.

13 Ibid., 80.

14 Ibid.

15 For a fairly comprehensive list of Stó:lõ petitions to the government, see 'Appendix II' in Carlson et al., eds., *Atlas,* 170–91.

16 Alexis' daughter was among the first literate Stó:lõ, having been the first to complete her studies at St Mary's Missionary School, in Mission. She taught her father rudimentary writing skills and went on to establish the first Native-run school in British Columbia. Within the small Catholic church on the Cheam Reserve she taught children (whose parents preferred a day school to the Church-run residential school) how to read and write.

17 Suttles and Jenness, *Katzie Ethnographic Notes,* 34.

18 Mayne, *Four Years in British Columbia and Vancouver Island.* Indeed, some contemporary Elders have suggested that the Semiamoo Tribe, who formerly lived in settlements located primarily on what after 1846 was to become the U.S. side of Mud Bay, chose to relocate to the British Columbian side in the 1860s precisely because they did not want to be relocated to collective reserves by U.S. authorities.

19 See, e.g., Joseph Trutch, Chief Commissioner of Lands and Works, to Col. Sec., 20 Sept. 1865, in *Papers,* 30. See also, *Journals of the Legislative Council,* 11 Feb. 1867, vol. 5: 25.

20 For an overview of Duncan's operation at Metlakatla, see Fisher, *Contact and Conflict,* 124–37.

21 Unless otherwise noted, the quotes in this and the following paragraph come from William Duncan's 'Letter on Indian Affairs' to the minister of the interior, Ottawa, May 1875, in Lenihan, 'Report of Indian Commissioner … 1875,' ix.

22 See esp. the discussion contained in Scott, 'Memorandum of 5 Nov. 1875, in *Papers,* 161–3; see also 'Executive Council Committee Report, approved by the Lt.-Gov. on 6 Jan. 1876,' in *Papers,* 169.

23 Emphasis in original.

24 William Duncan to the Hon. G.A. Walkem, 6 July 1875, in 'Report of the Government of British Columbia on the Subject of Indian Reserves (Appendix D),' in *Papers,* 16 (at back).

25 See Asst. Supt. of Indian Affairs James Lenihan to the Prov. Sec., 15 Oct. 1874, in *Papers,* 148–50; also Duncan to Walkem, 6 July 1875, in *Papers.*

26 Scott, 'Memorandum of 5 Nov. 1875.'

27 Lenihan, 'Report of Indian Commissioner ... 1875,' 37–8.

28 John A. Macdonald to the Marquis of Lorne, 11 July 1883, cited in Garth Stevenson, *Ex Uno Plures*, 141 (Montreal and Kingston: McGill-Queen's University Press, 1993). Also cited in W.S. McNutt, *Days of Lorne*, 110, 119 (Westport: Greenwood, 1955). Also, Br. Colonial Sec. Lord Kimberley referred to B.C. as the 'Spoilt Child of Confederation' two yars earlier – see Margaret Ormsby, *British Columbia* (Vancouver: Macmillan, 1958), 283.

29 The Marchioness of Dufferin and Ava, *My Canadian Journal, 1872–8, Extracts from My Letters Home, Written while Lord Dufferin was Governor-General* (London: John Murray, Albemarle Street, 1891), 271–2.

30 *Victoria Colonist* (10 Sept. 1976, 3) goes on to mention that on the departure at 9 p.m. his steamship was followed by 'upwards of 100 canoes each carrying from five to ten torches. The sight was most effective and at midnight the Vice Regal Party sailed for Yale.' The *Colonist* noted that at Yale there were addresses that day (10 Sept.) from the white, Chinese, and Indian population and at 'the scene of a third arch, erected by the Indian population, when they visited and the chief here, by means of an interpreter addressed the distinguished guests,' after which, 'the Royal party went to the Oppenheimer house.'

31 See I.W. Powell, Supt. of Indian Affairs, B.C., 'Synopsis of Reports on Proposed Municipal System for Indian bands,' c. 1881, LAC, RG 10, Vol. 2116, File 22155.

32 I am currently working on a book project that explores the role of the memories of the Crown's promise among Stó:lō and neighbouring Salish people. Preliminary research suggests several possibilities for the dichotomy between the oral and literate accounts of this event/non-event.

   Some of my early analysis on this subject was published in *Native Studies Review* 16/2 (2005): 1–38, under the title 'Re-thinking Dialogue and History: The King's Promise and the 1906 Aboriginal Delegation to London.'

33 Sumas and Chilliwack Methodist Chiefs, petition to Earl of Dufferin, 18 Aug. 1876; this petition is presented in full in Carlson et al., eds., *Atlas*, 174.

34 Address to the Governor-General Lord Dufferin, from the Indians of Yale, Frederick Temple Hamilton – Temple – Blackwood, 1st Marquess of Dufferin and Ava Fonds, Lord Dufferin Addresses, 1878-049, Address no. 289, LAC.

35 Frederick Edward Molyneux St John, *The Sea of Mountains*, vol. 2, *An Acount of Lord Dufferin's Tour through British Columbia in 1876* (London: Hurst and Blackett, 1877), 90–1.

36 Emphasis added. Address from the Indians at Thompson to Lord Dufferin,

Governor-General of Canada, at Lytton, B.C., 1876, Frederick Temple Hamilton – Temple – Blackwood, lst Marquess of Dufferin and Ava Fonds, Lord Dufferin Addresses, 1878-049, Address no. 290, LAC.

37 See Fisher, *Contact and Conflict*, 185–94.

38 G.M. Sproat to Supt. Gen., 29 July 1879, LAC, DINA, RG 10, Reel C-10117, Vol. 3669, File 10691.

39 Ibid.

40 See Wayne Dougherty and Dennis Madill, *Indian Act Government under Indian Legislation, 1868–1951*, 19–20 (Ottawa: DINA, Research Branch, 1980).

41 The Indian Reserve Commission hired Mischel as translator in 1878. See Harris, 'The Nlha7k·pmx Meeting at Lytton,' 8.

42 All information pertaining to the constitution for supra-tribal government come from letters Sproat wrote to the Superintendent General in 1879 (all in LAC, RG 10): 17 July, Vol. 3696, File 15316; 26 July and 27 Oct., Reel C-10117, Vol. 3669, File 10691; and from reports Sproat provided to the *Mainland Guardian*, 20 and 23 Aug. 1879, and to the *Daily British Colonist*, 21 Aug. 1879.

43 Harris, 'The Nlka7apmx Meeting,' 7.

44 Cole and Chaikin, *An Iron Hand upon the People*; see also Bracken, *Potlatch Papers*.

45 Sproat to Supt. Gen., 27 Oct. 1879, 5–6.

46 Sonny McHalsie, personal communications, Nov. 1993. Sonny's father was Nlakapamux, and his mother Stó:lō. He and his siblings relocated with their parents back and forth across the Stó:lō-Nlakapamux border many times while he was growing up. Sonny acquired his knowledge of Nlakapamux potlatching traditions principally through his father's relatives, but also through family friend and Spuzzum Elder Annie York.

47 Harris, 'Nlka7apmx Meeting,' 10.

48 Sproat to Supt. Gen., 29 July 1879, LAC, DINA, RG 10, Reel C-10117, Vol. 3669, File 10691.

49 See Elizabeth Vibert, 'Real Men Hunt Buffalo: Masculinity, Race and Class in British Fur Traders' Narratives,' *Gender and History* 8/1 (1996): 4–21.

50 Sproat to Supt. Gen., 29 July 1879; emphasis in original.

51 Jean Barman, *The West beyond the West: A History of British Columbia* (Toronto: University of Toronto Press, 1991), 374.

52 Undated enclosure from the *Daily Standard* (Amour De Cosmos, ed.), in correspondence from Sproat to Supt. Gen., 1 Dec. 1878, LAC, DINA, RG 10, Reel C-10117, Vol. 3669, File 10691.

53 James Lenihan to Supt. Gen., 28 Aug. 1879, and I.W. Powell to Supt. Gen., 29 Sept. 1879, both found in LAC, DINA, RG 10, Reel C-10117, Vol. 3669, File 10691.

54 Anderson et al., Petition, 25 Sept. 1879. It is important to note that the letter's salutation clearly identified Anderson as the former Dominion Reserve Commissioner who served with Sproat. Prior to that Anderson had been a ranking officer of the HBC and the first non-Native to explore overland routes between Kamloops and the lower Fraser, in 1846. William Duncan was prominently listed as 'the missionary from Metlakatla,' who, of course, was proposing the creation of centralized reserves (but under clear DINA control). I.W. McKay was the retired HBC trader (quoted in Chapter 2) who described pre-contact Coast Salish monotheism. Most of the other names were also those of retired HBC officers.

55 See Vic Satzewich and Linda Mahood, 'Indian Affairs and Band Governance: Deposing Indian Chiefs in Western Canada, 1896–1911,' *Canadian Ethnic Studies* 26/1 (1994): 40–58.

56 Sproat to Supt. Gen., 29 July 1879.

57 For a more detailed discussion of the events leading up to, and following, the lynching of young Louie Sam, see Keith Thor Carlson, 'The Lynching of Louie Sam,' *BC Studies* no. 109 (1996): 63–79.

58 P.M. McTiernan, Indian Agent, to I.W. Powell, Supt. of Indian Affairs, 14 March 1884, LAC, RG 10, Vol. 3679, File 12061.

59 For a discussion of the gathering, as reported by Canadian officials, see I.W. Powell, Supt. of Indian Affairs, to John Robson, Prov. Sec., 24 and 21 March 1884; Report of a Committee of the Hon. Privy Council, Approved by His Excellency, L'Marquis de Lansdowne, Gov. Gen. of the Dominion of Canada, 2 June 1884; McTiernan to Powell, 14 March 1884; Report of Indian Agent Patrick McTiernan, New Westminster, 15 Aug. 1884, all of which are located in LAC, RG 10, Vol. 3679, File 12061.

60 For a discussion of this gathering, as reported to Canadian officials at the time, see I.W. Powell, Superintendent of Indian Affairs for British Columbia, to John Robson, Provincial Secretary, 24 March 1884, and Powell to Robson, 21 March 1884, LAC, RG 10, Indian Affairs, Vol. 3679, File 12061; also Report of a Committee of the Hon. Privy Council, Approved by His Excellency, L'Marquis de Lansdowne, Gov. Gen of the Dominion of Canada, 2 June 1884, LAC, ibid.; also P.M. McTiernan, Indian Agent, to I.W. Powell, 14 March 1884, LAC, ibid., File 12063; Report of Indian Agent Patrick McTiernan, New Westminster, B.C., 15 Aug. 1884, LAC, ibid., File 12061.

61 Bruce G. Miller, *The Problem of Justice: Tradition and Law in the Coast Salish World* (Lincoln and London: University of Nebraska Press, 2001), 55–92.

62 Arranged marriages, on the other hand, expanded one's own family network and in the process necessarily reduced the number of outsiders who might consider harming you in an effort to bring balance to their lives.

63 *British Columbian*, 'The Sumas Tragedy' (in New Westminster), 15 March
   1884. The reporter cites Indian Agent Patrick McTiernan as his source.
   Interestingly, McTiernan never officially communicated this information to
   his superiors in Victoria or Ottawa.
64 The reports of the undercover detectives can be found in Russell to Roycroft, BCA, GR 431, Attorney-General Inquisitions, File 1884.
65 Report of McTiernan, 15 Aug. 1884.

10 Entering the Twentieth Century

1 Personal communication, 12 March 2001.
2 In the weeks leading up to his London trip Chief Joe came to be known as
   Joe Capilano by non-Natives who identified him with the Capilano River
   (where his village was situated) in North Vancouver. Capilano, however, was
   a hereditary name belonging to a family of the neighbouring Musqueam
   tribe – a community Joe had familial ties to through his mother. A controversy arose following Chief Joe's return over the legitimacy of his use
   of the Musqueam name. This tension reached a boiling point thirty years
   later (more than two decades after Chief Joe had passed away) when the
   Musqueam community held a potlatch to strip the name away from Chief
   Joe's son. In the early 1950s the controversy concerning who had the right
   to 'carry' the name Chief Joe had acquired as a result of his journey to
   London remained a topic of heated conversation in Aboriginal society. It
   was the principal topic associated with the 1906 trip that the delegation's
   official translator , Simon Pierre, wanted to discuss when interviewed by
   anthropologist Wayne Sutles half a century after the fact (personal communication, July 2003); moreover, it remains a controversial topic among
   certain members of the Squamish.and Musqueam tribes to this day (Crystal
   Johnston, personal communication, June 2003).
3 Robert Galois erroneously reports that the 1904 delegation was political and
   that the delegates tried to meet with King Edward VII. He also claims that
   they eventually met with Pope Leo XIII. In fact, as Fr. Le Jeune's daily diary
   shows, and the oral histories confirm, Chilihitza and Louie made no effort
   to meet with the British king or any other British political figures, and their
   papal audience was not with Leo XIII (who died in 1903) but with Pius X.
   See Robert Galois, 'The Indian Rights Association, Native Protest Activity
   and the "Land Question" in British Columbia, 1903–1916,' *Native Studies
   Review* 8/2 (1992): 1–34.
      I have discussed both these delegations in greater detail in Carlson, 'Re-
   thinking Dialogue and History.'

4 See esp. the delegates' petition as quoted in the *Victoria Daily Colonist,* 6 July 1906, and successive newspaper accounts from across Canada and London, of how Capilano refused to disclose the exact purpose of his mission to anyone other than the king. The High Commissioner's Office was particularly concerned over the political ramifications for the Laurier government, in terms of Ottawa-Victoria relations, should the publicity the delegates drew to the issue of their unjust treatment receive too much public scrutiny as a result of the London visit.

5 Interviews with Simon Pierre and the other delegates by British newspaper journalists immediately following the royal audience portray the Aboriginal delegates as extremely happy and excited. See from 13–14 Aug. 1906: 'King Receives Indian Chiefs,' *Vancouver Province*; 'Redskins to See the King,' *Daily Express*; 'Good, King Good,' *Daily Mail*; 'The King and the Indian Chiefs,' *Daily Graphic*; 'A Present for the Queen,' *Daily Gazette*; 'The King and the Indian Chiefs,' *Morning Post.*

6 Lord Strathcona in particular worked diligently to subvert the delegates' political objectives. A major part of his strategy was to over-awe the delegates with symbols of British power and authority, and to encourage the tabloid journalists to portray the Aboriginal spokesmen as quaint primitive buffoons in order to de-emphasize the political significance of their presence and message. See London, PRO, 'Colonial Correspondence,' 42/908 and 42/907, Original Despatches, 1906.

7 Steven Point, a distant relative of Simon Pierre's, shared this account with the author as it was told to him by his mother, Rena Point-Bolton.

8 See Carlson, 'Re-thinking Dialogue and History.'

9 Robert Galois' 1992 article, 'The Indian Rights Association,' astutely recognizes the implications of the delegation for Native public relations and comments on its effect on sparking greater supra-tribal political cooperation. He explains the delegation as being a response to the increased pressures on Aboriginal lands emerging after the completion of the transcontinental railway. He does not discuss the extent to which the delegation was the culmination of a trend towards greater supra-tribal identity that had been ongoing since first contact, nor that it was built upon earlier Coast Salish precedence for shared cooperative action and political identification.

10 See Tennant, *Aboriginal Peoples and Politics,* and Harris, *Making Native Space.*

11 Even within what had come to be regarded as Stó:lō territory, certain bands have been less inclined to identify with or participate in supra-reservation political organizations such as the Allied Tribes, the Union of B.C. Indian Chiefs, the B.C. Summit, the Lower Fraser Aboriginal Fishing Authority, the Stó:lō Tribal Council, or the Stó:lō Nation.

12 Marshall Sahlins, 'Past History,' in *Waiting for Foucault, Still* (Chicago: Prickly Paradigm Press, 2002 [1993]), 72.

13 For a discussion of the multifaceted ways in which this can occur, see the debate over late eighteenth-century Hawaiian interpretations of Europeans found in Gananath Obeyesekere, *The Apotheosis of Captain Cook: European Mythmaking in the Pacific* (Princeton: Princeton Univeristy Press, 1992), and Sahlins, *How 'Natives' Think.*

14 Coates and Fisher, *Out of the Background.*

15 Margaret A. Ormsby, *British Columbia: A History* (Vancouver: Macmillan, 1958).

16 Later it was revealed that the Yale First Nation had requested the change as part of their treaty settlement. In a subsequent 2009 decision, the federal government confirmed Shxw'ōwhámél's right to the canyon land. In a potlatch ceremony to celebrate their victory, a spokesperson for the Shxw'ōwhámél reminded the crowd that they needed to be ever vigilant against government attempts to define their community and territory in isolation of them; and in powerful rhetoric designed to undermine the cultural basis of the Yale claim, the speaker also referred to the political leaders of the Yale First Nation as 'people without memory.' Tyrone McNeil, 'speaker,' at Shxw'ōwhámél honouring ceremony, Seabird Island Community Hall, 3 May 2009.

17 Coast Salish people living on the U.S. side of the international border, in particular the Upper Skagit, were paid compensation by Seattle City Light and Authority.

18 Steven Point, personal communications, 16 May 1994.

19 During his shamanic training, Old Pierre's mother told him: 'The [Fraser] river is holy; it journeys day and night, coming no man knows whence, and travelling no man knows whither. Pray to it. Tell it that you are striving to be a medicine man, that for a long time you are going to fast, and ask it to help you. Then come back into the house.' Suttles and Jenness, *Katzie Ethnographic Notes,* 66.

References

Museums and Archives Abbreviations

ANA   American National Archives (Regional Branch, Bellingham, Washington)

BCA   British Columbia Archives (Victoria, BC)

BCPM   British Columbia Provincial Museum (Victoria, BC)

CPNS   Centre for Pacific Northwest Studies (University of Western Washington, Bellingham)

CA   Chilliwack Archives (Chilliwack, BC)

CMC   Canadian Museum of Civilization (Ottawa)

DINA   Department of Indian Affairs

HBCA   Hudson's Bay Company Archives (Winnipeg)

LAC   Library and Archives Canada (Ottawa)

OHS   Oregon Historical Society (Portland, Oregon)

PABC   Provincial Archives of British Columbia (Victoria, BC)

PCLV   Provincial Crown Lands Vault (Victoria, BC)

PRO   Public Records Office (London)

RAI   Royal Anthropological Institute (London)

RBCM   Royal British Columbia Museum (Victoria, BC)

SNA   Stó:lō Nation Archives (Chilliwack, BC)

VCM   Vancouver City Museum (Vancouver)

Archival and Manuscript Collections

Albers, Karen. 'Resource Sites in S'olh Temexw: Traditional Concepts of Ownership – Final Report for the Family-Owned Sites Project,' June 2000. SNA.

Anderson, Alexander C., William Duncan, Rod Finlayson, W.I. Macdonald,

I.W. Mckay, Archibald McKinlay, W.F. Tolmie, Charles A. Vernon, and Adm. Provost. Petition to the Hon. G.A. Walkem, Att. Gen. and Premier of B.C., 25 Sept. 1879. LAC, Department of Indian Affairs (DINA), Record Group (RG) 10, Reel C-10117, Vol. 3669, File 10691.

Ayessick, Pierre. 'Story of the First Whiteman.' BCA, Newcombe Family Papers, Add Mss 1077, Vol. 44:1.

Ball, Capt. H.M., to the Col. Sec., 4 Dec. 1869. BCA, Government Record (GR) 1372, File 397/1 B-1322.

Brew, Chartres, to Joseph Trutch, Chief Commissioner of Lands and Works, 26 Jan. 1866. BCA, GR 1372, File 943/13, Microfilm B-1339.

British Columbia. Colony. Lands and Works Department, 1859–72. BCA, GR 2900.

Canada, DINA. LAC, RG 10, Black Series, Vols. 2116, 3669, 3679, 3795, 7859, 10012.

– 'Indian Census of Yale Tribe, 1878.' LAC, RG 10, Vol. 10012A.

– 'Report of a Committee of the Hon. Privy Council, Approved by His Excellency, L'Marquis de Lansdowne, Gov. Gen. of the Dominion of Canada.' LAC, RG 10, Vol. 3679, File 12061.

Captain John. 'The Story of the Conversion and Subsequent Experiences of Capt. John, as Narrated by Himself,' translated from Chinook into English by Rev. W.H. Barraclough, B.A., 30 March 1898. CA, Add Mss 253.

Chief James of Yale. 'Testimony before the 1913–1916 Royal Commission.' SNA.

Douglas, James. Fort Victoria. Correspondence Out, 1856–1858. BCA, A/C/20/Vi4.

Douglas, James, to the Right Hon. Lord Stanley, M.P. Despatches, No. 26, Victoria, Vancouver's Island, 15 June 1858. Received, 9 Aug. 1858; answered, 14 Aug. 1858, Despatches, No. 8. *Papers Relative to the Affairs of British Columbia, Part I.* London: Her Majesty's Stationery Office, 1859.

Douglas, James, to the Right Hon. Sir E.B. Lytton, Bart. Victoria, Vancouver's Island, 12 Oct. 1858. Received, 14 Dec. 1858; Answered, 30 Dec. 1858, Despatches, No. 60. *Papers Relative to the Affairs of British Columbia, Part II.* London: Her Majesty's Stationery Office, 1859.

Douglas, James, to Edward B. Lytton, 15 Aug. 1859, Despatch No. 199. BCA, Colonial Office (CO), 60/5, 13; also PRO.

Dufferin, Lord. Canadian Addresses, 1878-049. LAC.

Evans, Elwood. 'The Fraser River Excitement, 1858.' BCA, copy of unpublished ms from Bancroft Library, Berkeley, California.

Fraser Valley Chiefs. 'Petition of Fraser Valley Chiefs to Gov. Musgrave Regarding Sale of Cranberry Patches,' in Holbrook to Gov. Musgrave, 7 Jan. 1870. BCA, Colonial Correspondence, F778/38, Reel B-1334.

Howse, A.R., to William McColl, 1864; and Report, 18 Dec. 1865. BCA, Colonial Correspondence, File 1030.

Jeffcott, Percival R. 'Collections.' CPNS, no. 981.

Jemmett, W.S. B.C. Fieldnotes Book, 31 July 1880. PCLV, B.C. Surveyor General's Office, W26.

Launders, J.B. Various Survey Maps. PCLV.

Lenihan, James, to the Supt. Gen., 28 Aug. 1879. LAC, RG 10, Reel C-10117, Vol. 3669, File 10691.

Lerman, Norman Hart. 'Lower Fraser Indian Folktales Collected by Norman Lerman, 1950–1951.' Chilliwack: Stó:lō Nation, SNA.

McColl, William, to Col. Moody, 13 May 1861. BCA, Royal Engineers Letterbooks, C/AB/30.6J.

McColl, William. Survey Map. PCLV, B.C. Surveyor General's Office, Ref no. 31-T1.

McDonald, Archibald. '1830 Census, Fort Langley.' HBCA.

McKay, J.W. 'Indian Tribes, Correspondence 1881, Regarding Festivals, Traditions, etc.' BCA, J.W. McKay Papers, Add Mss 1917.

McTiernan, P.M., Indian Agent to I.W. Powell, Supt. of Indian Affairs, 14 March 1884; and 'Report of Indian Agent Patrick McTiernan,' New Westminster, 15 Aug. 1884. LAC, RG 10, Vol. 3679, File 12061.

Moody, R.C. Letters and Enclosures, Colonial Correspondence – Indian Reserves on the Fraser River, 1860. BCA, GR 1372.

Nelson, Denys. 'Diary of a Trip up the Fraser.' Denys Nelson's Journal, 5 March 1925. VM, Hill-Tout Collection, General Files, B.XI.

Nonus, Sir Arthur. BCA, MSS 0061, Reel A00272, Box 2, File, 'Birch Papers.'

Passingham, F., to P. McTiernan, 21 Feb. 1891. LAC, RG 10, Reel C-10139, Vol. 3795, File 46607-1.

Powell, I.W., to Supt. Gen., 29 Sept. 1879. LAC, DINA, RG 10, Reel C-10117, Vol. 3669, File 10691.

– Supt. of Indian Affairs for B.C. 'Synopsis of Reports on Proposed Municipal System for Indian bands.' (c. 1881). LAC, RG 10, Vol. 2116, File 22155.

– to John Robson, Prov. Sec., 21 and 24 March 1884. LAC, RG 10, Vol. 3679, File 12061.

Russell, Charles, to Superintendent Roycroft. BCA, GR 431, Attorney-General Inquisitions, File 1884.

Scott, Robert Clyde. Scrapbook. Logbook entries. BCA, Add Mss 1299, Box 2/2.

Seymour, Frederick, to Edward Cardwell, 31 Aug. 1864. BCA, Colonial Despatches, CO 60/19, No. 30, Microfilm B-4034, 95–104.

Skw'atets Indians, Chilliwack, to H. Graham, 6 Dec. 1918. LAC, RG 10, Reel C-12144, Vol. 7859, File 30165-5(1).

Spalding, Henry and Eliza. 'Protestant Ladder.' OHS, Hi631, 632.

Sproat, Gilbert Malcolm. Papers. BCA, MS 0257.

– Field Minutes. LAC, Government of Canada, Department Indian and Northern Affairs, Vol. 18:309.

– to the Supt. Gen., Ottawa, 25 Nov. 1878. Letter entitled 'The Lower Fraser.' BCA, GR 1965.

– to the Supt. Gen., 1 Dec. 1878; 26 and 29 July 1879. LAC, DINA, RG 10, Reel C-10117, Vol. 3669, File 10691.

– to the Supt. Gen., 17 July 1879, LAC, RG 10, Vol. 3696, File 15316.

– to the Supt. Gen., 5 Aug. 1879, LAC, RG 10, Vol. 5/1:19.

– to the Supt. Gen., 27 Oct. 1879, LAC, DINA, RG 10, Vol. 3669, File 10691.

Strathcona, Lord. 'Colonial Correspondence.' PRO, 42/908 and 42/907, Original Despatches, 1906.

Teit, James A. 'Dream Book of a Stalo Prophet.' CMC, MS VII-G-19M (c. 1882).

Vowell, A.W., to the Supt. Gen., 19 May 1891. LAC, RG 10, Reel C-10139, Vol. 3795, File 46607-1.

Yale, James Murray. 'Census of Indian Population [from Fort Langley] and Crossing Over to Vancouver's Island and Coasting at about Latitude 50° from there Returning Southward along the Mainland and up the Fraser's River to Simpson Falls.' (1839). HBCA, B.223/2/1: 30–53.

Published Primary Documents

British Columbia. *Papers Connected with the Indian Land Question, 1850–1875.* Victoria: Richard Wolfenden, Government Printer, 1876 reproduction, 1987 (hereafter *Papers*). Especially:

– Ayessik, Peter, Chief of Hope and Other Chiefs, Petition to the Supt. of Indian Affairs, 14 July 1874.

– Ball, Capt. H.M., to the Col. Sec., 14 July and 15 Dec. 1869.

– Browning, Rev. A., to the Officer Administering the Government, 6 July 1869.

– Bushby, A.T., to B.W. Pearse, 28 June 1870, and Pearse to Bushby, 30 June 1870.

– Chessen, F.W., Sec. of the Aboriginal Protection Society, to the Right Hon. Sir Edward Bulwer Lytton, M.P., Her Majesty's Principal Sec. of State for the Colonies. Enclosed in Sir Edward Lytton to Gov. James Douglas, Despatch No.12, 2 Sept. 1858.

– Douglas, James, to Edward B. Lytton, 14 March 1859, and to R.C. Moody, 27 April 1863.

– Duncan, William, to the Hon. G.A. Walkem, 6 July 1875, in 'Report of the

Government of British Columbia on the Subject of Indian Reserves, Appendix D.'

– Goode, Charles B., for the Col. Sec., to R.C. Moody, 5 March 1861.
– Launders, J.B., to Joseph Trutch, Chief Commissioner of Lands and Works, 18 Dec. 1868.
– Lenihan, James, to the Prov. Sec., 15 Oct. 1874.
– Lytton, Edward, to Gov. James Douglas, 31 July, 30 Dec. 1858; 20 May 1859.
– McColl, William. Report to the Chief Commissioner of Lands and Works, 16 May 1864.
– Mohun, Edward, to Joseph Trutch, 3 Dec. 1868.
– Moody, R.C., to William Young, 27 May, 11 and 18 June, 2 July 1862; and to James Douglas, 28 April 1863.
– Pearse, B.W., to Joseph Trutch, 21 Oct. 1868.
– Scott, R.W., Memorandum of 5 Nov. 1875.
– Trutch, Joseph, Chief Commissioner of Lands and Works, to Col. Sec., 20 Sept. 1865; to Acting Col. Sec., 28 Aug. 1867; to Col. Sec., William Young. 19 Nov. 1867.
– Turner, George, to Joseph Trutch, 20 Oct. 1865.
– Vedder, V., and 27 others to His Excellency Anthony Musgrave, Gov. of B.C., 30 Nov. 1869.
– Young, William, to R.C. Moody, 18 June 1862, 11 May 1863; and to Joseph Trutch, 6 Nov. and 4 Dec. 1867.
Canada, Government of. *Report of the Deputy Superintendent General of Indian Affairs.* Ottawa: Government of Canada, 1875.
Carlson, Keith Thor, with David Shaege, Albert McHalsie, David Smith, Leanna Rhodes, and Collin Duffield, eds., *A Stó:lō-Coast Salish Historical Atlas.* 'Appendix II, Stó:lō Petitions and Letters.' Vancouver: Douglas and McIntyre, and Chilliwack: Stó:lō Heritage Trust, 2001. Especially:
– Chief Alexis of Cheam to James Lenihan, New Westminster, 5 Sept. 1875.
– Chiefs of Douglas Portage, the Lower Fraser and other Tribes on the Seashore, Petition to Supt. of Indian Affairs I.W. Wood Powell, 14 July 1874.
Great Britain. *Anno Vicesimo Primo et Vicesimo Secundo*, Victoræ Regina, CAP. XCIX. An Act to provide for the Government of British Columbia. [2 Aug. 1858.]
Hendrickson, James E., ed. *Journals of the Colonial Legislatures of the Colonies of Vancouver Island and British Columbia, 1851–1871.* 5 vols. Victoria: PABC, 1980.
Oblats de Marie Immaculée. Reports and Letters published in the annual series, *Missions de la Congrégation des Missionnaires Oblats de Marie Immaculée* (hereafter *Missions*). Rome: Maison Generale O.M.I., and Marseille: Typographie Veuve, Marius Olive. Reviewed vols. 1864 through 1906. Especially:

- Chirouse, Fr. Eugene Casimir, 16 July 1862 *(1862)*.
- D'Herbomez, Bishop Louis-Joseph, 30 May 1861 *(1862)*.
- Fouquet, Fr. Leon to Rev. Father Tempier, 8 June 1863 *(1864)*.
- Gendre, Fr. R.P., OMI *(1865)*.
- MacGugein, Fr. Edward, 'Report for 1886, Fraser Districts' *(1887)*.
- Marchal, Rev. Fr. Charles to Rev. Fr. Durieu, 12 Feb. 1871 *(1874)*.
- Peytavin, R.P. Eduard, 'Report of 1886' *(1887)*; and to R.P. MacGuckin, 21 Feb. 1887, 'Columbie Britannique: Lettre du R.P. Ed. Paytavin au R.P. MacGuckin, New Westminster, le 21 fevrier 1887, et 7 mars 1887' *(1887)*.

Unpublished Ethnographic Collections

Carlson, Keith Thor. Unpublished Fieldnotes (1992–2002).

Duff, Wilson. Unpublished Fieldnotes, Books 1–5. Unpublished bound volumes (1950). RBCM (copies at SNA).

Hill-Tout, Charles. 'Linguistic Selections.' Unpublished bound volume (1978). UBC Koerner Library Collection.

Lenihan, James. 'Report of Indian Commissioner James Lenihan, Mainland Division, British Columbia, 1875.' (Esp. William Duncan's letter to the Minister of the Interior, Ottawa, May 1875.) In *Report of the Deputy Superintendent General of Indian Affairs* (Ottawa: Government of Canada, 1875); copy in SNA.

Orchard, Imbert. Cassette tape recordings and transcripts. SNA.

Smith, Marian. Unpublished Fieldnotes. (Summer 1945). RAI, MS 268. Microfilm copy, BCARS.

Stó:lō Oral History Project Tapes. SNA.

Wells, Oliver. Oral History Audio Collection (1959–69). CA (copies and transcripts at SNA).

Court Decisions

Corbere v. *Canada (Ministrer of Indian and Northern Affairs)* [1999] 2 S.C.R. 1999 CanLII 687 (Supreme Court of Canada) Docket 25708.

Affidavit

Hope, Robert Norman, et al. 'Affidavit of Chief Robert Norman Hope in the Supreme Court of British Columbia.' *Chief Robert Hope et al.* v. *The Lower Fraser Fishing Authority and others,* July 1992, No. C92-4333, Vancouver Registry (67/62519/002).

Newspapers

British Columbia Guardian.

British Columbian. 'The Last Potlatch,' 27 April 1864.

– 'The Queen's Birthday,' 26 May 1865.

– 'The Sumas Tragedy,' 15 March 1884.

Chilliwack Progress. 'Family Feud: Stó:lō Say Fight Over Fishing Rights with Yale Band Comes Down to Respect for Traditional Fishing Rights,' 17 April 1998.

– 'Yale First Nation Shares in the Responsibility for Salmon Management,' 3 July 1999.

– 'Yale Territory Defended from Stó:lō Invasion,' 7 April 1998.

– 'Yale Territory Defended from Stó:lō Invasion,' 12 April 1998.

Daily British Colonist. 21 Aug. 1879.

Daily Express. 'Redskins to See the King,' 14 Aug. 1906.

Daily Gazette. 'A Present for the Queen,' 13 Aug. 1906.

Daily Graphic. 'The King and the Indian Chiefs,' 14 Aug. 1906.

Daily Mail. 'Good, King Good,' 14 Aug. 1906.

Mainland Guardian. 20 and 23 Aug. 1879.

Morning Post. 'The King and the Indian Chiefs,' 14 Aug. 1906.

Times of London. 'British Columbia,' 5 Aug., 30 Nov., 1 and 25 Dec. 1858.

Vancouver Province. 'King Receives Indian Chiefs,' 13 Aug. 1906.

Victoria Colonist. 'His Lordship Took His Place...' 10 Sept. 1876.

Victoria Daily Colonist. 'Chiefs in London.' 6 July 1906.

Published Sources

Akrigg, G.P.V. 'The Fraser River Gold Rush.' In *The Fraser's History, from Glaciers to Early Settlements: Papers from a Seminar Presented at the Annual Meeting of the British Columbia Historical Association on May 27, 1977, Burnaby, British Columbia.* Foreword by Blythe Eagles. Burnaby: Burnaby Historical Society, 1981.

Anderson, Benedict. *Imagined Communities: Reflections on the Origin and Spread of Nationalism.* London: Verso, 1983.

Arneil, Barbara. *John Locke and America: The Defence of English Colonialism.* Oxford: Clarendon Press, 1996.

Barman, Jean. *The West beyond the West: A History of British Columbia.* Toronto: University of Toronto Press, 1991.

Barnett, Homer Garner. 'The Nature of the Potlatch.' *American Anthropologist* 40/3 (1938): 349–58.

– *The Coast Salish of British Columbia.* Eugene: University of Oregon Press, 1955.

Barth, Fredrik. *Ethnic Groups and Boundaries.* Boston: Little Brown, 1969.

Basso, Keith H. *Wisdom Sits in Places: Landscape and Language among the Western Apache*. Albuquerque: University of New Mexico Press, 1996.

Benedict, Ruth. *Patterns of Culture*. Boston: Houghton Mifflin, 1934 (reprinted 1969).

Biersack, Aletta. 'History and Theory in Anthropology.' In A. Biersack, ed., *Clio in Oceania: Toward a Historical Anthropology*, 1991, 12: 1–36.

– ed. *Clio in Oceania: Toward a Historical Anthropology*. Washington, DC: Smithsonian Institution, 1991.

Bierwert, Crisca. *Brushed by Cedar, Living by the River: Coast Salish Figures of Power*. Tuscon: University of Arizona Press, 1999.

Birket-Smith, Kaj. 'An Analysis of the Potlatch Institution of North America.' *Folk* (1938) 6/2: 5–113.

– 'Potlatch and Feasts of Merit.' In K. Birket-Smith, ed., *Studies in Circumpacific Culture Relations*. Copenhagen: Munksgaard, 1967.

Bishop, Charles A. *The Northern Ojibwa and the Fur Trade: An Historical and Ecological Study*. Toronto: Holt, Rinehart and Winston, 1974.

Blackburn, Carole. *Harvest of Souls: The Jesuit Missions and Colonialism in North America 1632–1650*. Montreal and Kingston: McGill-Queens University Press, 2000.

Blake, Lynn A. 'Oblate Missionaries and the Indian Land Question.' *BC Studies* (1998) no. 119: 27–44.

Boas, Franz. 'Notes on the Ethnology of British Columbia.' *Proceedings of the American Philosophical Society* 24/126 (1887): 422–8.

– 'Indians of British Columbia.' *Transactions of the Royal Society of Canada for 1888* 6/2 (1888): 47–57.

– 'Notes on the Snanaimuq.' *American Anthropologist* 2/4 (1889): 321–8.

– 'First General Report on the Indians of British Columbia.' In *The 59th Report of the British Association for the Advancement of Science for 1889*. London, 1889, 801–93.

– 'Indian Tribes of the Lower Fraser River.' In *The 64th Report of the British Association for the Advancement of Science for 1890*, 454–63. London, 1894.

– 'The Social Organization and the Secret Societies of the Kwakiutl Indians.' In *Annual Report of the [U.S.] National Museum for 1895*, 315–655. Washington, DC: U.S. National Museum, 1895 (reprinted New York: Johnson Reprint, 1970).

– 'The Social Organization of the Haida.' In *The 68th Report of the British Association for the Advancement of Science for 1898*, 648–54. London, 1898.

– 'Tsimshian Mythology.' In *The 31st Annual Report of the Bureau of American Ethnology to the Secretary of the Smithsonian Institution, 1909–1910*. Washington, DC: Government Printing Office, 1916, 29–1037.

– *Indianische Sagen von der Nordpacifischen Kuste Americas.* Berlin: A. Asher, 1895.
Published in English as: *Indian Legends from the North Pacific Coast of America.*
Translated by Dietrich Bertz. Victoria: B.C. Indian Language Project, 1977,
and now also available as: R. Bouchard and D. Kennedy, eds., *Indian Myths
and Legends from the North Pacific Coast,* Vancouver: Talonbooks, 2002.
– *The Salish People: The Local Contribution of Charles Hill-Tout,* vol. 2, *The Squamish
and the Lillooet.* Vancouver: Talonbooks, 1978.
Boyd, Robert. *The Coming of the Spirit of Pestilence: Introduced Infectious Diseases and
Population Decline among Northwest Coast Indians, 1774–1874.* Seattle: University
of Washington Press, 1999.
Bracken, Christopher. *The Potlatch Papers: A Colonial Case History.* Chicago and
London: University of Chicago Press, 1998.
Braudel, Fernand. *The Mediterranean and the Mediterranean World in the Age of
Philip II,* 2 vols. Translated by Sian Reynolds. New York: Harper and Row,
1972–3 [1949].
Brealey, Ken. 'Travels from Point Ellice: Peter O'Reilly and the Indian Reserve
System in British Columbia.' *BC Studies* nos.115&116 (1997/98): 180–242.
Bunoz, E.M., Vic. Apost. 'Bishop Durieu's System.' *Etudes Oblates: Revue Trimes-
trielle.* Montreal: Maison Provinciale, 1942, 194.
Carlson, Keith Thor. 'The Lynching of Louie Sam.' *BC Studies* no. 109 (1996):
63–79.
– 'Smallpox: First Contact.' In Carlson et al., eds., *You Are Asked to Witness,* 1997,
27–40.
– 'Stó:lō Exchange Dynamics.' *Native Studies Review* 11/1 (1997): 30–5.
– 'Prophesy.' In Carlson et al., eds., *Atlas,* 2001.
– 'Re-thinking Dialogue and History: The King's Promise and the 1906 Aborigi-
nal Delegation to London.' *Native Studies Review* 16/2 (2005): 1–38.
– 'Innovation, Tradition, Colonialism, and Aboriginal Fishing Conflicts in the
Lower Fraser Canyon.' In S. Neylan and T. Binnema, eds., *New Histories for
Old,* 145–74. Vancouver: UBC Press, 2007.
– ed. *You Are Asked to Witness: The Stó:lō in Canada's Pacific Coast History.* Chilli-
wack: Stó:lō Heritage Trust: 1997.
Carlson, Keith Thor , with David Shaege, Albert McHalsie, David Smith, Leanna
Rhodes, and Collin Duffield, eds. *A Stó:lō-Coast Salish Historical Atlas.* Vancou-
ver: Douglas and McIntyre, and Chilliwack: Stó:lō Heritage Trust, 2001.
Carlson, Keith Thor, and John Sutton Lutz. 'Stó:lō People and the Develop-
ment of the B.C. Wage Labour Economy.' In Carlson, ed., *You Are Asked to
Witness,* 1996, 109–24.
Carlson, Keith Thor, with Sonny McHalsie. *I Am Stó:lō: Katherine Explores Her
Heritage.* Chilliwack: Stó:lō Heritage Trust, 1999.

Carlson, M. Teresa, et al. 'Stó:lō Oral Narratives.' In Carlson, ed., *You Are Asked to Witness*, 1997, 181–96.

Carter, Sarah. *Lost Harvest: Prairie Indian Reserve Farmers and Government Policy.* Montreal and Kingston: McGill-Queen's University Press, 1990.

– *Capturing Women: The Manipulation of Cultural Imagery in Canada's Prairie West.* Montreal and Kingston: McGill-Queen's University Press, 1997.

Coates, Ken, and Robin Fisher. *Out of the Background.* 2nd ed. Toronto: Irwin, 1998.

Codere. 'Fighting with Property: A Study of Kwakiutl Potlatching and Welfare, 1792–1930.' *Monographs of the American Ethnographic Society* (1950) 18

Cole, Douglas, and Ira Chaikin. *An Iron Hand upon the People: The Law against the Potlatch on the Northwest Coast.* Vancouver and Toronto: Douglas and McIntyre, and Seattle: University of Washington Press, 1990.

Collingwood, R.G. *The Idea of History.* New York: Oxford University Press, 1956.

Crosby, Thomas, Rev. *Among the An-ko-me-nums [Halkomelems] or Flathead Tribes of the Pacific Coast.* Toronto: William Briggs, 1907.

Cruikshank, Julie. *Do Glaciers Listen? Local Knowledge, Colonial Encounters, and Social Imagination.* Vancouver: UBC Press, 2005.

Cruikshank, Julie, with Angela Sidney, Kitty Smith, and Annie Ned. *Life Lived Like a Story: Life Stories of Three Yukon Native Elders.* Vancouver: UBC Press, 1990.

Curtis, Edward S. *The North American Indian; Being a Series of Volumes Picturing and Describing the Indians of the United States, and Alaska, Written, Illustrated, and Published by Edward S. Curtis; edited by Frederick Webb Hodge, Foreword by Theodore Roosevelt; Field Research Conducted under the Patronage of J. Pierpont Morgan, vol. 9, The Salishan Tribes of the Coast.* Seattle: E.S. Curtis, and Cambridge: Cambridge University Press, 1907–30.

– *The North American Indian; Being a Series of Volumes Picturing and Describing the Indians of the United States, and Alaska, Written, Illustrated, and Published by Edward S. Curtis,* vol. 10. Norwood, Mass.: Plimpton Press, 1930 (reprinted New York: Johnson Reprint, 1970).

Dawson, George. 'Notes and Observations on the Qwakiool People of the Northern Part of Vancouver Island and Adjacent Coasts, Made during the Summer of 1885.' *Transactions of the Royal Society of Canada.* Reprint. Fairfield, Wash.: Ye Galleon Press, 1973.

Deloria, Philip J. *Indians in Unexpected Places.* Lawrence: University Press of Kansas, 2004.

Dombrowski, Kirk. *Against Culture: Development, Politics and Religion in Indian Alaska.* Lincoln: University of Nebraska Press, 2001.

Donald, Leland. *Aboriginal Slavery on the Northwest Coast of North America.* Berkeley: University of California Press, 1997.

Dougherty, Wayne, and Dennis Madill. *Indian Act Government under Indian Legislation, 1868–1951.* Ottawa: DINA, Research Branch, 1980.

Douglas, James, to Gov. James Simpson, Fort Vancouver, 18 March, 1838. In E.E. Rich, ed., *The Letters of John McLaughlin from Fort Vancouver to the Governor and Committee, First Series,* vol. 4, *1825–38,* Appendix A, 280–1. Toronto: Champlain Society, 1991.

Drucker, Philip, and Robert F. Heizer. *To Make My Name Good: A Reexamination of the Southern Kwakiutl Potlatch.* Berkeley: University of California Press, 1967.

Duff, Wilson. *The Upper Stalo Indians of the Fraser Valley, British Columbia.* Victoria: BCPM, Anthropology in B.C., Memoir No. 1, 1952.

– *The Indian History of British Columbia,* vol. 1, *The Impact of the White Man.* 2nd ed. Victoria: RBCM, 1969.

– ed. *Anthropology in British Columbia.* Victoria: BCPM, Anthropology in B.C., Memoir No. 3, 1955.

Duffield, Colin. 'Constructing a Province, Clear-Cutting a Nation.' In Carlson et al., eds., *Atlas,* 2001, 112–13.

Dundes, Alan. 'Heads or Tails: A Psychoanalytic Study of the Potlatch.' *Journal of Psychological Anthropology* 2/4 (1979): 395–424.

Elliot, T.C., ed. 'The Journal of John Work, November and December, 1824.' *Washington Historical Quarterly* 3/3 (1912): 198–228.

Ferguson, R. Brian. 'A Reexamination of the Causes of Northwest Coast Warfare.' In R.B. Ferguson, ed., *Warfare, Culture, and Environment.* New York: Academic Press, 1984.

Fisher, Robin. *Contact and Conflict: Indian-European Relations in British Columbia, 1774–1890.* Vancouver: UBC Press, 1977 (2nd ed., 1992).

Fisher, Robin A., and Ken Coates. *Out of the Background: Readings in Canadian Native History.* Toronto: Irwin, 1988 (2nd ed., 1998).

Fleisher, Mark S. 'The Potlatch: A Symbolic and Psychoanalytic View.' *Current Anthropology* 22/1 (1981): 69–71.

Fogelson, Raymond. 'The Ethnohistory of Events and Nonevents.' *Ethnohistory* 36/2 (1989): 133–47.

Galloway, Brent. *A Grammar of Upriver Halkomelem.* Berkeley: University of California Press, 1993.

Galois, Robert. 'The Indian Rights Association, Native Protest Activity and the "Land Question" in British Columbia, 1903–1916.' *Native Studies Review* 8/2 (1992): 1–34.

– *Kwakwaka'wakw Settlements, 1775–1920: A Geographical Analysis and Gazetteer.* Vancouver: UBC Press, 1994.

Garfield, Viola. 'A Research Problem in Northwest Indian Economics.' *American Anthropologist* (1945) 47(4): 626–30.

Geary, Patrick J. *The Myth of Nations: The Medieval Origins of Europe*. Princeton: Princeton University Press, 2002.

Geertz, Clifford. 'Thick Descriptions: Toward an Interpretive Theory of Culture.' In C. Geertz, ed., *The Interpretation of Cultures: Selected Essays*. New York: Basic Books, 1973, 3–30.

Gibbs, George. 'Tribes of Western Washington and Northwestern Oregon.' In J.W. Power, ed., *Contributions to North American Ethnology* 1/2, 157–361. Washington: Department of the Interior, U.S. Geographical and Geological Survey of the Rocky Mountain Region, 1877 (reprinted Seattle: Shorey Press, 1970).

Goldman, Irving. *The Mouth of Heaven: An Introduction to Kwakiutl Religious Thought*. New York: Wiley, 1975.

Gough, Barry M. *Gunboat Frontier: British Maritime Authority and Northwest Coast Indians, 1846–90*. Vancouver: UBC Press, 1984.

Guilmet, George M., Robert T. Boyd, David L. White, and Nile Thompson. 'The Legacy of Introduced Disease: The Southern Coast Salish.' *American Indian Culture and Research Journal* 15/4 (1991): 1–32.

Hajda, Yvonne. 'Southwestern Coast Salish.' In Suttles, ed., *Handbook of North American Indians*, vol. 7, 1990, 503–17.

Harmon, Alexandra. *Indians in the Making: Ethnic Relations and Indian Identities around Puget Sound*. Berkeley: University of California Press, 1998.

Harris, R. Cole. *The Resettlement of British Columbia: Essays on Colonialism and Geographical Change*. Vancouver: UBC Press, 1997.

– 'Social Power and Cultural Change in Pre-Colonial British Columbia.' *BC Studies* nos. 115&116 (1997/8): 45–82.

– *Making Native Space: Colonialism, Resistance, and Reserves in British Columbia*. Vancouver: UBC Press, 2002.

Harris, Douglas. 'The Nlha7k·pmx Meeting at Lytton, 1879, and the Rule of Law.' *BC Studies* no. 108 (1995/6): 5–28.

Hazlitt, William Carew. *The Great Gold Fields of Cariboo: With an Authentic Description, Brought Down to the Latest Period, of British Columbia and Vancouver Island*. New York: Routledge, Warne, and Routledge, 1862.

Hendrickson, J., ed. *Journals of the Colonial Legislatures of the Colonies of Vancouver Island and British Columbia, 1851–1871*, vol. 4. Victoria: PABC, 1980.

Hill-Tout, Charles. 'Haida Stories and Beliefs.' In *The 68th Report of the British Association for the Advancement of Science for 1898*, 5–13. London, 1898.

– 'Ethnological Studies of the Mainland Halkomelem, a Division of the Salish of British Columbia.' In *The 72nd Report of the British Association for the Advancement of Science for 1902*, 416–41. London, 1903.

– *The Native Races of the British Empire, British North America I, The Far West, the Home of the Salish and Dene.* Toronto: Copp Clark, 1907.
– 'The Great Fraser Midden.' *Museum and Art Notes* 5 (Sept. 1930): 75–83.
– 'Prehistoric Burial Mounds of British Columbia.' *Museum and Art Notes* 5 (Dec. 1930): 120–6.
– *The Salish People: The Local Contribution of Charles Hill-Tout,* vol. 1, *The Thompson and Okanagan,* and vol. 2, *The Squamish and the Lillooet.* Edited by R. Maud. Vancouver: Talonbooks, 1978.
– 'Ethnological Studies of the Mainland Halkomelem.' In R. Maud, ed., *The Salish People: The Local Contribution of Charles Hill-Tout,* vol. 3, *The Mainland Halkomelem.* Vancouver: Talonbooks, 1978.
Jenness, Diamond. *Faith of a Coast Salish Indian.* W. Duff, ed. Victoria: BCPM, Anthropology in British Columbia, Memoir No. 3, 1955.
Kan, Sergei. *Memory Eternal: Tlingit Culture and Russian Orthodox Christianity through Two Centuries.* Seattle: University of Washington Press, 1999.
Kennedy, Dorothy, and Randall T. Bouchard. 'Bella Coola.' In Suttles, ed., *Handbook of North American Indians,* vol. 7, 1990, 323–39.
– 'Northern Coast Salish.' In Suttles, ed., *Handbook of North American Indians,* vol. 7, 1990, 441–52.
Knight, Rolf. *Indians at Work: An Informal History of Native Labour in British Columbia, 1848–1930.* Vancouver: New Star Books, 1978 (2nd ed., 1996).
Lamb, W. Kaye. *Simon Fraser: Letters and Journals, 1806–1808.* Toronto: Macmillan, 1960.
– ed. *A Voyage of Discovery to the North Pacific Ocean and around the World, 1791–1795.* London: Hakluit Society, 1984.
LaViolette, Forest. 'Missionaries and the Potlatch.' *Queen's Quarterly* 58 (1951): 237–51.
– *The Struggle for Survival: Indian Cultures and the Protestant Ethic in British Columbia.* Toronto: University of Toronto Press, 1961.
Ledell, John K. 'Narrative of a Miner's Trip to the Head Waters of the Gold Region.' In *Northern Light.* Whatcom: Bellingham Bay, 13 June 1858, 78–80 (reprinted from *Nooksack Tales and Trails,* ed. by P.R. Jeffcott, Ferndale, Wash.: Sedro-Wooley Courier Times, 1949).
LaJeune, Jean Marie Raphael. *Polyglot Manual – Stalo Manual; or Prayers, Hymns, and the Catechism in the Stalo or Lower Fraser Language.* Kamloops, B.C., c. 1896.
Lenihan, James. 'Annual Report of the New Westminster District, 1875.' In *Report of the Deputy Superintendent General of Indian Affairs.* Ottawa: Government of Canada, 1875.
Lerman, Norman Hart, and Betty Keller. *Legends of the River People.* Vancouver: November House, 1976.

Locke, John. *Two Treatises of Government.* Cambridge: Cambridge University Press, 1960.

Lutz, John Sutton. 'After The Fur Trade: The Aboriginal Labouring Class of British Columbia, 1849–1890.' *Journal of the Canadian Historical Association* 3/1 (1992): 69–93.

– *Makuk: A New History of Aboriginal-White Relations.* Vancouver: UBC Press, 2008.

MacLachlan, Morag, ed. *The Fort Langley Journals, 1827–30.* Vancouver: UBC Press, 1998.

Manne, Robert, ed. *Whitewash: On Keith Windschuttle's* Fabrication of Aboriginal History. Melbourne: Black Ink Agenda, 2003.

Marchioness of Dufferin and Ava. *My Canadian Journal, 1872–8, Extracts from My Letters Home, Written while Lord Dufferin was Governor-General.* London: John Murray, Albemarle Street, 1891.

Marshall, Daniel P. 'Document 1: H.M. Snyder, Letter to James Douglas, Fraser River, Fort Yale, 28 August 1858.' *Native Studies Review* 11/1 (1997): 140–5.

– 'Rickard Revisited: Native "Participation" in the Gold Discoveries of British Columbia.' *Native Studies Review* 11/1 (1997): 91–108.

– 'Mapping a New Social-Political Landscape: British Columbia, 1871–1874.' *Histoire Social / Social History* 31/61 (1998): 127–53.

– *Those Who Fell from the Sky: A History of the Cowichan Peoples.* Duncan, BC: Cowichan Tribes Cultural and Education Centre, 1999.

Maud, Ralph, ed. *The Salish People: The Local Contribution of Charles Hill-Tout,* vol. 3, *The Mainland Halkomelem,* and vol. 4, *The Sechelt and the South-Eastern Tribes of Vancouver Island.* Vancouver: Talonbooks, 1978.

Mauss, Marcel. *The Gift: Forms and Functions of Exchange in Archaic Societies.* Translated by Ian Cunnison. New York: Norton, 1967.

Mayne, R.C., Commander, R.N., FRGS. *Four Years in British Columbia and Vancouver Island: An Account of the Forests, Rivers, Coast Gold Fields, and Reasons for Colonization.* London: John Murray, 1862.

McHalsie, Albert 'Sonny.' 'Halq'eméylem Place Names in Stó:lō Territory.' In Carlson et al., eds., *Atlas,* 2001, 134–53.

McIntosh, Ian. 'Anthropology, Self-determination and Aboriginal Belief in the Christian God.' *Oceania* 67/4 (1997).

McNally, Vincent J. *The Lord's Distant Vineyard: A History of the Oblates and the Catholic Community in British Columbia.* Edmonton: University of Alberta Press, 2000.

Miller, Bruce G. 'Centrality and Measures of Regional Structure in Aboriginal Western Washington.' *Ethnology* 28/2 (1989): 265–76.

– *The Problem of Justice: Tradition and Law in the Coast Salish World.* Lincoln and London: University of Nebraska Press, 2001.

Miller, Bruce G., and Daniel Boxberger. 'Creating Chiefdoms: The Puget Sound Case.' *Ethnohistory* 41/2 (1994): 267–93.

– 'Evolution or History? A Response to Tollefson.' *Ethnohistory* 44/1 (1996): 135–7.

Miller, Jay. 'Back to Basics: Chiefdoms in Puget Sound.' *Ethnohistory* 44/2 (1997): 375–87.

– *Lushootseed Culture and the Shamanic Odyssey: An Anchored Radiance.* Lincoln: University of Nebraska Press, 1999.

Milloy, John. '"Our Country": The Significance of the Buffalo Resource for a Plains Cree Sense of Territory.' In K. Abel and J. Friesen, eds., *Aboriginal Resource use in Canada: Historical and Legal Aspects.* Winnipeg: University of Manitoba Press, 1991.

Molyneux St John, Frederick Edward. *The Sea of Mountains*, vol. 2, *An Account of Lord Dufferin's Tour through British Columbia in 1876.* London: Hurst and Blackett, 1877.

Morgan, Lewis Henry. *Ancient Society: Or, Researches in the Lines of Human Progress from Savagery, through Barbarism to Civilization.* New York: H. Holt, 1877.

Murdock, George. 'Rank and the Potlatch among the Haida.' *Yale University Publications in Anthropology* (1936) 13: 1–20.

Nelson, Diane M. *A Finger in the Wound: Body Politics in Quincentennial Guatemala.* Berkeley: University of California Press, 1999.

Newell, Dianne. *Tangled Webs of History: Indians and the Law in Canada's Pacific Coast Fisheries.* Toronto: University of Toronto Press, 1993.

Neylan, Susan Lynn. *'The Heavens Are Changing': Nineteenth-Century Protestant Missions and Tsimshian Christianity.* Montreal and Kingston, London, Ithaca: McGill-Queen's University Press, 2003.

Obeyesekere, Gananath. *The Apotheosis of Captain Cook: European Mythmaking in the Pacific.* Princeton: Princeton University Press, 1992.

Orchard, William C. *A Rare Coast Salish Blanket.* Leafletts of the Museum of the American Indian Heye Foundation, No 5. New York: Vreeland Press, 1926.

Ormsby, Margaret A. *British Columbia: A History.* Vancouver: Macmillan, 1958.

Peset, Jose Luis, ed. *Culturas de la Costa Noroeste de America.* Madrid: Turner Press, 1989.

Phillips, Mark Salber, and Gordon Schochet, eds. *Questions of Tradition.* Toronto: University of Toronto Press, 2004.

Power, John Wesley, ed. *Contributions to North American Ethnology.* Washington: Department of the Interior, U.S. Geographical and Geological Survey of the Rocky Mountain Region, 1877 (reprinted Seattle, Washington: Shorey, 1970).

Pratt, Mary Louise. *Authentic Indians: Episodes of Encounter from the Late-Nineteenth-Century Northwest Coast.* Durham: Duke Unversity Press, 2005.

Ray, Arthur J. *Indians in the Fur Trade: Their Role as Hunters, Trappers, and Middle-men in the Lands Southwest of Hudson's Bay, 1660–1870.* Toronto: University of Toronto Press, 1974.

Ray, Arthur J., and Donald Freeman. *'Give Us Good Measure': An Economic Analysis of Relations between the Indians and the Hudson's Bay Company before 1763.* Toronto: University of Toronto Press, 1978.

Reynolds, Henry. *The Law of the Land.* New York: Viking Penguin, 1987.

Sahlins, Marshall David. *Historical Metaphor and Mythical Realities: Structure in the Early History of the Sandwich Islands Kingdom.* Ann Arbor: University of Michigan Press, 1981.

– *Islands of History.* London: Tavistock, 1985.

– 'The Return of the Event, Again: With Reflections on the Beginnings of the Great Fijian War of 1855 between the Kingdoms of Bau and Rewa.' In A. Biersack, ed., *Clio in Oceania: Toward a Historical Anthropology,* 37–99. Washington, DC: Smithsonian Institution, 1991.

– 'Past History.' In *Waiting for Foucault, Still.* Chicago: Prickly Paradigm Press, 1993 (reprinted in 2002).

– *How 'Natives' Think: About Captain Cook for Example.* Chicago: University of Chicago Press, 1995.

– *With Apologies to Thucydides: Understanding History as Culture and Vice Versa.* Chicago: University of Chicago Press, 2005.

Satzewich, Vic, and Linda Mahood. 'Indian Affairs and Band Governance: Deposing Indian Chiefs in Western Canada, 1896–1911.' *Canadian Ethnic Studies* 26/1 (1994): 40–58.

Schaepe, David M. 'Rockwall Fortifications: Reconstructing a Fraser Canyon Defensive Network.' In Carlson et al., eds., *Atlas,* 2001, 52–3.

– 'Stó:lō Communication and Transportation Routes, c.1850.' In Carlson et al., eds., *Atlas,* 2001, 60–1.

– 'Rock Fortifications: Archaeological Insights into Pre-Contact Warfare and Sociopolitical Organization among the Stó:lō of the Lower Fraser River Canyon, B.C.' *American Antiquity* 71/4 (2006): 671–705.

Seaburg, William R., and Jay Miller. 'Tillamook.' In Suttles, ed., *Handbook of North American Indians,* vol. 7, 1990, 560–7.

Smart, James. *Sessional Papers.* Department of Indian Affairs, Annual Reports. Ottawa: Government of Canada, 1898.

Smith, Marian. *The Puyallup-Nisqually.* Columbia University Contributions to Anthropology No. 32. New York: Columbia University Press, 1940 (reprinted New York: AMS Press, 1969).

Sparks, Dawn, and Martha Border. *Echoes across the Inlet.* Deep Cove, BC: Deep Cove and Area Heritage Association, 1989.

Stanley, George F. *Mapping the Frontier: Charles Wilson's Diary of the Survey of the 49th Parallel, 1858–1862, While Secretary of the British Boundary Commission.* Toronto: Macmillan, 1970.

Street, Eloise. *Sepass Tales, the Songs of Y-ail-mihth.* Chilliwack: Sepass Trust, 1963 (2nd ed., 1974).

Sumas and Chilliwack Methodist Chiefs, Petition to Earl of Dufferin, 18 August 1876. Reproduced in Carlson et al., eds., *Atlas,* 2001.

Suttles, Wayne. 'Post-contact Change among the Lummi Indians.' *British Columbia Historical Quarterly* 18/1&2 (1954).

– *The Plateau Prophet Dance among the Coast Salish.* Albuquerque: University of New Mexico Press, 1957.

– 'Variations in Habitat and Culture on the Northwest Coast.' In *Proceedings of the 34th International Congress of Americanists.* Vienna: Ferdinand Berger, 1962.

– 'Affinal Ties': Subsistence, and Prestige among the Coast Salish.' *American Anthropologist* 62/2 (1960): 296–305.

– 'Coping with Abundance: Subsistence on the Northwest Coast.' In R.B. Lee and I. DeVore, eds., *Man the Hunter.* Chicago: Aldine, 1968.

– 'The Economic Life of the Coast Salish of Haro and Rosario Straits.' In D.A. Horr, ed., *Coast Salish and Western Washington Indians,* vol. 1. New York and London: Garlans, 1974.

– *Coast Salish Essays.* Vancouver: Talonbooks, 1987.

– '"They Recognize No Superior Chief": The Strait of Juan de Fuca in the 1790s.' In J.L. Peset, ed., *Culturas de la Costa Noroeste de America,* 251–64. Madrid: Turner, 1989.

– 'The Ethnographic Significance of the Fort Langley Journals.' In M. MacLachlan, ed., *The Fort Langley Journals, 1827–30,* 163–210. Vancouver: UBC Press, 1998.

– ed. *Handbook of North American Indians,* vol. 7, *The Northwest Coast.* Washington, DC: Smithsonian Institution, 1990.

Suttles, Wayne, and Diamond Jenness. *Katzie Ethnographic Notes, and the Faith of a Coast Salish Indian.* Victoria: BCPM, Anthropology in B.C., Memoir No. 2, 1955.

Suttles, Wayne, and Barbara Lane. 'Southern Coast Salish.' In Suttles, ed., *Handbook of North American Indians,* vol. 7, 1990, 485–502.

Tennant, Paul. *Aboriginal Peoples and Politics: The Indian Land Question in British Columbia, 1849–1989.* Vancouver: UBC Press, 1990.

Thompson, Nile. 'Journey through the Land: A Journal of a Voyage from Fort George Columbia River to Fraser River in the Winter of 1824 and 1825, by Francois N. Annance.' *Cowlitz Historical Quarterly* 32/1(1991): 5–44.

Tobias, John L. 'Protection, Civilization, Assimilation: An Outline History of Canada's Indian Policy.' *Western Canadian Journal of Anthropology* 6/2 (1976): 13–30.

Tollefson, Kenneth D. 'The Snoqualmie: A Puget Sound Chiefdom.' *Ethnology* 26/2 (1987): 121–36.

– 'In Defense of a Snoqualmie Political Chiefdom Model.' *Ethnohistory* 43/1(1996): 145–71.

Vancouver, George. 'Journal Entries.' In *A Voyage of Discovery to the North Pacific Ocean and around the World, 1791–1795*. Edited by W.K. Lamb. London: Hakluit Society, 1984.

Vansina, Jan. *Oral Tradition as History*. Madison: University of Wisconsin Press, 1985.

Vibert, Elizabeth. 'Real Men Hunt Buffalo: Masculinity, Race and Class in British Fur Traders' Narratives.' *Gender and History* 8/1 (1996): 4–21.

Waterman, Thomas T. *Notes on the Ethnology of the Indians of Puget Sound*. New York: Museum of the American Indian, 1973.

Weinberg, Daniela. 'Models of Southern Kwakiutl Social Organization.' In B.Cox, ed., *Cultural Ecology: Readings on the Canadian Indians and Eskimos*, 227–53. Toronto: McClelland and Stewart, 1973.

Wells, Oliver. *The Chilliwacks and Their Neighbours*. Edited by R. Maud and B. Galloway. Vancouver: Talonbooks, 1987.

Wickwire, Wendy. 'To See Ourselves as the Other's Other: Nlakapamux Contact Narratives.' *Canadian Historical Review* 75/1 (1994): 1–20.

Wike, Joyce A. *The Effect of the Maritime Fur Trade on Northwest Coast Indian Society*. New York: Columbia University Press, 1951.

Williams, Nancy M. *The Yolngu and Their Land: A System of Land Tenure and the Fight for Its Recognition*. Stanford: Stanford University Press: 1986.

Windschuttle, Keith. *The Fabrication of Aboriginal History*. Paddington, NSW: MacLeay Press, 2002.

Zellar, Gary. *African Creeks: Estlvste and the Creek Nation*. Norman: University of Oklahoma Press, 2007.

Unpublished Dissertations and Theses

Angelbeck, William. '"They Recognize No Superior Chief": Power, Practice, Anarchism and Warfare in the Coast Salish Past.' Doctoral dissertation in archaeology, University of British Columbia, 2009.

Blair, Hillary Kathleen. 'Settling Seabird Island: Land, Resources and Ownership on a British Columbia Indian Reserve.' M.A. thesis in history, Simon Fraser University, 1999.

Duff, Wilson. 'The Upper Stalo Indians: An Introductory Ethnography.' M.A. thesis, University of Washington, 1952.

Fehr, Amanda Beth. 'The Relationships of Place: A Study of Change and Continuity in Stó:lō Understandings of I:yem.' M.A. thesis, University of Saskatchewan, 2008.

Marshall, Daniel P. 'Claiming the Land: Indians, Goldseekers, and the Rush to British Columbia.' Doctoral dissertation in history, University of British Columbia, 2000.

Rohner, Ronald P., ed., *The Ethnography of Franz Boas: Letters and Diaries of Franz Boas, Written on the Northwest Coast from 1886 to 1931*. Chicago: University of Chicago Press, 1969.

Schaepe, David M. 'Recycling Archaeology: Analysis of Material from the 1973 Excavation of an Ancient House at the Maurier Site.' M.A. thesis in anthropology, Simon Fraser University, 1998.

Snyder, Sally. 'Skagit Society and Its Existential Basis: An Ethnofolkloristic Reconstruction.' Doctoral dissertation in anthropology, University of Washington, 1964.

Thom, Brian David. 'The Dead and the Living: Burial Mounds and Cairns and the Development of Social Classes in the Gulf of Georgia Region.' M.A. thesis in anthropology, University of British Columbia, 1995.

– 'Coast Salish Senses of Place: Dwelling, Meaning, Power, Property and Territory in the Coast Salish world.' Ph.D. dissertation in anthropology, McGill University, 2004.

Index

Index

Mary Anne (of Chehalis), 66

Matsqui prairie, 188, 325n24

Mayne, Lieutenant R.C., 59, 237

McColl, Sergeant William, 173–6, 188, 195, 215, 218, 222, 227, 322n67

McDonald, Archibald, 108, 109, 131, 148

McHalsie, Albert 'Sonny,' xvii, 23, 95, 96, 132, 288n34, 311n36, 314n74, 327n50, 327–8n56, 338n46

McKay, Joseph William, 145; on Salish monotheism, 60, 61

McKelvie, B.A., 106

McMillan, James, 103, 107, 305n94

McNally, Vincent, 182, 324n5

Mediterranean and the Mediterranean World, The, 27

metaphor, 22, 51, 54, 64, 86, 126, 139, 229

Methodists, 59, 63, 191, 192, 194, 198, 200, 236, 245, 325nn15 and 22

migration, 20, 30, 32, 50, 63, 97, 105, 169, 204, 213, 227, 272, 305n93, 317n11; event-facilitated, 86, 96, 99, 101, 106, 107, 114–21, 126, 127, 131, 132, 134, 135, 141, 142, 152, 154, 157, 270, 271, 274, 276; Chilliwack Tribe, 119, 120, 125, 126, 308n6

Miller, Bruce, xviii, 51, 308n4

Miller, Jay, xviii, 10, 48, 75, 96

Miller, J.R., xviii

Milloy, John, 63

Milo, Dan, xviii, 83, 85, 86, 89–91, 107, 117, 244, 299n8, 300n18, 309n8, 312n44, 324n6

Mischel, Chief, 213, 246, 248, 331n6, 338n40

Mission City, 182

missionaries, 16, 59–61, 135, 164, 173, 179–84, 186, 187, 189–92, 194, 198,

201, 202, 212, 213, 236, 237, 250, 266, 323n1, 325n15, 330n59, 339n54

Moody, R.C., xviii, 173

Morgan, Lewis Henry, 38–9

Mount Cheam, 79

Mount Golden-Ears, 79

Mount Tzuhalem, 79

'Mountain of God.' *See* Devil's Mountain

Myth of Nations: The Medieval Origins of Europe, 25

Nanoose, 134, 147

natural disasters: as impetus for migrations, 32, 87, 118, 126, 131. *See also* Great Flood

Nelson, Diane, 12

nested identity, 15, 29, 75, 116, 138, 158, 211, 270

New Westminster, 103, 105–7, 139, 162, 171, 182, 183, 195, 211, 215, 219–22, 227, 240, 241–5, 253, 255, 275, 305n89, 334n36

New York Times, 166

Nicamuns (Nicamous, Nicameus, Nicamoos, Nic,ca,ueus, Ni,cam. meus, Ni,ca.mous), 107

Nicomen. *See* Lakahamen

Nlakapamux constitution, 249, 251, 252

noble savage, 211

Nooksack language called 'Kluh Ch ihl ihs ehm,' 119

Nooksack Tribe, 38, 79, 81, 88, 90, 120, 297n27, 311n34

Nooksack (Washington), 255

Oblates of Mary Immaculate, xviii, 181–4, 186–9, 191, 192, 202, 219, 323n78, 325nn15 and 22; 'watch-

213, 332n9, 333n10; as merger of
STC and SNC, 17, 21

Stó:lō Nation Canada (SNC), 13, 14,
21

Stó:lō Tribal Council (STC), xiv, 12,
13–17, 21, 116, 213, 279, 303n60,
332n9, 341n11

stó:méx (warriors), 73

st'qwó:mpth ('those who speak our language'), 99

structural functionalism, 9, 115

sturgeon, 47, 48, 134; Shxw'ōwhámél
ancestor, 132–4; dance, 70

Sumas First Nation/Band (*Semá:th*),
xii, 21, 48, 91, 123, 127, 147, 176,
179, 245, 300nn17 and 19

Sumas Lake, 125, 300nn17 and 19

Sumas Mountain, 81, 83

Sumqeameltq, 65

Superintendent General of Indian
Affairs, 202

supratribal identity, 16, 54, 69, 75, 76,
189, 207, 214, 29, 270. *See also* tribal
identity

surveys/surveying, 8, 53, 94, 171–5,
195, 196, 215, 218, 228, 273, 276,
290n9, 322n67

Suttles, Wayne 25, 50, 97, 148; as an
influence on author, 26; on antiquity of word/idea 'Stó:lō,' 25, 212–
13; on food shortages and Coast
Salish culture, 87; on HBC census,
131; on Kwantlen nomenclature,
107; on smallpox epidemic, 92, 97,
98; on social class and status, 140;
on three-tiered social structure ('inverted pear'), 140; on tribal unity/
connections, 15, 38, 40–2, 48, 51, 54,
55, 87, 109, 127

Súx'yel (Captain Charlie), 204, 205

Swaniset, 65, 68, 69, 74, 84, 86, 93, 101,
103–5, 296–7n25, 306n103

sxa'yeqs. *See* Skayuk

sxá:sls ('historian,' 'one who keeps
track of everything'), 62, 68

sxwamecen, 69

Swí:lhcha, 120, 121, 123, 274

Sxóchaqel, 118

Sxwó:yxwela, 125

sxwó:xwey, 10, 31, 48, 63, 65, 68–71, 73,
76, 142, 297n28, 297–8n35

sxwōxwiyám, 63, 65, 68–70, 93, 144,
187, 294n12

sxwóxwiymelh ('a lot of people died at
once'), 96. *See also* smallpox

sxwòyeqs ('all dead' or 'tribe dead'),
105, 111

sxwsiyá:m ('wealthy men with property'), 48, 123

syewin or *yewin* (special prayers), 74

syewinmet or *yewinmet* ('one who knows
many prayers'), 74

syúwél or *ó:lkwlh* (guardian spirits). *See*
seven spirit entities

taboo. *See xa:xa* places

Tait Tribe, 14, 15, 116, 132, 144, 147,
151, 313n49, 315n92

Tamtami'uxwtan, 100

Tennant, Paul, 23

Tel swayel (sky-people), 64, 65

temperance societies, 184–8, 200, 202,
215, 216, 225, 236, 242, 248, 255,
258. *See also* alcohol

Tháthem:als, 120, 123, 309n13

Thelachiyatel, 14. *See also* Chilliwack
Tribe

Thelhatsstan, 101, 135

Thom, Brian, 10, 295n21

Times of London, 164, 166